The Adoption of Fintech

The term Fintech is a combination of the words "financial" and "technology," which is now a real business need. However, there are limited books covering holistic aspects from adoption to the future of Fintech. This book directs readers on how to adopt Fintech, develop regulation and risk frameworks, implement it in financial services, address ethical dilemmas, and sustain improvements. The anticipated challenges are developing trust, security, privacy, and a regulated environment without compromising profitability and financial stability. The anticipated solution is strengthening the governance, use of unbreachable technologies, risk management, consumer data protection, and sustainable practices.

This book is recommended for stakeholders, especially Fintech scholars, practitioners, and policymakers. It provides holistic insight and opportunities to support Fintech developments for the betterment of the economy and society. Fintech is defined as injecting technology into the area of finance for better security, speed, and customer experience. This book provides readers with direct case studies for better understanding. In addition, it explains regulation and usage of Fintech in daily transactions. Readers are shown how Fintech has an imperative role in financial analysis, Insurtech, and the share market.

The Adoption of Fintech
Using Technology for Better Security, Speed, and Customer Experience in Finance

Edited by
Syed Hasan Jafar, Hemachandran K,
Shakeb Akhtar, Parvez Alam Khan
and Hani El-Chaarani

Routledge
Taylor & Francis Group

A PRODUCTIVITY PRESS BOOK

First published 2024
by Routledge
605 Third Avenue, New York, NY 10158

and by Routledge
4 Park Square, Milton Park, Abingdon, Oxon, OX14 4RN

Routledge is an imprint of the Taylor & Francis Group, an informa business

ISBN: 9781032644158 (hbk)
ISBN: 9781032644141 (pbk)
ISBN: 9781032644165 (ebk)

DOI: 10.4324/9781032644165

Typeset in Garamond
by Deanta Global Publishing Services, Chennai, India

Contents

Preface

In the ever-evolving landscape of financial services, the emergence and rapid evolution of financial technology, or Fintech, have ushered in a transformative era that challenges traditional norms and reshapes the way we interact with money. *The Adoption of Fintech: Using Technology for Better Security, Speed, and Customer Experience in Finance* delves into the intricate dynamics of this technological revolution, exploring the nuanced relationship between Fintech and the established financial ecosystem.

As we stand at the crossroads of tradition and innovation, this book serves as a comprehensive guide to understanding the multifaceted impact of Fintech adoption. It is not merely a narrative of technological disruption but a thoughtful exploration of the symbiotic and, at times, antagonistic relationship between Fintech and traditional financial institutions. We navigate through the disruptive waves of digital currencies, decentralized finance, artificial intelligence, and blockchain, evaluating how these innovations challenge the status quo while presenting unprecedented opportunities.

The journey begins with an insightful examination of the historical context that birthed Fintech, tracing its roots from the early days of online banking to the present landscape dominated by mobile payments and robo-advisors. Through a blend of historical analysis and forward-looking perspectives, we aim to provide readers with a holistic understanding of the evolutionary trajectory of Fintech and its profound implications for the financial industry.

In the subsequent chapters, we scrutinize the key pillars of Fintech adoption, scrutinizing the regulatory frameworks that seek to balance innovation with consumer protection and financial stability. We explore the intricate dance between incumbents and disruptors, shedding light on the strategic collaborations and fierce competitions that define this new era of financial services.

Furthermore, *Adoption of Fintech* does not shy away from addressing the societal implications of this financial revolution. We probe the impact of Fintech on financial inclusion, assessing its potential to bridge the gaps that traditional banking systems have struggled to close. Additionally, we consider the ethical dimensions surrounding data privacy, security, and the responsible use of emerging technologies in finance.

As technology continues to weave itself into the fabric of our financial lives, this book serves as a compass, guiding readers through the complex terrain of Fintech adoption. It is a testament to the inevitability of change, the resilience of traditional finance, and the transformative power of innovation. Whether you are a seasoned financial professional, a curious observer, or an entrepreneur shaping the Fintech landscape, *The Adoption of Fintech: Using Technology for Better Security, Speed, and Customer Experience in Finance* invites you to embark on a thought-provoking exploration of the present and future of finance.

As editors, we sought to assemble a collection that would resonate with both seasoned professionals and newcomers to the field. Each chapter in this book delves into its respective area with rigour and depth, offering practical insights, theoretical underpinnings, and hands-on experiences that will inspire readers to explore the myriad of Fintech.

The handbook *The Adoption of Fintech: Using Technology for Better Security, Speed, and Customer Experience in Finance* is more than just a compilation of knowledge; it is a testament to the spirit of innovation that drives our society forward.

We extend our heartfelt gratitude to the contributors whose expertise and passion shine through in their work. Their dedication to pushing the boundaries of Fintech has made this book an invaluable resource for researchers, practitioners, and students alike.

We hope that this book provides a comprehensive overview of Fintech in diverse fields and how it is transforming different sectors. We believe that this book will be a valuable resource for academics, researchers, professionals, and policymakers who are interested in understanding the potential of Fintech.

We would like to thank all the contributors who have made this book possible, and we hope that readers will find it informative and thought-provoking.

Editors

Syed Hasan Jafar is an area chair of Finance at Woxsen University. He has around 13 years of experience in the field of finance and has worked as a research analyst, deputy research head, and corporate trainer. He appears on several national media channels as a financial expert, sharing his view on the financial market. His areas of expertise are security analysis, corporate finance, equity and derivative research, and valuation. He has taken several sessions at top universities in India and abroad. He was awarded Best Faculty Member of the year 2020–2021 at Woxsen School of Business, Woxsen University. He has conducted more than 50 investor awareness programs across the country and was awarded Best Research Analyst several times during his corporate experience.

Hemachandran K has been a passionate teacher with 14 years of teaching experience and five years of research experience. He is a strong educational professional with a scientific mind, highly skilled in artificial intelligence (AI) and machine learning. After receiving his PhD in embedded system at Dr MGR Educational & Research Institute, India, he started doing interdisciplinary research in AI. He has been published in more than more than 20 peer-reviewed journals and international conference publications. He served as an effective resource person at various national and international scientific conferences. He has a rich experience in mentoring undergraduate and postgraduate student research projects. He owns two patents and has lifetime memberships with estimable professional bodies. He was a pioneer in establishing the Single Board Computer lab at Ashoka Institutions, Hyderabad, India. His self-paced learning schedule and thirst for learning skills has earned him 15 online certificate courses conferred by COURSERA and other online platforms. He is an editorial board member to numerous reputed SCOPUS/SCI journals.

Shakeb Akhtar is an assistant professor and program director of the Master of Business Administration (Financial Services) at the School of Business, Woxsen University. He has been a passionate teacher with three years of teaching experience and five years of research experience He completed his PhD in Banking and Finance from Aligarh Muslim University, Aligarh, Uttar Pradesh, India. His PhD thesis concentrates on the comparison of performance of private and foreign sector banks in India. He was declared university topper in postgraduate and PhD course work examinations. His research has been featured in leading journals, including *Benchmarking: An International Journal, Quality and Quantity, Journal of Risk and Financial Management, International Journal of Sustainable Development and World Ecology*, and one case study in his area is published in *Emerging Economics Case Journal*. His research interests include banking, sustainability, Environmental, Social, and Governance (ESG), corporate governance, and green innovation practices. He teaches courses on corporate finance, accounting for managers, cost accounting, and banking and insurance practices.

Parvez Alam Khan is a lecturer at University Technology PETRONAS with four years of industry and five years of research experience He completed his PhD in Management from University Technology PETRONAS, Malaysia. His research has been featured in leading journals, including *Business Strategy and the Environment, Cogent Business & Management, Environmental Science and Pollution Research,* and *Journal of Risk and Financial Management.* His research interests include sustainable innovation, green innovation, social innovation, sustainable development goals (SDGs), and corporate governance. He teaches courses on accounting, sustainability, sustainable finance, corporate governance, and strategic management.

Hani El-Chaarani is a full professor of Finance. He is a financial consultant in many public and private institutions. He is a board member and financial advisor for many family firms in the Middle East and North Africa (MENA) region. He holds a PhD in Business Administration from the University of Bordeaux-IV (France), a Master of Science in Business Administration from the IAE-Bordeaux (France), and a Master of Science in Finance and Accounting from the Lebanese University. In addition, he holds a Rural and Economic Development diploma from Illinois University, USA, Excellence in Teaching diploma from Illinois University, USA, and Crisis Economic Leadership Diploma from London Business School-UK. He is a chartered accountant and visiting professor at various universities, research centres, and international organizations. He is the head of the Business School at Beirut Arab University, Lebanon. He acted as the keynote speaker and delivered professional talks on various international forums. He is head of the International Business and Economic Research Academy (IBERA). He has published close to 50 scientific works in high-ranked journals and international conferences. He is a reviewer in several ranked journals. His research interests include financial behaviour, corporate governance, Small and Medium Enterprises (SMEs) performance, blockchain, and big data management.

Contributors

Nomani Abuzar
CV Raman Global University
Bhubaneswar, India

David C. Adhing'a
Kenyatta University
Ruiru, Kenya

Mohd Afzal
VIT Business School
Vellore Institute of Technology
Vellore, India

Shakeb Akhtar
School of Business
   Woxsen University
Hyderabad, India

Mahfooz Alam
University of the People
Pasadena, CA, United States

Moses O. Aluoch
Kenyatta University
Ruiru, Kenya

Aleem Ansari
Symbiosis Centre for Management
   Studies
Symbiosis International (Deemed
   University)
Noida, India

Ezendu Ariwa
University of Wales Trinity Saint
   David
Lampeter, United Kingdom

Sunitha Purushottam Ashtikar
SR University
Hasanparthy, Warangal, Telangana,
   India

Medhansh Bairaria
Mahindra University
Hyderabad, India

K Balaji
Presidency University
Bangalore, India

Alberto Bettencourt
Chan Logistics Limited
Macao, SAR, China

Padmaja Bhujabal
School of Business
Woxsen University
Hyderabad, India

Ramona Birau
University Constantin Brancusi
Tg-Jiu, Romania

Sourav Biswas
School of Business
Woxsen University
Hyderabad, India

David Campbell
Manipal University
Jaipur, India

Randall Carolissen
Johannesburg Business School (JBS)
Johannesburg, South Africa

Hani El-Chaarani
School of Management
Beirut Arab University
Beirut, Lebanon

Prashant Subhash Chougule
School of Business
Woxsen University
Hyderabad, India

Chandan Dasgupta
School of Business Management
Narsee Monjee Institute of
    Management Studies
Mumbai, India

Chinna Swamy Dudekula
Northumbria University
Newcastle, United Kingdom

Humaira Fatima
VIT Bhopal University
Kothri Kalan, India

Sana Fatima
Symbiosis Centre for Management
    Studies
Symbiosis International (Deemed
    University)
Noida, India

Rachit Garg
School of Business Management
Narsee Monjee Institute of
    Management Studies
Mumbai, India

James M. Gatauwa
Kenyatta University
Ruiru, Kenya

Meghna Goel
KJ Somaiya Institute of
    Management
Somaiya Vidyavihar University
Mumbai, India

Syed Hasan Jafar
School of Business
Woxsen University
Hyderabad, India

Hemachandran K
School of Business
Woxsen University
Hyderabad, India

Vartika Kapooor
Symbiosis International (Deemed
   University)
Noida, India

Asif Khan
Institute of Management Technology
   (IMT)
Nagpur, India

Mohsin Khan
Vellore Institute of Technology
Katpadi, India

Nisha Khan
Mangalayatan University
Beswan, India

Akshay G Khanzode
School of Business Management
Narsee Monjee Institute of
   Management Studies
Mumbai, India

Bala Krishnamoorthy
School of Business Management
Narsee Monjee Institute of
   Management Studies
Mumbai, India

Pokala Pranay Kumar
University of Maryland
College Park, Maryland, USA

Neelam Kumari
Dublin Business School
Dublin, Ireland

Geetha Manoharan
SR University
Hasanparthy, Warangal, Telangana,
   India

Farhan Mustafa
Al Fayha College of Business
Saudi Arabia

Chitra Devi Nagarajan
VIT Business School
Vellore Institute of Technology
Chennai, India

G Nithya
N.G.P. Institute of Technology
Tamil Naidu, India

Pranjal Kumar Phukan
School of Business
Woxsen University
Hyderabad, India

Anil Audumbar Pise
University of the Witwatersrand
Johannesburg, South Africa

Hritvik Polumahanti
School of Business Management
Narsee Monjee Institute of
   Management Studies
Mumbai, India

Somnath Roy
School of Business Management
Narsee Monjee Institute of
   Management Studies
Mumbai, India

Rangapriya Saivasan
University of Mysore
Bangalore, India

Payal Sanan
ITM Business School
Navi Mumbai, India

Sindhukavi Senthilkumar
Woxsen University
Hyderabad, India

Musarrat Shaheen
School of Business
Woxsen University
Hyderabad, India

Muneer Shaik
Mahindra University
Hyderabad, India

Mushahid Ali Shamsi
Department of Commerce
Aligarh Muslim University
Aligarh, India

Harendra Singh
Manipal University
Jaipur, India

Vikrant Vikram Singh
Symbiosis Centre for Management
    Studies
Symbiosis International (Deemed
    University)
Noida, India

Monika Verma
School of Business Management
Narsee Monjee Institute of
    Management Studies
Mumbai, India

Farrah Zeba
ICFAI Business School
Hyderabad, India

Chapter 1

Introduction to Fintech in Industry 5.0: Companion or Antagonist

Mahfooz Alam, Shakeb Akhtar, and Alberto Bettencourt

The purpose of this introductory chapter is to sail through the financial technology (Fintech) that will be discussed in the rest of the book. The primary objective is to provide a glimpse of the overall global disruption that the advancement of Fintech companies is causing. Think back for a moment to the twentieth century, and you will be amazed by the innovations witnessed in the past few decades. The advancements in technology, globalization, and digitalization are all unsung heroes behind our lifestyle today. When was the last time you visited a bank to deposit or borrow funds? Maybe a month, quarter, or year ago?

All hail Fintech companies that we may avail ourselves of almost every bank service without even stepping foot inside the bank. We can transfer funds using mobile phone apps and even use a hassle-free "digital wallet" for payments. However, we all must agree that the world is transitioning fast, and we are all a part of it.

As with many emerging technology sectors, Fintech can be an ambiguous concept due to the sheer breadth of tools, platforms, and services that fall under its yawning umbrella. If you're still asking yourself, "Exactly what is Fintech?", then let's find out.

DOI: 10.4324/9781032644165-1

1.1 What Is Fintech?

Fintech is a portmanteau, a made-up word coined from the combination of the words *financial* and *technology*. Fintech is a relatively new term that refers to software, algorithms, and applications or any other technologies created to improve and automate traditional forms of finance for businesses and consumers alike. For example, a decade ago, we had to walk into the bank to request an account balance. Contrastingly, today, almost all banking services are at our fingertips in real time. Moreover, there exist several applications that help investors choose their portfolios as per their risk appetite. Notably, the era of physical currency is at stake, as coins and paper notes are now on the cusp of a transformation amid rising digital currency due to Fintech in action [1]. Lately, we have witnessed a paradigm shift in the financial sector landscape with key innovations driving the Fintech industry, such as blockchains, digital currency, robo-advisory, artificial intelligence (AI) and machine learning, mobile payments, crowdfunding, etc.

1.2 Background

The Fintech industry has undergone rapid technological transformations to meet evolving business needs and changing consumer habits, with COVID-19 accelerating digital disruption. Due to various restrictions to curb the pandemic, digital adoption has taken a quantum leap at both the organization and industry levels. With the sudden surge in digital adoption at work, education, business, healthcare, and other sectors, Fintech companies are posed with new challenges and have successfully triumphed over the COVID-19 pressure. For example, with rising cases and stricter measures to curb the spread of the pandemic, Zoom saw very high demand for its service, as people were working remotely but still needed to conduct business. Zoom was able to accommodate this huge spike in demand because it scaled up with its cloud provider.

While Fintech is now a buzzword, that doesn't mean that it's a brand new thing. The Fintech concept dates back to the 1860s when banks introduced signature-verifying technologies. However, credit cards, adopted in the early 1950s, are considered to be the first Fintech product that curtailed the need for physical currency. Similarly, the installation of automated teller machines (ATM) in the 1960s led to the evolution of Fintech services to the general public. The foundation of PayPal in 1998 pioneered the Fintech company that revolutionized banking operations. Since then, Fintech has come a long way, from mobile payment applications to digital banking and blockchains to cryptocurrencies, etc.

In a nutshell, Fintech's dramatic transformation can be categorized under five distinct "phases." The first phase of Fintech development can be attributed to the era of computers. Financial institutions replaced manual processes with machines, such as computers and mainframes, thereby improving the core financial industry. The digitization process helps the financial world to efficiently handle a higher volume of transactions. The advent of the internet marked the second phase of Fintech companies. With increasing outreach, internet banking facilities are now provided by almost every commercial bank. The third phase is associated with the introduction of mobile banking, allowing customers to use banking services from anywhere. In the fourth phase, Fintech companies used AI and the Internet of Things (IoT), such as robo-advisors, chatbots, and virtual assistants, to improve customer experience. The fourth wave has also led to an increase in financial literacy among individuals. Recently, we embarked on the fifth phase of Fintech with cloud computing and the cloud marketplace, which is driving digital change to enhance Fintech solutions for big data management, machine learning, blockchain, AI, cryptocurrency mining, and many other services being provided by prominent players such as Amazon Web Services (AWS), Microsoft Azure, Google Cloud Platform (GCP), IBM Cloud, and Alibaba Cloud.

The modern phase of Fintech is usually recognized as beginning after the financial crisis of 2008. The 2008 financial crisis triggered new regulatory initiatives, exposing the lack of more reliable and secured financial products to safeguard the interest of the investors. The emergence of new businesses and technologies, decentralized digital markets, and concern for financial literacy have paved the way for Fintech companies to take control of the steering wheel, creating an ideal environment for growth. Recently, the COVID-19 pandemic further accelerated the adoption of Fintech, and the world has witnessed a surge in Fintech payment concentration. Owing to social distancing and lockdown of economies to curb the spread of the pandemic, contactless payments and mobile banking became the norm. For example, online shopping and mobile payments were readily adopted by a majority of the people in India during the pandemic, making India the fastest growing market for Fintech products at an acceptance rate of 87% compared to 64% worldwide, post-COVID-19 period (Economic Survey 2022–23).[1] The sudden surge in the financial demands of Fintech demonstrates Fintech's significance.

1.3 Drivers of Fintech

In recent years, Fintech has been booming, and its ubiquitous status in the financial world is driven by a combination of factors (Figure 1.1) . Fintech is considered a significant facet of established and legacy financial institutions (FIs). Fintech is the epitome of financial development leading to the amalgamation of financial industries with Fintech firms. Global ventures and start-ups, in particular, are backing more Fintech companies by making large investments in Fintech products. According to the report published by Statista Research Department (2023), Fintech companies' total investment value has surged drastically in the past decade, totalling a whopping 216.8 billion US dollars.[2] The reasons for the upward trend in Fintech firms operating in the financial sector are manifold, including increased usage of smartphones, affordable and faster internet connectivity, improved infrastructural developments, and advancements in disruptive technologies such as blockchain, machine learning, AI, etc. We enlisted some of the key technologies driving Fintech developments and shaping the competitive landscape of the financial world [2].

1.3.1 Artificial Intelligence (AI)

AI is the simulation of human intelligence processed by machines. In a broader sense, the application of AI in Fintech companies improves overall efficiency by accomplishing routine tasks through machine learning. The development of AI has an enormous impact on Fintech companies, such as in the following areas:

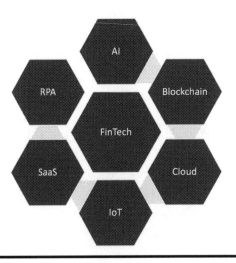

Figure 1.1   Drivers of Fintech

■ **Data Automation**: The application of AI has enormously improved the operational efficiency of the finance industry through data automation resulting in cost-effective and accurate results, such as robotic process automation (RPA) or software robots, and natural language processing (NLP).

■ **Credit Risk Assessment**: AI-based credit scores are considered to be the most reliable. The AI-generated credit scores enhance the overall risk management system by adhering to regulatory compliance based on real-time factors, thereby strengthening fraud detection, cybersecurity, etc.

■ **Automated Customer Services**: FIs are readily adopting AI chatbots and virtual assistance that simulate human interactions using machine learning to provide 24/7 customer support, answer queries, and assist with basic financial tasks. This not only improves efficiency but also enhances the overall customer experience.

■ **User Behaviour Analytics**: Fintech firms use AI and machine learning to analyze user behaviour, allowing them to identify patterns and gain insights into their data. Oftentimes referred to as AI application programming interfaces (AI-APIs), these user behaviour analytics can be used to create highly personalized and customized products and services that cater to individual needs.

■ **Financial Forecasts**: The use of AI is increasingly utilized to gather valuable insights into exchange rates, investments, and short- or long-term trend predictions. AI's ability to purge the data has successfully generated new models and processes, such as robo-advisory services, exchange rate prediction, claim processing, investment decisions, etc.

With its wider acceptance and enormous benefits, such as reduced costs, improved customer experience, increased operational efficiency, etc., Fintech is adopted by every FI to have a competitive edge. The use of AI has unfolded the productivity of Fintech companies, and it will unlock the hitherto untapped potential of ecosystem-based financing. The similarities between AI and Fintech are enormous [3].

1.3.2 Blockchain/Distributed Ledger Technology (DLT)

Blockchain creates a shared database, referred to as distributed ledger technology (DLT), that allows user data to be recorded and shared simultaneously across a synchronized distributed network. For storage and transmission of data, these DLTs use blockchains, which are generally immutable. However, a few blockchains, such as Bitcoin, can be mutated with control of more than

51% of nodes at a time. Blockchain enables the storage of financial transactions at multiple locations simultaneously, supporting ecosystem funding. A few of the DLTs are worth mentioning and are key to existing innovations, such as digital wallets, digital assets (cryptocurrencies), decentralized finance (DeFi), and non-fungible tokens (NFT), that have gained momentum and play a vital role in the Fintech industry. In addition, the authentication system based on zero-knowledge proof is also gaining significant attention for its ability to simplify authentication procedures. With the advent of blockchain technology, DeFi is ushering in a new era of modern finance, disrupting established traditional value chains and structures. As financial policies and regulations adapt, the expansion of DeFi will be inevitable [4].

1.3.3 *Cloud Computing*

Cloud computing offers an on-demand service to businesses that rely on remote servers rather than physical or local servers. It allows users to access resources and applications, such as analytics, databases, networking, storage, and many more, over the internet. Usually, consumers use cloud services to access their accounts from any device at any time. Cloud computing has revolutionized the Fintech industry and has significantly impacted user experience. Table 1.1 lists the key cloud characteristics.

Table 1.1   Key Characteristics of Cloud Computing

Item	*Descriptions*
Characteristics	• On-demand service • Easy availability and scalability • Broad network access • Improved security • Cloud-based solutions
Advantages	• Cost-effective and agile solutions • Easy deployment and time-efficient • Data loss prevention • Better collaboration and mobility • Unlimited resources
Disadvantages	• Heavy reliance on internet bandwidth • Less control over underlying cloud infrastructure • Security-risk concerns, such as data privacy and online threats • Integration complexity with existing systems • Risk of vendor lock-in

In general, there are three main types of cloud services, namely, public cloud, private cloud, and hybrid cloud. As the name suggests, public cloud refers to the infrastructure owned by cloud computing service providers who sell their cloud services to the general public or a wide array of businesses. Private cloud refers an exclusive infrastructure built and customized as per an organization's needs that is set up at data centres or via other hosting facilities. Lastly, a hybrid cloud is composed of both public and private clouds that is maintained separately but connected by proprietary technology.

Several key cloud computing trends for the near future include the following:

- **Edge Computing**: As 5G communication fosters new interactions and synergies across the IoT, cloud computing, AI, and other technologies in areas such as new retail, healthcare, industrial parks, smart cities, and industrial IoT, the development of edge computing is growing. Moreover, the interaction between data centres, edge computing, and cloud computing is significantly recognized.
- **Cloud Containers**: Cloud service providers are advocating for cloud container technology, enabling multiple workloads on a single operating system (OS). For example, platform as a service (PaaS) in cloud delivery is driven by a cloud container that has significantly reduced overhead costs and improves efficiency. Cloud developers are expected to emphasize building platforms that utilize container as a service (CaaS).
- **AI and Cloud Integration**: The integration of AI and cloud services is proliferating in the audio-visual industry, especially in the healthcare sector. Through cloud platforms, deep learning will continue to enhance services comprehensively.

Cloud service providers are the cornerstone in liberating FIs from non-core businesses. With its immense capacity and new formats being spawned, Fintech companies will continue to rely on cloud computing. In addition, the growing importance of big data stimulates cloud-based elastic computing with flexible scalability [5].

1.3.4 Internet of Things (IoT)

IoT is a term used to denote a collective network of interconnected devices or technologies. The IoT devices act as a catalyst to enable communication between linked devices and cloud services, such as wireless communication networks, sensor applications, and operations support. On the sensor front, radio-frequency identification (RFID) technology is widely used in the banking industry, FIs, and Fintech firms for identification, theft protection, user authentication, etc. The RFID technology has boosted the productivity and security of FIs and still has broad, untapped potential in the identification automation process. Among all other technologies, the IoT is at a maturing stage with significant ramifications for Fintech companies. Apart from identification, the IoT's communication solutions are also expanding immensely.

Meanwhile, FIs, such as the banking and insurance industry, are relying heavily on the IoT to determine and manage the risks as well as maintain records, etc. On a similar note, embedding banking services into wearables, such as digital payments, is an example of the IoT connecting banking services at the customer's ease. Overall, the IoT will be beneficial in customer relationship management (CRM), allowing FIs to provide niche products to targeted consumers. The scope of the IoT is limitless.

1.3.5 Open-Source Software/Software as a Service (SaaS)

In a fast-paced digital economy, scalability and speed are vital for the success of new-world businesses to gain a competitive edge. Technological advancements have committed FIs and other Fintech firms to adapt open-source software, known as software as a service (SaaS). It is a community-based intellectual property (software) created for the general public and made available via open collaborations. Open-source software emerges as a foundation technology of the internet, or personal or professional computing, such as Linux OS, Mozilla Firefox, VLC Media Player, etc. The availability of SaaS allows Fintech firms to rely on this type of software with serverless architecture. This helps companies to gain efficiency and reduce operating costs as well as provide the flexibility to customize the source code.

Nonetheless, open-source software may be cost-effective, but it can incur additional costs associated with network integration, end-user support, etc. However, a majority of companies consider open-source software as a trustworthy and reliable source. Traditional financial organizations need to scrutinize their information technology (IT) strategies and accentuate their Fintech innovation and development.

1.3.6 Robotic Process Automation (RPA)

RPA is the process of building, deploying, and managing software robots that boost work automation and decision-making capabilities. These robots can emulate human actions by relying on built-in software and machine-learning tools. RPA is a vital ingredient in digital transformation, extensively unravelling software robots, such as chatbots and virtual assistance services. RPAs core competency lies in handling big data for software robots, thereby automating complex processes and eliminating human error. The viability of RPA technology is found in its robust stability and high repeatability. In the future, the integration of RPA with AI will enhance its ability to deal with complex business decisions. RPAs are considered antecedents of Fintech operating at back-end offices, such as processing account payables or receivables, financial recording, work hour adjustments, etc. As a result, the automation of repetitive and time-consuming tasks increases the productivity and efficiency of FIs and eliminates errors. This helps businesses to focus on strategic formulation and better customer satisfaction. Though RPA is well established among market leaders, it is expected to profoundly penetrate various industries.

1.4 Role of Fintech in Industry 5.0

1.4.1 Background

The fifth industrial revolution, referred to as *Industry 5.0*, is an emerging phase of industrialization that builds upon Industry 4.0, emphasizing the integration of automation, data exchange, and advanced manufacturing technologies. Industry 5.0 puts forward a collaboration between humans and machines working alongside advanced technologies for more sustainable and socially responsible production. In the modern era, Industry 5.0 is a broader term than just manufacturing or processes, with the penetration of technological advancements such as AI, the IoT, machine learning, blockchain, robotics, etc. The advancement of technologies and constant evolvement of Fintech companies provide the foundation for growing digitization in businesses and economies across the globe. With the advent of automation technologies, the IoT, and the smart factory, Industry 4.0 emerged. Industry 5.0 advances by utilizing the synergy between ever-more precise, powerful, and intelligent machines and the distinctive creative capacity of the human being. However, the idea of Industry 5.0 goes beyond industry to encompass all organizations and business strategies to create a broader perspective than seen with Industry 4.0. Although we have not yet fully transitioned from Industry 4.0 to Industry 5.0, we still find a number of studies critically evaluating the role of Industry 5.0 in driving innovation and sustainability in the Fintech industry. Some major aspects of Industry 5.0 include the following:

- **Human–Machine Collaboration**: Industry 5.0 promotes the integration of human creativity and decision-making with advanced technologies. Development of Fintech products and services could lead to more efficient design processes, improved customer engagement, value co-creation, and enhanced safety features through human expertise combined with AI and robotics. The new paradigm change in this partnership promises to alter the realm of the Fintech industry.
- **Sustainable Production**: Industry 5.0 encourages the use of environmentally friendly materials and energy-efficient production processes. In the context of Fintech, this may lead to the adoption of sustainable manufacturing and the use of renewable energy sources for Fintech companies. Companies are embracing sustainable business practices aiming to reduce their carbon footprint. For example, Apple Inc. commits to be 100 per cent carbon neutral by 2030. At the heart of this sustainable development is the Fintech industry. To promote sustainability, FIs are creating financial products and services that incentivize companies to invest in energy-efficient technologies or sustainable development products.
- **Customization and Personalization**: As Industry 4.0 failed to accept the increasing demand for personalization, Industry 5.0 aims to amend this through greater customization and personalization of products. With a focus on personalized solutions, the Fintech industry engages in a customer-centric strategy, prioritizing customized financial products and services, such as robo-advisors, virtual chatbots, etc., potentially increasing their adoption. Industry 5.0 aims to offer niche solutions through mass customization with minimum cost and maximum accuracy.
- **Connectivity and Smart Infrastructure**: Industry 5.0 promotes the use of interconnected devices and smart infrastructure. In the case of Fintech, this could facilitate better financial viability, real-time future market performance, and improved overall efficiency.

1.4.2 *Financial Innovation and Industry 5.0*

In the era of Industry 5.0, Fintech companies develop new products and services allowing greater customization and adherence to sustainability. These financial innovations will cover a wide array of benefits to the business-to-business (B2B), business-to-consumer (B2C), and peer-to-peer (P2P) markets.

Some of the major Fintech innovations include PayTech, LendTech, digital banking, digital currency, WealthTech, and InsureTech.

1.4.2.1 *Digital Payments/PayTech*

In the past decade, the payment landscape has changed drastically from online payment (e.g., PayPal, Venmo) and mobile payment (e.g., ApplePay, GPay, WhatsApp Pay) to crypto-based payments (e.g., coinbase, Ripple). Cashless payments are the new norm and are expected to grow significantly with Industry 5.0. Since the onset of the pandemic, cashless payments have witnessed a sudden jump. In tandem, payment apps and services are widely accepted by individuals and businesses, as it is significantly less expensive than other payment methods. In the US, Plaid emerges as a major player in carrying out digital payments, while GPay and Paytm share a major portion of Paytech services in India. Digital payments are expected to be more secure, reliable, and convenient in Industry 5.0.

1.4.2.2 *Fintech Lenders/Lendtech*

Digital lending technology effectively provides accurate and faster decisions on loan approvals. Fintech lending companies provide loan services to applicants by collecting the required data and processing the information accurately with reliable decisions. The services include personal loans, auto loans, education loans, mortgage loans, and P2P lending. The digital lending app services are provided by banks and non-banking FIs. The prominent Fintech lenders are SoFi, Prosper, and SoLo, offering a range of lending and wealth management services. These Fintech companies use big data and the IoT in the lending process, stimulating consumer-friendly, personalized loan choices. For businesses, Lendtech firms provide fixed-term finance and trade finance.

1.4.2.3 Digital Banking

With the rise in digital banking, such as neobanks, the Fintech industry has changed the perspective on the most vital component of the financial system. Neobanks' services include, though are not limited to, application programming interfaces (API) providers and aggregators, conversational platforms, banking as a service (BaaS), and core banking. Digital banking simplifies banking services such as account opening and fund transfers with 24/7 availability. In turn, neobanks such as Varo offer traditional banking services, including personal accounts, saving accounts, and even secured credit cards; all these services are exempted from any surcharge that can hinder people from achieving their financial goals [6].

1.4.2.4 Digital Currency

Digital currency, also known as digital money, e-money, or e-currency, is exclusively available in electronic form, intangible in nature, but has the potential to serve as a medium of exchange or transaction. The electronic versions of currency are dominating the financial systems of a majority of developed economies, as they assist in fund flow simply and transparently. Digital currency can be categorized into three types: cryptocurrency, stablecoins, and central bank digital currency (CBDCs). The upsurge in the demand for Bitcoin (BTC), Ethereum (ETH), and thousands of other cryptocurrencies emerged as a new concept and was embraced by researchers, policymakers, and regulators alike. Unlike traditional paper notes and coins, digital currency is at the nascent stage and is still evolving. With a limited user base, vague regulatory framework, and incompetent infrastructure to support digital currency, its wider acceptance is dwindling. However, questions still abound. Moreover, volatility and regulatory compliance of digital currency limit the wider acceptance of digital money across the globe.

However, due to growing needs and tech-savvy consumers, digital currency is a debatable topic, and a majority of countries are exploring CBDCs. As of 2022, a few countries have made available CBDCs, namely, the Central Bank of Nigeria (e-Naira), the Central Bank of The Bahamas (Sand Dollar), the Eastern Caribbean Central Bank (DCash), and the Bank of Jamaica (JamDex). Interestingly, India has also launched its own CBDC, known as e-rupee, in response to the increase of digital payment systems based on blockchain technology. This e-rupee is a digital token and is considered a legal tender within Indian territory. Similarly, the US Federal Reserve and the People's Bank of China, along with other developed nations, are also exploring the possibilities of CBDCs.

1.4.2.5 Wealth and Investment Management/WealthTech

Robo-advisors and generative AI have dramatically altered the entire process of financial advisory. Robo-advisors are considered bias-free and emotionless wealth advisors based on AI and machine learning in delivering financial pieces of advice. In the Wealthtech segment, the robo-advisors' services include wealth and expense management such as income tax advice, retirement plans, and other holistic financial advice. For example, Stash provides easy and affordable access to financial advice products to users related to investment, education, etc.

While the robo-advisors may be just as safe as your human advisor, there are still a few precautions. The robo-advisors are generally recommended for basic investment decisions and may not be the best fit in complex scenarios that require human intelligence. Further, these robo-advisors rely on historical data in investment decision-making, there exists a possibility for errors, biases, or overfitting that could lead to suboptimal performance. Therefore, robo-advisors are susceptible to market declines and may incur losses in uncertain economic times.

1.4.2.6 Insurance/Insuretech

Insurance is one of the most conservative financial sectors, but Fintech companies are causing havoc in the global insurance market. A new term, *Insuretech*, was coined for the insurance industry employing Fintech. The Insuretech industry uses advanced technology to provide services such as digital insurance, virtual comparative analysis of investment schemes, e-insurance, P2P insurance, etc., with more precision and efficiency. These digitalized insurers such as Acko, Lemonade, PolicyBazaar, etc., are well-positioned to deliver customized policies, on-demand insurance solutions, automated claim processing, and real-time risk assessment that cater to evolving individual needs with better customer experience. The Insuretech industry is on the rise due to the support of innovative technologies such as AI, machine learning, the IoT, and blockchain that enable them to offer real-time surveillance and monitoring.

According to Future Market Insights, the Insuretech market is projected to be valued at 20.66 billion US dollars by the end of 2023 and further expected to rise to 210.6 billion US dollars by 2033, expanding at a significant compound annual growth rate (CAGR) of 26.1%.[3]

1.5 Risks and Challenges

The Fintech industry is considered one of the fastest-growing sectors in the world economy. With the growing competition and nascent financial innovations, the industry, nevertheless, faces various issues and challenges. The major challenges or risks faced by Fintech firms include the following:

■ **Regulatory Compliance**: FIs are one of the most regulated sectors. While government regulations and compliance vary from country to country, starting a Fintech firm is still challenging. Compliance and regulatory frameworks are implemented to safeguard the stakeholders from fraud and forgery. Fintech firms experienced various fraud alerts and data thefts, which lead to stricter regulations. These restrictions serve as a roadblock and make operations complex for Fintech firms.

■ **Data Security**: Data security and privacy leaks pose a major challenge for Fintech companies. As per the nature of business, Fintech firms store personal and financial data of users, such as social security numbers, credit card details, etc., and, thus, are often targeted by cyberattacks, data privacy violations, malware attacks, and fraudulent transactions. As Fintech services are widely adopted, data security and maintaining customer privacy will be of paramount importance. Therefore, Fintech companies should invest in research and development of cybersecurity for a brighter industry future.

■ **Lack of Tech Expertise**: A majority of the traditional FIs are reluctant to adopt Fintech solutions. Adoption of new technologies depends on economic status, education, and other social factors, and its contribution can only be realized when it is widely accepted and used. The problem looms larger in developing and emerging economies in which financial companies are still reliant on outdated and insecure software or applications. In a tech-savvy world, the consumers demand seamless and secure technologies. Although we may witness the constant focus shift to providing a better user experience, the process is still lengthy. However, the application of bots and conventional user interfaces (UI) have paved the way toward simplicity, transparency, and accessibility.

■ **Green Fintech**: Notwithstanding the fact that Fintech companies' inclination toward sustainability and green finance has swiftly changed in adherence to Industry 5.0, Fintech companies still need to cover a lot of ground. FIs should consider the planet and people and incorporate environmental, social, and governance (ESG) factors as well as financial factors when drafting long-term sustainable goals. Financing environmentally friendly projects and businesses, such as renewable energy, energy efficiency, sustainable agriculture, and clean technologies, can help to achieve these goals. To cope with the changing world and climate crisis risks, many Fintech companies, such as CarbonChain, Treelion, Tomorrow, etc., focus on building business models based on financial inclusion, sustainable investing, and green Fintech.

■ **Personalization**: In today's context, personalization is the primary and core strategy for Fintech firms to deliver hyper-relevant products and services. Owing to AI, the IoT, and deep learning, Fintech companies can provide tailored services as per the customer's profile, boosting loyalty, retention, and user experience. However, it is crucial to consider that personalized solutions require comprehensive user data, including financial data.

1.6 The Road Ahead

It is hard to predict for sure what Fintech innovations are on the horizon, as the Fintech industry is constantly evolving and emerging. The pandemic caused a serious setback for Fintech. Fintech companies are struggling with new regulations and complex government compliance measures. A few Fintech firms failed to secure the funding requirements, increasing the uncertainty of the business. At the same time, demand for Fintech has, perhaps, never been higher. Businesses and banking customers increasingly rely on technology to help navigate their financial livelihoods. Fintech is now so pervasive in FIs that it's all but ubiquitous, and it appears its influence will only grow in the future.

Notes

1. https://www.indiabudget.gov.in/economicsurvey/doc/echapter.pdf
2. https://www.statista.com/statistics/719385/investments-into-fintech-companies-globally/
3. https://www.futuremarketinsights.com/reports/insurtech-market

References

1. King, B. (2018). *Bank 4.0: Banking everywhere, never at a bank*. John Wiley & Sons.
2. Śledziewska, K., & Włoch, R. (2021). *The economics of digital transformation: The disruption of markets, production, consumption, and work*. Routledge.
3. Xu, J. (Ed.). (2022). *Future and fintech, the: Abcdi and beyond*. World Scientific.
4. Hassani, H., Huang, X., Silva, E. S., Hassani, H., Huang, X., & Silva, E. S. (2019). *Fusing big data, blockchain, and cryptocurrency* (pp. 99–117). Springer International Publishing.
5. Dorfleitner, G., Hornuf, L., Schmitt, M., Weber, M., Dorfleitner, G., Hornuf, L., … Weber, M. (2017). *The fintech market in Germany* (pp. 13–46). Springer International Publishing.
6. Nicoletti, B. (2021). *Banking 5.0: How fintech will change traditional banks in the 'new normal' post pandemic*. Springer Nature.

Chapter 2

Evolution of Fintech in the Financial Sector: Recent Trends and Future Perspectives

Asif Khan, Syed Hasan Jafar, and Hani El-Chaarani

2.1 Introduction

The landscape of the financial sector has undergone unprecedented changes in the past decade, largely owing to the advent and proliferation of financial technology, commonly known as Fintech (Chishti & Barberis, 2016; Murinde et al., 2022). This technology-driven transformation is fundamentally altering how financial products are designed, how markets function, and even the very concept of money itself. The integration of advanced technologies such as blockchain, artificial intelligence (AI), and data analytics into financial services has not just streamlined operations but has also expanded the reach of financial institutions (Arslanian & Fischer, 2019).

Fintech has made remarkable strides on a global scale, influencing not just advanced economies but also making substantial inroads in developing countries (Rodima-Taylor, 2022; Issami & Tandamba, 2023). Digital payment systems, peer-to-peer lending platforms, robo-advisors, and virtual currencies are some of the most ubiquitous Fintech applications (Ge et al., 2021). Traditional financial institutions are increasingly collaborating with Fintech start-ups to stay competitive and to meet the changing demands of

DOI: 10.4324/9781032644165-2

consumers. A notable trend is the growth of decentralized finance, challenging the centralized financial systems. Furthermore, the COVID-19 pandemic has accelerated the digitization of financial services, with many turning to Fintech solutions out of necessity (Soto-Acosta, 2020; Murinde et al., 2022). The banking sector development leads to the overall growth in the economy in every sector, particularly in service export (Azmi & Akhtar, 2023). In addition, AI has also made stock forecasting and predicting trends in the market easy based on the past data and current price movement (Jafar et al., 2023).

Despite its exponential growth and adoption, the Fintech sector presents a complex interplay of opportunities and challenges. While there is abundant literature on individual aspects of Fintech, such as digital payments or blockchain, comprehensive studies that cover its multifaceted impact on the financial sector, especially in the context of developing economies, are relatively scarce. Moreover, with rapid changes in technology, there is a pertinent need for up-to-date research that captures the current trends, benefits, and challenges.

This study aims to fill this gap by providing an in-depth analysis of the evolution of Fintech in the financial sector, focusing on its recent trends and future perspectives. It will delve into key areas such as financial inclusion, economic development, gender equality, and risk management. The study will also examine the regulatory frameworks that govern Fintech, proposing recommendations for balancing innovation and risk. Additionally, the study will contribute to the existing body of knowledge by integrating insights from real-world case studies, expert opinions, and statistical data, thereby offering a holistic view of the subject matter. In summary, the study aims to serve as a comprehensive resource for policymakers, financial institutions, researchers, and practitioners interested in understanding the transformative impact of Fintech on the financial sector and what the future holds in this exciting and ever-evolving landscape.

2.2 Fintech in Banking Sector

Fintech has transformed the banking industry, revolutionizing many elements of financial services and customer experience (Thakor, 2020; Sheng, 2021; Nguyen et al., 2021; Jain & Seth, 2023). Fintech has considerably improved ease and accessibility, from mobile banking and online account management to peer-to-peer payments and digital wallets. It has democratized financial services by reaching out to underserved and unserved people, particularly in rural and remote locations. Multifactor authentication, blockchain, and improved encryption methods have strengthened trust in digital transactions (Almadani et al., 2023). Automation, AI-driven analytics, and cloud computing have also significantly improved operational efficiency (Wajid et al., 2022; Ramachandran et al., 2022). To control this confluence of finance and technology, regulatory frameworks have arisen, with a focus on consumer protection, anti-money laundering, and data security. Overall, Fintech has challenged traditional banking structures while also paving the way for a more inclusive, efficient, and safe financial ecosystem (Taherdoost, 2023).

2.2.1 Enhancing Customer Experience in Banking through Fintech Innovations

Fintech platforms are fundamentally customer-focused, employing intuitive interfaces and user-friendly designs (Karim et al., 2022). Whether it is mobile banking apps or online dashboards, these platforms are making it easier for customers to carry out transactions, view account details, and manage their financial portfolios. The symbiosis between Fintech and traditional banking has been increasingly beneficial for the end-users, i.e., the customers (Chan et al., 2022). This relationship has significantly impacted the way banking services are accessed, utilized, and experienced by consumers. The following is a detailed discussion on how Fintech is enhancing customer experiences in the banking sector.

Fintech companies excel in delivering superior user interfaces that are intuitive, user-friendly, and visually appealing. By incorporating these elements into banking apps and websites, banks can offer a seamless digital experience that mimics the simplicity of consumer apps. Improved user interfaces (UI) and user experience (UX) ensures that customers can easily navigate through services, reducing friction and enhancing satisfaction. Advanced data analytics and machine learning algorithms enable banks to offer personalized financial products and advice (Taherdoost, 2023). Customers receive targeted offers based on their spending habits, investment choices, and risk tolerance. This high level of personalization makes banking more relevant to individual needs and lifestyles. Further, through chatbots and AI-driven customer service, banks can offer real-time assistance 24/7. This capability is especially useful for resolving simple queries or conducting basic transactions. It not only reduces the workload on human customer service agents but also ensures that customers have immediate access to help whenever needed. Fintech innovations have drastically reduced transaction times (Taherdoost, 2023). Whether it is fund transfer, loan approval, or investment transactions, processes that used to take days can now be completed almost instantaneously. The speed and efficiency add a layer of convenience that significantly improves customer experience. Fintech enables banks to offer multichannel accessibility to customers. Services can be accessed via mobile apps, websites, and even through third-party platforms using application programming interfaces (APIs). This omni-channel approach ensures that customers can conduct banking activities at their convenience, through the channel they are most comfortable with. Fintech has introduced various interactive tools that help customers to better manage their finances (Jain & Seth, 2023). Features such as expenditure tracking, budget-setting, and investment simulators empower customers to take charge of their financial health. These tools are often integrated into the banking apps, making it easier for customers to plan and manage their finances in one place.

The use of digital know your customer (KYC) and other identity verification technologies have simplified the customer onboarding process (Schlatt et al., 2022). New accounts can be created in minutes, with minimal paperwork, thereby making the initial interaction with the bank positive and hassle-free. With advanced features such as biometric authentication, two-factor authentication, and blockchain-based encryption, Fintech is strengthening the security framework of banking platforms. A secure environment enhances customer trust, which is crucial for a positive banking experience. Some banks are partnering with Fintech firms to offer educational content within their platforms. Short videos, articles, and tutorials on financial planning, investment strategies, and risk management educate customers, enriching their overall banking experience. Fintech's ability to automate several banking processes results in reduced operational costs. These savings often translate to lower service fees for customers, making banking more affordable.

2.2.2 Enhancing Operational Efficiency in Banks through Fintech Innovations

Fintech has transformed the banking business, improving customer service and operational efficiency (Dwivedi et al., 2021; Lee et al., 2021; Ni et al., 2023). These areas are where Fintech is making a big impact. Fintech solutions automate data entry, basic client questions, and some compliance checks. Automation speeds up procedures, minimizes human error, and frees up skills for more difficult activities that demand critical thought.

Fintech solutions using machine learning and advanced algorithms can anticipate loan, investment, and other financial risk using massive data sets (Fang et al., 2023; Ni et al., 2023). This predictive analysis is faster and more accurate than traditional methods, helping banks to make better judgements. Regtech, a subset of Fintech, helps financial firms comply with laws efficiently and cheaply. Automating compliance data collection and reporting helps banks to comply with legal obligations and reduce non-compliance risks. Fintech solutions track transactions, client interactions, and other variables in real time. In financial markets, where conditions can change in seconds, real-time decision-making is vital. Automation and process optimization cut operational costs significantly. Saving money by eliminating personnel, errors, or transaction times is one of Fintech's most immediate benefits (Lee et al., 2021). Security is a top priority for banks due to cyberthreats. Fintech cybersecurity solutions improve bank security through biometric authentication, end-to-end encryption, and blockchain-based verification. Chatbots and AI-driven customer service can solve many client issues without human participation. This gives customers instant support and frees up customer service professionals to handle more difficult situations. Fintech systems can track items and invoices in real time for supply chain finance banks, keeping all stakeholders informed of shipments, payments, and receivables. Transparency streamlines transactions and reduces fraud. Fintech systems are scalable, so banks can simply add services or features. The system is scalable to accommodate banking operations' expanding scale and complexity (Sheng, 2021). Modern Fintech solutions work with other platforms and systems, including old bank systems. Interoperability streamlines integration, saving time and money on technology upgrades. Cloud-based Fintech solutions provide strong disaster recovery and business continuity. This is essential for preserving operating efficiency through hardware breakdowns, natural catastrophes, and other disruptions (Taherdoost, 2023). In conclusion, Fintech is improving banking operational efficiency by converting outmoded models with dynamic, cost-effective ones.

2.2.3 Security Enhancements in Banking through Fintech Innovations

Security is a foundation of client trust and operational requirement in banking. Several creative Fintech solutions have improved this feature. This section provides a detailed look at how Fintech is improving banking security. Fintech has made two-factor and multifactor authentication possible (Singh et al., 2020). These solutions require password, device, or biometric verification, making unauthorized access more difficult. Fintech advances have added fingerprint, face, and retina scans to banking apps and systems. Biometrics increase account security by making them hard to copy. Secure, transparent, and immutable record-keeping uses blockchain technology. This system protects transactions, verifies assets, and reduces fraud. The decentralized data storage makes it tougher for thieves to modify data.

Fintech enables powerful encryption that secures data from start to finish. End-to-end encryption protects transaction integrity and confidentiality by preventing data interceptions and manipulation. AI and machine learning systems can detect suspicious transactions in real time. These tools can learn from prior data and accurately detect fraudulent transactions, flagging them for review before processing. Open banking projects use secure APIs to let third-party developers build financial institution apps and services. Data sharing with these APIs is compliant with rules and secure due to their sophisticated security mechanisms. Tokenization protects sensitive data by replacing it with unique symbols or tokens. Payment gateways and online transactions employ tokens to replace sensitive data such as credit card information, making it useless if intercepted. Advanced cloud security has accompanied financial operations' cloud migration. Data protection, vulnerability management, and regulatory compliance are offered by cloud security Fintech providers. Digital KYC and identity verification have simplified customer onboarding without compromising security. These systems accurately identify new consumers using machine learning and biometrics. Fintech has also developed banking-specific firewalls, intrusion detection systems, and anti-malware software. These cybersecurity procedures are updated to combat new threats. Financial institutions can meet security requirements with Regtech Fintech solutions. Automating compliance data tracking and reporting ensures the bank meets the newest regulatory requirements.

2.2.4 Regulatory Framework for Fintech in Banking Sector

Banking Fintech has evolved swiftly, requiring a dynamic regulatory framework to assure integrity, stability, and consumer safety (Ringe et al., 2020; Muganyi et al., 2022). While regulatory systems differ by state, there are numerous global themes and activities (Ni et al., 2023). Fintech enterprises that handle customer funds or provide bank-like financial services must get licenses in several jurisdictions. Licences usually have capital and operational requirements to assure stability and integrity. Enterprises must follow anti-money laundering (AML) and KYC compliance rules. Identity verification and continual surveillance ensure that the services are not utilized for money laundering or other criminal activity. Fintech organizations handle a lot of sensitive data; therefore, data protection rules, such as the General Data Protection Regulation (GDPR) and the California Consumer Privacy Act (CCPA), apply. These rules may force companies to hire a data protection officer and strictly control personal data. European open banking laws, such as the Revised Payment Service Directive (PSD2), require traditional banks to offer their APIs to third-party providers (including Fintech companies) for payment initiation and account information with client agreement. These rules promote competitiveness and innovation. Fintech regulations mainly include customer rights, transparent pricing, fair practices, and complaint resolution. In some jurisdictions, Fintech companies must contribute to a compensation fund to protect client savings or investments. Regulations often place prudential restrictions on Fintech enterprises that take deposits or offer loans to ensure financial stability (Eichengreen, 2023). Stress testing, capital adequacy, and liquidity ratios are examples. Given the risks of digital transactions and data storage, regulators have strict cybersecurity standards. These standards frequently follow worldwide best practises and require security incident reporting and audits. Fintech enterprises can test their innovations in a controlled environment without having to comply with all regulatory regulations in many jurisdictions (Muganyi et al., 2022). This promotes innovation and helps regulators to comprehend new technologies. Fintech companies generally operate internationally, making international regulatory collaboration crucial. The Global Financial Innovation Network (GFIN) seeks to standardize Fintech regulation in participating states. Regular inspection and reporting guarantee that Fintech companies follow regulations. Financial reporting, compliance checks, and notification of major operational changes may be required. The UK Financial Conduct Authority (FCA) has a unit dedicated to innovation and Fintech.

In conclusion, banking Fintech regulation is complex and developing. It promotes innovation while ensuring financial stability, consumer protection, and system integrity. Fintech regulation will change with it.

2.3 Fintech in Insurance Sector

Fintech has brought transformative innovations to the insurance industry, leading to the emergence of "Insurtech." These advancements have revolutionized traditional insurance models in multiple ways (Alfiero et al., 2022). Through machine learning and data analytics, insurers can now offer personalized policies based on more precise risk assessments. Automation and digital platforms have simplified administrative tasks, enabling customers to purchase policies, make payments, and file claims online, reducing the need for physical paperwork and office visits (Lee et al., 2021). Internet of Things (IoT) devices and telematics provide real-time behavioural data, allowing insurers, particularly in the auto industry, to offer dynamic, behaviour-based pricing models. Furthermore, advanced algorithms have enhanced fraud detection capabilities, leading to more efficient claims processing and reduced losses. Customer engagement has also been elevated through the use of AI-driven chatbots and mobile applications, which offer 24/7 support and personalized advice. Even in the realm of health insurance, virtual consultations and remote health monitoring via wearables are becoming increasingly common. Regulatory frameworks are evolving to keep pace with these innovations, focusing on consumer protection, data privacy, and cybersecurity (Chan et al., 2022). Overall, Fintech has made the insurance sector more efficient, customer-centric, and secure, while also demanding new approaches to regulation and oversight (Umasankar et al., 2023).

2.3.1 Enhancing Customer Experience in Insurance through Fintech Innovations

Fintech has greatly improved the customer experience by fixing long-standing problems and adding new, convenient features. Personalization of insurance goods is at the heart of this change. With the help of machine learning algorithms and big data analytics, insurers can now offer policies that are very specific to each person's risk profile and tastes (Bauer et al., 2021). This gets rid of the "one-size-fits-all" method, which makes insurance more useful and focused on the customer. Insurance methods have become more digital, which has also made the customer journey easier. Everything can be done online through easy-to-use tools, from finding and comparing policies to buying them and renewing them. This digital-first method saves time and makes it easy to take care of insurance issues from anywhere, at any time. This is even better now that there are mobile apps that offer features such as instant policy details, payment reminders, and even location-based services, such as finding nearby network hospitals for health insurance (Bauer et al., 2021). Automation and AI-driven analytics have made claims handling a lot better, which used to be a big source of trouble. Customers can now file claims online, share the necessary paperwork, and see how the process is going in real time. This makes things less stressful and uncertain during what is usually a tough time. Also, advanced algorithms can speed up the process of verifying claims, which makes the payment process go more quickly and clearly. Also, adding IoT devices, especially to health and auto insurance, lets companies reduce risk ahead of time and use dynamic price models (Kumar et al., 2023). For example, wearable tech can keep an eye on health metrics in real time, giving users information and even warnings that could help them to avoid big health problems. In the case of car insurance, telematics can encourage safer driving by tying it to lower premiums. AI-powered robots have also changed the way customer service is done. They can answer a wide range of questions 24/7, making service even more accessible and quick. These technological advances not only make insurance more effective, but they also make it more in line with what current customers expect, which makes the whole experience for customers a lot better (Trivedi, 2023).

2.3.2 Enhancing Operational Efficiency in Insurance Sector through Fintech Innovations

Insurtech, the integration of Fintech into the insurance sector, has greatly improved operational efficiency across several functions. One of the biggest improvements is automation. AI and machine learning algorithms have simplified underwriting, claims processing, and customer support. Automation cuts manual labour, human error, and time-consuming processes, cutting operational expenses. Big data and analytics improved risk assessment and pricing. Insurers may now use massive volumes of data from IoT devices and social media to improve risk profiles. Better pricing models, reduced high-risk asset exposure, and more profitability result. Analytics can also predict market trends, customer behaviour, and claims, helping insurers to make better judgements. Another breakthrough is blockchain technology, which makes contract management and transactions secure and transparent. Blockchain-enabled smart contracts can automate claim approvals and policy renewals, improving insurance efficiency and transparency.

With AI and data analytics, customer relationship management (CRM) systems have also improved greatly. These technologies enable targeted marketing and client retention by providing real-time customer behaviour and preference analytics. Finally, Regtech solutions automate regulatory compliance checks and reporting, simplifying insurers' regulatory compliance issues. This keeps the corporation compliant with new laws and frees up resources for key business activities. Overall, Fintech advances in the insurance industry are improving client experiences and altering operational efficiencies, making the industry more adaptable, cost-effective, and ready for new financial issues.

2.3.3 Security Enhancements in Banking through Fintech Innovations

The Fintech sector in India has undergone significant transformations over the past few years, evolving into a market projected to reach 150 billion US dollars by 2025. While the democratization of financial services through Fintech, particularly in rural India, has been well-documented, an often-overlooked but equally significant dimension is the strengthening of the security architecture in the banking sector. This aspect is particularly crucial given the sheer volume of digital transactions reported by the Reserve Bank of India (RBI), which stood at 6.2 billion transactions worth 10.6 trillion Indian rupees in July 2022 alone.

Traditional banking infrastructure has long been beleaguered by a range of security issues, from data breaches to fraudulent transactions. In response, regulatory bodies, such as the RBI, have been increasingly focusing on financial security, as evidenced by initiatives such as the "Financial Literacy Week" held in February 2022. Against this backdrop, Fintech innovations have been playing a pivotal role in enhancing security protocols. For instance, multifactor authentication (MFA) has become a standard feature in many Fintech solutions, providing a much-needed layer of security that also aligns with stringent regulatory requirements.

Additionally, breakthrough technologies, such as blockchain, are being employed to create tamper-proof ledgers for transactions, significantly reducing the scope of fraud. AI and machine learning algorithms are being implemented to monitor transactional behaviours in real-time, thereby flagging anomalies that may signify fraudulent activities. End-to-end encryption technologies secure data transmission, offering an added layer of protection for confidential information. Moreover, the advent of open banking has led to the use of secure APIs, allowing for a safer and more secure integration of third-party financial services applications.

Real-world applications further substantiate these advancements. Aadhaar-linked transactions, for instance, offer a robust identification method that minimizes identity theft, and the unified payments interface (UPI) incorporates built-in security features such as one-time-passwords (OTP) and Quick Response (QR) code scans. However, the Fintech sector also faces challenges in terms of data privacy and regulatory hurdles. The aggregation of large sets of financial data poses risks if not managed and encrypted effectively, and inconsistent regulatory frameworks can slow down the rapid deployment of newer and more effective security features.

In conclusion, the Fintech revolution in India, supported by government-led initiatives such as "Digital India," has had a transformative impact on the security landscape of the country's banking sector. Not only has Fintech democratized access to financial services, but it has also instilled robust security mechanisms that reduce risk and enhance consumer trust. Therefore, while Fintech's role in financial inclusion is undisputed, its legacy may well be defined by the heightened security standards it brings to banking – an area ripe for further academic inquiry.

2.3.4 Regulatory Framework for Fintech in Banking Sector

The increasing growth of Fintech in the global financial ecosystem, particularly in emerging economies such as India, has necessitated an evolved regulatory framework. This framework aims to balance the dual objectives of fostering innovation and ensuring consumer protection, financial stability, and data security. Regulatory bodies such as the RBI have been at the forefront of these efforts. This discussion aims to explore the contours of the regulatory landscape governing Fintech in the banking sector, focusing on key regulations, their implications, and existing challenges.

The first layer of regulation often involves licensing and registration requirements for Fintech companies. This ensures that only entities meeting specified criteria can offer financial services, thereby contributing to the sector's credibility. In India, the Payments and Settlement Systems Act, 2007, governs payment service providers, and the RBI has laid down guidelines for peer-to-peer lending platforms, thereby bringing them under its regulatory purview. Regulatory sandboxes have also been introduced to provide a controlled environment for testing new products and services, which is critical for fostering innovation without compromising on consumer safety. Further, the regulatory frameworks also focus heavily on consumer protection and data security (Ni et al., 2023). For example, the RBI's guidelines on data localization require Fintech companies to store payment data only in India, aimed at ensuring data security and facilitating regulatory supervision.

Similarly, guidelines on KYC procedures are increasingly being harmonized for banks and Fintech companies to minimize fraud and money laundering risks.

Open banking initiatives have led to regulations concerning APIs. The aim here is to create a secure and standardized way of data sharing between traditional banks and Fintech companies. Secure APIs not only foster a collaborative environment but also ensure that data transfer meets stringent security standards, thereby safeguarding consumer information. Additionally, the regulatory frameworks have evolved to keep pace with technological advancements, though challenges remain. One significant challenge is the fine balance between promoting innovation and ensuring stringent compliance, which can sometimes act as a deterrent for Fintech start-ups (Lessambo, 2023). The lack of a global regulatory framework also poses issues, given that Fintech is not confined by geographical boundaries (Ringe et al., 2020). Lastly, with rapid technological changes, regulations can quickly become outdated, requiring continual updates to stay relevant.

In summary, the regulatory framework governing Fintech in the banking sector has seen significant evolution, driven by the need to encourage innovation while ensuring consumer protection and financial stability. Regulations encompass a broad spectrum, from licensing and KYC norms to data localization and open banking standards. While challenges such as balancing innovation with compliance and the absence of a global framework exist, regulatory bodies are making concerted efforts to adapt and update guidelines in line with technological advancements. The efficacy of these regulatory frameworks will be instrumental in shaping the future trajectory of Fintech in the banking sector, thereby warranting continuous academic and policy-oriented scrutiny.

2.4 Conclusion and Policy Implications

The integration of Fintech into the financial sector has had transformative effects on the banking and insurance industries, offering a paradigm shift in how financial services are delivered and consumed. This study provided a comprehensive examination of the Fintech landscape, focusing on its multifaceted implications in financial inclusion, economic development, gender equality, and risk management. While the benefits are abundant, ranging from democratization of financial services to enhancements in operational efficiencies and security protocols, challenges such as data privacy, consumer protection, and financial stability cannot be overlooked. The COVID-19 pandemic has further emphasized the crucial role of Fintech, acting as an accelerant for digital transformation and showing its resilience in maintaining the continuity of financial services.

While Fintech operates in a dynamically evolving landscape, there is a pressing need for a harmonized regulatory framework that can adapt to technological advancements. Policymakers should aim for international collaboration to standardize regulations, particularly for services that transcend national boundaries. Regulatory bodies should strike a balance between promoting innovation and ensuring consumer protection and financial stability. The concept of "regulatory sandboxes" can be extended to provide a controlled environment for Fintech firms to test their innovations while adhering to conditional regulatory relaxations. Given the extensive use of data analytics in Fintech, policymakers must enforce stringent data protection laws akin to GDPR in Europe. This will not only protect consumer data but also enhance trust in digital financial services. Governments should collaborate with Fintech firms to extend financial services to underserved areas and marginalized communities. This has implications for economic development and poverty reduction.

Special attention should be given to developing Fintech services that empower women, particularly in sectors such as microfinance and digital savings. Policy incentives could encourage such social impact projects. As Fintech becomes more integrated into the mainstream financial ecosystem, policymakers should mandate the adoption of advanced cybersecurity measures to safeguard against potential threats to financial stability. Regulatory bodies and financial institutions should jointly conduct educational programs aimed at equipping consumers with the knowledge required to navigate the complexities of digital financial services, thereby promoting responsible usage.

Policymakers should encourage the development of interoperable systems to ensure seamless interaction between traditional financial institutions and Fintech companies. This enhances consumer choice and fosters a competitive environment. Regulatory bodies should institute robust mechanisms for regular monitoring and reporting of Fintech activities to anticipate and mitigate systemic risks effectively.

Fintech offers a promising future, replete with opportunities and challenges. Policymakers and regulators have a pivotal role to play in shaping this future, ensuring that the rise of Fintech serves to enhance, rather than disrupt, the broader objectives of financial stability, consumer protection, and economic development. Therefore, this study serves as a foundational resource for a broad range of stakeholders, encouraging informed policy dialogue and fostering academic research in this rapidly evolving field.

2.5 Limitations and Directions for Future Research Work

The present study, while comprehensive, has limitations that warrant acknowledgment. The scope is restricted by the availability of current data and the rapid evolution of Fintech technologies, making some findings potentially time-sensitive. Additionally, the research adopts a global perspective, which may not fully encapsulate country-specific regulations and market conditions.

Looking ahead, there are several avenues for future research. Country-specific analyses would add depth to the understanding of Fintech adoption and regulatory frameworks. Longitudinal studies could capture the long-term impacts of Fintech on the financial landscape. Given the fast pace of technological advancements, ongoing research is crucial to update the findings and recommendations periodically, especially in areas such as data privacy, consumer behaviour, and evolving regulatory standards.

References

Alfiero, S., Battisti, E., & Hadjielias, E. (2022). Black box technology, usage-based insurance, and prediction of purchase behavior: Evidence from the auto insurance sector. *Technological Forecasting and Social Change, 183*, 121896. https://doi.org/10.1016/j.techfore.2022.121896

Almadani, M. S., Alotaibi, S., Alsobhi, H., Hussain, O. K., & Hussain, F. K. (2023). Blockchain-based multi-factor authentication: A systematic literature review. *Internet of Things*, 100844. https://doi.org/10.1016/j.iot.2023.100844

Arslanian, H., & Fischer, F. (2019). *The Future of Finance: The Impact of Fintech, AI, and Crypto on Financial Services*. Springer.

Azmi, S. N., & Akhtar, S. (2023). Interactions of services export, financial development and growth: Evidence from India. *Quality and Quantity, 57*(5), 4709–4724. https://doi.org/10.1007/s11135-022-01566-8

Bauer, D., Tyler Leverty, J., Schmit, J., & Sydnor, J. (2021). Symposium on insure-tech, digitalization, and big-data techniques in risk management and insurance. *Journal of Risk and Insurance, 88*(3), 525–528. https://doi.org/10.1111/jori.12360

Chan, R., Troshani, I., Rao Hill, S., & Hoffmann, A. (2022). Towards an understanding of consumers' Fintech adoption: The case of open banking. *International Journal of Bank Marketing, 40*(4), 886–917.

Chishti, S., & Barberis, J. (2016). *The Fintech Book: The Financial Technology Handbook for Investors, Entrepreneurs and Visionaries.* John Wiley & Sons.

Dwivedi, P., Alabdooli, J. I., & Dwivedi, R. (2021). Role of Fintech adoption for competitiveness and performance of the bank: A study of banking industry in UAE. *International Journal of Global Business and Competitiveness, 16*(2), 130–138. https://doi.org/10.1007/s42943-021-00033-9

Eichengreen, B. (2023). Financial regulation in the age of the platform economy. *Journal of Banking Regulation, 24*(1), 40–50.

Fang, L., Li, X., Subrahmanyam, A., & Zhang, K. (2023, February 7). Does Fintech improve traditional banks' operating efficiency and risk exposure? Machine learning-based evidence from patent filings in China. In *Machine Learning-Based Evidence from Patent Filings in China.*

Ge, R., Zheng, Z., Tian, X., & Liao, L. (2021). Human–robot interaction: When investors adjust the usage of robo-advisors in peer-to-peer lending. *Information Systems Research, 32*(3), 774–785. https://doi.org/10.1287/isre.2021.1009

Issami, M. A., & Tandamba, B. (2023). A disruptive fintech for inclusive finance in Africa: Role and contribution of mobile money. In *Smart Technologies for Organizations: Managing a Sustainable and Inclusive Digital Transformation,* pp. 65–86. https://doi.org/10.1007/978-3-031-24775-0_4

Jafar, S. H., Akhtar, S., El-Chaarani, H., Khan, P. A., & Binsaddig, R. (2023). Forecasting of NIFTY 50 index price by using backward elimination with an LSTM model. *Journal of Risk and Financial Management, 16*(10), 423. https://doi.org/10.3390/jrfm16100423

Jain, R., & Seth, N. (2023). Fintech in banking: Bibliometric and content analysis. *Contemporary Studies of Risks in Emerging Technology, Part A,* 139–154. https://doi.org/10.1108/978-1-80455-562-020231010

Karim, R. A., Sobhani, F. A., Rabiul, M. K., Lepee, N. J., Kabir, M. R., & Chowdhury, M. A. M. (2022). Linking fintech payment services and customer loyalty intention in the hospitality industry: The mediating role of customer experience and attitude. *Sustainability, 14*(24), 16481. https://doi.org/10.3390/su142416481

Kumar, P., Taneja, S., Özen, E., & Singh, S. (2023). Artificial intelligence and machine learning in insurance: A bibliometric analysis. In *Smart Analytics, Artificial Intelligence and Sustainable Performance Management in a Global Digitalised Economy,* pp. 191–202. Emerald Publishing Limited. https://doi.org/10.1108/S1569-37592023000110A010

Lee, C. C., Li, X., Yu, C. H., & Zhao, J. (2021). Does fintech innovation improve bank efficiency? Evidence from China's banking industry. *International Review of Economics and Finance, 74,* 468–483. https://doi.org/10.1016/j.iref.2021.03.009

Lessambo, F. I. (2023). Banking regulation and fintech challenges. In *Fintech Regulation and Supervision Challenges within the Banking Industry: A Comparative Study Within the G-20,* pp. 1–26. Springer Nature Switzerland. https://doi.org/10.1007/978-3-031-25428-4

Muganyi, T., Yan, L., Yin, Y., Sun, H., Gong, X., & Taghizadeh-Hesary, F. (2022). Fintech, regtech, and financial development: Evidence from China. *Financial Innovation, 8*(1), 1–20. https://doi.org/10.1186/s40854-021-00313-6

Murinde, V., Rizopoulos, E., & Zachariadis, M. (2022). The impact of the Fintech revolution on the future of banking: Opportunities and risks. *International Review of Financial Analysis, 81*, 102103. https://doi.org/10.1016/j.irfa.2022.102103

Nguyen, L., Tran, S., & Ho, T. (2021). Fintech credit, bank regulations and bank performance: A cross-country analysis. *Asia-Pacific Journal of Business Administration, 14*(4), 445–466. https://doi.org/10.1108/APJBA-05-2021-0196

Ni, Q., Zhang, L., & Wu, C. (2023). Fintech and commercial bank risks-the moderating effect of financial regulation. *Finance Research Letters*, 104536. https://doi.org/10.1016/j.frl.2023.104536

Ramachandran, K. K., Mary, A. A. S., Hawladar, S., Asokk, D., Bhaskar, B., & Pitroda, J. R. (2022). Machine learning and role of artificial intelligence in optimizing work performance and employee behavior. *Materials Today: Proceedings, 51*, 2327–2331.

Ringe, W. G., & Christopher, R. U. O. F. (2020). Regulating fintech in the EU: The case for a guided sandbox. *European Journal of Risk Regulation, 11*(3), 604–629. https://doi.org/10.1017/err.2020.8

Rodima-Taylor, D. (2022). Platformizing Ubuntu? Fintech, inclusion, and mutual help in Africa. *Journal of Cultural Economy, 15*(4), 416–435. https://doi.org/10.1080/17530350.2022.2040569

Schlatt, V., Sedlmeir, J., Feulner, S., & Urbach, N. (2022). Designing a framework for digital KYC processes built on blockchain-based self-sovereign identity. *Information and Management, 59*(7), 103553. https://doi.org/10.1016/j.im.2021.103553

Sheng, T. (2021). The effect of fintech on banks' credit provision to SMEs: Evidence from China. *Finance Research Letters, 39*, 101558. https://doi.org/10.1016/j.frl.2020.101558

Singh, S., Sahni, M. M., & Kovid, R. K. (2020). What drives Fintech adoption? A multi-method evaluation using an adapted technology acceptance model. *Management Decision, 58*(8), 1675–1697. https://doi.org/10.1108/MD-09-2019-1318

Soto-Acosta, P. (2020). COVID-19 pandemic: Shifting digital transformation to a high-speed gear. *Information Systems Management, 37*(4), 260–266. https://doi.org/10.1080/10580530.2020.1814461

Taherdoost, H. (2023). Fintech: Emerging trends and the future of finance. In *Financial Technologies and DeFi: A Revisit to the Digital Finance Revolution*, pp. 29–39.

Thakor, A. V. (2020). Fintech and banking: What do we know? *Journal of Financial Intermediation, 41*, 100833. https://doi.org/10.1016/j.jfi.2019.100833

Trivedi, S. (2023). Blockchain framework for insurance industry. *International Journal of Innovation and Technology Management*, 2350034. https://doi.org/10.1142/S0219877023500347

Umasankar, M., Desai, K., & Padmavathy, S. (2023). Insuretech: Saviour of insurance sector in India. In *Emerging Trends and Innovations in Industries of the Developing World*, pp. 1–6. CRC Press.

Wajid, A., Sabiha, A., Akhtar, S., Tabash, M. I., & Daniel, L. N. (2022). Cross-border acquisitions and shareholders' wealth: The case of the Indian pharmaceutical sector. *Journal of Risk and Financial Management, 15*(10), 437. https://doi.org/10.3390/jrfm15100437

Chapter 3

Corporate Reputation and Reaction in Developing Risk Frameworks

Sindhukavi Senthilkumar and Padmaja Bhujabal

3.1 Introduction

In the rapidly evolving landscape of the financial services industry, the adoption of financial technology (Fintech) has become an integral aspect for financial institutions to stay competitive and relevant. The rise of Fintech in the past decades has seen indomitable growth, and the rapid adoption of Fintech into various industries is a testament to its growing dominance and popularity. As per a report by Ernst and Young (2019), the global adoption of Fintech services increased to a massive 64% in 2019 from 15% in 2015. Moreover, adoption of Fintech services continues to grow as its impact continues to grow, as corporations face an increasing need to establish robust risk frameworks to mitigate potential risks and maintain a positive reputation.

While Fintech comes with variegated advantages, the risks that Fintech brings to various stakeholders cannot be undermined. Despite the rules, safety, and security measures, determining how to guarantee data security is still a question that fails to be answered. Understanding these underlying threats is imperative to the different segments that rely on Fintech – be it consumers, financial institutions, government and investors – as each stakeholder comes with a different threat. For traditional financial institutions, the advent of Fintech has forced them to modernize their procedures and

 DOI: 10.4324/9781032644165-3

systems to stay relevant. This increased pressure has led to a series of different reactions from banks and financial institutions.

To answer the immediate call for a risk and regulatory framework that mitigates the risks of Fintech, both preventive and reactive measures need to be established to solve the limitations posed by the Fintech industry with respect to data protection and security. Due to the extreme dependence on Fintech, a small hindrance has the potential to create a systemic risk that cascades into risking not just the ones involved in the Fintech practice but other populations as well due to the interdependence of Fintech and the economy. These risks, when not treated carefully, will severely affect the performance of the company, for which the ultimate consequence is a tarnished corporate reputation and a firm on the verge of losing its business. Thus, it is of extreme importance to understand the interwoven nature of various factors that could damage a company as well as the possible threats that could increase the vulnerability of stakeholders.

In this chapter, we will explore the critical link between corporate reputation, the reaction of financial institutions to Fintech, and the development of risk frameworks in the context of developing economies. By understanding the symbiotic relationship between these elements, organizations can navigate the challenges of adopting Fintech as either a companion or antagonist more effectively.

3.2 Understanding Corporate Reputation

Corporate reputation is synonymous with a company's credibility in recent times; thus, it is a crucial aspect in businesses. It is the lens that provides companies with the stakeholders' perceptions of them – their public image and identity. In the simplest terms, it is the reputation a company holds amongst its stakeholders, including investors, shareholders, creditors, and customers. Depending on the stakeholder, this reputation shapes the varied interests of the firm, making it imperative for a company's ideal survival.

Corporate reputation stands as an intangible but invaluable asset for financial institutions. A positive reputation enhances customer trust, attracts investors, and paves the way for valuable collaborations with other industry players. Understanding the stakeholders helps cater to the company's wellbeing and growth fuelled by measures taken to enhance the company's reputation. It also contributes to increased customer loyalty, leading to improved profitability and market share.

Corporate reputation is not dependent on just one factor; rather, it is an accumulation of elements that lead to a favourable or unfavourable corporate reputation. The numerous elements that impact corporate reputation are financial management, general organizational management, company communication, and corporate marketing. These elements, when taken care of responsibly, lead to an advantageous corporate reputation.

The financial management of a company plays a crucial role in aiding the corporate reputation. The financial performance indicators establish a clear understanding of a company's revenue and profit, allowing investors to make an informed decision about investing in a company. Investors are restricted regarding the information available to them when deciding whether to invest in a company; thus, financial indicators emerge as a relatively more reliable parameter pertaining to investing. A favourable financial performance stems from better performance of the product or service in the market, which reflects the customers' willingness to buy. Sustaining in the market is classified as a financial performance indicator and is also synonymous with a dynamic organization that can inculcate futuristic practices and stay updated during times of volatility. The adoption of Fintech models into companies' regular practices is an imperative asset, as it influences investor confidence, customer satisfaction, and prospective partnerships. The financial reputation of a company is susceptible to serious damage if it fails to adhere to the dynamic market of Fintech.

In addition to that, the effect of corporate communications on corporate reputation is inevitable. This is primarily accomplished by maintaining relationships amongst the various stakeholders of the company, on whom it depends for survival. Large companies, upon realizing the potential and importance of public relations, have invested great amounts in the same. Corporate reputation retains and gains customers, and these quality customers are ready to spend adequately as well as return for further requirements. Richardson and Bolesh (2002) state that reputable organizations protect their corporate images by maintaining high standards of practice no matter the circumstances. This statement communicates the necessity of companies to integrate technology into the their practices to attain high performance. Reputations are not easy to imitate and, thus, provide an upper hand amongst competition, which is why companies work to keep their goodwill high. Furthermore, the organizational management element relies on the quality of management and leadership positions; the goodwill of the leader is imperative to an organization's goodwill.

3.3 Reaction of Financial Institutions

The rise of Fintech has not only been a boon to finance but has also been a threat to traditional financial institutions due to the disruptions in the financial industry. Fintech has been rapidly expanding into various domains not restricted only to seamless payments but also wealth and asset management, wholesale banking, regulatory technology, and trade finance. These innovations have allowed the introduction and transition to financial technology. Traditional financial industries are moving toward a collaborative approach from a competitive approach by understanding the underlying advantages that Fintech offers – from digital payments done through Fintech companies to reaching underserved populations, enabling financial inclusion.

Integrating Fintech into a financial institution can take place in one of numerous ways, including acquisition, alliances, investments, or building a Fintech model within the organization itself.

Acquisition: Many financial institutions resort to acquisition to cope with emerging financial trends. The example of the infamous Capital One acquiring almost a record 15 financial technologies, which was almost a record number of acquisitions. Some of the recent and notable Fintech notable acquisitions are Lola, a travel management Fintech company that offers travel solutions to small and medium enterprises, and Triple Tree, an investment banking platform with interests in specific industries, such as healthcare, and taking advantage of the benefits of investing in certain industries.[1]

Partnerships: While acquisitions are predominant, partnerships have also started gaining significance in recent times. Partnerships allow companies to reach a wider customer-base, access new market opportunities, and mutually grow revenue, thus making it an attractive option between Fintech and banks. The year 2022, saw major partnerships between credit service Fintech Yubi and public sector banks State Bank of India (SBI) and Indian Bank.[2] While the strategic partnership with Indian bank was to enhance the supply chain financing of huge corporations with small and medium enterprises, the alliance with SBI was to integrate the co-lending platform to cater to unserved and underserved communities, thus, fostering financial inclusion amidst the underprivileged.

Capital Investments: Investing in Fintechs offers companies pivotal support in gaining a deeper perspective about the potential threats from the disruptive forces of Fintech. In 2023, Citigroup invested in Peru's leading Fintech aimed at foreign exchange services[3] to strengthen Citibank's market in Peru. This strategic investment allows the clients to access high performance automation, quick payments, and advantageous rates.

Developing a Fintech Model: Financial institutions are involved in innovating financial procedures even further to stay relevant during times of intense competition. Although proven to be time-consuming and expensive, this enables banks to remain proactive in the industry and tap into the opportunity before other banks and financial institutions. The entry of Fintech has, in many circumstances, forced banks and financial institutions to integrate technology within their traditional approaches to sustain the financial industry due to growing customer preferences, advancements in technology, and legal requirements. Most Indian banks have developed apps of their own to offer clients an effortless banking experience. SBI's You Only Need One (YONO) is an e-banking platform and is one of the largest of its kind, with a staggering 52.5 million online users out of its 450 million users as of August 2022.[4]

Getting Acquired: It is not always a bank ensuring the higher authority over Fintechs, as banks can get acquired as well. An interesting example of this occurred when SoFi, a personal digital finance company, acquired Golden Pacific Bancorp in early 2022 as a way to get a bank charter that was approved by the Federal Reserve and the Office of the Comptroller of the Currency (OCC).[5] This case is testimony to the power a Fintech can possess in the present and times to come.

3.4 Risks Associated with the Adoption of Fintech

Before we delve into the different types of risks associated with Fintech, it is imperative to know the factors influencing these risks. These factors help to identify the cause behind the prevalence of risks that unsteady trust in Fintech. The various factors that lead to cybersecurity risks can be identified as follows.

The first layer of risk is associated with the rapid growth of the Fintech industry. It pertains to the increased usage of the same cloud computing services with extremely contracted data nodes that, consequently, leads to less variation in software. This directly calls for increased security measures, as this common exposure could be fatal to data privacy. Companies accumulate data from huge populations of clients and customers, and the failure to integrate cybersecurity measures with differentiated software could lead to the risk of a data breach. Moreover, relying on third-party entities in the process of integrating technologies that are interconnected with other technologies could lead to endangering data due to the availability of important data in different devices (World Bank, 2021).

The risk of endogenous and exogenous threats is extensively prevalent in this day and age. Endogenous threats are threats within the organization caused by compromised or unauthorized access to organizational data. On the other hand, exogenous threats arise from the fraudulent usage of data by outside entities that could be partner organizations or hackers. The persistent usage of unsafe or undiversified software without a necessary security-enabled cloud could lead to a data breach, which, in turn, could seriously tarnish the reputation of the company. A follow-up problem of the concentrated data nodes is the cybermonoculture, which pertains to large companies using the same information technology (IT) systems, including software, cloud computing services, and infrastructure. This resemblance or uniformity attracts risks and could result in a series of cascading cyberattacks in which institutions using the same IT model are easy targets to the risk of data extortion. Thus, using differentiated IT systems to protect and secure data from exposure to threats is of the utmost significance.

The second layer of Fintech risk stems from the varied and incompetent Fintech framework. This is due to the highly disintegrated Fintech framework both on a national and global level. From the domestic perspective, small- and medium-size enterprises are bound to face the consequences of inadequate regulatory framework. While Fintech is inclined toward extreme technological progression, the regulations are slow and inadequate, thus causing questions regarding the compatibility of the two.

While there are broad regulatory compliance measures for Fintech to abide by, disruptive innovations may not have laws governing them due to the uniqueness of their creation. However, it is vital for these companies to ensure a sustainable and reliable venture that stabilizes cybersecurity and customer and data protection to remain in the goodwill of the people.

Additionally, it is evident with the increasing magnitude of data that there isn't much clarity in the resulting consequences for the complex usage of data. A legal system that is not well-equipped fails to address the potential risks of the lack of data protection, especially due to the surge in evidence-based policy, which establishes effective policies based on already existing information. The flaw in an evidence-based model lies in the fact that it focuses on the past rather than the possible future threats that stem from the new disruptive innovations in technology, thus giving no parameters to limit the growth of new technologies. A shift in the regulations pertaining to the stringency in structuring the algorithms and data auditing is expected, which will prevent the establishment of narrow goals and regulations.

On an international level, the convergence of national security and stability plays a vital role in ensuring the protection of data. As technologies become borderless, there is an emergent need for transnational cooperation. It is imperative for countries to share intelligence and information to gain mutual benefits during times of crisis instead of being defensive toward each other. Although the issue of cybersecurity has been understood as a national issue, to ensure domestic protection of data, it is imperative to broaden the international mandate due to the nature of interdependence of interlinked data and transactions. Cyberspace, being devoid of a central authority, needs to be kept under check to be able to maintain order amongst the different players in the financial industry across various countries. New innovations can encourage the practices opposing anti-money laundering (AML) and combating the financing of terrorism (CFT) due to unregulated, decentralized ledgers created by anonymous users without accountability or regulatory backing. It is also important to establish a regulatory framework that supports in aiding a more protective data security step that is preventive, reactive, and proactive in addressing the needs of Fintech. Furthermore, the overdependence and overusage of money and data powered by Fintech could create a structure of interdependence that could seriously dwindle the cybersecurity of an organization, thus calling for an immediate, comprehensive legal framework to counter this interdependence.

A systemic risk that Fintech might attract is due to the rapid expansion into financial intermediation. These risks arise due to the size of Fintech, which can result in liquidity and credit problems. Using second-hand data to measure credit risk can itself lead to different degrees of risk while also discouraging a universal and uniform regulatory system. As Fintech payment systems gain widespread acceptance, their operators might transform into integral components within the payment ecosystem. Sizeable Fintech payment providers could become vital contributors to the broader financial network. In the event of a major Fintech payment provider experiencing a breakdown, it could substantially disrupt the operation of the payment infrastructure, even extending to government transactions if Fintech applications were adopted for public use. Such a breakdown could result in significant adverse effects on the wellbeing of retail users, including households and small-scale businesses, particularly in regions where Fintech serves as a catalyst for financial inclusion. When Fintech payments are deeply intertwined with the broader financial network, their potential failure could exert macroeconomic repercussions by disrupting sectors closely interconnected with Fintech payment systems. A thorough understanding of the possible factors leading to threats of data instability and piracy is vital to establish the risks associated with data.

3.5 Different Stakeholders, Different Risks

3.5.1 The Numerous Risks Awaiting Fintech Customers

Consumers are inevitable stakeholders to both corporations and Fintech; the growing demand for seamless and swift payment gateways has allowed Fintech to establish itself through the massive populations of consumers who prefer using Fintech as opposed to its conventional counterparts. The advent of Unified Payment Interface (UPI) in India, for example, has managed to seep into the large Indian population. These easy and timely systematic transaction systems have forced companies to integrate Fintech into their payment systems. Therefore, it is imperative to understand the increased risk to Fintech consumers.

3.5.1.1 Regulatory Deficiencies

Fintech customers face the problem of relatively inadequate protection compared to their conventional counterparts, which predominantly arises due to lack of coverage in consumer protection regulations. The consequence of this is that there are limited regulations to which Fintech must adhere with respect to consumer protection. Consumers are, thus, not provided with adequate relief mechanisms for complaints that encompass Fintech services. These services lead to customers being exposed to risks due to the uniqueness of the Fintech sector.

3.5.1.2 Fraudulent and Unethical Behaviour

As consumers become more aware of the threats of the data and internet realm, their growing apprehensions toward digital transactions due to potentially fraudulent activities or scams are evident. Consumers are afraid of the losses that can occur due to embezzlement of funds, identity theft, or phishing attempts. The threat of these miscreants are not only the financial service providers themselves but could also be the agents, staff, or outside entities. These could happen through remote locations, including cloud computing systems, and could even span international borders, making the process of enforcing regulations even more difficult, pertaining to the evidence. Predatory lending methods directed at communities without civil rights have not only breached banks' consumer protection obligations but also damaged their position (Agarwal and Zhang, 2020).

3.5.1.3 Instability and Unreliable Platforms

Fintech platforms without a concrete security system to protect consumer data are at an elevated risk of facing financial losses and other aspects of distress. The heightened reliance of technology is one of the prime reasons for risks. Another cause of vulnerability from the lack of cybersecurity is the reliance on third-party service providers or outsourced services due to compromises on data integrity. Reliability can also be influenced at large by the country's connectivity and telecommunications infrastructure. The increased vulnerability and heightened unreliability cause inconveniences to consumers and could also lead to monetary damages.

3.5.1.4 Financial Insolvency or the Failure of Business

The risk of Fintech of the potential failure of a business comes from the fact that Fintech is a new entrant into the market and is, thus, prone to discontinuing operations if it does not work as well as anticipated. For instance, consumers participating as lenders in peer-to-peer lending may be prone to losing their invested money if the funds are handled by a platform that becomes bankrupt or insolvent.

3.5.1.5 Inadequate Provision of Information to Consumers

Fintech introduces a variety of risks pertaining to information disclosure and transparency for consumers. Similar to the case of conventional offerings, the information available about the pricing, risks, and terms associated with Fintech products may be either incomplete or lacking in clarity. These conventional risks to consumers become more pronounced when consumers encounter unfamiliar elements such as new pricing structures, fees, product attributes, terms and conditions (T&C), and risks associated with Fintech products.

3.5.2 *The Risks that Financial Institutions and Banks Face*

There has been a dramatic surge in competition between the traditional banking industry and Fintech start-ups due to their flexible, cost-effective, and innovative services. The threat of this competition has the potential to drastically decrease the market share for banks and financial institutions. Owing to the seamless procedures, as opposed to the tiresome procedures of conventional banking, there has been an increasing preference toward choosing a Fintech service than the banking counterpart. Consumers find the customer experience derived from the Fintech services to be user-friendly, convenient, and swift, thus forcing traditional banking industries to modernize their practices.

The regulatory complexity is a rapidly evolving aspect that must be adhered to if the traditional banking sector decides to integrate Fintech or digitize financial procedures. Partnerships can be an attractive prospect for banks, but the corporate cultural differences, objectives, and operational processes differ greatly between the two, which could cause internal conflicts that could impair the collaboration. There are often differences in the type of employees they have, the process through which they are recruited, and so on. The nuances in modernizing the traditional industry requires the incorporation of transformative models that are innovative and dynamic in nature to withstand the market factors.

One of the major concerns of the economy is undoubtedly financial inclusion, and through the introduction of Fintech, financial inclusion is no longer a utopian vision. Banks and financial institutions must ensure that they are able to reach the underserved as much as possible in order to stay relevant in changing times of financial inclusion.

3.5.2.1 Data Privacy

Safeguarding consumer financial information is a fundamental aspect of Fintech regulation. Regulatory authorities responsible for data privacy can impose sanctions on companies that fail to implement appropriate risk management measures and adhere to standards regarding the protection of customer data. India has also enacted data protection regulations to safeguard the privacy and security of personal data, including financial information. The Personal Data Protection Bill of 2019 and the associated Data Protection Authority aim to establish comprehensive data protection standards and provide individuals with greater control over their data.

3.5.2.2 Anti-Money Laundering (AML)

Governments place significant emphasis on countering money laundering and recognize the potential for Fintech technology to be exploited for illicit financial activities. Consequently, various territories have established their own AML laws and regulations to combat money laundering effectively. India has implemented robust AML and CFT laws and regulations to combat money laundering and the financing of terrorism. These laws place obligations on financial institutions and Fintech companies to conduct due diligence, report suspicious transactions, and maintain records as part of their risk management and regulatory compliance measures.

3.5.2.3 Cybersecurity Threats

Cybersecurity attacks are deliberate and malicious actions carried out by cybercriminals or malicious actors with the intent to compromise the security, confidentiality, or availability of computer systems, networks, and digital assets. Both traditional banks and Fintech start-ups represent attractive targets for hackers and cybercriminals. In response, financial laws have been enacted to address these cyberthreats.

3.5.3 Threats of Being a Fintech Investor

While the disruptively innovating sector has its perks, it comes with risks. The dynamic nature of this industry calls for Fintech to be prompt in adapting to the latest trends and demands of the market. Thus, to ensure sustenance in the Fintech sector, the firm must diligently stay updated by investing in new technologies. Thus, market volatility is pivotal in making Fintech decisions due to its susceptibility toward the same.

Not every Fintech is bound to be successful, as there might be unfortunate circumstances in which Fintech fails. In case of a Fintech failure, the company's reputation could be destroyed, leading to a blockage in the continuous flow of operations. In a global economy, a small hindrance could deny vital services. Controversies and negative publicity have the ability to scar the company and, thus, bring down the value of an investor's stake in it.

Adding on, the excessive reliance on technology, which includes recent technologies such as artificial intelligence and machine learning, opens the door to unjust outcomes arising from decisions made by algorithms. It is evident that Fintech depends on certain algorithms to make decisions related to the business. These algorithms could occasionally lead to inequitable practices. A poor decision can lead to operational inefficiencies that can harm the company's performance. To remove these barriers, Fintech must ensure regular audits that test the algorithms to ensure that they are bias-free. Investors need to pay heed to these issues because the right decisions will ensure a better margin.

The risk of a product being deemed unsuitable is substantially high, especially in the Fintech domain. The only way to prevent this failure is to have a clear vision of the needs and requirements of the target audience. Bombarding consumers with too many features unknown to them and an unfriendly user interface could severely affect the consumer experience, thus slowing down the customer-adoption process in the Fintech market. Consumers may become reluctant to use the services due to the complexity that remains an unsolved mystery to them. Thus, it is essential to avoid this disaster through efficient decision-making criteria using appropriate analysis of the target market.

A significant aspect of the expansion of Finfech lies in its relevance to cater to different geographical locations. It is often observed that when a product is seemingly well-off in one place, the makers assume its success in a different location; however, quite often, they do not result in the same degree of success in different regions. It is also imperative to note the regulatory and technological investment banking system of the place before investing in it in order to make the right decision regarding its feasibility, security, and safety.

Political factors can impact Fintech industries as well, including trade disputes, sanctions, and shifts in global economic conditions. A noteworthy example is the adoption of India's UPI in France in 2023 following a meeting between Prime Minister Narendra Modi and French President Emmanuel Macron. Modi also stated that Indian tourists will be able to make payments in the Indian currency in the near future. Along with France, countries such as the United Arab Emirates (UAE), Saudi Arabia, Singapore, Bahrain, the Maldives, Oman, and Bhutan have enabled UPI for payment in their countries, thus enabling Indians to make rupee payments in the respective countries.

3.6 Building a Risk Management Framework

While the Fintech industry is prone to a wide range of risks that are detrimental to companies, there are various steps to that can be taken to mitigate the threats that can damage the firm. Fintech risk management can be defined as a collection of phases concerned with Fintech risk organizing and planning, risk assessment, risk reaction, and risk monitoring and control. While, at first glance, the rapidly booming industry has proven to be a boon, it comes with risks that are potentially undefined, which calls for diverse precautionary as well as responsive measures. As Fintechs pose numerous threats, there are a list of responsibilities that they must adhere to in order to maintain order in the industry.

3.6.1 Identifying All Possible Risks

As mentioned earlier, risks could stem from various reasons, including regulations and compliance (AML and CFT), data security, operational risks arising from human resources, and third-party problems. Detecting the possible threats helps Fintech to develop a response mechanism and contingencies to combat risks, thus saving the company from being unprepared. Fintech firms encounter a wide spectrum of potential risks, encompassing regulatory and compliance concerns due to the dynamic nature of financial regulations, data security threats associated with safeguarding confidential client data, operational challenges arising from internal processes and human fallibility, market-related risks tied to economic shifts and evolving customer preferences, and technological vulnerabilities linked to system breakdowns and cyberthreats. Effective monitoring and proactive mitigation measures within each of these risk domains are essential to ensure the sustained viability and prosperity of Fintech enterprises.

3.6.2 Ensuring Continuance after Outages

Fintech, being one of the most volatile and ever-growing industries, poses the threat of complete closure in the face of adversities. Because Fintech is being largely reliant on data, it must ensure that lost data is retrieved during times of distress through internal records, reliable tools, and third-party service providers/partners. Furthermore, it is imperative for Fintech to follow a procedural system of documenting and institutionalizing all necessary documents, along with implementing programs pertaining to secure design and application, resiliency, and approval. Cloud computing systems, such as Amazon Web Services (AWS) and MS Azure, prove to be of substantial importance due to the availability of nodes and decentralized data centres. Cloud-based systems help in keeping data intact while also ensuring the highest level of safety and security to confidential data.

It is crucial for Fintech to conduct a thorough risk assessment, including identifying the various types of risks and evaluating the magnitude of the risk and its corresponding impact on the industry along with the monetary repercussions that could arise due to the possible risk. It is imperative for Fintech firms to conduct comprehensive risk assessments, encompassing the identification of various risk types, an evaluation of their potential magnitude, and an assessment of their impact on the industry, including the financial implications that may arise as a result of these risks. Moreover, this meticulous risk assessment enables these companies to prioritize their risk management efforts efficiently. By quantifying the potential financial consequences linked to identified risks, these firms can judiciously allocate resources to implement robust mitigation strategies. This proactive approach fortifies their resilience and ensures the preservation of their reputation in the continually evolving financial landscape.

3.6.3 Testing over and over Again

It is possible to be able to check all the boxes needed to efficiently operate Fintech offerings, but it could be cumbersome. This can be achieved through numerous tests that are designed to evaluate regulatory compliance, data protection, utility, comprehensive measures that minimize the various risks, etc. Security testing comes in handy to identify potential risks and test the strength of the data encryption, ensuring its high resistance to threats and cyberattacks with appropriate and adequate authentication and appropriation. The commonly used security tests include penetration testing, which is used to mock cybersecurity attacks to detect any possible vulnerabilities that the application contains, and regular vulnerability scans, which are conducted to discover potential threats.

The purpose of a functionality test is to examine the application's efficiency in operation. This includes assessing its user-friendliness and performance, ensuring it adheres to predetermined standards, and verifying that it functions without any bugs or anomalies. The performance test, though similar to the functioning test, relates to assessing whether the offering is strong enough to withstand different tests, such as stress tests and load tests, and remain swift and responsive during high-traffic times. Similarly, the compatibility test is conducted to ensure that the app works as planned while remaining compatible with devices.

The usability test is conducted to evaluate whether the product is user-friendly and caters to the needs of the consumers without causing any potential frustrations that arise due to the incongruence between the app and user understanding. Usability refers to the efficiency of the app's design, layout, and interface. This comprehensive usability assessment plays a pivotal role in refining the product, making it more user-centric, and aligning it closely with consumer preferences and requirements.

Regulatory testing is done to ensure adherence to the various regulatory frameworks related to know your customer (KYC), AML, and data protection rules set by governing authorities. The company must ensure that the standards are met diligently and that the application is compliant with the requirements. This helps to identify any potential gaps with the established regulatory framework and the application.

3.6.4 Third-Party Risk Management

Though risky, most Fintech companies are reliant on third-party partnerships for various services. These partnerships, if not monitored carefully, can lead to negative repercussions that could involve serious data-related threats, such as breach of privacy, consumer-data leaks, cyberattacks, and so on. To prevent these possible threats from arising from third-party service providers, a variety of preventive and reactive measures can be taken.

   i) Completing due diligence in which in a thorough review regarding the background and operations of the partner company has been conducted.
  ii) Establishing clear contracts that mention the terms, expectations, and penalties pertaining to the deal/agreement.
 iii) Supervising the partner continuously is crucial to keep the partner and the long-term running of the partnership in check.
  iv) Adhering to the corresponding regulatory framework is an important step that Fintechs must take to supervise the gaps between the regulatory requirements and those that have been followed.

v) Preparing response and contingency plans to ensure that a backup plan is ready in case there are disruptions or discrepancies between the parties in terms of honouring the duties/responsibilities that ensure that company runs smoothly.

vi) Using insurance to cover potential damage from the risks posed by the third-party service provider.

Thus, in order to safeguard their operations and ensure sustained growth within the rapidly expanding Fintech industry, companies must adopt a comprehensive risk management framework. This framework encompasses various steps, including risk identification, business continuity planning, rigorous testing, and diligent third-party risk management. By taking a proactive stance toward risk mitigation and compliance, Fintech firms not only can protect their businesses but also contribute to the industry's overall resilience and success in an ever-evolving financial landscape.

3.7 Conclusion

Through the course of this chapter, we have explored varied dynamics involving the adoption of Fintech with respect to the corporate reputation, reactions of financial institutions, the different types of risks that come with Fintech, the impact of these risks to various stakeholders, and steps to ensure the safety and security against the potential risks.

Commencing from the corporate reputation, we saw the elements of corporate reputation that constitute the amalgamation of corporate reputation. Furthermore, the various reactions and the potential responses of financial institutions were described, turning the risk of Fintech into an opportunity. The different types of risks were identified, including cybersecurity to systemic risks that can significantly change the course of the economy. The various stakeholders have differentiated potential risks while involved in the Fintech industry, and each of them were described. The chapter also provided steps to establish a risk management system.

In summary, the Fintech industry is one that offers myriad opportunities that can be adopted for the betterment of companies as well as consumers while also presents complexities that need careful steps to mitigate. The careful adoption of Fintech can lead to sustained growth and resilience in the ever-evolving financial landscape.

Notes

1. Capital One acquires SME travel fintech Lola | Fintech Futures
2. Unified Credit Platform Yubi Partners With Indian Bank | Outlook India
3. Citi Makes Strategic Investment in Rextie, Peru's Leading Fintech for FX Services | Citigroup
4. Banks-Fintech relationship: From competition to collaboration - Banking & Finance News | The Financial Express
5. SoFi Completes Acquisition of Golden Pacific Bancorp, Inc. | SoFi

References

Agarwal, S., & Zhang, J. (2020). Fintech, Lending and Payment Innovation: A Review. *Asia-Pacific Journal of Financial Studies*, 49(3), 353–367.

Banks-Fintech Relationship: From Competition to Collaboration - The Financial Express. URL: https://www.financialexpress.com/business/banking-finance -banks-fintech-relationship-from-competition-to-collaboration-3241443/

Capital One Acquires SME Travel Fintech Lola. URL: https://www.fintechfutures .com/2021/10/capital-one-acquires-sme-travel-fintech-lola/#:~:text=Capital %20One%20has%20acquired%20Boston,be%20shutting%20down%20its%20 services.&text=In%20September%2C%20Lola%2C%20which%20offers,oper ations%20in%20its%20current%20form

Citi Makes Strategic Investment in Rextie, Peru's Leading Fintech for FX Services. URL: https://www.citigroup.com/global/news/press-release/2023/citi-strategic -investment-rextie-peru-leading-fintech-fx-services

Ernst & Young. (2019). *Global Fintech Adoption Index*. Ernst & Young, 44p. URL: https://www. EY-Global-Fintech-Adoption-Index-2019.pdf

Richardson, J., & Bolesh, E. (2002). Toward the See-Through Corporation. *Pharmaceutical Executive*, 22(11), 54–61.

SoFi Completes Acquisition of Golden Pacific Bancorp, Inc. | SoFi. URL: https:// www.sofi.com/press/sofi-completes-acquisition-of-gpb

Unified Credit Platform Yubi Partners with Indian Bank. URL: https://startup.out-lookindia.com/sector/fintech/unified-credit-platform-yubi-partners-with-indian -bank-news-8564#:~:text=Yubi%2C%20a%20unified%20credit%20platform,busi-nesses%20(SMEs)%20in%20India

World Bank. (2021). *Fintech Market Reports Rapid Growth During Covid-19 Pandemic*. World Bank. URL: https://www.worldbank.org/en/news/press -release/2020/12/03/fintech-market-reports-rapid-growth-during-covid-19 -pandemic

Chapter 4

India's Fintech and AI-Related Regulation Framework

G Nithya, Geetha Manoharan, and
Sunitha Purushottam Ashtikar

4.1 AI in Fintech

Artificially intelligent computer systems have the ability to learn from their environment and execute tasks that were previously done only by intelligent people (Al-Safi et al., 2023). Analyzing data and making decisions are done by artificial intelligence (AI) using algorithms, which has supported the development of a wide range of goods and services that may help us to automate daily chores. The term "Fintech" refers to the application of technology in the financial services industry (Lourens et al., 2022). This swiftly growing area of the economy is transforming how we access, use, and control our money. Because of research and development at the nexus of AI and Fintech, it is now feasible to create services and goods that can systematize and develop how we manage our finances. This crossing also creates a variety of legal difficulties that need to be addressed. The fusion of AI and Fintech is leading to the development of a new generation of services and solutions that might power and improve financial processes (Krishna and Mohammed, 2023). It also makes it easier for customers and companies to manage and access their money, giving enterprises more alternatives to better serve their customers.

Aldboush and Ferdous (2023) address the ethical issues surrounding the use of financial technology[1] (Fintech), with a specific emphasis on big data, AI, and privacy. The research identifies prejudice, discrimination, ownership, control, justice, openness, and privacy concerns as they apply to Fintech, using a methodical literature review process. The results underscore the significance of protecting consumer data, abiding by data protection rules, and encouraging corporate responsibility in digitalized era. The research makes specific recommendations for businesses, such as the use of encryption tools, openness about the gathering and use of customer data, the availability of consumer opt-out alternatives, and staff education on data security guidelines. The lack of research conducted in languages other than English and the need for more resources to go further into the results, however, restrict the study's scope. Future studies may broaden our understanding of the subject at hand and gather more detailed data to get around these constraints and better comprehend the complicated problems under study.

The purpose of the research, conducted by Azhar et al. (2023), was to determine whether Malaysian Millennials and Generation Z (Gen Z) are prepared to implement Fintech in accounting. Effort expectancy (EE), performance expectancy (PE), social influence (SI), and facilitating conditions (FC) are the four core elements of the unified theory of acceptance and use of technology (UTAUT), which served as the theoretical foundation for this research (FC). To collect data from 108 respondents throughout Malaysia, the study used a quantitative approach and an online survey. According to the data, consumers' inclination to embrace Fintech is strongly predicted by PE and FC (AI). Another finding indicated that EE and SI had little impact on consumers' decision to embrace Fintech (AI). Consumers' loyalty to continue utilizing Fintech services is also significantly impacted by AI. It has been shown that PE, followed by FC, is the best predictor of consumers' propensity to embrace Fintech and that, owing to their positive association, AI does have an impact on customer loyalty to Fintech. The outcome also shows that user loyalty to Fintech products is directly correlated with adoption intention. Building a customer base of loyalty is essential if one wants to persuade customers to use Fintech services in the future. One's presence may entice further consumers to utilize Fintech services and develop loyalty as a result. A percentage of Malaysian Millennials' and Gen Z's knowledge, Gen Z's adaptation, and acceptability of Fintech in accounting may be determined by the results of this research.

4.2 Indian AI–Fintech Landscape

According to Osei-Assibey et al. (2023), innovation in Fintech brings both enormous potential and problems for accounting practices all around the

globe. This study intends to investigate how Fintech has affected accounting procedures such as budgeting, financial reporting, auditing, performance
management, and risk and fraud management. The incorporation of AI
and big data analysis in accounting methods serves as a proxy for Fintech.
They picked African nations as their focal regions and polled qualified and
chartered accountants in Ghana and Nigeria. We used structural equation
modelling to examine how Fintech has affected accounting processes after
201 surveys qualified for our final analysis. The empirical findings demonstrate that AI and big data have a favourable and substantial influence on
accounting procedures, suggesting that Fintech may be able to reduce the
agency issue in accounting practices and promote improved accounting performance (Akhtar et al., 2022). It's interesting to note that big data has less
overall influence than AI. These findings provide important new information
to managers, politicians, and regulators concerning the potential adoption
of Fintech in the governance as well as macro- and micro-level regulatory
framework for accounting practice.

According to Chandrashekar (2018), the term "Fintech," or financial technology,[2] has gained popularity in the financial industry. Globally, Fintech
players are upending the status quo of the financial services sector by
bringing in a new trade on client issues as seen via a technological lens.
Consequently, Indian banks are on the verge of integrating AI into numerous banking applications to take advantage of this cutting-edge technology.
With this context, this chapter will concentrate on the current state of AI
tools in the banking sector (Akhtar et al., 2023) and analyze the potential for
its implementation in a variety of banking operations in the future, as well
as its benefits and key difficulties.

As Gonçalves et al. (2023) said, there are several active Fintech businesses operating in India across a range of sectors, including lending
(credit), payments (including product to customer (P2C) and peer-to-peer
(P2P) transfers), investments and trade, credit ratings, insurance, personal
finance and wealth, etc. India, which is now thought to have the third-
largest Fintech ecosystem in the world, is one of the Fintech markets with
the fastest development rates; by 2025, it is predicted that the industry will
be valued at around 150 billion US dollars. Because the bulk of Fintech
companies in India were founded in the previous five years, there has
been a lot of recent progress in this industry. Indian Fintech is now dominated by local companies, some of which have attracted international
investment. But, in recent years, a huge number of global businesses have
also joined the industry, as shown in Figure 4.1.

During the global COVID-19 pandemic, the Indian Fintech industry[3] kept growing despite a few early setbacks that generally hindered business. Fintech, which offers socially distant payment systems and digital health and insurance products, grew when the service economy recovered. The manufacturing sector fell for obvious reasons, but the service sector recovered. Fintech services offered in India include consumer financing, microfinance, small business loans, insurance distribution, digital payment solutions, investment commodities, and digital or e-wallets (Meenaakumari et al., 2022). Micro-credit solutions such as buy now, pay later (BNPL) and other Fintech technologies grew rapidly. After the outbreak, Amazon and Flipkart joined BNPL, which is expected to grow over the next few years. Neobanks, blockchain, open banking, growing cooperation between Fintech start-ups and traditional banks, and other significant themes have all demonstrated development and are anticipated to do so in the future. In its budget for 2022–2023, the Indian government allowed scheduled commercial banks, such as Yes bank (Akhtar et al., 2021), and post offices to build 75 digital banking units, making financial inclusion a trend to monitor.

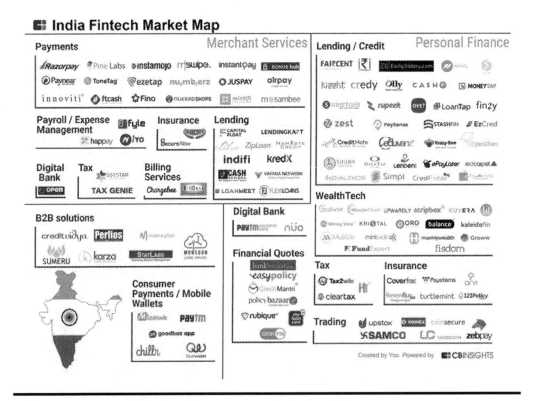

Figure 4.1   Indian Fintech market (Source: CBINSIGHTS)

In their study, "Examining the Factors Influencing Fintech Adoption Behaviour of Gen Y in India," Aggarwal (2023) found that information value drives Fintech adoption. The study expands the theory of planned behaviour by defining information quality as the component that prompts intent and action. After considering the effects of dynamic elements in a corporate context, the suggested framework was tested. The study examined India's Gen Y and identified key Fintech adoption factors. It will also help financial engineers to deliberately provide user-friendly products and services while using the enormous underlying potential of Fintech customers. Tertilt et al. (2018) and Kim et al. (2008) revealed that tech-savvy and demanding clients and business environment changes are fast transforming the wealth management sector's cost structure.

Duhaidahawi et al. (2021) defined Fintech and examined how it affects cybersecurity. The authors created hypotheses by statistical analysis of the research variables and discovered that all correlation coefficients were positive at a significance level of 0.01, which led them to accept the correlation hypotheses. At a significance level of 0.05, the findings also demonstrated that Fintech, an independent variable, had a favourable impact on cyber security.

Jackson et al. (2024) delves into improved customer service, including natural language processing (NLP), which has been used to increase the effectiveness and efficiency of customer service, enabling financial institutions to respond to client enquiries more quickly and accurately, and automated risk assessment, which is the automated process of risk assessment using NLP, enabling financial organizations to make better decisions about lending and investment activities.

A new generation of Fintech has been born as a result of how the digital revolution has altered interactions between consumers and service providers. Gonçalves et al. (2023) analyze customers' reactions to AI-made decisions against human ones. In two experimental tests with consumers of Fintech ($n = 503$), the authors validated their hypotheses. The findings demonstrate that customer reactions to credit choices made by AI (as opposed to humans) vary depending on the kind of credit product. When an AI provider rejects a request for a personal loan, this results in better levels of satisfaction than when the request is rejected by a credit analyst. Role congruity causes this effect. The results also indicate that customers' rejection sensitivity affects how they see the role congruity of financial services. To the authors' knowledge, this is the first Fintech study to examine role congruency and AI credit judgements vs humans.

4.3 Guiding Principles for AI

The four primary guiding principles for using AI in Fintech[4] are presented by Leslie (2019) in his study titled "Understanding AI Ethics and Safety." In that, he claims that AI is a creation of human design and implementation. Human mistakes in context, methodology, and implementation have a reasonable potential to be introduced during creation. It's crucial to keep them accountable for their veracity, dependability, and judgement. Hence, these four guiding principles – fairness, accountability, sustainability, and transparency – will correct the absence of moral accountability in AI robots, as shown in Figure 4.2.

4.3.1 Fairness

Fairness is the key tenet of AI. To guarantee data fairness, AI systems must be built on a dataset that accurately, relevantly, and generally reflects the population. Design fairness must be attained by using caution when using unreasonable goal variables, features, procedures, or analytical frameworks. Fairness in the result will be ensured by avoiding discriminatory or unequal influence factors. Implementation fairness may be achieved by

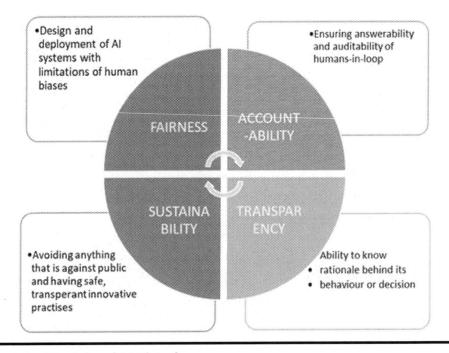

Figure 4.2 Principles of AI–Fintech

utilizing skilled people and AI systems that are deployed without prejudice. The following workflow method has to be put into place and communicated to team members in order to attain a high degree of fairness in AI. The workflow begins with issue conceptualization; goes through data extraction and capture, data pre-processing, modelling, testing, and validation; and concludes with deployment, monitoring, and reassessment of the data.

4.3.2 Accountability

The gear that supports statistical models and AI in finance[5] is not accountable for its choices or deeds. It must, thus, be helped by human accountability, which is difficult. Establishing a continuous chain of human accountability throughout the workflow delivery of AI projects is necessary. The system must be set up in such a manner that human involvement throughout the whole process ensures answerability and accountability.

4.3.3 Sustainability

In accordance with the sustainability concept, one should avoid behaviours that are against the public interest while developing and implementing AI in Fintech and guarantee the security and transparency of its operations. In order to prevent possible detrimental failures and preserve public confidence, AI's safety in financial services must be given top priority. With its operational goals, namely accuracy, dependability, security, and robustness, safety may be further realized. Hazards such as idea drift, brittleness, adversarial assault, and data poisoning must be reduced.

4.3.4 Transparency

Clarifying material and making it comprehensible or explicable are two aspects of AI transparency. It also covers the procedure's justifiability and the validity of the argument for its use. This may be accomplished by giving impacted stakeholders accurate explanations in comprehensible terms in a fair manner. Employees should adhere to principles of integrity, honesty, sincerity, neutrality, objectivity, and impartiality at every level of the AI process with the use of a regulated and managed framework. It's crucial to create and provide an effective, interpretable AI system.

4.3.5 Legal Implications in AI

The intersection of AI and Fintech has intricate and wide-ranging legal implications. There are several laws and regulations that must be considered while developing a product or service. With the help of an experienced Fintech law firm, these challenges may be resolved. This junction is creating a variety of legal concerns that need to be handled. The primary legal repercussions of the AI–Fintech nexus are in the areas of intellectual property rights, data protection, automated decision-making, contracts, and regulatory compliance. Experience has shown us that the interests of consumers cannot be adequately protected by market forces in the lack of regulation. Unregulated markets always result in outcomes that are inefficient for clients, whether it is the derivatives market or the London Interbank Offer Rate (LIBOR) setting. The Reserve Bank of India's (RBI) guidelines for the storage of payment data are projected to safeguard user payment information. Both the necessity to protect uninformed investors from being conned and the need to exercise policy autonomy drove the RBI's warnings on cryptocurrencies and its public position. The RBI[6] was perhaps the leading central bank to officially demand a complete ban on cryptocurrencies in India. A comprehensive ban is increasingly seen as a workable policy option on a global scale. The ambiguous or contradictory stances of the world's regulators may have had an impact.

4.4 Regulation of AI–Fintech in India

According to Mahindrakar (2020), the Indian government frequently encourages and supports the technology developments required to foster widespread digital inclusion. The study by Makkar et al. (2022) states that blockchain, AI, machine learning, biometric identification, and mobile banking/wallet services are made possible by cutting-edge technology such as blockchain. Numerous new digital products emerged from Fintech, digital finance companies, and digital financial services. These products quickly gained popularity among the general public due to their practical, quick, straightforward, and user-friendly functionalities.

According to Tiwari et al. (2022), Fintech should be supported by a strong legislative framework, supporting infrastructure, and appropriate regulatory policies from the government and financial institutions that oversee the industry. On the other hand, we discover that extensive and unequal access to digital infrastructure can also come with its own direct and indirect hazards, which can be harmful and lead to the onset of more financial exclusion.

Due of Fintech companies' overlapping and non-linear business models, India lacks a regulatory framework. The laws and regulations[7] that apply to a Fintech company sometimes depend on the type of business being run. The RBI, Securities and Exchange Board of India (SEBI), the Insurance Regulatory and Development Authority of India (IRDAI), and the Pension Fund Regulatory and Development Authority (PFRDA) often oversee financial sector undertakings, including Fintech companies.[8] The above organizations regulate online payments and transactions, payment aggregators and gateways, data and privacy, lending and deposit collection, securities and derivatives trading, insurance products and services, and more. Before a company can operate, permits are required for the start of various financial offerings, and it is required to get licenses from the RBI, SEBI, or IRDAI.

The following is a list of laws and rules to which Indian Fintechs may be subject.

The Consumer Protection Act, 2019

The Consumer Protection Act considers Fintech companies as providers. Section 2(47) (ix) of the Act states that "publishing of a consumer's personal information supplied in confidence, unless approved by law or in the public interest," is unethical. The Information Technology (Reasonable Security Policies and Processes and Sensitive Personal Data or Information) Regulations, 2011, prohibit the sharing of consumers' personal data without their consent unless required by law. Due to their sensitive client data, Fintech companies must comply with this rule.

The Prevention of Money Laundering Act, 2002

Know your customer (KYC) Master Instructions, the Prevention of Money Laundering Act of 2002 (PMLA), and the PMLA of 2005 are the main anti-money laundering laws for financial service providers. By following the requirements, banks, financial institutions, and intermediaries must verify client identities, keep records, and transmit information to the Financial Intelligence Unit-India (FIU-IND).

The Information Technology Act, 2000

Fintech platforms acquire and keep more user data, including behavioural and financial data. Protecting consumer privacy and data is important. There is currently no reliable data privacy system in India. The Information Technology Act of 2000 (IT Act) and the Regulations on IT (Reasonable Security Policies and Processes and Sensitive Personal Data or Information) are the major laws that protect personal data. Fintech firms must follow the IT Act. Companies may be held accountable for damages under Section 43A if they neglect to take the appropriate security measures to protect the sensitive personal data of their clients. Section 72A establishes fines for disclosing information in contravention of a valid contract. Personal data about people is essential to Fintech businesses. To avoid legal issues, it is necessary to abide by the applicable data security legislation.

4.5 RBI[9]

Payment and Settlement Systems Act, 2007

The Payments and Settlements Systems (PSS) Act of 2007 – also known as the PSS Act – is the legislation that controls payments in India. No "payment system" may be created or operated, according to the PSS Act, without first receiving RBI consent. Prepaid payment instruments (PPIs), money-transfer services, smart card operating systems, and debit and credit card operating systems are payment mechanisms; however, the PSS Act does not include a stock market. RBI clearance is needed to start a payment system. Thus, Fintech enterprises must comply with this law.

Master Directions on Prepaid Payment Instruments (MD-PPIs), 2021

Prepaid payment instruments, or PPIs, can be used to buy goods and services. PPIs may only be used with Indian rupees. No cash withdrawals are permitted in accordance with the PPI policy of the RBI. These instruments cannot be used to fund or settle the delivery of services by third parties. Such instruments are not regarded as payment systems that need RBI authorization or approval; hence, they are not governed or overseen by the RBI.

Framework for Scale Based Regulation for Non-Banking Financial Companies, 2021

The new regulatory framework for Non-Banking Financial Company (NBFC) is called scale-based regulation (SBR). These rules come into force on October 1, 2022, with the exception of the initial public offering (IPO) funding ceiling, which goes into effect on April 1, 2022. The IPO financial ceiling is a limit of Rs. 1 Crore per borrower for funding an IPO subscription.

Instructions for Account Opening, Account Operation, and Payment Settlement for Electronic Payment Operations Involving Intermediaries, 2009

Automated and online payment options for merchant purchases, including bills, internet shopping, and more, are growing nationwide. To safeguard consumers and ensure that intermediaries collecting electronic or online payments correctly account for them and promptly remit them to the businesses who provided the items and services. Thus, Section 18 of the Payment and Settlement Systems Act, 2007 (Act 51 of 2007) provides enough criteria for safe and orderly transactions.

The 2014 Payments Bank Licencing Guidelines and the 2016 Payments Bank Operating Guidelines

According to the RBI, a payment bank license application requires a minimum paid-up capital of Rs 100 crore. The least amount necessary to establish a payment bank is the paid-up equity capital. The promoter must also provide 40% of the paid-up equity capital for the first five years.

Framework for Recognising a Payment System Operator Self-Regulatory Organisation, 2020

The Central Bank has made available the framework and final regulations for creating a self-regulatory organization for payment system operators in line with its vision for payment and settlement systems. Using the framework, the central bank will be able to determine which Personal Security Officer (PSO)'s self-regulatory organization (SRO) it is. In order to protect consumers and advance moral and ethical behaviour, SROs are non-governmental organizations that establish and uphold standards for the conduct of its members.

*Regulation of Payment Aggregators and Payment Gateways, 2020 –
Guidelines.*

A new generation of payment processors that can function online, which
includes 19 organizations, among which the RBI has given in-principle clearance. Mswipe Technologies Pvt. Ltd., Zoho Payment Technologies Pvt. Ltd.,
and Tata Payments Ltd. are included in this.

*Processing of e-Mandate on Cards for Recurring Transactions, 2019
- Circular.*

An "e-mandate" is a standing order or repeated payment instruction on a
debit or credit card provided by the cardholder via a merchant platform,
such as a website or mobile application. An electronic mandate has been
provided to telecommunication service providers, over the top (OTT) platforms, insurance alliance partners, and other utility service providers.

Circular on Tokenisation – Card Transactions, 2019.

On January 8, 2019, the RBI released a circular granting authorization to
begin the card tokenization process in an effort to increase the security
of India's payment ecosystem. With the help of card networks, banks may
potentially provide tokenization services to owners of debit, credit, and
prepaid cards.

4.6 National Payments Corporation of India (NPCI)

4.6.1 Various Circulars on Unified Payments Interface (UPI) Payments

Multiple bank accounts, simple money routing, and merchant payments are
all included in a single mobile application (of any participating bank) thanks
to a mechanism called the Unified Payments Interface (UPI). "P2P" collection requests can be arranged and paid for. For example, users require an
account number, the Indian Financial System Code (IFSC), an alphanumeric

code that enables electronic transfers, the recipient's cell phone number, and a virtual ID or Aadhaar number (which is akin to a Social Security number) in order to transmit money.

4.7 Framework for AI–Fintech in India

Indian financial authorities and politicians promote Fintech innovation and technologically driven new entrants as long as they are outside of the established regulatory systems. Thus, disruptive innovation that doesn't fit within regulatory frameworks may be harder to manage. However, the government's development of the International Financial Services Centres Authority (IFSCA), in compliance with the IFSCA Act, 2019, shows an increased receptivity to Fintech innovation. The RBI, SEBI, IRDA, and Pension Fund Regulatory and Development Authority (PFRDAI) have handed their regulatory jurisdiction to the IFSCA, which regulates financial institutions, services, and products at the International Financial Services Centre in Gandhinagar, Gujarat.

4.7.1 RBI

The Enabling Framework for Regulatory Sandbox, which the RBI created in 2019, was used to announce the first cohort later that year with the topic "Retail Payments." By the end of 2021, six companies were supposed to have completed the testing process for the first cohort. The RBI launched the Reserve Bank Innovation Hub (RBIH) in late 2020 to encourage financial industry innovation through technology and creativity.

4.7.2 SEBI

In 2020, SEBI launched the Framework for Regulatory Sandbox to foster securities market innovation and give regulated entities the flexibility and resources to test Fintech ideas. SEBI's "Innovation Sandbox" promotes Fintech innovation online.

4.7.3 IRDAI

In 2019, IRDAI launched the IRDAI (Regulatory Sandbox) Rules to encourage insurance business innovation. One of the main aims of this sandbox is to promote innovation while achieving a stability between the logical expansion of the insurance business and the protection of policyholder interests.

4.7.4 Regulatory Barrier

Having a "local" presence in India is the biggest regulatory hurdle for a foreign Fintech[10] company. Foreign enterprises that seek to operate in India must also comply with foreign exchange control requirements, including limits on foreign ownership in Indian firms and subsidiaries. Additional concerns include cross-border payments and transactions; for example, a Fintech business that lends or extends credit may encounter regulatory restrictions on doing so. PayPal, another foreign Fintech company in India, recently announced it is winding down its internal payment's operation. Data storage may cause issues. For instance, the RBI mandates that all data relating to payment systems be stored in India and that all businesses participating in the payments ecosystem must comply with this obligation. International firms that automatically archive and process global payment data in centralized places or outside of India are affected by this. In reality, a few well-known corporations in the financial services sector had their operations in India shut down as a result of breaking data storage regulations.

4.8 Non-Financial Regulation

Despite a long-standing proposal and several changes, India[11] has no data protection law. Under the Information Technology Act, 2000, sensitive personal data concerning natural persons is collected, used, communicated, stored, and processed. Sensitive personal data and information (SPDI) includes passwords, bank account, credit card, debit card, or other payment instrument details, physical and mental health data, sexual orientation data, medical records and histories, biometric data, and more. Regarding the collection, storage, transmission, processing, and disclosure of SPDI, the SPDI Regulations impose a number of limitations.

Each corporate organization that collects SPDI from a person is obliged under the SPDI Regulations to get the person's prior written permission.

SPDI collection, purpose, data recipients, etc. require consent. Moreover, unless the transfer is mandated by a legally binding agreement between the parties, consent must be acquired before any SPDI is transferred or revealed. All corporate entities that collect, store, use, or transfer SPDI must follow reasonable security practises and procedures in accordance with the International Standard IS/ISO/IEC 27001 on "Information Technology, Security Techniques, and Information Security Management System Requirements" or other standards recognized and announced by the central government.

Each organization that collects SPDI is obliged by the SPDI Regulations to employ a grievance officer to report and resolve complaints from data subjects. The SPDI Regulations require SPDI managers to publish their privacy policies on their websites, including the types of SPDI gathered and their intended use.

The SPDI Guidelines would apply to financial data because it fits that description and is often collected by Fintech businesses. Together with the SPDI Regulations, a variety of privacy-focused policies have also been developed by Indian authorities to secure the security of financial information. For instance, the IRDAI requires insurers to (i) preserve policyholder privacy, (ii) store insurance records in Indian data centres, and (iii) retrieve all data provided by insurance service providers to their external service providers immediately after services are completed. The third-party administrators (TPAs) who receive insurance-related data for the servicing of insurance policies include insurance brokers, insurance web aggregators, common service centres, and insurance companies. These TPAs are subject to special rules regarding the confidentiality and protection of the data.

As previously indicated, the RBI has also mandated that all players in the payment ecosystem, including those that run payment systems, ensure that all data linked to such systems is kept only on equipment and in data centres located in India. The processing of payment-related data outside of India is not forbidden, but the data must be retrieved from such systems and returned to India no later than one business day or 24 hours after the completion of the payment. A full end-to-end transaction should be described in the data, together with any information that was obtained, transferred, or handled in relation to the payment instruction. If the transaction is international, a copy may be kept there. The RBI's Guidelines on Regulation of Payment Aggregators and Payment Gateways specify that authorized non-bank payment aggregators and merchants they have on boarded may no longer hold actual card data beyond June 30, 2022, except for the last four digits of card numbers for reconciliation.

4.9 Challenges in Regulating AI–Fintech

Most financial institutions use Fintech start-ups for large-scale tasks, including back-office operations, digital services, etc. These financial companies are only somewhat well-regulated for a number of reasons. Primarily because it is difficult to specify how cryptocurrencies and the blockchain technology that underpins them are governed. Due to its autonomy and decentralization, governments and third parties struggle to regulate the blockchain. Another contributing aspect is that Fintech is evolving swiftly, making it difficult to keep up with new developments and alterations. It is far more difficult to establish a precise regulatory framework. To put it another way, it is very challenging to develop a single, focused framework that can be used to account for every technological development and change in the banking business, both known and unknown.

Fintech is a benefit, but it is also producing complicated problems with few answers. The security of a person's data as well as their safety are substantially at risk. Are laws like the General Data Protection Regulation (GDPR) enough to address these threats? India is drafting a Personal Data Protection Law. Every time digital and electronic transactions are used, private information and sensitive data are put at risk. Businesses utilize these titbits of information to sell, buy, or otherwise profit from them in lieu of free services.

According to Inal (2023), the financial industry, established on knowledge, experience, and technology, thrives by taking advantage of innovations and potential while also feeling the strain of these changes and frequently being the first to use them. As with all technological advancement, AI algorithms, which bring about significant shifts and revolutions, are the ones that most compel the financial industry to adjust. Fintech risk management is increasingly using AI to discover, analyze, and mitigate financial risks such as fraud detection, credit risk assessment, operational risk management, and market risk management. AI in Fintech risk management might drastically change how financial institutions manage risk by offering more accurate and sophisticated risk assessments, reducing the time needed to identify and mitigate hazards, and boosting risk management efficiency. This study uses AI research in Fintech risk management to assess the scenario and make recommendations. In order to do this, a survey of the literature on AI algorithms used in risk management Fintech applications was done. According to expectations, the study will help inform future research and add to the body of knowledge.

4.10 Restrictions Imposed on Fintech

In light of the dangers posed by Fintechs, some instances of practises that RBI has limited or outright prohibited in the past year include:

- **Restricted Access, Use, and Storage of Data**: Data access, use, and storage are all subject to tight regulations by the RBI, which also prohibits the transfer of payments and lending data. RBI instructed payment service providers (PSPs) to exclusively store payment data on servers based in India in 2018. Through the Demand Loan (DL) Guidelines, RBI expanded this prohibition to include digital lending data in September 2023. There are additional limitations on data access and use imposed by the DL Guidelines. For instance, digital lenders must make sure that the data gathering by them or their logistics service providers (LSPs) is based on a legitimate necessity and with the borrowers' express consent.
- **Banned Credit-Loading of PPIs**: This was banned according to a notification that the RBI sent to PPI issuers in June 2022. According to RBI, PPIs loaded through credit lines functioned similarly to credit cards but were not subject to its regulations.
- **Banned Pass-through Accounts**: Regarding pass-through accounts, the RBI's DL Guidelines[12] required lenders to make direct payments to borrowers' bank accounts (without allowing the funds to go through any intermediaries' bank accounts). Following this, a number of participants in the digital lending space were compelled to modify their business strategies.

4.11 AI–Fintech and Financial Inclusion

Aggarwal et al. (2023) conducted a study to examine the Fintech adoption patterns of India's Gen Y people. This study counts exogenous elements, information quality (IQ), and willingness to pay for privileges to expand planned behaviour theory. Answers from the 349 higher education students chosen based on judgemental sampling were gathered from many reputable Indian institutions. The Smart PLS 4 software bootstrapping approach was used to assess the proposed framework. In addition to the idea that observable behavioural control (OBC) and real intention are directly related, it was discovered that a number of other research hypotheses also have a significant influence (AI). The study supports the use of planned behaviour theory for India's successful adoption of Fintech. Information quality affects Fintech adoption. The study expands a theory of planned behaviour by identifying information quality as a factor affecting intent and behaviour. After considering the effects of the dynamic forces that are always changing in a business environment, the validity and reliability of the proposed framework were examined. The research focused on Indian Gen Y Fintech adopters and their major drivers. Moreover, it will assist financial technologists in strategically launching more user-friendly products and services while using the vast underlying capabilities of Fintech consumers to the fullest.

The possibility of financial inclusion is also being expanded by this technology. Products and services in the AI–Fintech sector that make it easier for underserved populations to access financial services are enabling a more equitable allocation of financial resources. The risks associated with financial inclusion, however, must be recognized by businesses. To protect clients from fraud and abuse, businesses must have adequate security.

4.12 Conclusion

Fintech has helped financial institutions expand their reach into rural and underdeveloped communities. Both locally and globally, it has helped to develop a strong financial infrastructure. It's critical to create regulations that increase Fintech's positive aspects while minimizing any negative effects or risks. Regulations are needed to prevent unauthorized collection and storage of consumers' financial data. In the case of data breaches or the discovery that a third party obtained users' private information without their consent, strict regulations should be in place to hold Fintech businesses responsible. Transactions should be safe and straightforward thanks to the regulations. Consumers should be able to file complaints against these institutions through a specialized, independent, and focused grievance redressal system, similar to an ombudsman. Fintech's fast development makes it obviously challenging to manage but not impossible.

Despite the fact that unstable geopolitics and a recession have made things challenging, the Fintech ecosystem is quite promising. The Fintech sector is constantly shifting as a result of technological progressions and alterations in consumer behaviour. Significant advances in AI and machine learning, blockchain, mobile and digital payments, cybersecurity, and fraud prevention, as well as open banking and API connectivity, will emerge in 2023. Most importantly, Fintechs used to growth above all else will understand reason in 2023. We can anticipate new regulations that assist in moulding the sector into one that is sustainable, responsible, and compliant, as Indian regulators become more aware of the interaction between Fintechs and their clients. Additionally, Fintechs will be more cautious about wasting money and concentrate on producing money sustainably.

References

Aggarwal, M., K. Nayak, and V. Bhatt (2023). Examining the factors influencing Fintech adoption behaviour of gen Y in India. *Cogent Economics and Finance*, vol. 11, no. 1, 2197699.

Akhtar, S., M. Alam, and M. S. Ansari (2022). Measuring the performance of the Indian banking industry: Data envelopment window analysis approach. *Benchmarking: An International Journal*, vol. 29, no. 9, pp. 2842–2857. doi: 10.1108/BIJ-03-2021-0115.

Akhtar, S., M. Alam, and M. M. Khan (2021). Yes Bank fiasco: Arrogance or negligence. *Emerging Economies Cases Journal*, vol. 3, no. 2, pp. 95–102. doi: 10.1177/25166042211061003.

Akhtar, S., M. Alam, A. Khan et al. (2023). Measuring technical efficiency of banks vis-à-vis demonetization: An empirical analysis of Indian banking sector using CAMELS framework. *Quality and Quantity*, vol. 57, pp. 1739–1761. doi: 10.1007/s11135-022-01431-8.

Aldboush, H. H., and M. Ferdous (2023). Building trust in Fintech: An analysis of ethical and privacy considerations in the intersection of big data, AI, and customer trust. *International Journal of Financial Studies*, vol. 11, no. 3, pp. 90.

Al Duhaidahawi, H. M. K., J. Zhang, M. S. Abdulreda, M. Sebai, and S. Harjan (2021). Financial Technology (Fintech) and cybersecurity. *International Journal of Research in Business and Social Science (2147-4478)*, vol. 9, no. 6, pp. 123–133, Jan. 2021. doi: 10.20525/ijrbs.v9i6.914.

Al-Safi, J. K. S., A. Bansal, M. Aarif, M. S. Z. Almahairah, G. Manoharan, and F. J. Alotoum (2023). Assessment based on IoT for efficient information surveillance regarding harmful strikes upon financial collection. *International Conference on Computer Communication and Informatics (ICCCI)*, Coimbatore, pp. 1–5.

Azhar, A. N., N. Zakaria, S. M. Foo, and A. Aziz (2023). Fintech adoption in accounting: A study of MILLENNIALS' and GEN-ZS' readiness in Malaysia. *Quantum Journal of Social Sciences and Humanities*, vol. 4, no., 3, pp. 48–61.

Chandrashekar, K. (2018). Embracing artificial intelligence-an inevitable challenge for banking industry in India. *Journal of Emerging Technologies and Innovative Research*, vol. 5, no. 10, pp. 79–83.

Gonçalves, A. R., A. Breda Meira, S. Shuqair, and D. Costa Pinto (2023). Artificial intelligence (AI) in Fintech decisions: The role of congruity and rejection sensitivity. *International Journal of Bank Marketing*.

İnal, İ. H. (2023). Use of artificial intelligence in fintech tools in terms of risk management. *Social Science Development Journal*.

Jackson, I., M. Jesus Saenz, and D. Ivanov (2024). From natural language to simulations: Applying AI to automate simulation modelling of logistics systems. *International Journal of Production Research*, vol. 62, no., 4, pp. 1434–1457.

Jaichandran, R., S. H. Krishna, G. M. Madhavi, S. Mohammed, K. B. Raj, and G. Manoharan (2023). Fuzzy evaluation method on the financing efficiency of small and medium-sized enterprises. *2023 International Conference on Artificial Intelligence and Knowledge Discovery in Concurrent Engineering (ICECONF)*, Chennai, pp. 1–7. doi: 10.1109/ICECONF57129.2023.10083731.

Kim, D. J., D. L. Ferrin, and H. R. Rao (2008). A trust-based consumer decision-making model in electronic commerce: The role of trust, perceived risk, and their antecedents. *Decision Support Systems*, vol. 44, no. 2, pp. 544–564.

Leslie, D. (2019). *Understanding Artificial Intelligence Ethics and Safety: A Guide for the Responsible Design and Implementation of AI Systems in the Public Sector*. The Alan Turing Institute. doi: 10.5281/zenodo.3240529.

Lourens, M., R. Raman, P. Vanitha, R. Singh, G. Manoharan, and M. Tiwari (2022). Agile technology and artificial intelligent systems in business development. *5th International Conference on Contemporary Computing and Informatics (IC3I)*, Uttar Pradesh, pp. 1602–1607. doi: 10.1109/IC3I56241.2022.10073410.

Mahindrakar, S. (2020). Technological aspects and digital finance uprising in India. *International Journal for Research in Applied Science and Engineering Technology*, vol. 8, no. IX, pp. 856–859.

Makkar, S., T. Bajpai, M. Bhola, D. Mahesh, and G. Manoharan (2022). Blockchain disruption in banking sector. *AIP Conference Proceedings*, vol. 2418, p. 020019. doi: 10.1063/5.0082288.

Meenaakumari, M., P. Jayasuriya, N. Dhanraj, S. Sharma, G. Manoharan, and M. Tiwari (2022). Loan eligibility prediction using machine learning based on personal information. *5th International Conference on Contemporary Computing and Informatics (IC3I)*, Uttar Pradesh, pp. 1383–1387. doi: 10.1109/IC3I56241.2022.10073318.

Osei-Assibey Bonsu, M., Y. Wang, and Y. Guo (2023). Does Fintech lead to better accounting practices? Empirical evidence. *Accounting Research Journal*, vol. 36, no. 2/3, pp. 129–147.

Tertilt, M., and P. Scholz (2018). To advise, or not to advise—How Robo-advisors evaluate the risk preferences of private investors. *The Journal of Wealth Management*, vol. 21, no. 2, pp. 70–84.

Tiwari, K., M. Ramchandani, and V. Jain (2022). Inclusion of financial technology and artificial intelligence in management and development of human resource in India. *International Journal of Research in Engineering and Science*, vol. 10, no. 7, pp. 585–589.

Websites

https://www.rbi.org.in/Scripts/BS_Fintech.aspx

https://rbi.org.in/scripts/fs_notification.aspx?id=5379&fn=9&Mode=0

https://www.pwc.in/consulting/financial-services/Fintech/point-of-view/financial-regulatory-technology-insights-newsletters-vinyamak/february-2018.html

https://corporatefinanceinstitute.com/resources/knowledge/finance/Fintech-financial-technology/

https://www.investopedia.com/terms/f/Fintech.asp

https://builtin.com/Fintech

https://corporatefinanceinstitute.com/resources/knowledge/finance/Fintech-financial-technology/

https://corporatefinanceinstitute.com/resources/knowledge/credit/swift/

https://www.bis.org/fsi/publ/insights23.pdf

Magazines

Top 10 trends for the Fintech industry for 2023. Online. Available at: https://www.avenga.com/magazine/top-10-trends-for-the-Fintech-industry-for-2023/

The project INFINITECH. Online. Available at: https://www.infinitech-h2020.eu/

Economic survey 2020-21, Indian Government, vol. 2. Online. Available at: www.indiabudget.gov.in/budget2021-22/economicsurvey/doc/echapter_vol2.pdf\

Notes

1. https://corporatefinanceinstitute.com/resources/knowledge/finance/Fintech-financial-technology/
2. https://corporatefinanceinstitute.com/resources/knowledge/finance/Fintech-financial-technology/
3. "Top 10 trends for the Fintech industry for 2023" Available online at: https://www.avenga.com/magazine/top-10-trends-for-the-Fintech-industry-for-2023/
4. https://www.bis.org/fsi/publ/insights23.pdf

5. https://corporatefinanceinstitute.com/resources/knowledge/credit/swift/
6. https://rbi.org.in/scripts/fs_notification.aspx?id=5379&fn=9&Mode=0
7. https://www.pwc.in/consulting/financial-services/Fintech/point-of-view/ financial-regulatory-technology-insights-newsletters-vinyamak/february-2018. html
8. https://www.investopedia.com/terms/f/Fintech.asp
9. https://www.rbi.org.in/Scripts/BS_Fintech.aspx
10. THE PROJECT INFINITECH" Available online at: https://www.infinitech-h2020 .eu/
11. Economic Survey 2020-21, Indian Government, Vol - 2" Available online at: www.indiabudget.gov.in/budget2021-22/economicsurvey/doc/echapter_vol2 .pdf\
12. https://builtin.com/Fintech

Chapter 5

Ethical and Sustainability Considerations for Fintech

Farhan Mustafa, Mushahid Ali Shamsi, and Anil Audumbar Pise

5.1 Introduction

The financial landscape has been radically reshaped and has undergone remarkable transformation due to technological advancements. This led to the emergence of the Fintech industry, which is entirely automated. This transformation is redefining how we manage our money, invest, and access financial services (Gomber et al., 2017).

The emergence of Fintech has brought about a significant transformation in the financial services sector in recent years. Fintech has introduced novel methods of accessing and managing financial products and services, ranging from peer-to-peer (P2P) lending platforms to robo-advisors. This shift has resulted in heightened competition, reduced costs, and increased convenience for consumers.

Fintech has gained significant traction, particularly in P2P financial transactions, enabling individuals to conduct electronic money transfers without needing physical currency or in-person interactions (Mallat, 2007). Moreover, it has simplified bill payments, eliminating the necessity for handling physical checks or visiting payment centres. Fintech has also facilitated customer-to-business (C2B) payments for essential services, offering a seamless and contactless payment experience. These factors have fuelled Fintech's growing acceptance and adoption, providing secure, efficient, and convenient alternatives to traditional cash-based transactions.

DOI: 10.4324/9781032644165-5

This financial technology-based wave offers remarkable opportunities and unprecedented convenience for stakeholders. However, it also presents substantial ethical and sustainability challenges. In this chapter, we will explore multifaceted considerations, including how demonetization and COVID-19 acted as a catalyst for the rise in Fintech transactions how Fintech stakeholders can navigate them responsibly.

5.2 Ethical Considerations for Fintech

The ever-increasing reliance, integration, and continuous growth of Fintech underscore the pressing need for ethical and sustainable frameworks to guide its development. Adhering to ethical practices not only boosts fairness and inclusiveness but also establishes trust and credibility for the Fintech industry-based products (Mustafa & Sharma, 2023).

Fintech, an abbreviation for financial technology, covers a diverse range of technologies and services that harness digital advancements to offer financial solutions. This includes digital payment systems, P2P lending platforms, robo-advisors, blockchain-based cryptocurrencies, and mobile banking applications. While these innovations hold the promise of positively transforming the financial industry, they also bring forth significant ethical considerations and sustainability challenges that require careful examination.

One of the major ethical considerations in Fintech revolves around data privacy and security (Chen & Kim, 2021). Fintech companies, in their quest to streamline financial processes and offer tailored services, collect vast volumes of personal and financial data from users. The guardianship of this sensitive data is a moral obligation, and the consequences of failing to safeguard it can be catastrophic.

Another ethical dimension lies in Fintech's potential to foster financial inclusion. By extending services to previously marginalized and underserved populations, Fintech can bridge the financial divide. However, ethical concerns emerge when biases in algorithms or access barriers inadvertently exclude certain communities.

Another significant ethical dimension are algorithms, which that are lifeblood of Fintech applications, powering credit scoring, investment recommendations, and fraud detection. However, when these algorithms harbour biases, they can perpetuate discrimination and inequality – a major ethical concern.

Finally, transparency and accountability are fundamental ethical principles that guide Fintech companies. They entail providing clear terms and conditions, disclosing fees, and openly communicating business practices. Ethical Fintech companies embrace these principles and hold themselves accountable for their actions and decisions.

5.3 COVID-19 and Demonetization Reshaped Fintech

The year 2020 witnessed the global COVID-19 outbreak, while in 2016, the Indian government initiated demonetization measures aimed at combating corruption and promoting digital transactions, thereby fostering a shift toward a cashless economy (Akhtar et al., 2020). These two significant events have not only accelerated the adoption and evolution of Fintech solutions but have also reshaped the way financial transactions are conducted, fostered financial inclusion, and addressed various challenges in the financial ecosystem.

Demonetization invalidated high-value currency notes, compelling individuals and businesses to explore and embrace digital payment alternatives. Fintech companies seized this opportunity by providing user-friendly digital wallets, mobile banking apps, and payment gateways, which became indispensable tools for daily transactions. Demonetization prompted the government to drive financial inclusion through initiatives such as Jan Dhan Yojana. Fintech companies complemented these efforts by offering digital identity verification and biometric authentication services, simplifying access to financial services.

Furthermore, the COVID-19 pandemic accelerated the global transition to a cashless economy, driven by concerns about hygiene and the potential transmission of the virus through physical currency. Contactless payment methods, exemplified by Apple Pay, gained popularity as they offered secure and convenient transactions without the need for physical contact. In India, Fintech companies offering mobile wallets, digital payment platforms, and unified payments interface (UPI) services experienced a surge in usage. This trend accelerated the government's vision of transitioning to a cashless economy.

Statistics indicate that during the COVID-19 crisis, 27% of small businesses in the United States reported an upsurge in contactless payments, underscoring the preference for cashless transactions (Balch, 2020). While in India, contactless transactions in total face to face (F2F) transactions grew by more than six times, from 2.5% in December 2018 to 16% in December 2021 (Visa, 2022). This shift was propelled by social distancing, heightened awareness of hygiene practices, and the convenience of digital payment options (Balch, 2020).

Notably, the increased reliance on digital payments during the pandemic not only reshaped consumer behaviour but also prompted businesses to adopt Fintech services to meet evolving customer preferences. This pattern is expected to endure as we progress toward a more technologically driven future.

Although these two major events pushed considerable growth in Fintech, a series of ethical challenges remains, including the heightened concerns over users' sensitive information and its privacy. Fintech firms must implement transparent data collection and usage policies, along with user consent mechanisms, as they are essential to maintain trust and ethical data practices.

5.4 Flexibility and Simplicity

The ascendancy of Fintech can be attributed to its simplicity, flexibility, and security in executing electronic transactions complemented by distinctive features such as customization and rapid communication (Osakwe & Okeke, 2016). However, the adoption of Fintech services in India, especially in rural areas, is still in its infancy due to pervasive infrastructure-related challenges, including the high cost of smartphones and limited internet access. These challenges are compounded by behavioural and infrastructural factors, as highlighted by Kumari and Mary (2019), who emphasized the influence of complexity, cost, faith, safety, perceived ease of use, and benefits on the adoption decisions of rural entrepreneurs. Rachna and Singh (2013) further underscored the critical role of security and privacy in ensuring the success of Fintech.

5.5 Concerns over Sustainability in Fintech

Sustainability considerations take into account primarily environmental, financial, social, and economic impact. The Fintech industry's environmental impact is an emerging concern. Sustainable Fintech firms develop viable business models, diversify revenue streams, and avoid predatory lending practices that can lead to customer debt spirals. These mission-driven entities operate with a dual purpose: to create positive social and environmental impact while achieving financial sustainability.

The proliferation of data centres and computing infrastructure contributes to energy consumption and greenhouse gas emissions. Sustainable Fintech companies are taking steps to assess and reduce their environmental impact by adopting energy-efficient technologies, utilizing renewable energy sources, and implementing responsible data management practices. One such example is of Klarna, a Swedish Fintech company committed to making its operations climate-neutral by 2025. Klarna is investing in renewable energy, optimizing data centres for energy efficiency, and promoting carbon footprint reduction among its employees.

Sustainability in Fintech extends to social and economic dimensions. Ethical Fintech companies consider the broader impact of their services on society, striving to create positive economic outcomes, empower individuals, and support local communities.

Sustainable Fintech companies navigate regulatory challenges responsibly. They collaborate closely with regulators to ensure compliance with financial laws and regulations, promoting a stable and trustworthy financial ecosystem. These companies actively engage in discussions around regulatory frameworks to promote innovation while safeguarding consumer interests.

5.6 Organizational Efforts for Sustainability in Fintech

As societal concerns about sustainability gain traction, Fintech companies are proactively adjusting their business models and operations to align with the principles of environmental responsibility and social equity. These companies adopt social responsibility measures to contributing toward benefits to stakeholders (Chaturvedi et al., 2021; Jones & Patel, 2019).

Fintech firms are actively seeking ways to minimize their carbon footprint, reduce energy consumption, and adopt ecofriendly practices (Brown & Green, 2021). Strategies such as green data centres, energy-efficient technologies, and the integration of renewable energy sources have gained prominence as Fintech organizations strive to lower their environmental impact.

Fintech companies are at the forefront of exploring innovative solutions to extend financial services to underserved populations, effectively narrowing the gap between the banked and unbanked segments (Chen & Kim, 2020).

5.7 Stakeholder Engagement and Transparent Communication

Stakeholder engagement and transparent communication are underscored as essential components of sustainable Fintech initiatives (Smith & Davis, 2017). Cultivating trust among consumers, investors, and regulatory authorities is a primary objective. Fintech firms are proactively engaging with stakeholders to elicit feedback, exhibit their unwavering commitment to sustainability, and instil a sense of accountability. Effective communication strategies are pivotal in conveying the value of sustainability endeavours and garnering support from stakeholders across the spectrum (Gupta & Patel, 2018).

5.8 Awareness

Despite being considered the future of the financial system (Singh & Gupta, 2016), Fintech's awareness and literacy levels remain moderate in rural areas of India. Additionally, the perception of financial risk among rural consumers is a deterrent to adopting digital payment systems (Pauchard, 2019). Even with numerous initiatives and programs aimed at promoting a cashless economy, a significant portion of the rural population in India still relies on traditional payment methods. According to the *Economic Times*, 80% of rural India and 20% of urban India have yet to embrace digital mediums of exchange. Rai and Sharma (2019) assert that the literacy level regarding digital financial services and the Fintech industry significantly influences consumers' intentions to adopt them. Previous studies have consistently highlighted financial risk as a pivotal factor that consumers carefully consider when contemplating the adoption of digital payments (Pauchard, 2019; Ryu, 2018; Yang et al., 2015). Consequently, consumer perceptions of risk and levels of digital literacy wield substantial influence over Fintech adoption.

5.9 Digital Financial Literacy (DFL) for Fintech

Digitalization positively affects organizational performance. Digital financial literacy (DFL) encompasses an individual's comprehension of various

Fintech services, including online purchases, online payments using diverse methods, and online banking systems (Prasad et al., 2018). Morgan et al. (2019) have attempted to delineate DFL across four conceptual dimensions: awareness of the risks associated with digital financial products and services, understanding of digital financial products and services, knowledge of consumer rights and redress procedures, and knowledge of digital financial risk management.

Social traits, such as age, income, and education, significantly influence an individual's financial literacy regarding digital tools and Fintech (Setiawan et al., 2020). Studies by Wangmo (2015) and Nanziri and Olckers (2019) have supported that income levels correlate with financial literacy. Moreover, research by Tony and Desai (2020) aimed to elucidate the broader connection between financial inclusion and DFL. Prasad et al.'s (2018) study focused on charting the level of DFL in Indian households, while Liew et al. (2020) engaged 252 farmers from the Sarawak region to assess their DFL. Rai and Sharma (2019) explored the awareness levels of higher education institutions regarding digital financial services, revealing considerable variation in literacy levels based on geographical areas, namely rural and urban regions (Krishnakumar, 2023).

5.10 Perceived Financial Risk (PFR) in Fintech

Perceived financial risk (PFR) encapsulates the potential monetary loss stemming from using Fintech (Yang et al., 2015). This risk, attributed to concerns about financial fraud and elevated transaction costs, negatively impacts the adoption of Fintech and digital payment systems (Ryu, 2018). Incidents of fraud and monetary losses tied to user accounts in digital payment systems have engendered consumer apprehension. Scholarly literature consistently underscores the centrality of PFR as the primary consideration for consumers when contemplating digital payments – a factor that profoundly influences their adoption of Fintech services (Pauchard, 2019; Ryu, 2018; Yang et al., 2015). In a study by Park et al. (2019), the effects of perceived risk, perceived benefits, and trust on users' intention to embrace digital payments were examined, revealing a negative relationship between perceived risk, trust, and consumer intention to use digital payment services. Therefore, PFR emerges as a prominent factor inhibiting the adoption of Fintech services.

5.11 Tangible Business Benefits of Sustainable Fintech Practices

Research underscores that organizations incorporating sustainability into their core strategies often witness an enhanced brand reputation, heightened customer loyalty, and an expanded investor base (Liu & Chen, 2021). As consumers become increasingly environmentally and socially conscious, they are more likely to favour businesses that demonstrate a commitment to sustainability. Fintech companies that proactively adopt ecofriendly policies and promote ethical conduct can build a reputation for responsibility and trustworthiness, leading to increased consumer loyalty. Also, Fintech companies that embrace sustainability are more likely to attract a broader investor base. Investors recognize that sustainable practices can contribute to long-term financial stability and resilience in a rapidly changing business landscape.

Furthermore, sustainable Fintech practices frequently stimulate innovation, resulting in the development of novel products and services that cater to evolving consumer preferences and, in turn, create a competitive advantage in the market (Wang & Jackson, 2019).

5.12 Conclusion

In the ever-evolving realm of Fintech, the pursuit of responsible and sustainable practices is as pivotal as the technological advancements themselves. This chapter has embarked on a comprehensive journey to explore the intricate ethical and sustainability considerations intrinsic to Fintech, emphasizing their fundamental role in shaping the industry's future.

From digital payments to blockchain-driven solutions, Fintech has unlocked unprecedented levels of convenience, accessibility, and financial inclusion. Yet, beneath this veneer of progress lies a complex terrain of ethical and sustainability challenges that merit our attention and engagement.

First, centred on ethical considerations at its core, Fintech obliges companies to safeguard user data with utmost diligence, recognizing the moral imperative of data privacy and security. It underscores a commitment to financial inclusion, seeking to bridge digital divides and ensure that financial services are universally accessible. These ethical touchpoints serve as a moral compass, urging Fintech entities to uphold the highest standards of integrity and foster unwavering user trust.

The other significant consideration was focused on sustainability considerations, extending the discourse to encompass environmental, financial, social, and regulatory dimensions.

Finally, this chapter calls for collective commitment and collaboration among Fintech professionals, regulators, researchers, and users, all converging to chart a course for an industry defined by trust, innovation, and societal welfare.

Bibliography

Akhtar, S., Niazi, M. H., & Khan, M. M. (2020). Cascading Effect of COVID 19 on Indian Economy. *International Journal of Advanced Science and Technology*, 29(9), 4563–4573.

Annapurna, R. (2024). *How India is using the Internet*. The Economic Times. Retrieved from https://economictimes.indiatimes.com/tech/technology/how-india-is-using-the-internet/articleshow/108354854.cms?from=mdr.

Azmi, S., Akhtar, S., & Nadeem, M. (2020). Impact of Digitalisation on Bank Performance: A Study of Indian Banks. *Test Engineering and Management*, 83, 23678–23691.

Balch, O. (2020). Are Digital Payments COVID Winners? Raconteur. On Interventions. *Decision Sciences*, 39(2), 273–315. https://doi.org/10.1111/j.1540-5915.2008.00192.x.

Brown, A., & Green, R. (2021). Sustainable Practices in the Fintech Industry. *Journal of Sustainable Finance*, 8(2), 101–120.

Chaturvedi, K., Akhtar, S., Azhar, N., & Shamshad, M. (2021). Impact of Corporate Social Responsibility on Financial Performance of Selected Banks in India: Based on Camel Model. *Studies in Economics and Business Relations*, 2(2).

Chen, L., & Kim, J. (2020). Fintech and Financial Inclusion: Empowering the Unbanked. *Journal of Financial Innovation*, 12(3), 45–67.

Garcia, M., & Smith, T. (2019). Diversity and Inclusion in Fintech: Strategies for Equitable Growth. *Fintech Journal*, 6(1), 21–38.

Gomber, P., Koch, J. A., & Siering, M. (2017). Digital Finance and Fintech: Current Research and Future Research Directions. *Journal of Business Economics*, 87(5), 537–580.

Gupta, S., & Patel, R. (2018). Effective Communication Strategies for Sustainable Fintech Initiatives. *Journal of Sustainable Finance and Innovation*, 4(4), 89–108.

Hansen, E., & Jensen, M. (2022). Navigating Regulatory Challenges in Sustainable Fintech. *Journal of Financial Compliance*, 9(1), 77–95.

Johnson, K., & Anderson, L. (2018). Regulatory Frameworks and Compliance in Sustainable Fintech. *Fintech Regulation Review*, 7(3), 55–72.

Jones, R., & Patel, S. (2019). Fintech Evolution: Adapting Business Models for Sustainability. *International Journal of Fintech Research*, 15(2), 123–142.

Krishnakumar, P. (2023). *Digital Wallets: The Genesis, Current Usage, and Future Use Healthcare Payments in India Prashanthi Krishnakumar.* Access Health – Nonprofit Healthcare Organisation. https://fintechforhealth.sg/digital-wallets -the-genesis-current-usage-and-future-use-healthcare-payments-in.

Kumari, I. N. N., & Mary, A. I. V. (2019). Factors Affecting the Adoption of Mobile Payments of Rural Entrepreneurs - A Qualitative Study. *International Journal of Economic Research*, 16(1), 161–171.

Liew, T., Lim, P., & Liu, Y. (2020). Digital Financial Literacy: A Case Study of Farmers From Rural Areas in Sarawak. *International Journal of Education and Pedagogy*, 2(4), 245–251. Retrieved from https://myjms.mohe.gov.my/index.php/ ijeap/article/view/11612.

Liu, H., & Chen, Q. (2021). The Business Benefits of Sustainable Fintech: A Case Study of Innovation Impact. *Journal of Sustainable Financial Strategies*, 9(4), 33–50.

Mallat, N. (2007). Exploring Consumer Adoption of Mobile Payments–A Qualitative Study. *The Journal of Strategic Information Systems*, 16(4), 413–432.

Morgan, P. J., Huang, B., & Trinh, L. Q. (2019). The Need to Promote Digital Financial Literacy for the Digital Age.

Mullins, D., & Carter, J. (2021). Regulatory Complexities in Sustainable Fintech: A Comparative Analysis. *Fintech Law Journal*, 14(2), 87–105.

Mustafa, F., & Sharma, V. (2023). Factors Enabling Pervasiveness of Belief and Ethics-Based Marketing Practice: An Interpretive Structural Modeling Approach. *Journal of Islamic Marketing*, 14(10), 2429–2449.

Nanziri, L. W., & Olckers, M. (2019). *Financial Literacy in South Africa.* Cape Town: SALDRU. UCT (SALDRU Working Paper Number 242 Version 1/ NIDS Discussion Paper 2019/9). Retrieved from http://www.opensaldru.uct.ac.za/ handle/11090/957.

Osakwe, C. N., & Okeke, T. C. (2016). Facilitating m-Commerce Growth in Nigeria through mMoney Usage: A Preliminary Analysis. *Interdisciplinary Journal of Information, Knowledge, and Management*, 11, 115–139. https://doi.org/10 .28945/3456.

Park, J., Amendah, E., Lee, Y., & Hyun, H. (2019). M-Payment Service: Interplay of Perceived Risk, Benefit, and Trust in Service Adoption. *Human Factors and Ergonomics in Manufacturing and Service Industries*, 29(1), 31–43. https://doi .org/10.1002/hfm.20750.

Pauchard, L. (2019). *A Comparison of the Different Types of Risk Perceived by Users That Are Hindering the Adoption of Mobile Payment.* Springer International Publishing. https://doi.org/10.1007/978-3-030-23943-5_14.

Perez, A., & Turner, B. (2020). The Business Case for Sustainability in Fintech: Evidence from Industry Leaders. *Journal of Sustainable Innovation*, 11(1), 67–84.

Prasad, H., Meghwal, D., & Dayama, V. (2018). Digital Financial Literacy: A Study of Households of Udaipur. *Journal of Business and Management*, 5, 23–32. https://doi.org/10.3126/jbm.v5i0.27385.

Rachna, & Singh, P. (2013). Issues and Challenges of Electronic Payment Systems. *International Journal for Research in Management and Pharmacy*, 2(9), 1–6.

Rai, K., & Sharma, M. (2019). A Study on Awareness About Digital Financial Services Among Students. *SSRN Electronic Journal*. https://doi.org/10.2139/ssrn.3308732.

Ryu, H.-S. (2018). Understanding Benefit and Risk Framework of Fintech Adoption: Comparison of Early Adopters and Late Adopters. *Proceedings of the 51st Hawaii International Conference on System Sciences*. https://doi.org/10.24251/hicss.2018.486.

Setiawan, M., Effendi, N., Santoso, T., Dewi, V. I., & Sapulette, M. S. (2020). Digital Financial Literacy, Current Behavior of Saving and Spending and Its Future Foresight. *Economics of Innovation and New Technology*, 1–19. https://doi.org/10.1080/10438599.2020.1799142.

Singh, J., & Gupta, M. (2016). An Empirical Study of Customer Adoption of Mobile Wallet Payment Services: A Case Study of the City Kurali of Punjab. *Splint International Journal of Professionals*, 3(12), 88.

Smith, H., et al. (2020). The Evolution of Fintech and Sustainability: An Analytical Perspective. *Journal of Financial Technology Trends*, 14(3), 109–128.

Smith, R., & Davis, P. (2017). Stakeholder Engagement and Communication in Sustainable Fintech Initiatives. *Sustainable Finance Review*, 5(2), 45–62.

Smith, T., & White, E. (2022). Organizational Commitment to Sustainability in the Fintech Sector. *Sustainability and Innovation Journal*, 18(1), 23–40.

Tony, N., & Desai, K. (2020). Impact of Digital Financial Literacy on Digital Financial Inclusion. *International Journal of Scientific and Technology Research*, 9(1), 1911–1915.

Visa. (2022). *Contactless Payments Witnessed a 6x Growth in the Last 3 Years: Visa and Worldline India Whitepaper*. https://www.visa.co.in/about-visa/newsroom/press-releases/contactless-payments-witnessed-a-6x-growth-in-the-last-3-years-visa-and-worldline-india-whitepaper.html.

Wang, Y., & Jackson, M. (2019). Innovation and Sustainable Fintech Practices: A Comparative Study. *Journal of Financial Innovation and Technology*, 13(4), 87–104.

Wangmo, P. (2015). Assessing the Level and Impact of Financial Literacy on Individual Saving and Spending Habits in Royal Institute of Management. *PGDPA Research Report 2018*. Bhutan.

Yang, Y., Liu, Y., Li, H., & Yu, B. (2015). Understanding Perceived Risks in Mobile Payment Acceptance. *Industrial Management and Data Systems*, 115(2), 253–269.

Chapter 6

Robo-Advisory and Investor Trust: The Essential Role of Ethical Practices and Fiduciary Responsibility

Rangapriya Saivasan

6.1 Introduction

The financial landscape has witnessed a remarkable transformation with the emergence of robo-advisory services, marking a paradigm shift in investment management. Robo-advisory platforms use advanced computer programs and artificial intelligence (AI) that provide automatic help with investing and managing investment portfolios. The worldwide robo-advisory market has a valuation of 7.9 billion US dollars as of 2022, and it is estimated that it will reach 129.5 billion US dollars by 2032 (compound annual growth rate [CAGR] of 32.5% for the period between 2023 and 2032) (Allied Market Research, 2023; Grand View Research, 2022). Robo-advisory's rapid growth highlights its potential impact, making ethics crucial for investor trust and safeguarding their interests. It's set to define modern investment strategies (Chong, 2017). These platforms utilize algorithms to analyze investors' financial goals, risk tolerance, and preferences, crafting personalized investment portfolios that align with these factors. With the integration of machine learning and data analytics, robo-advisors

 DOI: 10.4324/9781032644165-6

continually optimize portfolios to adapt to market changes, ensuring a dynamic investment approach. The convenience, accessibility, and cost-efficiency offered by robo-advisory services have garnered significant attention, attracting both tech-savvy Millennials and traditional investors alike (Beilfuss, 2018). Forecasts suggest that the global assets under management (AUM) within robo-advisory platforms are projected at 3 trillion US dollars in 2023, and the robo-advisors market anticipates a 13.99% annual growth rate (CAGR 2023–2027), aiming for 5 trillion US dollars by 2027 (Statista, 2023). This projection is underpinned by the allure of low fees, simplified investment processes, and the increasing recognition of robo-advisory's potential to democratize investment opportunities for broader demography. As more investors embrace these platforms, their influence on the financial landscape is set to reshape traditional investment practices (Matthews, 2023). Robo-advisory services, despite clear advantages, grapple with ethical and fiduciary challenges. Algorithmic bias, transparency issues, and the absence of human interaction pose concerns. Data privacy is crucial, necessitating responsible handling for investor trust and regulatory compliance in this era of vast data collection (Wipro, 2020; Severino, 2022).

Numerous literary works demonstrate the Indian financial system's susceptibility to severe financial crises, eroding trust in the country's economic structure. These crises often originate from inadequate ethical standards and deficient fiduciary oversight (Akhtar, Alam, & Khan, 2021; Ansari, Akhtar, Khan, & Shamshad, 2023). Balancing innovation and ethics is vital in the evolving robo-advisory landscape. This study delves into inherent ethical considerations, including algorithmic bias, transparency, suitability assessment, data privacy, conflicts of interest, and accountability. It highlights the importance of fair, transparent practices, client suitability, data protection, and fiduciary responsibility in the robo-advisory ecosystem. Subsequent sections will analyze these ethical concerns and their broader implications for investors, robo-advisory firms, regulators, and the investment industry. In an era of tech-driven financial innovations, upholding ethical principles is key to maintaining trust and delivering long-term value to investors and society. The rest of this work is organized as follows: Section 6.2 covers the literature review, Section 6.3 presents the research methodology, Section 6.4 outlays the data analysis and results, Section 6.5 presents the implications of the study and the future research areas, and Section 6.6 provides the conclusion.

6.2 Literature Review

The literature review encompasses an examination of approximately 63 relevant papers, with a focus on the most prominent ones featured herein. Notably, a distinct scarcity of literature pertains to the intersection of ethics and fiduciary responsibility within the context of the examined subject.

The rise of robo-advisory (RA) services has disrupted the conventional fund and wealth management industry, driven by factors such as competitive pricing, transparency, and services. The study by Rasiwala and Kohli (2021) focuses on understanding the perception of financial experts regarding digital disruption's impact and strategies employed by financial service providers to counter Fintech challengers. Through structured content analysis of interviews with experts from diverse financial backgrounds, key themes emerged, including competition, vulnerability of segments, ecosystem challenges, asset complementarity, and disruption coping strategies. Experts acknowledge the potential for disruption from Fintech but emphasize the importance of collaboration between traditional financial institutions and Fintech companies. It is recommended that banks embrace a hybrid platform that integrates both traditional and disruptive financial services, allowing improved customer experiences and access to underserved segments while leveraging complementary assets of both sectors. Regulatory flexibility is also deemed necessary for fostering successful collaboration. Robo-advisors, algorithm-driven online advisory platforms, are gaining popularity due to their cost-effective investment recommendations. However, their unique client–machine interaction raises legal and regulatory concerns. This article asserts that while RA services differ from traditional financial advice, existing regulations, such as the European Union's (EU) framework for financial intermediaries, can address most issues. The key is applying rules that don't hinder robo-advisors' potential to widen access to financial services. Market efficiency requires adapting regulations to suit robo-advisors' distinct characteristics, without imposing uniform rules on all participants. Currently, robo-advisors don't pose systemic risks, and investor protection should focus on maintaining a certain quality level and effective error redress. Modifying licensing requirements and even considering direct licensing for robo-advisors may be relevant moving forward (Maume, 2018).

The study by Piotrowski (2022) provides evidence that application of AI, particularly RA services, in financial services has the potential to enhance accessibility and cost efficiency. This study focuses on the limited adoption of RA services in Polish banks, attributing it to customer resistance, particularly among older age groups and those hesitant toward new technologies. Lack of experience with investment advisory services and apprehensions about data misuse also hinder acceptance. Through a survey of 911 individuals aged 18–65, the study employs a multinomial logit model to identify these significant barriers, offering insights for banks to encourage wider adoption of RA services and AI in financial services. Another study aims to assess Indian individual investors' awareness and perceptions of robo-advisors in wealth management. Robo-advisors are automated platforms suggesting portfolio allocations based on algorithms. Conducted through qualitative methods, the research used focused group discussions with purposive sampling of active Indian stock market investors. Content analysis of discussions highlighted factors such as cost-effectiveness, trust, behavioural biases, data security, and sentiments impacting investor perception. Participants suggested ways to enhance awareness. Some investors viewed robo-advisors as quantitative analysis alternatives, believing human intervention essential for understanding emotions. Presently, robo-advisors are seen as supplementary rather than substitutive to financial advisors in the Indian stock market (Bhatia, Chandani, Atiq, Mehta, & Divekar, 2021). The work by Shanmuganathan (2020) utilized behavioural analysis in the context of AI-driven robo-advisors to comprehend the impact of AI solutions on investor choices. Through a longitudinal case study design focused on wealth management and market dynamics, the research explored robo-advisor performance analysis and customer decision-making patterns. Leveraging AI and machine learning in robo-advisors enabled an enhanced understanding of customer behaviour and its interplay with market dynamics. By tracking actions and identifying behavioural trends, the study provided valuable insights for fund managers. This work extends behavioural finance theories by integrating AI-driven robo-advisors, highlighting the link between behavioural patterns and portfolio strategies. The study identifies that the success of robo-advisors relies on three key factors. First, selecting the right technology and pricing approach for offering RA services, involving decisions on fee structures such as Charles Schwab's free model or the 25 to 35 basis points range. Second, an effective distribution strategy matters, considering whether to leverage existing trademarks or create new ones for RA services. Lastly, firms with advisor forces should integrate their capabilities with robo-advisors to enhance service provision. These elements collectively shape the prosperous implementation and operation of RA platforms. This study examined how Swiss-based robo-advisors present information on their websites to ensure retail investor protection. Data from 11 RA websites were collected, categorized, and analyzed, revealing several weaknesses. The services provided by RA services were ambiguously defined, risk information was poorly presented compared to benefits, and explanations about automation and algorithms were insufficient. While recent regulations such as the Swiss Financial Services Act (FinSA) might partially address these issues, RA services still need to enhance disclosures. Best practices for RA services include clarifying services, presenting balanced risk and benefit information, disclosing algorithm use, and communicating their compliance with customer protection standards. However, this analysis couldn't assess RA services' real-world performance or their ability to comply with complex legal requirements, highlighting areas for future research on RA services and investor literacy (Mezzanotte, 2020). As per Steennot (2022), the advent of RA services highlights their potential benefits in offering enhanced protection to retail investors through suitability tests. However, it acknowledges the risks posed by limited human interaction and algorithmic use. The paper emphasizes the need for clear explanations of robo-advice, effective questioning, ensuring accurate algorithmic advice, and providing transparent information. It suggests that financial regulators should be able to scrutinize algorithms and propose compensation for retail investors who receive unsuitable advice without needing to prove algorithm flaws.

From the literature review, it is evident that many papers mention that ethical and fiduciary challenges exist in RA services; however, prevalent literature lacks an in-depth exploration of these challenges, hindering a focused and thorough addressing of these issues. A comprehensive analysis that intricately identifies and examines these challenges is needed to enable a more nuanced and effective approach to address them within the context of RA services.

6.3 Research Methodology

Qualitative research formed the foundation of this study, aiming to comprehensively explore the dynamics of the evolving phenomenon (Patton, 2002). Employing thematic analysis and user observation as key methodologies, a holistic understanding emerged, shedding light on the phenomenon's development within real-life contexts. Thematic analysis unveiled recurring patterns and meanings in collected data, uncovering nuanced insights within the evolving landscape. User observation, conducted in authentic settings, provided direct insight into user behaviours and challenges, which are crucial for understanding practical implications (Clarke, 2015; Baker, 2006).

Supplementing empirical findings with peer-reviewed articles and industry reports enhances the analysis of an evolving subject. This flexible methodology, incorporating qualitative methods and user observation, accommodates emergent patterns and deepens understanding, acknowledging the subject's complexity.

6.4 Data Analysis and Results

Through a thorough literature review, the key RA enablers and operational strengths were identified. This forms the basis for exploring ethical challenges and fiduciary responsibility. Integrating these perspectives aims to enhance understanding, inform decision-making, and build industry trust in RA services.

The framework highlights key elements vital for the growth and success of RA services. It focuses on advanced technological infrastructure, including algorithms and AI, for efficient data processing. User accessibility and convenience are paramount, achieved through user-friendly interfaces and 24/7 availability. Personalization is crucial, tailoring investment advice to individual aspirations and risk preferences and crafting diversified portfolios. Cost efficiency is achieved through reduced fees and automated processes, enabling scalability to accommodate numerous clients and diverse portfolios. Robust data security and privacy measures, along with regulatory compliance, are essential. Clear communication and transparency in investment strategies, along with explanations for algorithm-driven decisions, build investor trust. Continuous learning and improvement, with regular algorithm updates and user feedback integration, enhance the overall experience. Commitment to research and innovation ensures competitive adaptability in the dynamic financial landscape. Promoting investor education and collaborating with financial institutions and technology providers enrich capabilities. Continuous evolution of the financial system on the backdrop of innovation and collaboration often drives the constructive consolidation of inefficient financial institutions, resulting in positive synergies that ultimately benefit the end customers (Akhtar, Alam, Khan, & Shamshad, 2023; Akhtar, Alam, & Ansari, 2022). Lastly, enhancing the user experience through intuitive design and user feedback loops ensures an interactive and user-centric approach. These components form the basis for successful RA services, meeting evolving market demands and user expectations (see Figure 6.1) (Raut, 2017; CGI, 2016).

6.4.1 Critical Ethical Considerations in Robo-Advisory Services

6.4.1.1 Algorithmic Bias

A significant challenge revolves around algorithmic bias in RA platforms. Despite their efficiency, these algorithms can unintentionally perpetuate biases present in historical data. Such biases lead to unequal treatment, impeding the platforms' ability to offer impartial and equitable advice to investors from diverse backgrounds. Some of the possible biases include gender bias (biased toward male investors, disregards female preferences), socioeconomic bias (favours high-income options, excludes lower-income

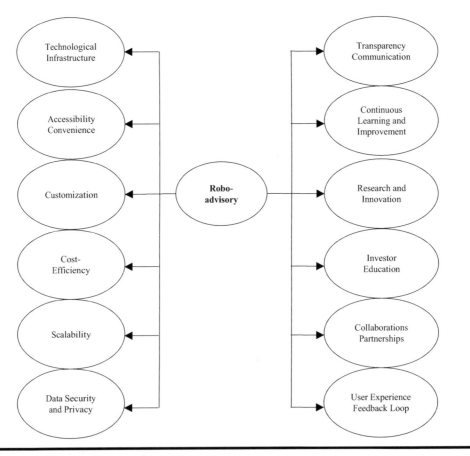

Figure 6.1   Key enablers of robo-advisory. Source: Adapted from Fan & Chatterjee (2020), Research Nester (2023)

choices), ethnic bias (lacks diversity, neglects different ethnicities' needs), age bias (overlooks age differences, misaligns with life stages), geographical bias (ignores regional nuances, non-inclusive), educational bias (assumes high literacy, excludes less-educated users) (Draws, Szl'avik, & Timmermans, 2021; Deo, 2021; Li, 2022).

6.4.1.2 Transparency Gap

The cornerstone of ethical investment practices, transparency, can be compromised in the automated realm of RA services. Machine learning (ML) and AI systems can function as "black boxes," complicating their interpretability due to complexity. This opacity raises transparency and bias concerns (Eschenbach, 2021). Investors often struggle to grasp the complexities of algorithms, creating a transparency gap between platform recommendations and investor comprehension. This gap raises concerns about accountability, urging platforms to transparently communicate their processes and decisions to investors. This gap, stemming from intricate algorithm workings, hinders investor understanding (Zhu & Pysander, 2023). Lack of insight into recommendations undermines informed decision-making, potentially leading to suboptimal choices and reduced trust. Clear communication is pivotal for empowering investors with the necessary knowledge.

6.4.1.3 Lack of Human Interaction

The absence of human interaction in RA services raises concerns about accurately assessing nuanced financial situations and risk tolerance. Algorithms replace personalized human advice, potentially resulting in suboptimal investments. This relates to the broader challenge of fiduciary responsibility, in which automated platforms may appear less accountable. AI cannot grasp emotional nuances and biases crucial to investing, potentially affecting choices and the fulfilment of fiduciary duties. Buczynski, Cuzzolin, and Sahakian (2021) insist on the need for "human-in-the-loop" approaches for investment decisions made by the ML system. This could address the issue of responsibility and accountability effectively. The work by Pomerol (1997) explores AI's ties to decision-making, particularly in diagnosis and look-ahead reasoning. While AI is well-connected to diagnoses through methods such as expert systems, it lacks attention to look-ahead reasoning involving uncertainty and preferences, thus calling for human expertise to bridge this gap.

6.4.1.4 Data Privacy Concerns

RA platforms' extensive collection of personal and financial data raises serious privacy concerns. Mishandling this data could lead to breaches, enabling identity theft, financial fraud, and unauthorized access to sensitive information. Such exposure of personal financial details poses risks to investors' reputations and financial well-being. Furthermore, the misuse of this data might result in targeted marketing or manipulation of investment decisions, infringing on individual autonomy. Inadequate data protection measures can erode trust in these platforms, undermining their credibility. Therefore, robust security measures and ethical practices are imperative to prevent these risks and uphold investor privacy and trust in RA services. The issue of data privacy in RA systems has two sides. While concerns exist about sensitive data handling, blockchain technology, a secure and decentralized digital ledger, holds promise for enhancing data security and privacy. Blockchain's cryptographic features enable secure data storage, significantly reducing the risk of unauthorized access. It is being explored to ensure transparent and tamper-proof data storage, secure identity management, and efficient sharing of financial information in the RA sector. This is especially relevant in the face of hacking threats, which could lead to severe misappropriation of funds and the compromise of personal information (Aw et al., 2023; Abraham, Schmukler, & Tessada, 2019; An, Choi, & Huang, 2021).

Tackling the challenges of ethical considerations and fiduciary responsibility in RA services hinges on the responsible utilization of explainable AI (XAI) and a robust regulatory framework overseen by experts. By incorporating fairness-aware algorithms and rigorous data preprocessing techniques, RA platforms can mitigate algorithmic bias, ensuring equitable treatment across diverse user backgrounds. Transparent model explainability tools can bridge the transparency gap, fostering investor comprehension of algorithmic recommendations and holding platforms accountable for their decisions. Digmayer (2022) examines AI-driven RA services supporting economic decisions, revealing transparency concerns across phases and suggesting explanations, design enhancements, and communication to alleviate adoption barriers.

To address the lack of human interaction, AI can be supplemented with human-in-the-loop approaches, enabling expert human oversight for more nuanced assessments of investor financial situations and risk preferences (Buczynski, Cuzzolin, & Sahakian, 2021). Furthermore, a comprehensive regulatory framework, guided by industry experts and authorities, can enforce data privacy measures, algorithmic auditing, and investor protection standards (Maume, 2018; Scholz, 2020). Collaboration among regulators, industry stakeholders, and AI experts is crucial for RA platforms to maintain fiduciary responsibility, and ethics, that align with investor interests and preserve trust in finance.

6.5 Implications and Future Research

This study's implications span various stakeholders in RA services. As these services transform investment management, recognizing ethical and fiduciary aspects is crucial.

- **RA Firms**: The study emphasizes integrating ethics into algorithms, promoting transparency and responsibility. Firms can gain trust and loyalty by aligning platforms with investor and regulatory needs.
- **Regulators and Policymakers**: Regulatory bodies can leverage study insights to formulate comprehensive guidelines that ensure algorithmic fairness, data privacy, and investor protection.
- **Investors and Industry Professionals**: The study equips investors with awareness about potential pitfalls, fostering informed decision-making while navigating the RA landscape. Industry professionals gain deeper insights into addressing ethical challenges, upholding fiduciary responsibilities, and maintaining high standards of service.
- **Advancements in Fintech**: By highlighting the ethical dimensions and the role of AI in RA services, the study encourages Fintech innovation that prioritizes fairness, transparency, and accountability. This emphasis contributes to a sustainable and trustworthy Fintech ecosystem.
- **Academic and Research Community**: Researchers can build upon the study's findings, exploring novel methodologies to assess algorithmic bias, transparency, and the interplay of AI in investment management.

The following are the potential research studies that can be pursued within the realm of ethical and fiduciary challenges in RA services.

- Quantify the impact of algorithmic bias on investment recommendations across diverse groups.
- Investigate user comprehension of algorithmic advice and its influence on trust and decisions.

- Compare investment performance between algorithmic and human-assisted RA services.
- Conduct perception study on investors regarding data privacy's role in RA engagement.

6.6 Conclusion

RA services have disrupted the investment management landscape with promises of convenience and efficiency. These platforms, driven by advanced algorithms and AI, have transformed traditional practices. This study delves into the complex intersection of technology, ethics, and financial stewardship, examining the ethical considerations and fiduciary responsibilities associated with RA services. Key enablers of RA growth, including technological infrastructure, accessibility, customization, and scalability, offer advantages such as reduced fees and broader accessibility but also present challenges. Automated systems can perpetuate algorithmic bias, hinder transparency, and lack personalized human interaction. Addressing these challenges emphasizes responsible AI deployment and regulatory oversight. This study calls on industry players, regulators, and the investment community to adopt ethical practices and shape compliance frameworks. Investors can make informed decisions, and the community benefits from a trustworthy financial ecosystem. In an algorithm-driven digital age, the findings stress the importance of aligning technology with ethics and regulations. Trust in financial technology relies on responsible innovation that safeguards investor interests and fosters transparency. By advocating for responsible AI practices and comprehensive regulation, this study charts a path that harmonizes technological advancement with ethical integrity. This pathway not only enhances investor trust but also sustains the financial ecosystem's vitality for generations to come.

References

Abraham, F., Schmukler, S. L., & Tessada, J. (2019). *Robo-Advisors: Investing Through Machines*. Washington, DC: World Bank Research and Policy Briefs No. 134881.

Akhtar, S., Alam, M., & Ansari, M. (2022). Measuring the Performance of the Indian Banking Industry: Data Envelopment Window Analysis Approach. *Benchmarking: An International Journal, 29*(9), 2842–2857. https://doi.org/10.1108/BIJ-03-2021-0115.

Akhtar, S., Alam, M., & Khan, M. M. (2021). Yes Bank Fiasco: Arrogance or Negligence. *Emerging Economies Cases Journal, 3*(2), 95–102. https://doi.org/10.1177/25166042211061003.

Akhtar, S., Alam, M., Khan, A., & Shamshad, M. (2023). Measuring Technical Efficiency of Banks Vis-à-vis Demonetization: An Empirical Analysis of Indian Banking Sector Using CAMELS Framework. *Quality and Quantity, 57*(2), 1739–1761. https://doi.org/10.1007/s11135-022-01431-8.

Allied Market Research. (2023). *Robo Advisory Market Research, 2032.* Allied Market Research.

An, Y. J., Choi, P., & Huang, S. (2021). Blockchain, Cryptocurrency, and Artificial Intelligence in Finance. In P. H. Choi (ed.), *Blockchain Technologies* (pp. 1–34). Singapore: Springer. https://doi.org/10.1007/978-981-33-6137-9_1.

Ansari, M. S., Akhtar, S., Khan, A., & Shamshad, M. (2023). Consequence of Financial Crisis on Liquidity and Profitability of Commercial Banks in India: An Empirical Study. *Studies in Economics and Business Relations, 3*(2), 36–50. https://doi.org/10.48185/sebr.v3i2.367.

Aw, E. C.-X., Leong, L.-Y., Hew, J.-J., et al. (2023). Counteracting Dark Sides of Robo-Advisors: Justice, Privacy and Intrusion Considerations. *International Journal of Bank Marketing.* https://doi.org/10.1108/IJBM-10-2022-0439.

Baker, L. (2006). Observation: A Complex Research Method. *Library Trends,* 171–189. https://doi.org/10.1353/lib.2006.0045.

Beilfuss, L. (2018, June 19). The Future Robo Adviser: Smart and Ethical? *The Wall Street Journal.* https://www.wsj.com/articles/the-future-robo-adviser-smart-and-ethical-1529460240.

Bhatia, A., Chandani, A., Atiq, R., Mehta, M., & Divekar, R. (2021). Artificial Intelligence in Financial Services: A Qualitative Research to Discover Robo-Advisory Services. *Qualitative Research in Financial Markets,* 632–654. https://doi.org/10.1108/QRFM-10-2020-0199.

Buczynski, W., Cuzzolin, F., & Sahakian, B. (2021). A Review of Machine Learning Experiments in Equity Investment Decision-Making: Why Most Published Research Findings Do Not Live Up to Their Promise in Real Life. *International Journal of Data Science and Analytics,* 221–242. https://doi.org/10.1007/s41060-021-00245-5.

CGI. (2016). *Beyond Robo-Advisors: Using Technology to Power New Methods of Client Advice and Interaction.* CGI Group Inc.

Chong, D. (2017). *Ethics on Robo-Advisors and Its Big Data.* Singapore: Chong, Darren.

Clarke, V. B. (2015). Thematic Analysis. In J. A. Smith (ed.), *Qualitative Psychology: A Practical Guide to Research Methods* (pp. 222–248. New York: SAGE Publications Ltd.

Deo, S. (2021). *The Under-Appreciated Regulatory Challenges Posed by Algorithms in Fintech Understanding Interactions Among Users, Firms, Algorithm Dec.* Berlin: Hertie School.

Digmayer, C. (2022). Automated Economic Welfare for Everyone? Examining Barriers to Adopting Robo-Advisors from the Perspective of Explainable Artificial Intelligence. *Journal of Interdisciplinary Economics.* https://doi.org/10.1177/02601079221130183.

Draws, T., Szl′avik, Z., & Timmermans, B. (2021). Disparate Impact Diminishes Consumer Trust Even for Advantaged Users. *International Conference on Persuasive Technologies* (pp. https://doi.org/10.1007/978-3-030-79460-6_11). Maastricht: arXiv.

Eschenbach, W. J. (2021). Transparency and the Black Box Problem: Why We Do Not Trust AI. *Philosophy and Technology*, 1607–1622. https://doi.org/10.1007/s13347-021-00477-0.

Fan, L., & Chatterjee, S. (2020). The Utilization of Robo-Advisors by Individual Investors: An Analysis Using Diffusion of Innovation and Information. *Journal of Financial Counseling and Planning*, 130–145. http://doi.org/10.1891/JFCP-18-00078.

Grand View Research. (2022). *Robo Advisory Market Size & Share Analysis Report, 2030*. San Francisco: Grand View Research.

Li, F. (2022). *Artificial Intelligence in Finance: A Change in Direction*. London: BNY Mellon.

Matthews, I. I., & K. L. (2023, March 17). What Is a Robo-Advisor? Understanding the Pros and Cons of Letting a Robot Manage Your Investment Portfolio. *Fortune Recommends*. https://fortune.com/recommends/investing/what-is-a-robo-advisor/.

Maume, P. (2018). Regulating Robo-Advisory. *SSRN Electronic Journal*. https://doi.org/10.2139/ssrn.3167137.

Mezzanotte, F. E. (2020). An Examination into the Investor Protection Properties of Robo-Advisory Services in Switzerland. *Capital Markets Law Journal*, 489–508. https://doi.org/10.1093/cmlj/kmaa024.

Patton, M. Q. (2002). *Qualitative Research and Evaluation Methods*. Thousand Oaks: Sage Publications.

Piotrowski, D. (2022). Demographic and Socio-Economic Factors as Barriers to Robo-Advisory Acceptance in Poland. *Annales Universitatis Mariae Curie-Skłodowska, Sectio H Oeconomia*, 109–126.

Pomerol, J.-C. (1997). Artificial Intelligence and Human Decision Making. *European Journal of Operational Research*, 3–25. https://doi.org/10.1016/S0377-2217(96)00378-5.

Rasiwala, F. S., & Kohli, B. (2021). Artificial Intelligence in Fintech: Understanding Stakeholders Perception on Innovation, Disruption, and Transformation in Finance. *International Journal of Business Intelligence Research (IJBIR)*, 48–65. https://doi.org/10.4018/IJBIR.20210101.oa3.

Raut, S. (2017). *Digital Transformation and High-Tech Robo-Advisor - Do You Need One?* Noida: Nasscom.

Research Nester. (2023). *Robo Advisory Market*. Noida: Research Nester.

Scholz, P. (2020). *Robo-Advisory: Investing in the Digital Age*. Berlin: Springer Nature.

Severino, F. T. (2022). Robo-Advisors: A Big Data Challenge. In T. D. Walker (ed.), *Big Data in Finance*. Cham: Palgrave Macmillan. https://doi.org/10.1007/978-3-031-12240-8_7.

Shanmuganathan, M. (2020). Behavioural Finance in an Era of Artificial Intelligence: Longitudinal Case Study of Robo-Advisors in Investment Decisions. *Journal of Behavioral and Experimental Finance*, 1–13. https://doi.org/10.1016/j.jbef.2020.100297.

Statista. (2023). *Robo-Advisors - Worldwide*. Statista.

Steennot, R. (2022). Robo-Advisory Services and Investor Protection. *Law and Financial Markets Review*. https://doi.org/10.1080/17521440.2022.2153610.

Wipro. (2020). *Future of Robo-Advisors in Investment and Wealth Management*. Bangalore: Wipro.

Zhu, H., & Pysander, E.-L. (2023). Not Transparent and Incomprehensible: A Qualitative User Study of an AI-Empowered Financial Advisory System. *Data and Information Management*. https://doi.org/10.1016/j.dim.2023.100041.

Chapter 7

The Intersection of Fintech and Sustainability: A Catalyst for Positive Change

Pranjal Kumar Phukan and Pokala Pranay Kumar

7.1 Introduction

The junction of financial technology (Fintech) and sustainability constitutes a significant and multifaceted convergence that is changing the financial landscape and its implications for sustainable development. This junction goes beyond the world of financial services to include a complex interplay between technologically driven financial advances and the requirements of environmental, social, and governance (ESG) sustainability (Cambridge Centre for Alternative Finance, 2021). This chapter delves into this intersection from a scientific angle, examining its varied aspects and the implications it has for addressing urgent global concerns.

A potent force for good change emerges in a society where economic development, technical advancement, and environmental responsibility collide. A change in the financial landscape has been sparked by the combination of Fintech with sustainability principles, transforming how we invest, conduct business, and tackle pressing global issues. The way we think about finance and environmental stewardship has changed fundamentally as a result of this convergence, which is more than just a trend. In this introduction, we set out on an exploration of the profound effects of the convergence of Fintech and sustainability, revealing

   DOI: 10.4324/9781032644165-7

its potential to spur improvement in several facets of our global society (Gomber et al., 2018).

Fintech, a disruptive movement that uses technology to transform financial services, has seen a remarkable rise in the twenty-first century. Concurrently, rising worries about social inequity, resource scarcity, and climate change have made sustainability a primary focus on a worldwide scale. The fusion of these two revolutionary developments provides a dynamic environment in which financial innovation and environmentally friendly practises come together, advancing us toward a more fair, resilient, and sustainable future (Mavrotas & Semuel, 2019).

This convergence has a fundamental shift in how we view finance at its core. With little consideration for its broader societal and environmental effects, finance has traditionally been considered as a driver of profit. The incorporation of sustainability into the financial industry, however, puts this conventional way of thinking to the test. It forces us to reconsider the role that finance should play in promoting favourable social and environmental outcomes (Barbier, 2020).

The rise of impact investing and sustainable investments is one of the most notable examples of the junction between Fintech and sustainability. To provide investors with personalized portfolios that meet ESG standards, Fintech platforms and robo-advisors use data analytics and machine learning (Cambridge Centre for Alternative Finance, 2021). This change equips people and organizations to invest in businesses that prioritize sustainability, ultimately fostering ethical business practises and societal advantages.

Blockchain, smart contracts, and digital identity verification are examples of technological advancements that have made sustainable finance possible (World Bank, 2020). For instance, supply chain transparency and trust are improved by blockchain technology, which is a crucial component of sustainability. It enables customers to check the legitimacy of organic certifications, establish fair labour practises, and trace the origins of items.

Investments are just one aspect of the Fintech–sustainability nexus. Additionally, it strengthens initiatives to promote financial inclusion and deal with social problems. Peer-to-peer lending platforms, digital banking services, and mobile payment systems give unbanked and underbanked people all over the world access to financial services. This increase in financial accessibility promotes social welfare, poverty alleviation, and economic growth (Barbier, 2020).

As we explore the interface between Fintech and sustainability, we embark on a journey of inquiry and understanding. We examine the original solutions, revolutionary technologies, and ethical dilemmas that characterize this dynamic environment. We seek to understand how finance, which has historically been seen as contributing to social and environmental issues, is changing and becoming a powerful force for change (Mavrotas & Semuel, 2019).

On this journey, we will see real-world examples of businesses, institutions, and individuals leveraging the potential of sustainability and Fintech to address pressing global issues. These instances, which range from blockchain-based supply chain transparency initiatives to green bonds that support renewable energy projects, demonstrate how the convergence of finance and sustainability is a powerful force driving change (Mavrotas & Semuel, 2019).

The junction of Fintech and sustainability in this era of convergence is clearly not a passing fad; it represents a fundamental shift in how we think about money and solve global problems (Kshetri, 2017). It is a call to action for people, organizations, governments, and institutions to rethink their duties in a society in which finance is a force for good.

7.2 Environmental Sustainability: A Broad Overview

The protection and preservation of the natural world while addressing the demands of the present and future generations are achieved through environmental sustainability. It covers a broad range of ideas, methods, and projects meant to slow down environmental deterioration, protect natural resources, and promote peace on Earth. It is a broad term with several facets that includes ideas, routines, and programmes designed to safeguard the environment and ensure a sustainable future. Responsible resource management, biodiversity preservation, tackling the climate crisis, and fair sharing of environmental benefits are all part of it. Governments, corporations, people, and the entire world must work together to achieve environmental sustainability (World Economic Forum, 2019).

By upholding the values of environmental sustainability, we may decrease these risks, restore ecological balance, and create a society in which current needs are met without endangering the ability of future generations to meet their own needs. It is a rallying cry that transcends political lines and ideologies, reminding us of our shared responsibility to protect the environment and secure a healthy and peaceful future for all species on Earth. Environmental sustainability is a necessity, not just a desirable outcome, for the survival and development of humans and the natural world (World Bank, 2020).

7.3 Southeast Asia's Green Finance and Impact Assessment

Southeast Asia is seeing a rise in green finance as the area struggles to address urgent environmental issues such as deforestation, air pollution, and the effects of climate change. It entails allocating money for financially sound environmental activities and projects. Impact assessment in this context performs a rigorous analysis of the concrete environmental advantages of these investments (Volz, 2018). Impact evaluation and green finance are essential tools for tackling environmental issues and advancing sustainable practises in Southeast Asia. These examples show how financial resources are allocated to projects and programmes that have a good influence on the environment, and scientific evaluations offer measurable proof of these advantages (UN Environment Programme, 2020).

The region's efforts to strike a balance between economic growth and environmental sustainability are aided by this fusion of finance and research (United Nations, 2015; Yeow et al., 2021).

7.4 Sustainable Energy Investments

Example: Vietnam's Wind and Solar Projects

1. **Green Finance**: To fulfil their rising energy needs and cut carbon emissions, Southeast Asian nations such as Vietnam are increasingly turning to renewable energy. Green bonds have been released in order to finance significant wind and solar projects. These bonds draw environmentally aware investors seeking both financial gains and a favourable influence on the environment (Global Sustainable Investment Alliance, 2021).
2. **Impact Assessment**: When evaluating the effects of these projects, scientists consider things such as decreased greenhouse gas emissions, better air quality, and the preservation of natural habitats. For instance, the ability of a solar farm in Vietnam to cut carbon dioxide (CO_2) emissions by a specific amount each year may be evaluated and reported (World Economic Forum, 2019).

7.5 Initiatives in Sustainable Agriculture

Example: Sustainable Palm Oil Production in Indonesia

1. **Green Finance**: Palm oil is a significant export for nations such as Indonesia, yet its production can result in habitat degradation and deforestation. To assist the sustainable production of palm oil, green finance projects have evolved. These programmes consist of loans and investments for businesses that agree to adopt sustainable practises (Global Sustainable Investment Alliance, 2021).
2. **Impact Assessment**: Scientific evaluations examine the effects of sustainable palm oil efforts by examining indicators such as preserved biodiversity, preserved forests, and decreased carbon emissions. The success of these projects is evaluated by tracking changes in land use using satellite imagery and geographic information system (GIS) technology (World Economic Forum, 2019).

7.6 Clean Transportation Initiatives

Example: Electric Vehicle (EV) Adoption in Thailand

1. **Green Finance**: Green financing for electric car initiatives has increased significantly in Thailand. The development and acceptance of electric vehicles as well as the infrastructure for charging them are supported by financial institutions through loans and funding. These expenditures help to lessen air pollution and reliance on fossil fuels (Global Sustainable Investment Alliance, 2021).
2. **Impact Assessment**: The reduction in greenhouse gas emissions brought on by greater EV adoption is measured through scientific impact analyses. Additionally, evaluations consider air quality improvements, particularly in metropolitan areas where pollution levels can have a substantial influence on public health (World Economic Forum, 2019).

7.7 Actions Taken to Conserve the Ocean

Example: Coral Reef Restoration in the Philippines

1. **Green Finance**: Rich marine biodiversity is commonly found in the Philippines and other Southeast Asian nations. Overfishing, pollution, and climatic change, however, pose dangers to coral reefs. Coral reef restoration initiatives receive green funding to safeguard and revitalize these ecosystems (Global Sustainable Investment Alliance, 2021).
2. **Impact Assessment**: Monitoring coral health, biodiversity levels, and the regeneration of damaged reef areas are all included in scientific evaluations of coral reef restoration initiatives. Concrete indicators of effectiveness include information on fish populations, coral colony regeneration, and improved water quality (World Economic Forum, 2019).

7.8 Investments Linked to ESG

Example: ESG Funds in Singapore

1. **Green Finance**: ESG investments are increasingly popular in Singapore. Financial institutions provide ESG-linked investment products and funds to entice socially conscious investors. These funds invest capital in businesses that exhibit good ESG performance (Global Sustainable Investment Alliance, 2021).
2. **Impact Assessment**: A company's ESG practises and their quantifiable consequences are assessed as part of impact evaluations for ESG-linked investments. For instance, assessments could consider a company's decreased trash production, water use, or involvement in community development (World Economic Forum, 2019).

7.9 Supply Chain Transparency with Blockchain Technology

A potent instrument for improving openness and traceability in supply chains is emerging: blockchain technology. It provides decentralized, immutable ledgers that are impermeable to tampering and record all transactions and events. Blockchain is being used to address important supply chain concerns such as traceability, provenance, and sustainability in Southeast Asian nations, including India. These in-the-wild examples show how blockchain improves sustainability, authenticity, and traceability across a range of sectors, including trade, pharmaceuticals, agriculture, and fisheries (Bai & Sarkis, 2020). Blockchain will be extremely important in advancing moral behaviour, decreasing fraud, and preserving the integrity of supply chains in the area as these projects continue to develop (Cambridge Centre for Alternative Finance, 2021).

7.10 Food Reliability and Safety

Example: Thailand's Seafood Traceability

1. **Challenge**: Illicit fishing, mislabelled products entering overseas markets, and labour exploitation were problems for the Thai seafood industry. One of the main concerns was making sure the fish was, indeed, supplied responsibly (Khan et al., 2021).
2. **Blockchain Approach**: A blockchain-based network for seafood traceability was developed through a collaboration between Systems, Applications and Products in Data Processing (SAP) and Thai Union Group, one of the biggest seafood producers in the world. Customers can use this platform to scan QR codes on seafood goods to access details such as the product's origin, fishing vessel, processing information, and sustainability certifications (Raj & Bhatt, 2018).
3. **Impact**: Consumers can now make educated decisions, and the platform aids in the fight against illegal fishing and labour abuse by monitoring the entire supply chain (Cambridge Centre for Alternative Finance, 2021).

7.11 Sustainable Farming

Example: Coffee Supply Chain in Vietnam

1. **Challenge**: The Vietnamese coffee industry worked to increase traceability and transparency so that sustainably cultivated coffee beans could be verified (Global Sustainable Investment Alliance, 2021).
2. **Blockchain Solution**: Blockchain is used by the Kiri Innovation platform in Vietnam to validate data about the coffee supply chain. Farmers document information about the production, processing, and

transportation of their coffee beans on the blockchain (UN Environment Programme, 2020).

3. **Impact**: To ensure fair trade practises and sustainable sourcing, coffee buyers and consumers can track the coffee's journey from farm to cup (Barbier, 2020).

7.12 Ethics in Procurement

Example: Indian Tea Industry

1. **Challenge**: Fair labour practises, pesticide use, and the veracity of organic tea products were issues that the Indian tea business had to deal with (Global Sustainable Investment Alliance, 2021).
2. **Blockchain Solution**: Blockchain technology has been used by Indian tea producers to keep detailed records of tea production and processing. Customers can get this information by scanning the QR codes on tea packaging (UN Environment Programme, 2020).
3. **Impact**: As technology helps to improve working conditions and reduce the use of dangerous pesticides, customers can confirm the authenticity of tea that is organic and ethically sourced (Barbier, 2020).

7.13 Finance for the Supply Chain

Example: Singapore's Trade Trust

1. **Challenge**: Singapore and other nations in Southeast Asia serve as centres for international trade. A major problem was ensuring transparency in trade documentation and minimizing fraud (Global Sustainable Investment Alliance, 2021).
2. **Blockchain Technology**: The blockchain-based platform Trade Trust offers a digital trade document verification mechanism. It guarantees the validity and immutability of shipping, customs, and other trade-related papers (UN Environment Programme, 2020).
3. **Effect**: Transparency and trust between trading partners are improved because of the platform's reduction of delays and fraud in trade transactions (Barbier, 2020).

7.14 Healthcare and Pharmaceuticals

Example: Pharmaceuticals in Malaysia

1. **Challenge**: Significant health hazards were created by fake medications and a lack of openness in the pharmaceutical supply chain in Malaysia (World Bank, 2020).
2. **Blockchain Technology**: Blockchain technology is being studied by Malaysian businesses for drug traceability. With the use of a blockchain-based unique identification attached to each pharmaceutical product, consumers and healthcare professionals may confirm the product's validity and track its path from maker to consumer (Nguyen, 2023).
3. **Effect**: The use of blockchain technology improves patient safety by lowering the prevalence of fake medications and preserving the integrity of pharmaceutical supply networks (United Nations, 2015).

7.15 Sustainability and Fintech: Implications for Social Wellbeing

Science has important consequences for social welfare when it comes to the convergence of Fintech and sustainability. This convergence creates a variety of advantages and opportunities that have a positive influence on people, communities, and society at large (Chueca Vergara & Agudo, 2021). The author examines how Fintech, and sustainability interact to improve social wellbeing in this article (World Bank, 2020).

7.16 Economic Accessibility and Inclusion

1. **Fintech**: Peer-to-peer lending platforms, digital banking, and mobile wallets have expanded access to financial services for previously under-represented groups. These advancements make it simpler for people living in rural or underdeveloped areas to access banking, savings, and credit services (Barbier, 2020).
2. **Sustainability**: By lowering poverty and income inequality, financial inclusion is in line with sustainability objectives. Access to financial services enables people and communities to invest in sustainable

livelihoods, healthcare, and education (Global Sustainable Investment Review, 2021).

3. **Impact on Social Wellbeing**: The improvement of economic stability, decreased vulnerability to shocks, and opportunity for people to make plans are all benefits of greater financial inclusion for society (Kshetri, 2017).

7.17 Cross-Border Transactions and Remittances

1. **Fintech**: Cross-border transactions and remittances are less expensive and take less time thanks to Fintech technologies. To help migrant workers and their families, digital remittance companies provide lower fees and quicker transfers (UN Environment Programme, 2020).
2. **Sustainability**: Cross-border transactions that are inexpensive and effective encourage financial stability and economic resiliency in areas that depend on remittances for their livelihood (Global Sustainable Investment Alliance, 2021).
3. **Impact on Social Wellbeing**: Remittance recipients' families enjoy higher living standards, better access to education and healthcare, and less financial stress, all of which contribute to greater social wellbeing (United Nations, 2015).

7.18 Philanthropy and Humanitarian Assistance

1. **Fintech:** Humanitarian help and philanthropic donations are streamlined by cryptocurrencies and blockchain technology. Aid efficiently reaches beneficiaries thanks to secure, transparent transactions that reduce fraud and corruption (Volz, 2018).
2. **Sustainability:** Effective philanthropic and humanitarian initiatives assist sustainable development objectives such as poverty reduction, disaster relief, access to clean water, and access to healthcare (Global Sustainable Investment Alliance, 2021).
3. **Impact on Social Wellbeing**: Improved social wellbeing for disadvantaged communities is a result of quick and secure aid distribution during emergencies and open charitable practises (Gomber et al., 2018).

7.19 Ethics-Based and Impact Investing

1. **Fintech**: By linking investors with ventures and companies that share their values, Fintech platforms support ethical and impact investing. Investors have the option to fund initiatives that are sustainable, socially responsible, and environmentally friendly (Mavrotas & Semuel, 2019).
2. **Sustainability**: By promoting efforts relating to renewable energy, clean technology, fair labour practises, and social enterprises, ethical and impact investments help to improve social and environmental conditions (Global Sustainable Investment Alliance, 2021).
3. **Impact on Social Wellbeing**: By investing in projects that address social challenges, generate jobs, and support equitable economic growth, ethical and impact investing supports social wellbeing (Raj & Bhatt, 2018).

7.20 Services Access and Digital Identity

1. **Fintech**: To have access to a variety of services, such as financial, healthcare, and educational services, people need to be able to authenticate their identity online (Raj & Bhatt, 2018).
2. **Sustainability**: Access to essential services such as healthcare, education, and government aid programmes is made possible using digital identities, which improves social wellbeing (Global Sustainable Investment Alliance, 2021).
3. **Impact on Social Wellbeing**: Especially for remote and marginalized people, digital identification lowers access barriers to important services, improving social inclusion and wellbeing (Mavrotas & Semuel, 2019).

7.21 Education and Financial Sensitivity

1. **Fintech**: Educational elements that support financial literacy and good financial behaviour are frequently included in Fintech apps and platforms (Mavrotas & Semuel, 2019).
2. **Sustainability**: Sustainable development is largely dependent on financial literacy. Individuals who are empowered can make wise financial decisions that enhance their wellbeing and financial security (Global Sustainable Investment Alliance, 2021).

3. **Impact on Social Wellbeing**: Improved financial stability and social stability result from more financial literacy, which gives people the knowledge and abilities to successfully navigate complicated financial institutions (Yeow & Ng, 2021).

7.22 Sustainability and Fintech's Role in Economic Transformation

A catalyst for economic change is the nexus of sustainability and Fintech. It encourages effective resource allocation, evaluates and reduces climate risks, fosters digital innovation and entrepreneurship, makes it easier to access capital for sustainable projects, fosters financial inclusion, and encourages sustainable investment strategies, all of which contribute to economic transformation (Raj & Bhatt, 2018). By boosting innovation, enhancing resource allocation, and promoting sustainable growth, this convergence reshapes economic systems (United Nations, 2015).

7.23 Effective Resource Allocation

1. **Fintech**: Fintech systems can use advanced data analytics, artificial intelligence (AI), and machine learning to make data-driven judgements. Optimizing capital allocation, risk assessment, and investment tactics are among these (World Economic Forum, 2019).
2. **Sustainability**: Reducing waste, protecting natural resources, and advancing the ideas of the circular economy are all aspects of sustainable practises (Raj & Bhatt, 2018).
3. **Economic Transformation Impact**: Resource allocation in organizations and economies is improved when data-driven decision-making from Fintech and resource-efficiency principles from sustainability are combined. Costs are decreased, productivity is increased, and sustainable economic growth is supported (Kshetri, 2017).

7.24 Climate Risk Evaluation

1. **Fintech**: Fintech platforms evaluate climate-related risks in investment portfolios using complex modelling and data analytics. Financial

institutions can use these tools to better determine how exposed they are to physical and transitional hazards related to climate change (Yeow & Ng, 2021).

2. **Sustainability**: Sustainability efforts focus on comprehending and reducing climate-related risks to ensure long-term economic stability (Raj & Bhatt, 122018).

3. **Economic Transformation Impact**: Businesses and governments may proactively manage and minimize the financial effects of climate change thanks to a climate risk assessment that relates to Fintech. This aids in the change and resilience of the economy (Kshetri, 2017).

7.25 Capital Access for Sustainable Projects

1. **Fintech**: Access to money for sustainable initiatives and companies is made possible via crowdfunding platforms, peer-to-peer lending, and digital investment channels (Raj & Bhatt, 2018).

2. **Sustainability**: Research, development, and scaling costs for sustainable initiatives are frequently covered through grants. The advancement of these efforts depends on having access to cash (Yeow & Ng, 2021).

3. **Economic Transformation Impact**: Innovation in green technologies, sustainable agriculture, and clean energy is sparked by the availability of funding through Fintech platforms for sustainable initiatives. By diversifying the economy and lowering reliance on conventional, resource-intensive industries, this results in economic transformation (Kshetri, 2017).

7.26 Microcredit and Financial Inclusion

1. **Fintech**: Through mobile banking, digital wallets, and microfinance platforms, Fintech solutions provide financial services to underbanked and unbanked communities (Bai & Sarkis, 2020).

2. **Sustainability**: Reduced poverty and income disparity, improved social wellbeing, and increased economic involvement are all aspects of financial inclusion that are consistent with sustainability goals (Kshetri, 2017).

3. **Economic Transformation Impact**: Fintech has a revolutionary impact on economies by facilitating financial inclusion. By encouraging entrepreneurship, consumption, and general economic growth, it

unleashes the economic potential of previously underutilized populations (Raj & Bhatt, 2018).

7.27 Investments in Sustainability

1. **Fintech**: ESG parameters are considered by robo-advisors and Fintech platforms that provide sustainable investment solutions (Bai & Sarkis, 2020).
2. **Sustainability**: Investments with a focus on sustainability projects and companies with good ESG performance should be given priority (Raj & Bhatt, 2018).
3. **Economic Transformation Impact**: Fintech-enabled sustainable investment techniques direct money to companies that adopt sustainable business practises. This promotes economic transformation by promoting ethical business practises and promoting expansion of sustainable enterprises (Kshetri, 2017).

7.28 Conclusion

The nexus of sustainability and Fintech represents a turning point in the development of the world's economies and financial systems. Unquestionably, this convergence – driven by social responsibility, environmental awareness, and technical innovation – is a catalyst for improvement in many facets of our society. We must consider the significant consequences and the bright future it holds as we come to the end of our examination of this transformational juncture (Global Sustainable Investment Alliance, 2021).

Economic systems may undergo a transformation because of the convergence of sustainability and Fintech. It improves the distribution of resources, encourages digital entrepreneurship, and advances financial inclusion. Economic systems can become more effective, resilient, and varied by utilizing technology to address sustainability issues. Economic transformation is not merely a goal; it is a feasible result of this convergence (Khan et al., 2021).

The empowering of marginalized groups is one of the partnership's outstanding successes in the field of sustainability and Fintech. Microbusinesses receive capital, the unbanked have access to financial services, and people develop their financial literacy. This increased financial inclusion promotes social wellbeing, lowers income inequality, and greatly expands the economy's potential (Chueca Vergara & Agudo, 2021).

The powers of Fintech and the dedication to sustainability meet the imperative of combating climate change head-on. The junction of climate risk assessment and funding for green projects helps society to lessen the effects of a changing climate and adapt to its challenges. To promote environmental stewardship and the transition to a sustainable future, the financial sector assumes a crucial role (Volz, 22018).

There are significant ethical and economic ramifications to the rise of Fintech-driven platforms for ethical and impact investing. It gives people and organizations the power to invest in accordance with their principles by allocating money to businesses that place a high priority on social and environmental responsibility. This change in investment behaviour may encourage businesses to adopt more sustainable practises and have advantageous social effects (Barbier, 2020).

Social wellbeing is ultimately prioritized at the point where sustainability and Fintech converge. It improves monetary stability, employment prospects, and accessibility to necessities. It enables people and groups to make wise financial decisions and take part in the larger economy (Bai & Sarkis, 2020). It advances sustainable objectives such as poverty alleviation, access to education, and healthcare. It strengthens the inclusiveness, equity, and prosperity of our societies.

References

Bai, C., & Sarkis, J. (2020). A supply chain transparency and sustainability technology appraisal model for blockchain technology. *International Journal of Production Research*, 58(7), 2142–2162. https://doi.org/10.1080/00207543.2019.1708989.

Barbier, E. B. (2020). Greening monetary policy. *Nature Climate Change*, 10(1), 9–11.

Cambridge Centre for Alternative Finance. (2021). *Global cryptoasset regulatory landscape study*. Cambridge Judge Business School.

Chueca Vergara, C., & Agudo, F. L. (2021). Fintech and sustainability: Do they affect each other? *Sustainability*, 13(13), 7012. https://doi.org/10.3390/su13137012.

Global Sustainable Investment Alliance. (2021). *Global sustainable investment review 2020*. Global Sustainable Investment Alliance.

Gomber, P., Kauffman, R. J., Parker, C., & Weber, B. W. (2018). On the fintech revolution: Interpreting the forces of innovation, disruption, and transformation in financial services. *Journal of Management Information Systems*, 35(1), 220–265.

Khan, P. A., Johl, S. K., & Akhtar, S. (2021). Firm sustainable development goals and firm financial performance through the lens of green innovation practices and reporting: A proactive approach. *Journal of Risk and Financial Management,* 14(12), 605.

Kshetri, N. (2017). Can blockchain strengthen the internet of things? *IT Professional,* 19(4), 68–72.

Mavrotas, G., & Semuel, H. (2019). Impact of fintech on sustainable development: Evidence from sub-Saharan Africa. *Fin.Tech. and Sustainable Development in the Digital Age,* 51–68.

Nguyen, T. T. H. (2023). Improving and optimizing the performance of the supply chain: The case of coffee production in Vietnam. Business administration. Université Polytechnique Hauts-de-France; Institut National des Sciences Appliquées Hauts-de-France.

Raj, R. G., & Bhatt, D. (2018). Fintech for inclusive and sustainable digital economic growth in India. *International Journal of Applied Business and Economic Research,* 16(3), 315–330.

UN Environment Programme. (2020). *Digital technologies for sustainable development: Enabling trade, finance, and trust in a digital economy.* United Nations.

United Nations. (2015). *Transforming our world: The 2030 agenda for sustainable development.* United Nations General Assembly.

Volz, U. (2018). *Blockchain technology for enhancing transparency in the green finance sector.* UNEP Inquiry Working Paper, 12.

World Bank. (2020). *Fintech for financial inclusion: A framework for digital financial transformation.* World Bank Group.

World Economic Forum. (2019). *Mitigating the impact of climate change on financial stability: How can financial services, regulators and central banks respond?* World Economic Forum White Paper.

Yeow, K. E., & Ng, S.-H. (2021). The impact of green bonds on corporate environmental and financial performance. Managerial Finance, 47(10), 1486–1510. https://doi.org/10.1108/MF-09-2020-0481.

Chapter 8

Fintech Services and Corporate Sustainability in Commercial Banks in Kenya

James M. Gatauwa, Moses O. Aluoch, and David C. Adhing'a

8.1 Introduction

Attainment of the United Nations Sustainable Development Goals by the year 2030 have increasingly raised the attention of governments, institutions, and individuals in ensuring that the environment is sustainable. This is further exacerbated by the impact that climate change is having on communities the world over. It is against this backdrop that corporate sustainability has recently become the focus of firms. According to Rahman and Rahman (2020), sustainability refers to the long-term cultural, socio-economic, and environmental wellness of a society. It is worth noting that corporate sustainability derives its description from the broader term of sustainability or sustainable development. It is also worth noting that corporate entities the world over have been embracing sustainability reporting with varying speeds in their quest to achieve sustainable business and a better environment. The Global Reporting Initiative (GRI) Standards Report (2016) defines sustainability reporting as an entity's practice of publicly reporting on its economic, environmental, and social impacts with the agenda of attaining sustainability.

Feyen et al. (2021) define Fintech services as financial services, including the ongoing wave of digital financial services, that rely on technology for

DOI: 10.4324/9781032644165-8

customer use. In this study, Fintech services are the independent variables that are composed of internet banking, mobile banking, blockchain technology, and Fintech lending. These four independent variables were chosen because they encompass the financial services offered by Kenyan banks, and they rely on financial technology. It is worth noting that Fintech services are offered not only by commercial banks but also by Fintech firms, savings and credit cooperative societies, micro-finance institutions, and other financial institutions.

In Kenya, as of 2023, there are 39 actively trading commercial banks that are regulated by the Central Bank of Kenya (CBK). There are a few other banks placed under receivership. Ten out of 39 Kenyan banks have their shares/stocks publicly trading at the Nairobi Securities Exchange (NSE) whereby individuals and institutional investors have a chance to purchase or sell these shares. These 39 banks are expected to comply with prudential regulations issued by the CBK, the Basel requirements, and the International Financial Reporting Standards (IFRS) in publishing their quarterly, semi-annual, and annual reports. Furthermore, these financial institutions are categorized as Tier I, II, and III based on asset size. These commercial banks have their branch networks geographically spread throughout the country whilst having banking models with robust agency banking, mobile banking, internet banking, and Fintech services.

8.1.1 The Statement of the Problem

The Fintech services industry in Kenya has been on a growth trajectory since 2016 when the CBK introduced interest-rate capping, even though it was short-lived, ending in 2019. Nevertheless, corporate sustainability among commercial banks has been raising numerous concerns, especially considering the impact these banks have on society and their stakeholders at large. In addition, corporate sustainability is a relatively new phenomenon among commercial banks in Kenya, which has come into play against the backdrop of the climate change and sustainability debate taking place globally. The first climate change conference in Africa, dubbed "Africa Climate Week Summit," was hosted in Nairobi, Kenya, from 4 to 6 September 2023, in an effort to raise awareness about carbon emissions, green financing, and environmental sustainability. The issue here is that Tier II and III banks with a mixed trend in financial performance over the past five years find that fully focusing on corporate sustainability is a challenge. Nevertheless, the majority of Tier I commercial banks have had a strong record of growth in their financial performance as well as their efforts in corporate sustainability.

In the empirical literature, the link between Fintech services and corporate sustainability indicates a broadly positive relationship (Forcadell, Aracil, & Ubeda, 2020; Guang-Wen & Siddik, 2022; Kim, Kwon & Kim, 2023; Wanjiru, Mutiso, & Maina, 2022; Wu & Pea-Assounga, 2022; Mhlanga, 2023; Toumi et al., 2023). However, these studies have not clearly explained the possibility of a reverse causality whereby corporate sustainability affects the adoption of Fintech services. Furthermore, a number of studies have relied on a critical review of literature research approach (Solanki & Rana, 2019; Mir & Bhat, 2022; Gioia, 2022), yet this poses the key concern of whether this relationship between Fintech services and sustainability would be ultimately weak, positive, or negative if empirical modelling were applied.

In the contextual perspective, there is a growing body of empirical literature on Fintechs and sustainability, especially in the Asian economic context. Some of these studies, such as Solanki and Rana (2019), Naruetharadhol et al. (2021), Mir and Bhat (2022), Guang-Wen and Siddik (2022), and Kim, Kwon, and Kim (2023), generally find that Fintech services have a significant effect on corporate sustainability in commercial banks, which agrees with similar studies done in other parts of the world. However, it is notable that there is no single study apart from this one that has integrated internet banking, mobile banking, blockchain technology, and Fintech lending against corporate sustainability, thus making it unique and much poised to contribute to the body of knowledge in this study area.

8.1.2 Objectives and Organization of the Study

The general objective of this study is to examine the link between Fintech services and corporate sustainability in commercial banks in Kenya. The specific objectives are to test the effect of internet banking, mobile banking, blockchain technology, and Fintech lending on corporate sustainability of commercial banks in Kenya. This chapter is organized in several sections. Section 8.2 contains the theoretical literature review that discusses the theories that underpin the study and the empirical literature review discussing the academic debate on Fintech services and corporate sustainability, conceptual framework and the study hypotheses. Section 8.3 highlights the research methodology, while Section 8.4 captures the data analysis approach. Finally, Section 8.5 captures the summary, conclusions, and recommendations.

8.2 Literature Review

8.2.1 Theoretical Review

The theoretical literature of this study entails a review of the key theories that underpin the link between Fintech services and corporate sustainability, including financial intermediation theory, technology acceptance theory, and diffusion of innovation theory. First, financial intermediation theory proponents Gurley and Shaw (1960) argued that intermediaries have played a key role in the financial sector. Consequently, Diamond (1984) argued that intermediaries overcome challenges on asymmetric information by acting as a monitor. This means that financial intermediaries play a fundamental role in enabling savers and depositors to transact efficiently at low costs.

Second, the technology acceptance model developed by Davis (1989) argues that users of technology can forecast whether new innovations will be accepted when considering the interactions between beliefs and attitudes. This implies that developers of innovations in Fintech services can estimate their adoption amongst users.

Finally, the diffusion of innovation theory was developed by Rogers (1962). He sought to explain the reasons behind new ideas and innovations being adopted by users and other stakeholders and that there are four elements that affect the adoption of innovation. In this study, the theory underpins the aspect of Fintech services being adopted by corporate stakeholders with the key goal of achieving sustainability of their businesses.

8.2.2 Empirical Review

There exists a growing, though not substantive, body of empirical literature on Fintech services and sustainability in the corporate sector. However, there is a larger body of research in this area in the Asian context, such as Bangladesh, India, Korea, Malaysia, Singapore, Thailand, and others. This could probably be explained by the comparative advantage that several Asian countries possess in the area of information technology. For example, Guang-Wen and Siddik (2022) examined the link between Fintech adoption, green finance, and performance among banks. The study was conducted in Bangladesh involving 302 bank respondents during the COVID-19 pandemic period. Structural equation modelling was used with findings indicating that Fintech adoption greatly affects green finance, innovation, and performance.

These results imply that Fintech services have a positive impact on the corporate sustainability of banks in an emerging economy. In addition, there are related studies focusing on sustainability in the banking sector in Asia, such as Akhtar et al. (2023); Akthar, Alam, and Ansari (2022); and Ansari et al. (2022).

In Korea, Kim, Kwon, and Kim (2023) tested the effect of mobile banking on sustainability of banks in Korea that offer internet banking services. The study findings indicate that mobile banking services substantially impact the sustainability of financial services in banks. Similarly, in Thailand, Naruetharadhol et al. (2021) examined the factors contributing to the sustainable use of mobile banking among 688 mobile banking users using online questionnaires. The study findings show that there is a positive relationship between technology service qualities, perception, and sustainability in the context of mobile banking. In India, Solanki and Rana (2019) examined the link between mobile banking and corporate sustainability using a descriptive approach. The study contends that commercial banks have been successful in reducing carbon emissions through their green finance initiatives. More particularly, these Indian banks have adopted green initiatives such as reducing paper usage, issuing online bank accounts, e-banking, and other Fintech banking services. Ultimately, these efforts have led to the achievement of corporate sustainability of banks. Nevertheless, a critique to this study is that it lacks an elaborate approach to statistical modelling in which data is actively used to demonstrate the link between Fintech services and sustainability. Furthermore, the study is limited to commercial banks only, yet Fintech services have broadly been adopted by other financial institutions.

There are also conceptual studies that entail a critical review of literature on Fintech services and corporate sustainability, including studies conducted by Bai and Sakis (2019), Gioia (2022), and Mir and Bhat (2022). For instance, Gioia (2022) reviewed 260 research papers from the Scopus database with a subsequent thematic analysis that yielded 80 research papers on Fintech services and sustainability. Specifically, the study focused on blockchain and cryptocurrency technology with its effects on the environment and sustainability. The findings generally indicate that Fintech firms need to partner with other financial institutions such as commercial banks in order to enhance the extensive adoption of Fintech services amongst customers. On the other hand, Mir and Bhat (2022) reviewed green banking and sustainability using a systematic literature review. The study further focused on the adoption of best practices for green banking. The study was also supplemented by data from a Malaysian and an Indian financial institution. The findings generally indicate that governments, firms, and individuals should play an active role in creating a sustainable environment. Furthermore, green banking is a key source of sustainability, especially in relation to the firms and individuals that are funded with the ultimate goal of ensuring a sustainable environment. Nevertheless, these two studies are limited to a systematic literature review, which calls into question whether involving the further extent of data collection and modelling would have yielded different results.

In the African context, studies argue that Fintech services would lead to corporate sustainability. In Kenya, Wanjiru, Mutiso, and Maina (2022) examined the link between internet banking and the sustainability of commercial banks while using primary data collection via questionnaires. The study found a significant effect, implying that for banks need to have fully adopted internet banking to achieve sustainability. Similarly, in the Congolese context, Wu and Pea-Assounga (2022) studied the effect of internet banking on investment decisions through sustainability. The study adopted primary data collection and found that internet banking – in essence Fintech services – affect corporate sustainability. Nevertheless, in Nigeria, Onyekwere, Ogwueleka, and Irhebhude (2023) examined the sustainability of bitcoins and block technology using a survey approach involving 320 respondents. The findings indicate that bitcoins are highly adopted as a form of Fintech service, implying that it is expected to lead to the corporate sustainability. However, with all these African studies arguing in favour of Fintech services leading to corporate sustainability, there is need to also examine the drawbacks associated with these Fintech innovations and their impact on society.

In Europe, a few continental studies have examined the link between Fintech services and sustainability. Mizra, Umar, Afzal, and Firdousi (2023) sought to establish the interrelationship between Fintech, green finance, and profitability. The study involved a sample of European banks for the study period between 2011 and 2021, using panel data modelling. The findings show that investment in Fintech and green lending have a positive relationship. This further means that Fintech and green financing, to a great extent, contribute to the sustainability of these banks. Similarly, Forcadell, Aracil, and Ubeda (2020) studied corporate sustainability and digitalization in 112 international banks across 10 European countries as well as the United States and Australia. The study period spanned from 2003 to 2016 using a feasible generalized least squares model. The findings indicate that corporate sustainability and digitalization lead to market performance and efficiency of international banks. Further, Hoepner et al. (2016) contend that corporate sustainability reduces the problem of information asymmetry among customers.

The conceptual framework for this study entails the relationship between Fintech services and corporate sustainability. The independent variables are internet banking, mobile banking, blockchain technology, and Fintech lending. The dependent variable is corporate sustainability.

8.2.2.1 Null Hypotheses

The null hypotheses for this study are as follows:

H₁: There is no statistically significant effect of internet banking on corporate sustainability in commercial banks in Kenya.

H₂: There is no statistically significant effect of mobile banking on corporate sustainability in commercial banks in Kenya.

H₃: There is no statistically significant effect of blockchain technology on corporate sustainability in commercial banks in Kenya.

H₄: There is no statistically significant effect of Fintech lending on corporate sustainability in commercial banks in Kenya.

8.3 Research Methodology

This study adopted the descriptive analytical research design, as it permits using descriptive and inferential statistics analysis. The population involved 39 commercial banks in Kenya. Primary data was collected using a questionnaire from top managers of these commercial banks. Data was analyzed using descriptive statistics analysis, which entails analyzing measures of central tendency, such as the mean and standard deviation, and inferential statistics analysis, which involved first undertaking diagnostic tests, namely correlation analysis, multicollinearity testing, normality testing, heteroscedasticity testing, analysis of variance, and ordinary least squares (OLS) regression modelling. The regression model used was as follows:

$$CS_{it} = \beta_0 + \beta_1 IntB_{it} + \beta_2 MB_{it} + \beta_3 BT_{it} + \beta_4 FL_{it} + \varepsilon_{it} \tag{i}$$

where:

CS_{it} = Corporate sustainability
β_0 = Constant
β_{1-4} = Coefficients
$IntB_{it}$ = Internet banking
MB_{it} = Mobile banking
BT_{it} = Blockchain technology
FL_{it} = Fintech lending
ε_{it} = Error term

8.4 Data Analysis

First, the data analysis approach entailed determining the response rate on the primary data collection, which was approximately 80%. Based on existing research literature, the response rate is deemed appropriate. The target respondents were the top managers in commercial banks, a majority of whom were between the ages of 31 to 50 and had a university degree. All the respondents had the relevant experience in Fintech services.

Second, the diagnostic tests were conducted in preparation of regression modelling. For instance, normality testing was conducted in order to determine whether the data fit a normal distribution, as indicated in Table 8.1. From the results in Table 8.1, the data is normally distributed at 0.05 level of significance, as the p-values of the variables are above 0.05, with the exception of corporate sustainability. Consequently, linearity tests were also conducted in order to determine whether the data follows a linear pattern and,

Table 8.1   Normality Test Results

Variable	Shapiro-Wilk[a]		
	Statistic	df	Sig.
Corporate Sustainability	0.232	31	0.000
Fintech Lending	0.139	31	0.247
Mobile Banking	0.135	31	0.101
Internet Banking	0.198	31	0.450
Blockchain Technology	0.159	31	0.400

(*Source*: Data Computations, 2023)

further, whether the data fits a line of best fit. The results indicated that the level of linearity between each of the study variables was significant, implying that Fintech lending, mobile banking, internet banking, blockchain technology, and corporate sustainability have a linear relationship.

A heteroscedasticity test was undertaken to establish whether the regression model can predict the dependent variable in a consistent pattern for all the coefficients of the independent variables (Wooldridge, 2002; Gatauwa, 2020). The results show that there is an absence of heteroscedasticity, which implies that the data is homoscedastic. Lastly, the analysis of variance was undertaken to determine the level of interrelationship between the independent variables and the dependent variable. The analysis of variance results is shown in Table 8.2, in which the degrees of freedom total to 30, while the sum of squares is 19.52. However, the results indicate a p-value of 0.004 at 0.05 level of significance, which means that the independent variables have a statistically significant effect on the dependent variable.

Finally, the data analysis involved ordinary least squares modelling considering the nature of the data and the diagnostic test results, indicating compliance to the assumptions of classical linear regression modelling. The model summary and regression model results are shown in Table 8.3, respectively. The results indicate that the value of R is 0.75, while the adjusted R^2 is 0.55. This implies that 55% of the change in the dependent variable is explained by the independent variables. The R^2 is also referred to as the coefficient of determination. Furthermore, Table 8.3 indicates the regression analysis results. The regression model results show that mobile banking, internet banking, blockchain technology, and Fintech lending have a statistically significant effect on corporate sustainability, as indicated by the p-values of less than 0.05. This is considering that the level of significance is 0.05.

Table 8.2   Analysis of Variance Results

	Model	Sum of Squares	df	Mean Square	F	Sig.
1	Regression	10.71	4	2.68	7.66	0.004[a]
	Residual	8.81	26	0.35		
	Total	19.52	30	–	–	–

(*Source*: Data Computations, 2023)

[a.] Predictors: (Constant), mobile banking, internet banking, blockchain technology, Fintech lending

Table 8.3 Regression Model Summary and Coefficients

Model	Unstandardized Coefficients		Standardized Coefficients		
	Beta	*Std. Error*	*Beta*	*T-Statistic*	*Sig.*
1(Constant)	0.880	0.416	–	0.192	0.847
Mobile Banking	0.308	0.100	0.383	3.08	0.002
Internet Banking	0.140	0.214	0.171	0.82	0.045
Cryptocurrency	0.202	0.086	0.112	1.80	0.037
Fintech Lending	0.455	0.107	0.396	1.15	0.049
Dependent variable: Corporate sustainability					

Model	R	R Square	Adjusted R Square	Std. Error of the Estimate
1	0.75	0.56	0.55	0.33

(*Source*: Data Computations, 2023)

8.5 Summary, Conclusion, and Recommendations

From the data analysis undertaken in the previous section, we take note that Fintech services through mobile banking, internet banking, blockchain technology, and Fintech lending positively affects corporate sustainability in commercial banks in Kenya. Considering that commercial banks are among the leading financial institutions in Kenya to adopt a mix of Fintech services, this implies that other financial institutions, such as Fintech firms, savings and credit cooperative societies, micro-finance institutions, and others, would also attain sustainability if they fully adopted Fintech services. That notwithstanding, there are studies that also found that Fintech services positively impact corporate sustainability (Forcadell, Aracil, & Ubeda, 2020; Guang-Wen & Siddik, 2022; Kim, Kwon, & Kim, 2023; Wanjiru, Mutiso, & Maina, 2022; Gatauwa, 2022; Wu & Pea-Assounga, 2022). However, these study findings are of some entities in other economic sectors that are lagging behind in the implementation of proper mechanisms that enhance corporate sustainability.

This study recommends that governments and industry regulators should operationalize mechanisms that allow corporate entities across various sectors of an economy to achieve corporate sustainability, considering that leading agencies, such as the United Nations and the World Bank, among others, have already set the foundation and momentum for governments, entities, and individuals to achieve sustainability. This is vital because there are just a few years to the year 2030, when the whole world over ought to have achieved sustainability on a larger scale.

This study recommends the following with regard to further contribution to knowledge. First, future studies could undertake the same study area but cover a regional country context whereby several countries are covered in the survey. Second, future studies could pursue similar research areas but cover different sectors or study contexts such as manufacturing, real estate, investment services, and others in order to ascertain the level of similarity or deviation from banking studies. Third, different research methodologies could be applied, such as time series modelling or panel data modelling, with a view to observe the points of departure from existing studies that cover OLS modelling.

References

Akhtar, S., Alam, M., & Ansari, M.S. (2022). Measuring the performance of the Indian banking industry: Data envelopment window analysis approach. *Benchmarking: An International Journal* 29(9), 2842–2857.

Akthar, S., Alam, M., Khan, A., & Shamshad, M. (2023). Measuring technical efficiency of banks vis-à-vis demonetization: An empirical analysis of Indian banking sector using CAMELS framework. *Quality and Quantity* 57, 1739–1761.

Ansari, M.S., Akhtar, S., Khan, A., & Shamshad, M. (2022). Consequence of financial crisis on liquidity and profitability of commercial banks in India: An empirical study. *Studies in Economics and Business Relations* 3(2), 36–50. https://doi.org/10.48185/sebr.v3i2.367

Bai, C. & Sarkis, J. (2019). Green supplier development: A review and analysis. In *Handbook on the Sustainable Supply Chain*. Edward Elgar Publishing, 542–556.

Davis, F.D. (1989). Perceived usefulness, perceived ease of use and user acceptance of information technology. *MIS Quarterly* 13(3), 319–339.

Diamond, D. (1984). Financial intermediation and delegated monitoring. *Review of Economic Studies* 51(3), 393–414.

Feyen, E., Frost, J., Gambacorta, L., Natarajan, H., & Saal, M. (2021). *Fintech and the Digital Transformation of Financial Services: Implications for Market Structure and Public Policy*. BIS Papers No. 117. The Bank for International Settlements and the World Bank Group.

Forcadell, F.J., Aracil, E., & Úbeda, F. (2020). The impact of corporate sustainability and digitalization on International Banks' performance. *Global Policy*. http:/doi.org/10.1111/1758-5899.12761

Gatauwa, J.M. (2020). Does fiscal policy stance affect public expenditure? Evidence from Kenya. *International Journal of Public Finance* 5(2), 295–310.

Gatauwa, J.M. (2022). Private equity financing and financial performance: A critical review of the literature. *African Development Finance Journal* 1(2), 95–103.

Gioia, A. (2022). Blockchain and cryptocurrency innovation for a sustainable financial system. *International Journal of Industrial Management (IJIM)* 15(1), 1–16. https://doi.org/10.15282/ijim.15.1.2022.8994

GRI Standards. (2016). *Global Reporting Initiative 101: Foundation*. Amsterdam, The Netherlands.

Guang-Wen, Z. & Siddik, A.B. (2022). The effect of Fintech adoption on green finance and environmental performance of banking institutions during the COVID19 pandemic: The role of green innovation. *Environmental Science and Pollution Research* 30(10), 25959–25971. https://doi.org/10.1007/s11356-022-23956-z

Gurley, J.G. & Shaw, E.S. (1960). *Money in a Theory of Finance*. Washington, DC: Brookings Institution.

Hoepner, A., Oikonomou, I., Scholtens, B., & Schroeder, M. (2016). The effects of corporate and country sustainability characteristics on the cost of debt: An international investigation. *Journal of Business Finance and Accounting* 43(1–2), 158–190.

Kim, S., Kwon, H., & Kim, H. (2023). Mobile banking service design attributes for the sustainability of internet-only banks: A case study of Kakao Bank. *Sustainability* 15(8), 6428. https://doi.org/10.3390/su15086428

Mhlanga, D. (2023). Block chain technology for digital financial inclusion in the industry 4.0, towards sustainable development. *Frontiers: Section Blockchain Economics* 6. https://doi.org/10.3389/fbloc.2023.1035405

Mir, A.A. & Bhat, A.A. (2022). Green banking and sustainability. *Arab Gulf Journal of Scientific Research* 40(3), 247–263. Emerald Publishing Limited. https://doi.org/10.1108/AGJSR-04-2022-0017

Mirza, N., Umar, M., Afzal, A., & Firdousi, S.F. (2023). The role of fintech in promoting green finance, and profitability: Evidence from the banking sector in the euro zone. Economic Analysis and Policy 78, 33–40. https://doi.org/10.1016/j.eap.2023.02.001

Naruetharadhol, P., Ketkaew, C., Hongkanchanapong, N., Thaniswannasri, P., Uengkusolmongkol, T., Prasomthong, S., & Gebsombut, N. (2021). Factors affecting sustainable intention to use mobile banking services. *SAGE Open*, 1–13. https://doi.org/10.1177/21582440211029925journals.sagepub.com/home/sgo

Onyekwere, E., Ogwueleka, F.N., & Irhebhude, M.E. (2023). Adoption and sustainability of bitcoin and the blockchain technology in Nigeria. *International Journal of Information Technology* 15(5), 2793–2804. https://doi.org/10.1007/s41870-023-01336-1

Rahman, M.M. & Rahman, M.S. (2020). Green reporting as a tool of environmental sustainability: Some observations in the context of Bangladesh. *International Journal of Management and Accounting* 2(2), 31–37.

Rogers, C. R. (1962). *The interpersonal relationship: The core of guidance.* Harvard educational review.

Solanki, R.S. & Rana, R.S. (2019). Go clean go green: E-Banking and its sustainability. *International Conference on Sustainable Computing in Science, Technology & Management (SUSCOM-2019)*, 710–713. https://ssrn.com/abstract=3354490

Toumi, A., Najaf, K., Dhiaf, M.M., Li, N.S., & Kanagasabapathy, S. (2023). The role of Fintech firms' sustainability during the COVID19 period. *Environmental Science and Pollution Research* 30(20), 58855–58865. https://doi.org/10.1007/s11356-023-26530-3

Wanjiru, P.W., Mutiso, A.N., & Maina, M. (2022). Internet banking and sustainability of registered Commercial Banks in Kenya. *IOSR Journal of Business and Management (IOSR-JBM)* 24(8), 9–15. http://www.iosrjournals.org

Wooldridge, J.M. (2002). *Econometric Analysis of Cross Section and Panel Data* (2nd ed.). London: The MIT Press.

Wu, M. & Pea-Assounga, J.B.B. (2022). Assessing the relationship between internet banking and investment decision through sustainability and competitive advantage: Evidence from Congolese Banks. *Frontiers in Psychology* 13, 869646. https://doi.org/10.3389/fpsyg.2022.869646

Chapter 9

Ethical Implications and Sustainable Practices in Digital Payment Systems

Akshay G Khanzode, Meghna Goel,
Hemachandran K, and Randall Carolissen

9.1 Introduction

With the advent of new technologies, methodologies, and frameworks the financial technology (Fintech) sector is undergoing rapid transformations, offering novel entrepreneurial opportunities and exponential growth trajectories. It is well known that both the economies and social development goals of countries that were bold enough to prioritize the artificial intelligence (AI) agenda as a national priority have accelerated advancement (reference Oxford insights). The core outcomes of these advancements emanated in streamlined financial processes, ensuring that they are more efficient, accessible, and user-friendly to, inter alia, democratize access to all of a country's citizenry. It has been universally accepted that leveraging AI is critical toward globally attaining the United Nation's Sustainable Development Goals (SDGs). This is particularly significant for developing countries suffering large economic divides and crippling sovereign debt.

The primary thesis of this chapter revolves around a meticulous examination of the ethical implications inherent in digital payment systems and the relentless pursuit of sustainable practices within this domain. Ethical

DOI: 10.4324/9781032644165-9

considerations are important guardrails, as they ensure that the rights, privacy, and security of vulnerable users are safeguarded amidst digital transactions. For instance, the ethical handling of personal and financial data is a cornerstone of trust and legality in digital payment platforms. Concurrently, sustainability within digital payment systems is paramount to ensure that these platforms not only facilitate financial transactions but also contribute positively to broader economic and environmental frameworks (Oláh et al., 2018).

Digital payment systems sit at the confluence of technology, finance, and ethics. This attained synergy has the potential to drive financial inclusion, which itself aligns intrinsically with SGD 3, offering a pathway to better health and wellbeing through economic stability (Tay et al., 2022). The examination unfolded a spectrum of initiatives that digital payment platforms can undertake to minimize their environmental impact (poverty and inequality) while promoting economic inclusivity and intergenerational wealth creation.

A significant outcome of this evolution is the development and expansion of digital payment systems, which unequivocally enhanced democracy and inclusivity of especially marginalized communities, the uninterruptible power supplies (UPS) payment system rolled out in India being a case in point. This encompasses various mechanisms ranging from online banking, e-wallets, to contactless payments through mobile devices. These digital payment systems are at the heart of modern financial transactions, significantly altering how individuals and businesses manage and move money. They represent a shift from traditional cash-driven financial systems, driving economic modernization and ease of financial accessibility (Gomber et al., 2018).

Despite the obvious benefits, this modernization provides some sobering insights which underscore the importance of addressing ethical dilemmas, such as data privacy, algorithmic biases, and the digital divide, and emphasized the significance of fostering sustainable practices within the Fintech ecosystem (Diaz-Rodriguez et al., 2023). However, each sub-domain within Fintech presents unique challenges and opportunities, necessitating a more nuanced analysis. Thus, this chapter aims to narrow down the focus to one of the crucial segments within Fintech: digital payment systems.

Aligning with SDG 3, ensuring healthy lives and promoting wellbeing for all at all ages, financial inclusion is a pivotal aspect. It is fundamental to understand that financial health is intricately linked to overall wellbeing of citizens of a country. Digital payment systems, by virtue of their ease of access and operation, play a pivotal role in enhancing financial inclusion (Demirgüç-Kunt & Klapper, 2012). They enable individuals, especially those from traditionally underserved or unserved communities, to meaningfully partake in the financial ecosystem, thereby promoting economic stability and individual wellbeing. The journey toward comprehensive financial inclusion through digital payment systems is laden with ethical quandaries and demands a robust framework of sustainability to ensure that the growth and benefits of these systems are long-term and equitable.

Furthermore, the intersection of ethics, sustainability, and digital payment systems is a fertile ground for academic exploration. It presents a myriad of questions and avenues for investigation. For instance, how are digital payment platforms ensuring the ethical handling of user data? What measures are in place to guarantee the accessibility of these platforms to all demographics? On the sustainability front, how are digital payment systems contributing to the reduction of the carbon footprint traditionally associated with the financial sector? Are these systems designed to foster economic resilience, especially in times of financial downturns or global crises? How do regulatory frameworks across different jurisdictions address the ethical and sustainability concerns inherent in digital payment systems?

This chapter endeavours to explore these questions, offering a granular analysis of the ethical implications and sustainable practices within digital payment systems. By dissecting various real-world examples, regulatory frameworks, and initiatives taken by stakeholders in this domain, the chapter aims to present a comprehensive yet lucid understanding of the topic. Through this focused examination, readers will garner insight into how digital payment systems are evolving to align with ethical standards and sustainable practices, contributing to the broader goal of financial inclusion under SDG 3. Through the subsequent sections, a detailed exploration of the ethical dilemmas, sustainable practices, regulatory landscapes, and illustrative case studies concerning digital payment systems will be undertaken.

9.2 Ethical Implications in Digital Payment Systems

9.2.1 Data Privacy and Security

9.2.1.1 Examination of Data Privacy Challenges Peculiar to Digital Payment Systems

The modern economy has increasingly transitioned to digital payment platforms, with companies such as PayPal and Square leading the charge. These systems offer convenience and efficiency, yet they also evoke substantial data privacy challenges. With each transaction, a trove of personal and financial data is collected, processed, and stored with the concomitant exposure to criminality. The Equifax breach of 2017 stands as a poignant reminder of the risks involved, as a significant lapse in data security led to the exposure of sensitive data of 143 million individuals (NYT, 2017).

9.2.1.2 Discussion of Ethical Questions Surrounding Data Breach and Identity Theft

The ramifications of data breaches extend beyond mere financial loss, potentially leading to a more damaging outcome, namely identity theft. The Capital One breach in 2019 further underscores the ethical onus on digital payment platforms to uphold robust data security measures and to provide transparent communication and redress to affected individuals (CapitalOne, 2019).

9.2.1.3 Case Studies Illustrating Significant Data Privacy Dilemmas and Their Resolution

The responses to the aforementioned breaches by Equifax and Capital One, inter alia, provide a spectrum of strategies employed by companies to address data privacy dilemmas. These instances demonstrate the necessity of evolving security infrastructures, maintaining open communication with stakeholders, and proactively working toward preventing future breaches.

9.2.2 Fraud Prevention and Ethical Conduct

9.2.2.1 Discussion on the Responsibility of Digital Payment Platforms in Preventing Fraud

Digital payment systems lend themselves to algorithmic targeting for fraudulent use by less than honourable actors in the system. PayPal's adaptive measures to identify and mitigate fraud exemplify a commitment toward safeguarding user interests. However, the challenge extends beyond mere fraud detection to establishing a culture of ethical conduct within the digital payment ecosystem.

9.2.2.2 Examination of Ethical Dilemmas in Fraud Detection and User Verification

The development of robust interventions to eradicate fraud has the potential to encroach upon user privacy. The challenge is to strike a judicious balance between ensuring adequate security whilst respecting privacy norms. Real-world instances, such as the scrutiny faced by various digital payment platforms over their user verification processes, highlight these ethical dilemmas.

9.2.2.3 Real-world Examples of Fraud Incidents and Measures Taken to Prevent Future Occurrences

Various incidents of phishing scams targeting digital payment platforms elucidate the myriad forms and sophistication of fraud to which these systems are susceptible. The measures taken post-incident, encompassing enhanced user verification, educational campaigns, and improved monitoring capabilities, reflect a multidimensional approach toward fostering ethical conduct and mitigating fraud risks.

9.2.3 Inclusivity and Accessibility

9.2.3.1 Analysis of How Digital Payment Systems Can Bridge or Exacerbate Financial Inclusion Gaps

M-Pesa, a mobile phone-based money transfer service in Kenya, exemplifies how digital payment systems can significantly bridge financial divides, especially in regions with underdeveloped banking infrastructures (Van Hove & Dubus, 2019). Conversely, if implementation is not mindfully inclusive, these systems could exacerbate existing disparities.

9.2.3.2 Examination of Ethical Considerations in Making Digital Payments Accessible to All Demographics

The drive toward inclusivity necessitates a thorough examination of ethical considerations. The accessibility of digital payment systems to a diverse user base is a testament to the principle of equality and non-discrimination, which is pivotal to ethical conduct within this domain.

9.2.3.3 Illustrative Cases of Initiatives Aimed at Improving Inclusivity in Digital Payment Systems

Globally, various initiatives emphasize the potential for digital payment systems to foster inclusivity. For instance, the advent of contactless payment systems in public transportation across numerous urban settings showcases a deliberate effort toward enhancing inclusivity and accessibility.

In conclusion, the discourse on ethical implications in digital payment systems entails a nuanced examination of data privacy, fraud prevention, and inclusivity. Through a robust understanding of these ethical dimensions, stakeholders within the digital payment ecosystem are better positioned to navigate the associated challenges and opportunities, thereby contributing to the broader socio-economic development and attainment of sustainable development goals.

9.3 Sustainable Practices in Digital Payment Systems

9.3.1 Tracing the Environmental Contours

The narrative around the environmental sustainability of digital transactions unveils a sharp and contrasting comparison against traditional payment methods. The digital shift is celebrated as a green segue from the cumbersome physical infrastructure, paper trails, and carbon emissions of the transportation entailed in traditional methods. This is especially illuminating as one begins to factor in the carbon footprints emanating from digital transactions, rooted in the energy-hungry corridors of data centres and networks. A comparative tableau lays bare the carbon imprints, fostering a fertile ground for discourse on sustainable practices in the digital payment dominion.

As the digital economy evolves, it leads us through a plethora of initiatives within the digital payment arena, each striving to roll back and mitigate against adverse environmental impacts. This digital revolution highlights the requisites for energy-efficient data processing systems, incorporation of renewable energy sources, and a thoughtful embrace of electronic waste management practices. Further, blockchain technology shows much promise for lower energy consumption in digital transactions. As a thorough exploration of these green initiatives unfolds, their effectiveness in rendering the digital payment realm green begins to take shape.

The novelty offered by digital payment platforms further reveal real-world green shoots, each a case study in environmental sustainability. Whether it is the desire for carbon-neutral data centres or the bold strokes of blockchain for energy-efficient transaction verification, each case narrates the potential for environmental resonance within digital payment systems.

9.3.2 *Economic Resilience and the Embrace of Inclusivity*

Insofar as economic resilience pertains, digital payment systems' ability to stabilize local and global economic landscapes and mitigate fraudulent practices in social welfare systems are alluring. Their cadence resonates through seamless borderless transactions, lowered transaction costs, and an embrace of financial inclusivity, painting an enabling picture for small and medium enterprises (SMEs) accessing the global marketplace. A thoughtful analysis endeavours to elucidate the economic harmony composed by digital payment systems.

Economic inclusivity provides digital payment bridges that transcend financial inclusion chasms. They empower the underserved and unserved, offering them real and meaningful participation in formal economic activities and a chance to improve their economic stature. This discourse navigates through the mechanisms and challenges in optimizing inclusivity through digital payments.

The recent global COVID-19 health crisis amplified the role of digital payment systems in the furtherance of economic resilience. Digital payment systems provided the fuel for continued economic activities and the survival of the poor during lockdown, enabled remote transactions, and orchestrated an efficient disbursement of financial aid. Through real-world examples, the indispensable role of digital payment systems in bolstering economic resilience during global catastrophes is undeniable and futuristic in its impact.

9.3.3 *Navigating the Growth Spectrum*

As digital payment systems become pervasive and their growth trajectory assumes an exponential nature, questions of sustainability remain vexing. The explosive growth exemplifies changing economic transaction drivers, yet at the same time, invites an inquiry into the longevity of the radical innovation, given potential market saturations, technological harmonies, and the evolving regulatory strictures. This discourse aims to delve into these nuances, seeking to understand the sustainability of the growth symphony of digital payment systems.

Taking the country case studies in Oxford Insights, appropriate regulatory compliance is an absolute necessity, but it must be developed judiciously as an enabling mechanism. It must provide the compass guiding this pervasive ecosystem toward sustainable growth and ethical conduct. Hence, adherence to data protection cantatas, including anti-money laundering (AML) and other financial compliance regulations, must orchestrate a sustainable and ethical symbiosis within digital payment realms.

Digital payment platforms underwrote many developmental plans based on sustainable principles. Case studies unveil tales of robust user verification processes combatting fraud and initiatives nurturing financial literacy among marginalized populations. These real-world narratives render a profound understanding of how digital payment platforms can embody sustainability whilst responding affirmatively to the complexity of the Fintech landscape.

9.4 Regulatory Compliance and Future Trends

9.4.1 Overview of Key Regulatory Frameworks Governing Digital Payment Systems Globally

The domain of digital payment systems intrinsically spans across multifarious jurisdictions, each with its country specific regulatory framework. Several global frameworks were meticulously crafted to ensure the safety, security,

Table 9.1 Comparative Table Showcasing Data Privacy and Security Measures Employed by Select Digital Payment Platforms

Feature/Platform	Paytm	PhonePe	Google Pay
Encryption Standard	AES-256	AES-256	AES-256
Two-Factor Authentication	Yes	Yes	Yes
PCI Compliance	Level 1	Level 1	Level 1
Data Masking	Yes	Yes	Yes
Fraud Detection	Machine learning-based algorithms and models.	Machine learning for real-time fraud prevention.	Utilizes a set of machine learning models.
Privacy Policy	Transparent about data usage and adheres to legal requirements.	Transparent; adheres to legal requirements regarding data sharing.	Transparent; follows legal guidelines on data sharing.

and efficacy of digital payment transactions. Among these, the Payment Card Industry Data Security Standard (PCI DSS) is worth mentioning, as it was designed to mandate a secure environment for companies engaging with credit card information. Within the realm of the European Union (EU), there are Payment Services Directive 2 (PSD2) and the General Data Protection Regulation (GDPR). The PSD2 is aimed at fostering competition and participation in the payment industry. The GDPR imposes a stringent framework on data management for payment platforms in the European domain. In the United States (US), there are AML, know your customer (KYC), and the Consumer Financial Protection Bureau (CFPB) regulations. The quintessential and probably most pervasive scheme is Unified Payments Interface (UPI) of India, which provided empowerment and inclusion to the entire populace. It is enabled by the highly progressive and sophisticated Adhaar biometric system, which combines operational, technical innovation with responsive, yet enabling, ethical standards.

9.4.2 Emergence of Regulatory Trends

Emerging trends in regulation follows a dialogue of evolution, centring on ethical and sustainable digital payment practices. There is a growing emphasis on data privacy that has been propelled by a string of high-profile data breaches. Open banking trends, as illustrated in the EU's PSD2, illustrates infractions on transparency and competition, showing how banks are covertly coaxed to share customer data with authorized and, in some cases, unauthorized third-party providers. As the regulatory lens sharpens on consumer protection and sustainable finance, the imperative of aligning financial services regulations with broader societal objectives is brought into sharp relief. Digital payment platforms must factor in environmental sustainability and social inclusivity (Azmi & Akhtar, 2023). Cross-border regulatory harmonization paves the way for a cohesive global digital payments ecosystem, preparing for inevitable global integration and harmonization of regulatory frameworks.

9.4.3 Reflective Exposition on Regulatory Implications

The evolving regulatory landscape significantly shapes the digital payment systems' future, underpinning trust, stability, and innovation. A reflective exposition reveals how stringent data protection, anti-fraud, and consumer protection standards are paramount in crafting a reputation of reliability and safety for digital payment platforms. Emerging regulatory trends such as open banking and cross-border regulatory harmonization are identified as catalysts, fostering fertile ground for innovation, competition, and the evolution of digital payment systems (Wajid et al., 2022). Alignment with broader societal goals provides encouraging financial inclusivity and environmental sustainability in a protective envelope. The global interoperability facilitated by regulatory harmonization, alongside the adaptation to technological advancements such as blockchain and cryptocurrencies, are depicted as critical mileposts in ensuring a secure, ethical, and efficient operation of digital payment systems. Through this kaleidoscope of established and emerging regulatory frameworks, the digital payment sector is envisaged to tread a path aligning robust operational standards with broader societal and ethical objectives.

Table 9.2   Overview of Financial Inclusion Initiatives Launched by Select Digital Payment Platforms

Digital Payment Platform	Initiative	Description	Year Launched
Paytm	Paytm Payments Bank	A mobile-first bank with zero charges on all online transactions and no minimum balance requirement.	2017
Google Pay	Google Pay for Business	Simplifies digital payments for businesses and enables financial inclusion for small business owners.	2019
PhonePe	PhonePe for Business	Provides a range of payment solutions to help merchants digitize their business.	2018
BharatPe	BharatPe for Business	Offers a single interface for all UPI apps, allowing merchants to accept UPI payments from any app.	2018
Airtel Payments Bank	Banking Points	Expands banking services to unserved regions through a vast network of banking points across India.	2017

9.5 Case Studies

9.5.1 *In-depth Analysis of Selected Case Studies Demonstrating Ethical and Sustainable Practices in Digital Payment Systems*

The digital payment ecosystem is replete with examples in which ethical and sustainable practices provided for massive advancement operations. In this section, we discuss real-world case studies to elucidate.

9.5.1.1 *Adyen: Upholding Data Privacy in the European Digital Payments Landscape*

A noteworthy exemplar of ethical conformity and data privacy is Adyen, a digital payment platform based in Europe. Adyen's stringent adherence to the GDPR showcases effective legal compliance and strategic orientation toward bolstering user trust. By deploying cutting-edge encryption technologies, Adyen ensures data integrity both in transit and in use. Its comprehensive data management system facilitates meticulous control and monitoring of data processing activities. Adyen witnessed an uptick in user engagement and retention rates, reflecting burgeoning trust and robust risk mitigation against data breaches (Adyen, 2015).

9.5.1.2 *GCash: Bridging Financial Inclusion in the Philippines*

GCash in the Philippines epitomizes the effort toward bridging the financial inclusion chasm. GCash has invested in user-friendly digital interfaces and community outreach programs to educate potential users. Collaborations with local financial institutions were forged, aiming for a seamless integration of services to promote financial inclusivity. The socio-economic repercussions, user adoption rates, and operational challenges that were encountered shed light on the pragmatic dynamics of fostering financial inclusion in emerging markets, which are well documented (Uña et al., 2023).

9.5.1.3 *Google Pay: Venturing into Eco-Conscious Operations*

On a global scale, Google Pay embarked on an ecoconscious voyage by committing to operate carbon-free by 2025 by increasing investments in renewable energy sources. Encouraging ecofriendly practices among users

Table 9.3 Overview of Key Regulatory Frameworks Governing Digital Payment Systems Globally

Region/ Country	Regulatory Framework	Governing Body	Key Objectives
Global	Payment Card Industry (PCI) Standards	PCI Security Standards Council	Establishes security standards for processing, storing, and transmitting credit card information.
European Union	Payment Services Directive 2 (PSD2)	European Commission	Enhances consumer protection, promotes innovation, and improves the security of payment services.
United States	Dodd-Frank Wall Street Reform and Consumer Protection Act	Federal Reserve	Establishes rules to reduce risks in the financial system, including payment and settlement activities.
India	Unified Payments Interface (UPI) Guidelines	Reserve Bank of India (RBI)	Provides a regulatory framework for the UPI payment system, promoting interoperability and real-time payments.
China	Non-bank Payment Institution Online Payment Business Regulation	People's Bank of China (PBOC)	Regulates non-bank payment institutions to ensure the security and stability of online payment services.
Australia	Payment System (Regulation) Act 1998	Reserve Bank of Australia	Provides a framework for the regulation and reform of the payment system to improve safety and efficiency.

and stakeholders, Google Pay crafted a narrative of environmental stewardship in the digital payment sector.

9.5.2 Lessons Learned and Best Practices from These Case Studies

The analysis of these case studies provides insightful lessons and best practices examples. The cases underscore the importance of a holistic data protection strategy, routine security audits, and a culture of data privacy awareness. It emphasizes the importance of forging partnerships with local financial institutions, governmental bodies, and non-governmental organization (NGOs) to foster a conducive ecosystem for financial inclusion. Moreover, it resonates with the long-term perspective toward sustainability underpinned by investments in green technologies and sustainable business practices.

9.5.3 Comparative Analysis of Different Digital Payment Platforms and Their Approach Toward Ethics and Sustainability

The comparative lens provides the building blocks for a framework for sustainable digital payment platforms, carving a robust set of criteria encompassing data privacy and security measures, financial inclusion initiatives, environmental sustainability practices, and adherence to regulatory compliance. The analysis unpacks the distinct approaches, achievements, and shortcomings concerning ethical and sustainable practices across selected platforms grounded on established industry benchmarks for ethics and sustainability. Evaluating each platform against these benchmarks unveils their relative performance, spotlighting the leaders and laggards in ethical and sustainable practices within the digital payment domain. This analysis accentuates the actionable insights and best practices, significantly enriching the discourse on the nexus between ethics, sustainability, and digital payments, thereby contributing to an informed dialogue among stakeholders in the Fintech ecosystem.

This section provides a comparative analysis of three major digital payment platforms – Adyen, GCash, and Google Pay – focusing on their approach toward data privacy and security, financial inclusion, environmental sustainability, and regulatory compliance.

9.5.3.1 Adyen

Data Privacy and Security: Adyen demonstrates a strong commitment to data security, being fully PCI DSS v3.2.1 compliant as a Level 1 Service Provider. This compliance ensures the confidentiality, integrity, and availability of data and systems, thus safeguarding merchant and user data.

Financial Inclusion Initiatives: While Ayden's specific initiatives toward financial inclusion are not detailed in the available data, its global reach suggests an impact on broader market access.

Environmental Sustainability Practices: Adyen invests in social responsibility with activities such as waste disposal prevention through environmental projects and extensive volunteer work aligned with the UN's SDGs.

Regulatory Compliance: Adhering strictly to the GDPR and other regulations, Adyen sets a high standard for legal and ethical compliance in the European digital payments landscape.

9.5.3.2 GCash

Data Privacy and Security: Specific details on GCash's data privacy and security measures were not available, but its widespread use implies a foundational level of security.

Financial Inclusion Initiatives: GCash is a frontrunner in financial inclusion in the Philippines, with efforts to extend banking services to unserved regions. Its expansive user base and partnerships with private and public sectors underscore its commitment to inclusive financial services.

Environmental Sustainability Practices: Through initiatives such as GForest, GCash contributes to environmental conservation, encouraging users to participate in reforestation efforts and carbon footprint reduction.

Regulatory Compliance: GCash's collaboration with government agencies for fund distribution during the pandemic highlights its adherence to local regulations and commitment to transparent operations.

9.5.3.3 Google Pay

Data Privacy and Security: As a significant entity in the global digital payment sector, Google Pay is expected to have robust security measures, though specific details are not provided in the available data.

Financial Inclusion Initiatives: Google Pay plays a pivotal role in facilitating mobile transactions worldwide, indicating its contribution to global financial inclusion.

Environmental Sustainability Practices: Committed to ecoconscious operations, Google Pay's pledge to operate carbon-free by 2025 exemplifies its dedication to environmental sustainability.

Regulatory Compliance: Operating across multiple global markets, Google Pay adheres to a range of regional regulations, showcasing its commitment to legal compliance.

This comparative analysis reveals distinct approaches and contributions of each platform toward ethics and sustainability in the digital payment domain. Adyen excels in data security and environmental initiatives, GCash stands out in financial inclusion and eco-conservation, and Google Pay demonstrates significant global reach and a commitment to sustainability. Each platform, in its unique way, contributes to shaping a more ethical and sustainable future in digital payments. This analysis not only highlights the strengths but also points to areas in which further improvements can be made, enriching the discourse on the nexus between ethics, sustainability, and digital payments.

9.6 Conclusion

The ethical considerations accompanying the pervasive and rapidly evolving nature of Fintech, particularly digital payment systems, has been the main thrust this chapter. Traversing through the multifaceted ethical implications, the emphasis on sustainable practices, and the crucible of regulatory frameworks, a nuanced understanding of the subject matter become possible. Digital payment systems, being the linchpin of contemporary economic transactions, exhibit a profound potential to foster financial inclusivity, uphold data privacy, and propel sustainability agendas.

The analysis underscored the exigency of robust data protection mechanisms to ensure user trust and regulatory adherence. The paramount importance of fraud prevention spotlighted the quintessential role of ethical conduct in managing digital transactions securely. Sustainable practices within digital payment platforms burgeoned as a compelling narrative. The environmental footprint of digital transactions vis-à-vis traditional payment methods highlighted the exigency for green Fintech solutions. Moreover, the emphasis on economic resilience showcased how digital payment systems could be leveraged to foster economic stability, especially in times of crisis.

A pivotal takeaway was the dynamic interaction between regulatory frameworks and digital payment platforms. The emergent regulatory trends underline a concerted effort toward fostering an ethical and sustainable digital payment ecosystem.

As we delineate the contours of a more ethically sound and sustainable Fintech ecosystem, the imperative for continuous dialogue among stakeholders resonates unequivocally. The synergy between regulatory bodies, digital payment platforms, and the end-users is vital for fostering a culture

of ethical compliance and sustainability. The dissemination of best practices, informed discourse around regulatory compliance, and a shared vision
for sustainable growth are instrumental in navigating the ethical labyrinth
inherent in the digital payment domain. Moreover, the reflection on the case
studies and comparative analysis propels the narrative forward, providing a
real-world exemplification of the theory discussed. It underscores the criti-
cality of empirical examination and the sharing of knowledge across the
Fintech landscape to foster an environment of continuous improvement and
ethical adherence.

As the Fintech arena continues to burgeon, the ethical and sustainability
compass must remain steadfast, guiding the sector toward practices that not
only enhance economic prosperity but also uphold the ethical and environmental ethos. This chapter, we trust, will contribute and catalyze informed
discussions, further research, and actionable initiatives that inch the Fintech
sphere closer to a harmonious blend of ethics, sustainability, and unparalleled innovation.

References

Adyen. (2015). The global e-commerce payments guide. San Francisco. Retrieved
    from https://www.adyen.com/de/business-intelligence/global-ecommerce-
    payments-guide.
Azmi, S. N., & Akhtar, S. (2023). Interactions of services export, financial develop-
    ment and growth: Evidence from India. *Quality & Quantity, 57*(5), 4709–4724.
Demirgüç-Kunt, A., & Klapper, L. F. (2012). Measuring financial inclusion: The
    global findex database. *World Bank Policy Research Working Paper, 6025*.
Diaz-Rodriguez, N., Del Ser, J., Coeckelbergh, M., de Prado, M. L., Herrera-Viedma,
    E., & Herrera, F. (2023). Connecting the dots in trustworthy artificial intel-
    ligence: From AI principles, ethics, and key requirements to responsible AI
    systems and regulation. *Information Fusion, 99*, 101896.
Equifax says cyberattack may have affected 143 million in the U.S., NYT, 2017.
    https://www.nytimes.com/2017/09/07/business/equifax-cyberattack.html
GDPR: What it means for customer payment data, Adyen, 2018. https://www.adyen
    .com/en_GB/knowledge-hub/gdpr-customer-data
Gomber, P., Kauffman, R. J., Parker, C., & Weber, B. W. (2018). On the fintech revo-
    lution: Interpreting the forces of innovation, disruption, and transformation in
    financial services. *Journal of Management Information Systems, 35*(1), 220–265.
Information on the capital one cyber incident, 2019. https://www.capitalone.com/
    digital/facts2019/

Oláh, J., Kitukutha, N., Haddad, H., Pakurár, M., Máté, D., & Popp, J. (2018). Achieving sustainable e-commerce in environmental, social and economic dimensions by taking possible trade-offs. *Sustainability, 11*(1), 89.

Tay, L.-Y., Tai, H.-T., & Tan, G.-S. (2022). Digital financial inclusion: A gateway to sustainable development. *Heliyon, 6*(8).

Uña, G., Griffin, N., Verma, A., & Bazarbash, M. (2023). *Fintech Payments in Public Financial Management: Benefits and Risks.* International Monetary Fund.

Van Hove, L., & Dubus, A. (2019). M-PESA and financial inclusion in Kenya: Of paying comes saving? *Sustainability, 11*(3), 568.

Wajid, A., Sabiha, A., Akhtar, S., Tabash, M. I., & Daniel, L. N. (2022). Cross-border acquisitions and shareholders' wealth: The case of the Indian pharmaceutical sector. *Journal of Risk and Financial Management, 15*(10), 437.

Chapter 10

Banking 4.0 and its Role in Fintech

Nisha Khan, Sourav Biswas, and Neelam Kumari

10.1 Introduction

The Industrial Revolution started during the eighteenth century with the origination of mass production, and during nineteenth and twentieth centuries, the Second Industrial Revolution came into force in the form of the automobile, steel, and electric industries. Later on, with the involvement of digital technology, including big data analytics, cloud computing, and artificial intelligence (AI), the Third Industrial Revolution began; however, it suffered due to the 2008 global financial crisis (Iqbal & Yadav, 2021). The present "Fourth Industrial Revolution," or Industry 4.0, started with the merging of latest technologies, and it was regarded as the best revolution in every aspect. As it creates a large impact on each sector globally, one of the most influential sectors is the financial banking sector (Gupta, 2021). Banking 4.0, born from the fusion of Industry 4.0 and the Fintech revolution, signifies a paradigm shift in banking. It embraces digital transformation, prioritizes customer-centric approaches, fosters innovation, relies on data analytics and AI, explores blockchain and cryptocurrency, upholds regulatory compliance and security, and promotes ecosystem integration. This evolution marks a transition towards a more agile, customer-focused, and technologically advanced banking landscape, reshaping traditional practices in response to emerging trends and disruptive forces. Fintech's advancement in technology is considered one of the noteworthy revolutions in the area of finance (Kumar et al., 2022).

DOI: 10.4324/9781032644165-10

Fintech is the amalgamation of the words "finance" and "technology," which describes the correlation of modern or internet-related technologies such as AI and cloud computing with the established business activities of financial industries such as the banking industry (Roy et al., 2022). The advent of Fintech starts during the 1950s with the invention of first credit card. The second age of Fintech, or Fintech 2.0, which is regarded as when the financial sector made a real shift toward technology and digitalization, began in 1967 when Barclays Bank installed its first ATM. The financial sector remained in Fintech 2.0 until the Great Recession in 2008, and it mainly focused on providing cost-effective technologies for service industries (Roy et al., 2022).

In the third age of Fintech, or Fintech 3.0, digital banking transformed the banking industry and, as Fintech encourages financial inclusion through competent financial services, played a pivotal role in the overall economic development of nations. With its easy access, end users can manage their monetary transactions, including investment, and savings (Lestari & Rahmanto, 2021). While Fintech 3.0 is still in progress, Fintech 4.0 is arriving with technological enhancements that reduce, and in some cases eliminate, the need for human resources. Fintech development is high in developing nations such as India, China, Indonesia, Pakistan, and Nigeria and is improving their economic growth (Demirguc-Kunt et al., 2018). When the effects of these revolutions are combined, they generate the concept of Fintech banking in which the banking industry adopts Fintech to deliver their products and services to customers through technology, such as AI and blockchain security (Kumar et al., 2022). According to the World Bank (2020), the growth of Fintech and digital technology during the COVID-19 pandemic was high, as it provided access to financial services all around the world while complying with regulations imposed by governments, i.e. social distancing and minimal face-to-face interaction.

In light of these facts, the present chapter highlights the evolution and growth of Banking 4.0 and the role of Banking 4.0 in Fintech. It also covers the competition from Fintech firms that banks overcame during the Fintech revolution. Lastly, this chapter further exhibits different aspects of Banking 4.0 and Fintech from the viewpoint of various previous studies.

10.2 Literature Review

Presently, the world is going into the quarter stage of the Industrial Revolution referred to as Industry 4.0, which has had a multifaceted impact on every sector, the most profound of which is found in the financial sector, including banks. The concept of Banking 4.0 came under the purview of Industry 4.0 in which traditional banking was converted into branchless banking with the advent of sophisticated technology for conducting financial transactions (Lauren, 2021), providing a speedy, precise, and superior experience to end users, which is regarded as the top priority of digital banks globally (Gupta, 2021). Due to digitalization and through the use of innovative technologies such as blockchain, big data, AI, and cloud computing, banks are not only enhancing efficiency and the value of products but also changing customer habits, as they are becoming well informed about the potential and opportunities derived from technology (Kuchciak & Warwas, 2021; Wajid et al., 2022). From the consumer perspective, the most proven dimensions of Banking 4.0 are functional quality, innovation, trust, value, security and risk mitigation (Abdillah et al., 2020). Further, a study was conducted in Bangladesh to analyze the customers' readiness to adopt Fintech, which found a wide range of readiness dimensions, such as financial wellbeing, rate of literacy, demography, mental readiness, and sentiment, attached with Fintech are needed (Mahmud et al., 2023).

During the Banking 4.0 period, Fintech has also offered a large range of services with a high-tech invention. Kumar et al. (2022) conducted a bibliometric analysis of 3,268 documents from 1966–2021, and the result displayed that the use of AI and blockchain expertise in banking organizations was the most trending topic of research. A descriptive research study performed in Indonesia analyzed how banks had been collaborating with Fintech firms but that, in near future, integration with big tech industries will be used to achieve the aim of Banking 4.0 (Legowo et al., 2021). The penetration of Fintech not only acts as the driving force behind the financial development of emerging economies but also impacts economies with weak financial sector performance and low levels of financial inclusion, as they grow at a faster rate due to availability of digital technology and extensive smartphone penetration (Karsh & Abufara, 2020; Azmi & Akhtar, 2022; Aduba et al., 2023). Apart from that, as a new entrant, Fintech challenges existing financial industries, i.e. the banking sector, in particular, as it pushes banks in their core areas of business, i.e. credit (Al-Ajlouni & Al-Hakim, 2018), and the cointegration between Fintech lending and banks would help to improve banks' credit quality and encourage banks to diversify their risks (Junarsin et al., 2023). Alshater et al. (2022) provide an insight on Fintech in Islamic finance on the basis of content analysis. They found that through Fintech, Islamic finance may improve the socio-economic development of underdeveloped and unserved populations and act as a government support system, enhancing financial inclusion and achieving sustainability. Fintech also helps in strengthening the sustainability in agriculture by allowing innovative services and digitalization in the marketplace and forming avenues to improve financial steadiness and ensure enduring success for economic sustainability (Anshari, 2019; Azouaoui et al., 2023). But Aysan et al. (2022), in connection with digital transformation in Islamic banks, reveals two main challenges: the size and level of technology in the operating region.

Further, Mhlanga (2020) investigated the impact AI has on digital financial inclusion under the umbrella of Industry 4.0 and found that AI had created a large impact in digitally improving the arena of financial inclusion in the area of risk and fraud detection, cybersecurity, and customer support or help-desk-like chatbots and had the capability to provide financial services to the unserved population. One of the studies examines the role of innovative services as an intermediary between business growth and Fintech adoption and found that human competence has positively impacted the adoption of Fintech (Bhutto et al., 2023). Due to current environmental issues, economies are moving toward sustainability and need a sustainable economic model that include Fintech and Industry 4.0 (Ferraro et al., 2022). Technological innovations are not without their challenges or risks. Mamta and Goyal (2022) identify the risk linked with the acceptance of Fintech, particularly in the Indian banking sector, and found that the main risks or challenges include cybersecurity risks, operational risks, data privacy risks, technological risks, training and development challenges, and customer retention risks, as the banks also need to upskill and reskill their existing employees to effectively adopt the technological changes required for Fintech adoption (Mazurchenko et al., 2022). Further, it was found that there was a significant and negative relationship of perceived risk with the acceptance of AI technology in the banking industry, particularly in Asian nations (Noreen et al., 2023). The main bottlenecks to the success of Fintech adoption in financial industries, such as the Indian banking sector, is unequal access to Fintech applications, as they mostly favoured wealthy, urban, and male and populations, and were not highly adopted by the rural population until they began using the internet for online payments and arranging for their basic necessities for the first time during the COVID-19 pandemic (Akhtar et al., 2020; Dabbeeru & Rao, 2021; Gupta & Agrawal, 2021). Due to the pandemic, the inhibition toward Fintech adoption has been lifted, as it enhances the creation of bank liquidity to meet uncertainty, thereby staking its role in bank diversification (Chaturvedi et al., 2021; Tang et al., 2023).

10.3 Evolution and Growth of Banking 4.0

With the fast pace of human civilization, the world is also changing its technological requirements, shifting toward embedded technology. The concept of Industry 4.0 emanates from Germany, as it has the top manufacturing industry in the world (Gupta, 2021), and the term was first coined in 2011 at the Hannover Fair. Industry 4.0 came with technological advancements, including robotics, the Internet of Things (IoT), AI, and machine learning to reduce or, in some cases, eliminate the use of human resources (Schwab, 2018). The evolution of Industry 4.0 has created an impact on all sectors across world economies, including the banking sector, considered an important pillar of economic development, as it provides strength to the overall financial system and delivers financial stability during times of crisis. Today, the world is witnessing a significant transition from traditional banking models to digital banking, with an increasing emphasis on integrating Internet of Things (IoT) technologies. This shift reflects a broader trend towards leveraging digital platforms and connectivity to enhance banking services and customer experiences. With IoT, devices are interconnected and capable of transmitting data, enabling banks to offer innovative solutions such as smart banking, automated transactions, and personalized services tailored to individual needs. This evolution not only streamlines banking processes but also opens up new opportunities for financial inclusion and efficiency in the digital age (Sharma et al., 2023).

The evolution and growth of Banking 4.0 are described in the sections that follow.

10.3.1 Banking 1.0

The first generation of banking spans from 1942 to 1980. Banking at this time provided services in a traditional way through bank branches. It also consisted of various financial mediators that acted as main players at that time. It suffered from certain drawbacks, such as delays or systems that took a long time to process, lack of proper access to financial services, large amounts of paperwork, and decentralized transactions. These Banking 1.0 bottlenecks cleared the way for Banking 2.0 (Mehdiabadi et al., 2020; Sharma et al., 2023).

10.3.2 Banking 2.0

The second generation of banking evolution, or Banking 2.0, started in 1980 and ended in 2007, just before the period of global financial crises. It starts with the advent of self-service banking or off-shore banking, when banks started pushing their services outside of bank branches. It commences with the introduction of ATM machines and card readers, and its growth accelerated in 1995 with the use of the internet in commercial banking (Mehdiabadi et al., 2020; Sharma et al., 2023).

10.3.3 Banking 3.0

The third generation of banking, or Banking 3.0, saw a surge in cash-less transactions which required a lot of technological advancement and the emergence of smartphones in 2007. Considered an era of portable banking, usage of mobile phones and the internet allowed even previously hesitant customers to use technology to habitually perform banking transactions, such as transferring funds digitally (Mehdiabadi et al., 2020; Sharma et al., 2023). Banking 3.0 lasted until 2015.

10.3.4 Banking 4.0

The fourth generation of banking, or Banking 4.0, started in 2015 and is continuing to move forward. Banking 4.0 arose because of the maturity and growth of new technologies such as machine learning, big data, AI, cloud computing, and robotics that mainly consist of virtual reality systems, such as chatbots (the intelligent banking assistant) (Mehdiabadi et al., 2020; Kaur et al., 2020). This has transformed the whole banking system, revolutionizing traditional banking toward modern-day digital banking. Due to the COVID-19 pandemic, financially illiterate people, especially those who live in rural areas, began adopting online fund transfers and availing themselves of the basic online banking facilities (Sharma et al., 2023). From the figure 10.1, Banking 4.0 is highly impacted by IoT, as it enables different devices to work together and provide customers with a number of applications to connect with the bank within digital platforms (Böhmer, 2020).

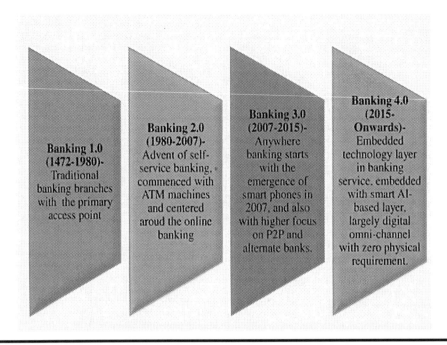

Figure 10.1 Evolution and growth of Banking 4.0 (Based on Kumar et al., 2022)

10.4 Banking 4.0: The Role of Fintech

Due to the expansion in information technology and digitalization, the service sector, particularly Fintech, has undergone a third phase of evolution that deals with the use of technology to provide financial services directly to customers without any human interaction. After the 2008 global financial crises, Fintech created a new landscape for financial institutions such as banks (Azmi et al., 2020; Thakor, 2020). The Basel Committee on Banking Supervision (BCBS) accepted the Financial Stability Board's (FSB) definition of Fintech as a technically enabled financial innovation (Bank of International Settlement, 2018). The use of technological advancements through Fintech benefited the banking sector, in particular, with lower search costs, economies of scale, inexpensive and safer transactions, and reduced verification costs (Thakor, 2020). No doubt, Fintech has transformed the realities of vigorous business houses and economies at large, but for banking services, the main field of Fintech development is the payment side (Omarini, 2017). The BCBS provides the sectoral innovations made by Fintech in different

Table 10.1 Fintech Products and Services by Sectoral Innovations

Market Support Services	Sectoral Innovation				
	Credit, Deposit and Capital-Raising Services	*Payments, Clearing and Settlement Services*		*Investment Management Services*	*Insurance*
	Crowdfunding	**Retail**	**Wholesale**	High-frequency trading	Link to mobile devices
	Lending marketplaces	Mobile wallets	B2B point of sale	Copy trading	Big data
	Mobile banks	Peer-to-peer transfers	FX wholesale	E-trading	Improved risk pricing
	Credit scoring	Digital currencies	Digital exchange platforms	Robo-advice	New contracts
	Portal and data aggregators				
	Ecosystems (infrastructure, open source, APIs)				
	Data applications (big data analysis, machine learning, predictive modelling)				
	Distributed ledger technology (blockchain, smart contracts)				
	Security (customer identification and authentication)				
	Cloud computing				
	Internet of Things/mobile technology				
	Artificial intelligence (bots, automation in finance, algorithms)				

(*Source*: BSBS, Bank of International Settlements, 2018)

areas (Table 10.1) and conducted a survey for finding the highest number of service providers in four categories. They found that most of the providers belong to services such as payment, clearing and settlement after that deposit, and credit and capital raising services (Bank of International Settlement, 2018; Thakor, 2020).

The Fintech revolution, with the greater involvement of market support services through AI, IoT, and cloud computing, helps banks to more easily adopt the technology associated with Banking 4.0. The emergence of AI-based technology in the financial field provides a new paradigm in Banking 4.0, as its integration of financial services and effectiveness, precision, and mechanization has enhanced a large range of banking activities (Jafar et al., 2023). It also expands the data that enables banks to make data-driven decisions and optimize the risk management and advancements in fraud detection. Thanks to AI algorithms, automated and personalized advice related to investment decision, wealth administration, and financial planning are available through chatbots to a wider range of customers; these chatbots play a crucial role in enhancing remote banking with a customized customer experience at a minimal cost (Bhat et al., 2022; Kumar et al., 2023).

Apart from that, the Fintech revolution also provides technologies such as machine learning, big data, peer-to-peer finance, open banking, mobile banking/payments, blockchain, and robo-advisory (Aysan, 2022). AI-enabled peer-to-peer (P2P) trade and lending, along with the incorporation of blockchain technology, allow customers to validate transactions, evaluate different borrowers' perspectives of online lending to analyze fraud risks, and safeguard against cyberattacks (Thakor, 2020; Cao et al., 2020; Bhat et al., 2022). In the payment segment (deposits and lending), blockchain-based technology provides new and easy methods of payment without centralized authorities (Renduchintala et al., 2022). With the aid of cloud computing, banks are provided with a platform that helps them in managing, storing, and retrieving data with greater safety and minimizes the cost of infrastructure, and ultimately, the banks are able to develop resilient operational activities (Albastaki et al., 2021). The changing dynamics of open banking, driven by the integration of application programming interfaces (APIs), are reshaping the financial landscape. Banks now have the capability to offer payment initiation services independently, bypassing traditional payment systems. This marks a departure from the past, where banks typically shared customer data with Fintech firms. Today, this collaboration fosters the development of more customer-centric approaches to banking services (Feyen et al., 2021). Lastly, it is noteworthy to provide an insight on the big data that enabled the banks to develop personalized customer profiles which bridge the communication and conviction gap among banks and its clients (Singh et al., 2022). So, the role of the Fintech revolution is considered as a main pathway for adopting the successful implementation of Banking 4.0, as it not only increases the effectiveness of banks to provide services to the users through more customer centric approach, but it also helps to meet banking customers' satisfaction (Huparikar & Shinde, 2022).

10.5 Focus Area of Banks under Fintech Revolution

Due to the Fintech revolution all over the world, the banking and financial sector have experienced numerous changes, as they start offering products and services in the most innovative and digitalized ways. The main focus area lies in consumer and commercial lending and payment space. Despite the benefits of the Fintech revolution, the banks, particularly, are facing a high level of competition from Fintech start-up firms due to issues such as highly regulated norms, high operating costs, traditional business lines, low investment and collaboration for innovations and technological upgrades, and neutral approaches. The report entitled "Fintech Revolution in Banking: Leading the Way to Digital" by Infosys highlights the main focus area for banks in order to overcome the competition from Fintech start-ups.

10.5.1 Investment

Compared to other industries, the banking industry allocates a huge part of their annual budget toward investment in technology and innovation. But it was found that the main focus of this investment is to resolve awaiting proposals and not for the digital transformations needed to apply the advances of Banking 4.0 in the most efficient way. So, in order to overcome the competition from Fintech firms, banks should start investing in their digital transformation and allow reinvention at each stage of operation in order to remain relevant in a market with high competition.

10.5.2 Innovation

Innovation in traditional banking leads the banking sector toward the adoption of Banking 4.0, but banks are less focused on constantly infusing innovation practices in real-time situations. To overcome issues encountered from Fintech competition, banks need to learn and start working on innovations at every level of banking. If banks start recruiting the talented and innovative minds at the right place and at the right time, it is possible. It also reduces the operating and human resource costs and provides protection against digital risk with constant innovation.

10.5.3 Customer Experience

To overcome the high level of competition from the Fintech revolution, particularly due to the involvement of digitalization in financial services, banks need to provide more elevated or upgraded technology in products and services to enhance the customer experience; through the help of progressive customer relationship management (CRM) tools, as customers indicate that they are dissatisfied with the prevailing line of products and services, it is necessary for banks to focus on customer demands and the personalization of their offerings to continuously delight their customers.

10.5.4 Integrate Fintech Ideas

Banks have large, sometimes devoted, customer bases, making them financially robust enough to invest in recent innovative ideas formulated by Fintech firms. Therefore, assimilating the innovative and disruptive Fintech ideas into their banking models, banks can face competition without making alliances with Fintech companies. The upsurge of Banking 4.0 can help the banking sector to shed the loopholes in its legacy systems and can, ultimately, speed up their efficiency toward Fintech competitors (Singh, 2020).

10.5.5 Collaboration

Apart from integration, banks are required to collaborate with Fintech firms in those areas in which they cannot work alone. When collaborating, banks should recognize areas for growth prospects and select the most appropriate Fintech partner to help fill the gap in services and make them compatible in market. Banks can also identify their strengths and weaknesses in core segments and make final decisions regarding collaboration with Fintech firms; ultimately, this has led banks toward the era of digitalization.

Apart from the previously mentioned focus areas, the banking sector also requires adoption of technological changes in order to develop a banking business model that will work in the face of challenging Fintech patterns. Kobler et al. (2016) suggested a banking business model that can be applied under the Banking 4.0 concept is shown in figure 10.2.

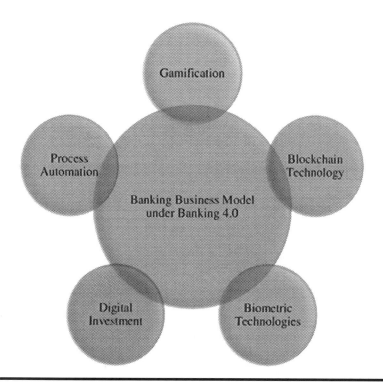

Figure 10.2   Banking business model under Banking 4.0 (Source: Kobler et al., 2016)

10.6 Conclusion

Banking 4.0 is considered a constructive destruction that is the result, particularly, of innovative technologies and Fintech companies. Fintech involvement makes traditional banking less effective, and banks need to change their business models and may need to create alliances with Fintech firms in order to follow the more customer-centric approach in providing access to financial services to the end users (Mekinjić, 2019). The present chapter identified the four phases in the evolution and growth of Banking 4.0 as part of the Fourth Industrial Revolution and also examined the role of Fintech in the acceptance of Banking 4.0. It has been clearly shown that the Fintech revolution plays a pivotal role in the adoption of Banking 4.0 through enhanced technologies (AI, blockchain technology, cloud computing, open banking, mobile payment, P2P lending, and big data analytics) in each area of banking, but the most profound segment affected by the Fintech revolution is payment, clearing, and settlement service providers. The chapter also provides insight on how banks should face severe competition from Fintech industries and determines the focus area for the banking sector in particular.

While banks are required to make huge investments toward digital transformation in innovative technologies that targeting a wide range of customers, it should mainly follow the progressive CRM and concentrate on customers' demand areas. Lastly, banks need to conducts a Strengths, Weaknesses, Opportunities, and Threats (SWOT) analysis to evaluate weaknesses in its core segment, and based on that, they should take proper action to collaborate with Fintech firms, as this will, ultimately, ease the path of the banking sector in adoption of Banking 4.0.

References

Abdillah, L., Hussein, A.S., & Ratnawati, K. (2020). Identification of the dimensions of bank 4.0 experiential quality based on millennial customer perceptions. *Asia-Pacific Management and Business Application*, 9(1), 67–82.

Aduba, J.J., Asgari, B., & Izawa, H. (2023). Does Fintech penetration drive financial development? Evidence from panel analysis of emerging and developing economies. *Borsa Istanbul Review*, 23(5), 1078–1097.

Akhtar, S., Niazi, M.H., & Khan, M.M. (2020). Cascading effect of COVID 19 on Indian economy. *International Journal of Advanced Science and Technology*, 29(9), 4563–4573.

Al-Ajlouni, A.T., & Al-Hakim, M. (2018). Financial technology in banking industry: Challenges and opportunities. *International Conference on Economics and Administrative Sciences*, 1–18.

Albastaki, Y.A., Razzaque, A., & Sarea, A.M. (2021). Innovative strategies for implementing Fintech in banking. *IGI Global*. DOI: 10.4018/978-1-7998-3257-7.ch006

Alshater, M.M., Saba, I., Supriani, I., & Rabbani, M.R. (2022). Fintech in Islamic finance literature: A review. *Heliyon*, 8(9), e10385.

Anshari, M., Almunawar, M.N., Masri, M., & Hamdan, M. (2019). Digital marketplace and Fintech to support agriculture sustainability. *Energy Procedia*, 156, 234–238.

Aysan, A.F., Belatik, A., Unal, I.M., & Ettaai, R. (2022). Fintech strategies of Islamic Banks: A global empirical analysis. *Fintech*, 1(2), 206–215.

Azmi, S.N., & Akhtar, S. (2022). Interactions of services export, fnancial development and growth: Evidence from India. *Quality and Quantity*, 57, 4709–4724.

Azmi, S., Akhtar, S., & Nadeem, M. (2020). Impact of digitalisation on bank performance: A study of Indian banks. *Test Engineering and Management*, 83, 23678–23691.

Azouaou, A., Berjaoui, A., & Houssain, A. (2023). Banks 4.0 in the context of sustainable development: A literature review and research framework. *E3S Web of Conference*, 412.

Bank of International Settlements. (2018). Implications of fintech developments for banks and bank supervisors. Basel Committee on Banking Supervision (BCBS). Retrieved from: https://www.bis.org/bcbs/publ/d431.pdf

Bhat, J.R., Alqahtani, S.A., & Nekovee, M. (2022). Fintech enablers, use cases and role of future internet of things. *Journal of King Saud University – Computer and Information Sciences*, 35(1), 87–101.

Bhutto, S.A., Jamal, Y., & Ullah, S. (2023). Fintech adoption, HR competency potential, service innovation and firm growth in banking sector. *Heliyon*, 9(3), e103967.

Böhmer, H.M. (2020). Banking 4.0 - The impact of Industry 4.0 on current business banking business models in a big South African Bank [Master Report, University of the Witwatersrand]. Johannesburg, South Africa.

Cao, L., Leung, T., Yuan, G., & Zhang, W. (2020). Special issue on AI and fintech: The challenge ahead. *IEEE Intelligent Systems*, 35(2), 3–6.

Chaturvedi, K., Akhtar, S., Azhar, N., & Shamshad, M. (2021). Impact of corporate social responsibility on financial performance of selected banks in india: Based on camel model. *Studies in Economics and Business Relations*, 2(2), 17–31.

Dabbeeru, R., & Rao, D.N. (2021). Fintech applications in banking and financial services industry in india, 1–12. 3881967

Demirguc-Kunt, A., Klapper, L., Singer, D., & Ansar, S. (2018). *The Global Findex Database 2017: Measuring financial inclusion and the fintech revolution.* World Bank Publications.

Ferraro, G., Ramponi, A., & Scarlatti, S. (2022). Fintech meets Industry 4.0: A systematic literature review of recent development and future trends. *Technology Analysis and Strategic Management*, 1–17.

Feyen, E., Frost, J., Gambacorta, L., Natarajan, H., & Saal, M. (2021). Fintech and the digital transformation of financial services: Implications for market structure and public policy. BIS Papers No 117.

Fintech Revolution in Banking: Leading the Way to Digital. (n.d.). Infosys. Retrieved from: https://www.infosys.com/industries/financial-services/white-papers/Documents/fintech-revolution-banking.pdf

Gupta, R. (2021). Industry 4.0 adaption in Indian Banking Sector—A review and agenda for future research. *MDI Sage*, 27(1), 1–9.

Gupta, S., & Agrawal, A. (2021). Analytical study of Fintech in India: Pre-& Post Pandemic COVID-19. *Indian Journal of Economics and Business*, 20(3), 33–71.

Huparikar, A., & Shinde, N. (2022). A study on influence of Fintech on consumer satisfaction of Bank in Pune. *Journal of Positive School Psychology*, 6(5), 989–995.

Iqbal, B.A., & Yadav, A. (2021). FOURTH industrial revolution: Its role and contribution in employment generation and skills development. *Journal of Global Economy, Trade and International Business*, 1(1), 85–96.

Jafar, S.H., Akhtar, S., El-Chaarani, H., Khan, P.A., & Binsaddig, R. (2023). Forecasting of NIFTY 50 index price by using backward elimination with an LSTM model. *Journal of Risk and Financial Management*, 16, 423.

Junarsin, E., Pelawi, R.Y., Kristanto, J., Marcelin, I., & Pelawi, J.B. (2023). Does fintech lending expansion disturb financial system stability? Evidence from Indonesia. *Heliyon*, 9(9), e18384.

Karsh, S.A., & Abufara, Y. (2020). The new era of financial technology in banking industry. *Journal of Southwest Jiaotong University*, 55(4), 1–13.

Kaur, N., Sahdev, S.L., Sharma, M., & Siddiqui, L. (2020). Banking 4.0: "The influence of artificial intelligence on the banking industry & how AI is changing the face of modern-day banks". *International Journal of Management*, 11(6), 577–585.

Kobler, D.D., Bucherer, D.S., & Scholtmann, J. (2016). Banking business models of the future. *Deliotte*. Retrieved from: https://www2.deloitte.com/content/dam/Deloitte/tw/Documents/financial-services/tw-banking-business-models-of-the-future-2016.pdf

Kuchciak, I., & Warwas, I. (2021). Designing a roadmap for human resource management in the Banking 4.0. *Journal of Risk and Financial Management*, 14, 615.

Kumar, A., Patel, N., & Jain, N.K. (2023). The impact of AI technology on the financial sector and how AI is modifying the state of modern-day financial institutions by Banking 4.0. *European Chemical Bulletin*, 12(Si6), 5448–5459.

Kumar, A., Srivastava, A., & Gupta, P.K. (2022). Banking 4.0: The era of artificial intelligence- based fintech. *Strategic Change*, 31(6), 1–11.

Lauren, E.A. (2021). The fourth industrial revolution in banking sector: Strategies to keep up with financial technology. Retrieved from: https://papers.ssrn.com/sol3/papers.cfm?abstract_id=4049913

Legowo, M.B., Subanidja, S., & Sorongan, A. (2021). Fintech and bank: Past, present, and future. *Journal Teknik Komputer AMIK BSI*, 7(1), 94–98.

Lestari, D., & Rahmanto, B.T. (2021). Fintech and its challenge for banking sector. *The Management Journal of BINANIAGA*, 6(1), 55–70.

Mahmud, K., Joarder, M.M.A., & Sakib, K. (2023). Customer Fintech Readiness (CFR): Assessing customer readiness for fintech in Bangladesh. *Journal of Open Innovation: Technology, Market, and Complexity*, 9(2), 100032.

Mamta, D., & Goyal, P. (2022). Fintech in Indian banking sector: Overview and challenges. *International Journal of Advanced Research in Commerce, Management &Social Science*, 5(4), 197–200.

Mazurchenko, A., Zelenka, M., & Maršíková, K. (2022). Demand for employees' digital skills in the context of banking 4.0. *E+M Business Administration and Management*, 25(2), 41–58.

Mehdiabadi, A., Tabatabeinasab, M., Spulbar, C., Yazdi, A., & Birau, R. (2020). Are we ready for the challenge of banks 4.0? Designing a roadmap for banking systems in Industry 4.0. *International Journal of Financial Studies*, 8(2), 32.

Mekinjić, B. (2019). The impact of Industry 4.0 on the transformation of the banking sector. *Journal of Contemporary Economics*, 1(1), 6–28.

Mhlanga, D. (2020). Industry 4.0 in finance: The impact of Artificial Intelligence (AI) on digital financial inclusion. *International Journal of Financial Studies*, 8(3), 45.

Noreen, U., Shafique, A., Ahmed, Z., & Ashfaq, M. (2023). Banking 4.0: Artificial Intelligence (AI) in banking industry & consumer's perspective. *Sustainability*, 15(4), 3682.

Omarini, A. (2017). The digital transformation in banking and the role of Fintechs in the new financial intermediation scenario. MPRA Paper No. 85228, 1–12.

Renduchintala, T., Alfauri, H., Yang, Z., Pietro, R.D., & Jain, R. (2022). Survey of blockchain applications in the Fintech sector. *Journal of Open Innovation: Technology, Market, and Complexity*, 8(4), 185.

Roy, P., Rai, P., & Singh, S.K. (2022). Fintech 4.0 & emerging challenges in the segments of the Fintech ecosystem. *International Journal of Advanced Research in Commerce, Management &Social Science*, 5(4), 163–174.

Schwab, K. (2018). The fourth industrial revolution. World Economic Forum. Retrieved from: https://www.weforum.org/about/the-fourth-industrial-revolution-by-klaus-schwab

Sharma, P., Rani, P., Nagpal, N., & Ghangas, P.S. (2023). A study on development of technology and customer acceptance of banking 4.0. *European Chemical Bulletin*, 12(9), 2737–2747.

Singh, A.K. (2020). Banking 4.0-Era of innovation. *International Journal of Advanced Research in Management and Social Sciences*, 9(3), 56–60.

Singh, J., Singh, G., Gahlawat, M., & Prabha, C. (2022). Big data as a service and application for Indian Banking Sector. *Procedia Computer Science*, 215, 878–887.

Tang, M., Hu, Y., Corbet, S., Hou, Y., & Oxley, L. (2023). Fintech, bank diversification and liquidity: Evidence from China. *Research in International Business and Finance*, 67(Part A), 102082.

Thakor, A.V. (2020). Fintech and banking: What do we know? *Journal of Financial Intermediation*, 41, 100833.

Wajid, A., Sabiha, A., Akhtar, S., Tabash, M.I., & Daniel, L.N. (2022). Cross-border acquisitions and shareholders' wealth: The case of the Indian pharmaceutical sector. *Journal of Risk and Financial Management*, 15(10), 437.

World Bank. (2020). Fintech market reports rapid growth during COVID-19 pandemic. Retrieved from: https://www.worldbank.org/en/news/press-release/2020/12/03/fintech-market-reports-rapid-growth-during-covid-19-pandemic

Chapter 11

Banking in the Future: An Exploration of Underlying Challenges

Prashant Subhash Chougule and Chinna Swamy Dudekula

11.1 Introduction

The advent of novel technologies in recent decades has significantly contributed to enhancing organizational efficiency (Maddikunta et al., 2021). The advent of industrialization has precipitated significant advancements in technology, resulting in profound transformations in the realm of business development. Therefore, these effects may be classified as industrial revolutions. Organizations demonstrate a keen interest in leveraging the advantages of innovation to effectively address customer requirements and acquire valuable insights from them (Rao et al., 2022). During the course of the industrial revolutions, scholars have identified five significant transformations that have occurred in the realm of industry throughout history. The future industrial age represents the most recent significant advancement in the industrial sector and is widely regarded as the forthcoming phase of industrial development. Its primary objective is to harness the ingenuity of human experts in conjunction with efficient, intelligent, and precise machines, thereby facilitating the attainment of production solutions that are both resource-efficient and user-friendly, surpassing the capabilities of Industry 4.0 (Motienko, 2020).

DOI: 10.4324/9781032644165-11

Let's take a look at these previous industrial flashpoints. The initial phase of industrialization, commonly referred to as the First Industrial Revolution, was characterized by the development and implementation of the steam engine, which occurred between the years 1760 and 1840. The Second Industrial Revolution, spanning from 1870 to 1969, is characterized by the incorporation of electricity into various industrial operations. The onset of the Third Industrial Revolution occurred during the 1970s, marked by the adoption of technological advances in communication and information as well as industrial automation. Subsequently, the Fourth Industrial Revolution, commonly referred to as Industry 4.0, originated from collaborative efforts between various developed nations. Notably, Germany spearheaded this public–private initiative with the aim of constructing intelligent factories that seamlessly integrate physical objects with digital technologies (Brettel, Friederichsen, Keller, & Rosenberg, 2014; Hermann, Pentek, & Otto, 2016).

The primary characteristic that delineates the phases of Industry 4.0 is the significant transformation in the interconnection of manufacturing systems resulting from the incorporation of data, information, and communication technology, the Internet of Things, cyber–physical systems, big data analytics, three-dimensional (3D) printing, advanced robotics, intelligent sensors, augmented reality, cloud computing, artificial intelligence (AI), nanotechnology, and human–machine interfaces (Mehdiabadi, Shahabi, Shamsinejad, Amiri, Spulbar, & Birau, 2022). The industry has experienced a notable influence from the advancement toward Industry 4.0, which is primarily attributed to the development of smart factories, smart products, and intelligent services that rely on the integration of the IoT and industrial internet-connected services (Kagermann, 2015). Various strategic initiatives have been implemented in numerous countries, such as the Industrial Internet Consortium in the United States, Industry 4.0 in Italy, Production 2030 in Sweden, Made in China 2025, and Society 5.0.

However, many researchers are already looking beyond the current industrial revolution. Xu et al. (2021) have demonstrated in their research that the initial phase of the transition from Industry 4.0 to the next level involves acknowledging the capacity of the industrial sector to contribute to societal objectives that go beyond employment and economic expansion. This transition aims to establish a resilient framework for prosperity by ensuring that production practises adhere to the ecological limits of our planet while prioritizing the wellbeing of industry workers as the focal point of the production process (Breque, De Nul, & Petridis, 2021).

The next step after Industry 4.0 is expected to have the following characteristics:

1. Establish, as a primary objective, a resilient entity that promotes prosperity through the implementation of production practises that adhere to the ecological limits of our planet.
2. Prioritize and place at the core of the production process the wellbeing of industry workers.
3. Strive to attain societal objectives that extend beyond mere employment and economic expansion.
4. Harness the distinctive creative abilities of human experts in collaboration with advanced, intelligent, and accurate machines.
5. Indulge in mass personalization via tailored and individualized products based on individual preferences and requirements of the customers.
6. Enhance production quality via the allocation of repetitive and standardized tasks to robots or machines while reserving tasks that necessitate analytical thinking for human workers.
7. Shift from viewing robots and AI as competitors to collaborators.

These characteristics are also the features that banks of today will need to tackle in order to resiliently weather the current storm of disruptions and stake its claim as a bank of the future. Thus far, banks and other financial institutions have been engaged in a process of trying to keep pace with these disruptions, primarily reacting rather than proactively responding. This is evident from the evolution of banking from Banking 1.0 to Banking 4.0. Table 11.1 illustrates the evolution of industry along with banks.

The significant question to be posed is whether it is enough to aspire to Banking 4.0 status. One wonders if the wheels of disruption will stop turning once the coveted Banking 4.0 status is achieved. One also has to ponder about the ethical and sustainability issues that are not fully considered in this framework until Banking 4.0.

Many banks today aspire to attain Banking 4.0 status. These banks are confronted with significant market challenges stemming from uncertain monetary policies, a decline in credit quality, and the burdens of regulation and compliance. In order to successfully navigate these challenges, the banks of today have no alternative but to look beyond Banking 4.0. This will require fundamental changes in not only how banks harness technology but also how they make money, communicate with customers and employees, and even appoint leadership.

Table 11.1 Evolution of Industry Vis-à-Vis Banks

Evolution Level	Industry	Bank
1.0	Characterized by the development and implementation of the steam engine, industrial production and transportation.	Similar to traditional banking, which also provides services through physical branches during designated operating hours. Characterized by central banks and clearing houses.
2.0	Characterized by the incorporation of electricity into various industrial operations, telegraph, and division of labour.	Characterized by the advent of growing branch networks, automated teller machines (ATMs), and card scanners that facilitated the establishment of off-branch operations at different intervals.
3.0	Marked by the adoption of technological advances in communication and information as well as industrial automation and enterprise resource planning (ERP).	Characterized by the general understanding that banking can be done on the go with credit cards, electronic payments, mobile card readers, or even through apps on a smartphone platform.
4.0	Characterized by the development of smart factories, smart products, and intelligent services that rely on the integration of the Internet of Things and industrial internet-connected services.	Refers to industry-wide change brought on by data, technology, and changing consumer demands. In addition to providing more individualized, efficient, and dependable financial services, it seeks to encourage collaboration as well as creativity within the financial ecosystem. Fintech, mobile banking, online banking, etc. are parts of this.
5.0	Characterized by AI, robotics, resurgence of human touch in manufacturing, and sustainability.	Characterized by Exchange Traded Funds (ETFs), cryptocurrency, high-frequency trading, cognitive banking, robo-advisors and cobots, responsible banking, and embedded banking.

This chapter is focused on the fundamental question: What strategies can modern banks implement in order to not only successfully endure the current period of disruptions but also establish themselves as the banks of the future, actively shaping the future rather than simply reacting to it?

11.2 Objectives of the Chapter

1. To understand the essential characteristics of the banks of the future.
2. To discuss the challenges faced by modern banks of today.
3. To discuss the responses to challenges faced by current banks so as to become the banks of the future.

We will begin with what banks of the future will look like. This will be followed by the challenges faced by contemporary banks and possible responses will then be proposed for the same along with the discussion of the problems.

11.3 Theoretical Background

11.3.1 Understanding Banking 5.0

According to a statement often attributed to Darwin, the survival of a species is not determined by its strength or intelligence but, rather, by its ability to adapt to changes in its environment. This assertion pertains suitably well to the field of banking. Innovation is imperative within the financial services sector. Alternatively, the organizations would experience adverse consequences or face potential dissolution.

Let's start with banking itself. Banking refers to the process of exchanging value, encompassing both tangible assets and intangible trust, between individuals or organizations and financial institutions (Zhou, 2009).

The banking sector is responsible for the management and facilitation of various financial transactions, including the handling of cash and credit. Financial institutions provide a secure avenue for individuals to deposit surplus funds and access credit facilities. The banking industry provides a range of financial products and services, including savings accounts, certificates of deposit, and checking accounts. Financial institutions utilize these deposits to provide credit. The loans in question encompass various types, such as mortgages for residential properties, loans secured by assets, and financing for automobile purchases. Financial institutions are responsible for the management of information and, as a result, are significantly impacted by advancements in information and communication technologies. Banking institutions have undergone a persistent process of transformation throughout history. The macro changes can be categorized into five distinct periods, which bear resemblance to the widely recognized industrial revolutions. The aforementioned alterations have been of considerable magnitude and have resulted in notable economic and societal transformations. Throughout a series of subsequent disruptive changes, there has been a consistent and ongoing process of improvement (Nicoletti, 2021).

The Fifth Industrial Revolution in banking is expected to be characterized by the integration of AI, collaborative robots (cobots), and a strong emphasis on sustainability. Each of these aspects will exert a significant influence on the banking industry. The likelihood of banks experiencing significant disappearance is low, as they are expected to undergo substantial transformation and establish partnerships with start-up companies. The level of competition is expected to be intense. The proliferation of fifth-generation technologies is expected to facilitate the adoption and dissemination of novel banking models. Andrew Ng drew a parallel between the profound impact of AI and electricity, asserting that similar to how electricity revolutionized numerous domains a century ago, he finds it difficult to envision an industry that will remain untouched by AI's transformative influence in the coming years (Azmi, Akhtar, & Nadeem, 2020).

The coming disruptions are expected to bring down the barriers between the real word and the virtual one and provide opportunities to customers to demand highly personalized banking services at a relatively lower price. This will require banking and financial services providers to shift from a mindset characterized by mere addition of value to reinvention and creation of value. The primary strategic objective is to restructure the roles and relationships within a network of stakeholders (including vendors, partners, and customers) in order to generate value through novel combinations and the integration of various players and services. The term "value constellation" has been used to describe this emerging organizational paradigm (Normann & Ramirez, 1993). This will necessitate further movement away from a mindset that distinguishes between products and services and move toward considering them as "offerings" which will allow customers to create value for themselves (Nicoletti, 2017).

Industry 5.0 is characterized by increased speed, scalability, and a higher level of stakeholder involvement compared to previous industrial revolutions (Rundle, 2017). This scenario is expected to occur due to the increasing emphasis on the development of sophisticated person–machine interfaces that facilitate enhanced integration, as well as the improved automation of robots, combined with the cognitive capabilities and ingenuity of individuals (Shelzer, 2017). This innovation is expected to result in enhanced productivity.

Banking 5.0 will entail a heightened level of collaboration between individuals and intelligent systems, such as robots. According to the European Economic and Social Committee (EESC), Industry 5.0 is characterized by the integration of human creativity and craftsmanship with the efficiency, productivity, and reliability of robotic systems (Aslam, Aimin, Li, & Ur Rehman, 2020). This advancement in technology facilitates the delegation of monotonous and repetitive tasks to automation, thereby allowing individuals to focus their efforts on the more emotional and creative aspects of their work. Individuals will assume greater levels of responsibility and enhanced oversight of systems in order to enhance the overall quality of service.

The novelty of this concept is not unprecedented, as evidenced by the survey conducted by Accenture, which involved 512 manufacturing executives from various regions across the globe. By the year 2020 and beyond, a significant majority of the participants, specifically 85%, anticipate the implementation of a collaborative production line within their plants in which both humans and robots work together.

Furthermore, on the customer side, it is expected that they will exhibit a preference for services and products that possess discernible attributes of personalized attention and expertise, as observed in the realm of wealth management consultancy. Consequently, they are inclined to be willing to pay a higher monetary value for such offerings. The increasing demand for personalized experiences is expected to continue in the future, as customers seek to express their unique identities through the products and services they consume (Nicoletti, 2021). Financial institutions can effectively and efficiently meet this demand by integrating both human workers and intelligent robots. The effective collaboration between individuals and solutions will have an impact on the economy, ecology, and the social sphere. In contrast, AI and robots will necessitate a greater amount of electrical energy in order to power their computer systems. Therefore, it is crucial to implement all available measures in order to ensure the long-term viability of the environment through the adoption of environmentally friendly practises (Baldwin & Forslid, 2020).

11.3.2 Challenges to be Overcome

After providing an overview of the anticipated developments beyond Banking 4.0, it is pertinent to examine the obstacles that contemporary banks must surmount to attain a desirable position in which they are ahead of future advancements rather than lagging behind.

These challenges are enumerated as follows:

1. Dealing with technology disruptions.
2. Changing demographics of customers.
3. Changing demographics of employees.
4. Finding new ways of earning revenue.
5. Transitioning from single or multiple channels to omnichannel way of connecting to customers and/or stakeholders.
6. Transitioning from physical banking to branch-less banking (BLB) and open banking (OB).
7. Successfully integrating completely novel concepts such as interest-free lending, cryptocurrencies, and crowdfunding into daily operations.
8. Ensuring data integrity and cybersecurity for all stakeholders.
9. Dealing with costly legacy systems.

Let us systematically examine each of these challenges.

11.3.2.1 Dealing with Technology Disruptions

The banking sector was the initial industry to effectively harness the capabilities of an electronic network for conducting business-to-business (B2B) and business-to-customer (B2C) collaborations through technological means (Muaz, Jayabalan, & Thiruchelvam, 2020). Currently, certain sectors within the commercial banking industry continue to utilize business operating systems. This phenomenon rapidly leads to the fragmentation and duplication of business processes, a lack of support for marketing initiatives by client managers, and an unregulated increase in operational risk. The information systems employed by financial institutions exhibit both distinct and interconnected functionalities. The proliferation of bank companies in recent years has led to a significant increase in the volume of data and information stored within banks. The quantity and dependability of data storage are significantly required (Jiang & Yang, 2011). The predominant storage technologies employed by commercial banks are network attached storage (NAS) and storage area networks (SAN). The utilization of the same network by NAS in conjunction with other programmes often results in network bottlenecks, while the high cost of the SAN infrastructure poses financial challenges for banks (Aymerich, Fenu, & Surcis, 2008). In the present scenario, it is the customers who possess influence, as opposed to the bank. Customers play a pivotal role in driving the development of new business concepts. The process of business transformation is driven by the integration of technology and the modification of social and household relationships. In order to effectively respond to the evolving customer-centric landscape, banks are required to undertake the modernization of their business models, operations, and information technology infrastructure. Banks possess a considerable capacity to provide customers with reliable services across various branches and geographical regions as well as to consolidate and analyze a vast amount of dispersed customer data and analytics (Awadallah, 2016). In order to effectuate changes to the banking system, it is imperative for banks to initially undertake a comprehensive analysis of the client's standpoint. In light of the significant transformations taking place in the banking sector, there is a need for the implementation of novel approaches aimed at enhancing profitability and revenue generation (Asadi, Nilashi, Husin, & Yadegaridehkordi, 2017).

The recent years have been rife with many disruptions, which can be attributed to the following technologies.

11.3.2.1.1 Cloud Computing

Cloud computing has emerged as a disruptive phenomenon in the banking industry, presenting a dynamic model for information technology (IT) service delivery that holds the potential to deliver enhanced speed, flexibility, and the capacity to swiftly respond to evolving requirements. This chapter examines the implementation of cloud computing within the banking industry, with a specific emphasis on its impact on improving performance, accuracy, efficiency, security, and availability of IT infrastructure. Although the notion of cloud computing is not novel, its utilization within the banking sector has grown, facilitating a diverse array of advantages such as enhanced client relationship management (CRM), extensive data storage, and adaptable execution capabilities. This chapter explores the various complex aspects of cloud computing in the banking sector, emphasizing its importance and potential consequences.

The cloud is an IT service delivery model that provides customers with the potential for expedited deployment, enhanced adaptability, and the ability to promptly address emerging needs (Asadi, Nilashi, Husin, & Yadegaridehkordi, 2017). The banking industry is expected to witness a multitude of applications for cloud computing in the future, as technological advancements continue to progress. Banks have the ability to adopt cloud computing technologies in their subsidiary companies and gradually integrate these solutions into their central operations. Large banks can enhance the security and high availability of their IT infrastructure and offer on-demand IT infrastructure services by implementing a private cloud solution. Large financial institutions have the opportunity to gradually explore the utilization of hybrid and public cloud computing models. In comparison to larger banks, small banks require increased access to cash, technology, expertise, and various other resources. The banks are unable to establish their own data centres due to the significant financial burden associated with such an endeavour. Therefore, a considerable number of small banks exhibit a preference for implementing the public cloud. Cloud service providers must prioritize the provision of security measures and conduct further research on the specific requirements of the banking industry in order to develop cloud computing applications that possess exceptional flexibility, business continuity, and resilience (Rana & Ji, 2023).

11.3.2.1.2 The Entire Suite

The term "Internet of Things" (IoT) was initially introduced by Kevin Ashton at the Massachusetts Institute of Technology (MIT) in 1998. Ashton defined it as a concept that enables the connection of people and objects at any time, in any location, utilizing any network or service (Sundmaeker, Guillemin, Friess, & Woelfflé, 2010). The evolution of the IoT can be delineated into five distinct phases; this progression commences with the initial connection of two computers, subsequently expanding to encompass a substantial network of computers through the advent of the World Wide Web.

Subsequently, the mobile-internet refers to the integration of mobile devices with the internet, followed by the people–internet, which pertains to the connectivity facilitated by social networks. Eventually, it has evolved into the IoT, which refers to the interconnected network of objects (Perera, Liu, Jayawardena, & Chen, 2014).

The implementation of the IoT is considered a crucial component in facilitating the digital transformation of a bank. The integration of connected objects is unquestionably a strategic imperative for banks in order to maintain competitiveness. In contemporary times, consumers possess high expectations regarding innovation in the banking sector, particularly in relation to the emergence of digital banks. These consumers anticipate that such banks will provide them with suitable services that align with their modern, interconnected lifestyles (Petracek, 2018). There exist seven digital trends that employ the IoT and significantly influence the financial services sector. These trends encompass mobile banking, M-banking, crowd-based financing, virtual currency, high-frequency trading firms, cybercriminal activities, and the utilization of big data and IT analytics.

11.3.2.1.3 Blockchain

Blockchain is an emerging technology that has garnered significant attention in recent years. It is exceedingly challenging to discuss contemporary technologies without acknowledging the concept of "blockchain." Blockchain is a technological innovation that facilitates the storage of digital data within a publicly accessible and collectively maintained database. The subject matter can be understood as a sequence of unchanging entities (Muaz et al., 2020). Various types of banking applications can be supported by these immutable blocks. The utilization of blockchain technology holds the capacity to revolutionize the banking system, transforming it into a secure and efficient process that offers a level of transparency far surpassing that of traditional methods. The technology in question is widely recognized as the foundational technology behind the cryptocurrency known as Bitcoin. In 2018, the utilization of blockchain technology was observed across various sectors, encompassing gaming, banking, and other industries. The "jump-out-of-the-cake" event on blockchain took place in 2017. In contemporary times, the pervasive presence of blockchain is evident across various domains and within the realm of technology, as indicated by its frequent references (Fueled, 2017). Prior to this, it was not widely recognized or acknowledged. In recent times, blockchain has garnered significant attention due to its promising capabilities, resulting in increased familiarity among a wide range of individuals. In a wide range of industries, individuals are actively engaged in harnessing the potential of this remarkable technology to address their challenges (Chowdhury, Suchana, Alam, & Khan, 2021).

In recent times, the banking sector has undergone notable transformations as a result of the implementation of blockchain technology. The utilization of blockchain technology enables individuals to reach consensus on the state of a dataset without relying on trusted intermediaries for conducting transactions. The innovation of blockchain provides financial services, such as payments, without the involvement of intermediaries such as banks. The utilization of blockchain technology has the potential to facilitate faster payment processing and reduce transaction costs in comparison to traditional banking systems. This is primarily attributed to the decentralized nature of blockchain networks, which enable efficient and secure payment settlements. Open blockchains provide mechanisms for establishing safeguards such as stocks, bonds, and optional assets. This facilitates the enhancement of productivity within capital-intensive industries. This sub-section outlines several key advantages of implementing blockchain technology within the banking sector, such as cost reduction, faster transactions, improved security, improved information quality, access to digital currencies, enhancing accountability, aiding with reconciliation, and ensuring compliance (Chowdhury, Suchana, Alam, & Khan, 2021).

11.3.2.1.4 Big Data and Business Intelligence

Big data refers to the amalgamation of various processes and tools that are involved in the management and utilization of extensive collections of data. The emergence of the big data concept can be attributed to the imperative need to discern trends, preferences, and patterns within the vast database that is generated through human interactions with various systems and entities. Business organizations can leverage big data to employ analytics and visualization techniques in order to identify and prioritize customers who are likely to generate the highest profits and yield the greatest benefits (More & Moily, 2021).

According to finance industry experts, big data is a tool that enables organizations to effectively handle and control extensive datasets within a specified timeframe along with the necessary storage capacity to accommodate the large volume of data. These datasets are typically characterized by their variety, volume, and velocity (Nobanee, Dilshad, Dhanhani, Al Neyadi, Al Qubaisi, & Al Shamsi, 2021).

The advent of the big data revolution in the twenty-first century has garnered significant attention from banking institutions, given the wealth of valuable data they have accumulated over several decades. The analysis of this data has revealed previously undisclosed insights into the patterns of financial transactions, thereby aiding in the prevention of significant calamities and acts of theft as well as enhancing our comprehension of consumer actions and preferences.

Banks are able to derive significant advantages from the utilization of big data, as they can efficiently and expeditiously extract valuable insights from their data and subsequently translate them into meaningful benefits for both their own operations and their clientele. Banks on a global scale are increasingly leveraging data to enhance their operations in multiple areas, including sentiment analysis, product cross-selling, regulatory compliance management, reputational risk management, financial crime management, and other related functions. Indian banks are making progress in aligning themselves with global banks, although there is still significant potential for further improvement (Srivastava & Gopalkrishnan, 2015).

The advantages include, fraud detection and prevention, customer segmentation in new and insightful ways, enhanced risk prediction and management, insightful study of the economic and social factors affecting the bank, past financial data utilization and performing predictions based on the same in areas of fraud prevention, credit default prediction, etc. (More & Moily, 2021).

The implementation of big data analytics is currently being observed in multiple domains within the banking sector. This utilization is aiding banks in enhancing their service delivery to both internal and external customers. Additionally, it is facilitating improvements in their active and passive security systems.

11.3.2.1.5 Artificial Intelligence

The utilization of machine learning and AI technologies in the financial industry has experienced significant growth in recent years. The institutions have effectively utilized their significant power to provide business solutions for both front-end and back-end processes, resulting in enhanced efficiency and improved customer experience (Donepudi, 2017).

AI pertains to the capacity of computer programmes to autonomously acquire and employ knowledge without the need for human intervention or involvement. AI systems derive conclusions and execute suitable actions by autonomously observing their surroundings and analyzing information. Individuals acquire knowledge and enhance their performance through the process of reflecting upon their past judgements and making adjustments based on the level of accuracy achieved (Kaya, Schildbach, AG, & Schneider, 2019).

AI is currently undergoing testing in know your customer (KYC) procedures as a means of authenticating the identities of clients. AI algorithms are employed to analyze client documents and assess the credibility of the information contained therein by juxtaposing it with data obtained from the internet. In the event that AI algorithms detect inconsistencies, they signal a warning and prompt bank employees to conduct a more comprehensive KYC verification process (Kaya, Schildbach, AG, & Schneider, 2019).

Chatbots are computerized aides that engage with customers through written or spoken communication with the objective of fulfilling their inquiries or needs without the intervention of a human bank representative (Kaya, Schildbach, AG, & Schneider, 2019).

Financial institutions are also actively investigating the utilization of AI for the purpose of visually representing information derived from legal documents and annual reports. Additionally, they are exploring AI's potential to extract crucial clauses from such documents. AI tools autonomously generate models by observing data and conducting back testing in order to enhance accuracy through learning from past errors (Kaya, Schildbach, AG, & Schneider, 2019).

Robo-advisors, which facilitate complete automation in specific asset management services, and online financial planning tools, which assist customers in making more informed decisions regarding consumption and saving, are notable advancements in the field. As financial technology solutions continue to evolve, they are increasingly employing autonomous techniques to search and analyze data, enabling them to identify patterns and trends (Kaya, Schildbach, AG, & Schneider, 2019).

Banks are predominantly focusing on the exploration of AI applications as a means to enhance efficiency by replacing activities that are characterized by high costs, labour-intensive processes, and repetitive tasks. The primary emphasis lies in the acquisition of gains pertaining to operational risk management, such as the detection of fraudulent activities or the enhancement of KYC processes. Additionally, there is a focus on identifying opportunities for cost reduction, such as the utilization of chatbots or robo-advisors.

11.3.2.1.6 Robots and Cobots

The proliferation of technologies such as AI and virtual reality (VR) is giving rise to novel possibilities and opportunities. The individuals in question will undergo a transition in their employment. Mixed teams will be formed, consisting of both individuals and smart technologies. By employing this approach, it becomes feasible to integrate individual experiences with AI. According to a survey conducted among Italian manufacturing subject matter experts (SMEs), 43% of them hold this viewpoint (Gianderico & Di Gilio, 2018).

When AI is integrated with human ingenuity and creativity, it enables both individuals and financial institutions to accomplish significantly greater outcomes. Accenture refers to this concept as "applied intelligence." Financial institutions possess the capacity to effectively address intricate challenges, innovate novel products and services, and penetrate existing or establish novel markets (Shook, Knickrehm, Mcintyre, Woolf, Browne, & Lavelle, 2022).

The organization has either implemented or plans to implement cutting-edge solutions and processes, such as information and communication technology security, cloud computing, collaborative robotics, and the IoT.

The current developments in automation and robotics have resulted in a fundamental transformation of human interaction with robots. These robots are constructed using advanced technologies such as AI, which are undergoing significant fluctuations. Robotic devices that possess computational capabilities, particularly those that exhibit enhanced performance through human interaction, are commonly referred to as cobots. While robots excel in efficiently producing large quantities of identical products, their inability to engage in critical thinking limits their capacity to personalize and customize products. Hence, it is proposed by Industry 5.0 that the integration of human and robotic collaboration can lead to the production of personalized goods with enhanced efficiency and precision. Today's customers have a strong desire for precise and efficient personal banking services. Therefore, the utilization of cobots presents an opportunity for banks to provide error-free and expeditious personalized banking services to a vast customer demographic (Soomro, Ali, & Parveen, 2022).

The utilization of cobots is expected to experience a significant rise in the future. The term "cobot" is a portmanteau of the words "collaborative" and "robot." Cobots possess the ability to effectively interact with both the work environment and the operators, thereby exhibiting a combination of operational and integrative flexibility while ensuring a secure working environment. Cobots are a type of power tool that enhance the capabilities of operators in terms of speed, accuracy, and precision while still maintaining a human-like touch. Financial institutions have shown a keen interest in the utilization of virtual or software cobots. The uses of cobots are as follows:

■ The process of generating and dispatching documentation requests is automated.

- The utilization of smart contracts facilitates the creation and enforcement of agreements. The aforementioned solutions refer to computer protocols that serve the purpose of facilitating, validating, enforcing, negotiating, or executing a contractual agreement.
- The utilization of automated systems for the purpose of performance management and monitoring. The topic of interest is fraud detection. The utilization of automated systems for conducting customer assessments.
- The manufacturing of automated dashboards and the implementation of automated indicators for improvement actions.
- The provision of tailored services.

11.3.2.1.7 Augmented Reality

Augmented reality (AR) is occasionally mischaracterized as a device that solely enhances the viewing experience. However, AR refers to the broader scope of developing applications that aim to enhance the physical world by incorporating virtual information and facilitating real-time user interaction with it. The utilization of AR offers a user-friendly and visually based form of support that effectively mitigates the intricacy associated with various tasks. Similar to other domains of innovation, the concept of AR is frequently characterized by a lack of precise definition and can encompass various scopes or interpretations contingent upon the specific context, occasionally with deliberate intent. The lack of specificity frequently leads to inflated anticipations, which subsequently lead to disillusionment, thereby tarnishing the reputation of this concept – one that is both valuable and intriguing – among the broader population (Heng, Hörster, Karollus, Slomka, AG, & Hoffmann, 2015).

In order to foster client loyalty and encourage continued utilization of their services, banks are endeavouring to implement innovative strategies aimed at providing transparent and convenient banking solutions for their clientele. In contemporary times, clients possess distinct and specific demands, necessitating a particular quality of service, thereby presenting challenges for banks to maintain a competitive advantage. Banks are currently prioritizing the adaptation of emerging technologies and exploring innovative approaches to enhance their ability to provide improved customer experiences. AR refers to the continuous integration of data and virtual enhancements with real-world objects (Rose, 1993).

The ability to integrate digital and physical entities has the potential to revolutionize customer experiences, seamlessly integrating banking services into everyday interactions. The implementation of visually captivating AR can enhance the overall client experience through the provision of location-based offers, ATM locators, direct communication with a relationship manager, property searches, and payment processing capabilities. The anticipated growth in the utilization of AR for managing account capacities is expected to be observed over time. However, it is worth noting that certain banks have already introduced multiple applications in this regard. The Commonwealth Bank of Australia has developed a mobile application that, when directed toward a property, provides comprehensive listing details and additional information that can be utilized to make informed decisions regarding real estate. Standard Chartered China has developed an AR application that offers location-based services, such as discount coupons. Westpac has developed an AR application that enables its customers to conveniently access features such as checking card balances, making payments, and locating nearby bank or ATM branches. Citibank dealers have been experimenting with the utilization of Microsoft HoloLens as a virtual workstation in order to enhance the bank's existing technological devices and operational procedures (Malini & Menon, 2017).

11.3.2.1.8 Smart Contracts and DApps

In 1994, Nick Szabo, a computer scientist and legal scholar, coined the term "smart contract" and provided the following definition: "A smart contract is the individual conceptualized a method for enhancing the effectiveness of written agreements by implementing an automated enforcement mechanism." Consider a vending machine. In the absence of a shop clerk, the vending machine effectively upholds the contractual agreement of selling a beverage to the customer at the price advertised, provided that the customer inserts sufficient money (Metcalfe, 2020).

Decentralized applications (DApps) are frequently characterized as trustless or peer-to-peer, as they lack a central server or controlling entity, distinguishing them from the traditional client–server model. There are appealing characteristics of the smart contract and the adaptable nature of the platform (Metcalfe, 2020).

DApps and smart contracts have applications in fundraising (Via ICOs), traversing marketplaces (which include exchanges too), ensuring compliance with Know Your Customer-Anti-Money Laundering (KYC-AML) norms, asset securitization, and financial inclusion.

In the contemporary context, individuals increasingly rely on innovation and technology as a means to accomplish tasks in a more efficient and expeditious manner. Frugal innovations that possess sustainability and accessibility characteristics have the potential to generate higher revenue and enhance firm value, while concurrently reducing resource demands, costs, and positively impacting the environment (Shivdas & Chandrasekhar, 2016). Financial technology (Fintech) is an innovative and cost-effective field that aims to resolve the challenges associated with the accessibility and utilization of financial services, regardless of geographical limitations (Nair & Menon, 2017).

The aforementioned trends are expected to result in increased customer satisfaction within the banking industry. These trends encompass the following:

■ Banks are engaging in collaborations or partnerships with Fintech firms in order to establish an ecosystem that fosters innovation and fulfils the constantly evolving demands of customers. This approach views Fintech firms as potential partners rather than competitors.

■ Organizations can leverage application programming interfaces (APIs) as a means to generate revenue from their digital assets and data. Open APIs facilitate the seamless integration of banking institutions' offerings with external applications, thereby granting customers access to a diverse range of products and services within the banking ecosystem. Furthermore, these APIs can be leveraged for monetization purposes in numerous instances. The proposed business model in question pertains to the banking industry, wherein banks are envisioned to undergo a transformation.

■ Banks as a platform (BaaP) represents a significant transformation in the banking industry, serving as a conduit for numerous Fintech firms. This model establishes direct connections between banks and Fintechs, facilitating the integration of their innovative solutions. Consequently, BaaP enables banks to offer customers a comprehensive range of services in a single location.

■ The proliferation of digitization and connectivity has resulted in a rise in cyberthreats, leading banks to enhance their security systems. Cloud services have gained popularity due to their ability to offer flexibility and agility. There is a growing trend among banks to adopt public cloud-based banking infrastructures, driven by a diminishing perception of security and regulatory risks.

■ Banks are currently making investments in AR technology with the aim of enhancing the customer experience. By leveraging AR, banks can offer seamless solutions to their customers, thereby differentiating themselves from their competitors.

■ Banks are currently engaged in the exploration of applications pertaining to distributed ledger technology through various means such as collaboration, partnership with start-ups, and the establishment of incubators and innovation labs.

■ The utilization of AI and cognitive technology in the banking sector facilitates the acceleration of digitization efforts and the provision of tailored and personalized offerings, thereby granting banks a competitive advantage over their rivals.

■ Robotic process automation (RPA) is a technologically advanced approach that enables banks to effectively minimize their IT expenditures while maintaining the quality-of-service provision. The utilization of biometric authentication tools can effectively address the issues of identity theft and fraud within the banking sector.

By implementing such tools, banks can bolster their security measures, ensuring a higher level of protection for transactions and, ultimately, enhancing the overall customer experience.

11.3.2.2 Changing Demographics of Customers

Many of the previously mentioned methods will help banks to segment their customers into various segments based on demographics, needs, capacities, etc. It becomes important to understand the bank customer of the future due to the very simple fact that by the advent of Banking 5.0, the current customer demographics will undergo a huge change.

In the past, the customer could be dictated with respect to banking and financial services in terms of time of service, place of service, terms of service, and fees of service. The older customers, i.e. before Millennials, would more or less accept the dictation of how the banking services will be delivered to them. However, the current demographics are changing, and so are the attitudes of the customers.

Currently, a substantial demographic of bank clientele comprises young and middle-aged individuals who possess distinct expectations and preferences in comparison to the preceding generation. The current banking models are inadequate for meeting the expectations and preferences of customers. To address this issue, the adoption of fourth-generation tools, technologies, and mechanisms is necessary. The advent of Industry 4.0

encompasses two distinct aspects: first, the fulfilment of emerging demands through the development of novel products and processes and, second, the attainment of enhanced productivity through the integration of process innovations (Zambon, Cecchini, Egidi, Saporito, & Colantoni, 2019). The integration of the emerging cohort of customers into the marketplace and conducting business in this era of transformation necessitates a comprehensive reassessment of prevailing banking services and products. The utilization of technology in banks has resulted in several benefits, including increased productivity, the introduction of innovative products, expedited transactions, seamless fund transfers, the implementation of real-time information systems, and the facilitation of efficient risk management (Saravanan & Lakshmi, 2016).

A noteworthy aspect, particularly relevant to the Banking 5.0 era, pertains to the demographic commonly referred to as Millennials. Millennials, also known as Generation Y, encompass individuals born between the years 1980 and 2000. Generation Z, also known as Gen Z, refers to the demographic cohort that follows the Millennial generation. These segments exhibit significant levels of activity across various digital platforms, including the internet, social media platforms, and mobile devices. Generations Y and Z collectively account for more than 25% of the global population (Bassett, 2018). Acquiring these market segments poses a substantial yet pertinent challenge for financial institutions. The individuals in question represent the prospective clientele.

In contemporary society, individuals belonging to the Millennial generation exhibit a strong desire for immediate mastery over various aspects of their lives, while concurrently seeking out novel and inventive offerings in the realm of goods and services. A significant number of individuals belonging to the Millennial generation residing in urban areas do not possess personal automobiles. These consumers do not depend on their personal network, such as family or friends, for acquiring information.

Millennials exhibit a predilection for online reviews and social communities, such as specialized forums and other digital platforms. Various factors and features contribute significantly to the acquisition of these segments, such as expeditious transactions and transparency, the convenience of online shopping, time efficiency, cost-effectiveness, and the provision of high-value incentives such as discount coupons (Deshpande, 2020).

The widespread adoption of mobile phones and other mobile devices has had a significant impact on the behaviour of older generations of customers, as influenced by Millennials. This phenomenon is commonly referred to as "equalization." The potential impact of this phenomenon could be significant for the banking industry, which has historically focused on a customer base that is not accustomed to digital technologies. There is a limited number of financial institutions that have demonstrated a management mindset, a proactive attitude, and successfully implemented digital solutions (Nicoletti, 2021).

This scenario is particularly favourable for agile, digitally focused innovators, such as Fintech entities. According to the findings of a survey, it was observed that individuals belonging to the Millennial and Gen Z generations possessed the highest number of Fintech accounts in comparison to other age groups (Krivkovich, White, Townsend, & Euart, 2020). The Gen Z demographic witnessed a notable surge of 14% in the number of inexperienced users, which can also be expressed as a 27% increase. Similarly, the Millennial cohort experienced a rise of 8%, or a 17% increase. A notable proportion of individuals belonging to the Baby Boomer generation (26%) utilize Fintech accounts, thereby challenging the prevailing notion that digital financial tools are primarily utilized by younger demographics (Krivkovich, White, Townsend, & Euart, 2020).

It is not just the buying habits or attitudes but also the intellectual makeup of the new generation. They are also worried about the planet and their community. They are asking whether the products and services being offered to them are made through sustainable processes. They worry about the corporate social responsibility (CSR) practices of the providers of these services. In order to win over these customers, it is essential that the banks of the future start positioning themselves as desirable providers of ethical, sustainable, and planet-friendly banking services.

11.3.2.3 Changing Demographics of Employees

Just as the demographics of the future employees are expected to change, we can expect similar changes for employees, too. The employees in the banks of the future will need to be of a different mould from before.

The employees in the banks of the past, who are mostly experts at risk management, will simply not be the most effective people for the future job. For example, banks mostly reject 80% of entrepreneurial funding proposals they receive, while cutting edge Fintech service providers, such as ALIPAY, were providing more loans than ever before and at very competitive rates with easy delivery mechanisms (Lu, 2018). Successfully competing (or even collaborating) with such agile players requires acquisition of a workforce with a completely different attitude and skill set.

The new employees will need to be young, either Millennials or Gen Z. They will need to be as tech-savvy as (if not more) their customers. This change has to start at the top, at the C-suite level. It is advisable that the board composition must undergo a change to include more people from technology and start-up backgrounds. The ideal technologists for this context are those who possess a strong network within the realm of emerging technologies. It is preferable that they have prior experience in launching their own start-up or have effectively navigated digital transformations in the past (King, 2018).

It is also advisable that banks fill their ranks with a large number of Millennials and Gen Z employees who are expected to be at the forefront of the transition to Banking 5.0. This is not only because they represent a huge segment of the population the bank will try to cater to but also because a majority of them have been hailed to be more entrepreneurial, individualistic, and open-minded (Sachs, 2015). It is imperative that this group leads the banks of the future.

It should also be noted that even though it is desirable to have younger people in the ranks of the future banks, it is not an easy task to achieve. The recent COVID-19 pandemic; the work from home (WFH) phase and; their individualistic nature, inclination toward work-life balance, and attraction to environmental, social, and governance (ESG) values have come together to produce a generation with a pronounced set of core values. Banks of the future cannot hope to hold on to the talent of the future if they do not consider ESG concerns, CSR integrity, and passion factor of the younger generations (King, 2018).

11.3.2.4 Finding New Ways of Earning Revenue

Traditionally, banks have earned incomes from banking activities such as community-banking model, net interest income, fees, and commissions. However, considering the rising costs of banking and related activities, banks can no longer afford to just limit their income sources.

They are now expected to raise sufficient income at the strategic business unit (SBU) level from ancillary activities such as cross-selling, APIs, etc. (Mehdiabadi, Tabatabeinasab, Spulbar, Karbassi Yazdi, & Birau, 2020). This is where the enterprising nature of young employees is expected to come in handy. The banks of the future will need to find new and innovative ways to connect and reconnect with the community and redefine new ways of earning income if they expect to witness the coming of the new banking age.

11.3.2.5 Transitioning from Single or Multiple Channels to an Omnichannel Way of Connecting to Customers and/or Stakeholders

As the level of industrial evolution progressed, so did the levels of the customer engagement channels.

11.3.2.5.1 Single Channel

For centuries, the most rudimentary method of establishing a connection between businesses and customers has persisted. In this manner, customers establish a singular connection with the business primarily through face-to-face interactions, such as visiting a physical store, bank branch, insurance office, and similar establishments (Mehdiabadi, et al., 2020).

11.3.2.5.2 Multichannel

In this manner, enterprises possess the ability to engage in various modes or channels of communication with their clientele. However, it is important to note that each of these channels operates autonomously and is not interconnected with the others. The proliferation of electronic devices, including phones, mobile phones, and computers, has significantly facilitated the expansion of communication methods. In the contemporary business landscape, the multichannel approach is widely adopted by most organizations to engage with their clientele. The introduction of various technological systems, such as ATMs, telephone banks, internet banking, and mobile banking, has significantly transformed the way customers interact with banks and financial institutions. This has resulted in a multichannel approach to customer–bank relationships (Mehdiabadi, Tabatabeinasab, Spulbar, Karbassi Yazdi, & Birau, 2020).

11.3.2.5.3 Cross-Channel

This represents an advanced level of multichannel communication. According to the multichannel method, each communication port operates independently from the other ports. Consequently, a single client is perceived as a distinct and separate entity within each port. In contrast, the cross-channel approach entails the establishment of a singular identity for each customer, which is universally recognized across all ports. It is important to acknowledge that within the cross-channel method, communication ports remain autonomous from one another (Mehdiabadi, Tabatabeinasab, Spulbar, Karbassi Yazdi, & Birau, 2020).

11.3.2.5.4 Omnichannel

In this particular scenario, the customer maintains a consistent identity across all ports, thereby establishing a sense of uniformity and cohesion within the system. The omnichannel (OC) style facilitates customer communication in a seamless manner, allowing for accessibility at any time, from any location, across all devices. The customer and their activities play a central role in the provision of services to them. Consequently, the provision of service to individual customers is tailored to their specific needs and preferences, taking into account their engagement with various ports. Consequently, the system not only addresses the explicit requests of the customers but also takes into consideration their interests and underlying needs (Mehdiabadi, Tabatabeinasab, Spulbar, Karbassi Yazdi, & Birau, 2020).

The primary distinction between multichannel and OC lies in the prioritization of the brand within the strategic framework, wherein multichannel places the brand at the core and ensures consistent messaging across all communication channels.

Nevertheless, the OC approach prioritizes the customer channel as the focal point of the overall strategy. The manner in which the message is transmitted to the customer is altered, thereby aligning it with the customer's preferred mode of communication across various channels. This will be the hallmark of how banks of the future engage with customers of the future.

11.3.2.6 *Transitioning from Physical Banking to Branch-less Banking (BLB) and Open Banking (OB)*

It is not enough to generate new sources of income, as saving on costs is also important. In this case, BLB will surely help.

To enhance customer service, a viable approach is to allocate resources toward the specialized training and development of branch staff, while also implementing cost-cutting measures. This strategy offers a convenient and economically efficient means of achieving the desired outcome.

The transformation of BLB necessitates both internal and external modifications within bank branches in order to redefine the traditional role of physical branches. To achieve this, it is imperative to adopt contemporary technology and leverage various payment tools such as the internet, telephony, mobile devices, ATMs, point-of-sale systems, and virtual teller machines (VTMs) (Dzombo, Kilika, & Maingi, 2017).

BLB refers to the provision of financial services through non-traditional bank channels, wherein retail agents or other intermediaries act as the primary interface with customers. This approach relies on the utilization of technologies such as card-reading point-of-sale (POS) terminals and mobile phones to facilitate the transmission of transaction information (CGAP, 2011).

BLB has made a substantial impact on financial inclusion in developing nations, as evidenced by its early experiences. A significant competitive strategy employed by numerous financial service providers involves engaging in collaborations and forming partnerships with businesses that possess a considerable local retail presence. This particular form of banking is employed as a distribution channel strategy in order to offer financial services. BLB provides customers with the opportunity to achieve cost reduction by offering instant access. The implementation of this banking model within organizations effectively mitigates the expenses linked to the execution of low-volume transactions as well as the costs associated with maintaining a physical presence. Currently, there exist two primary advantages associated with contemporary banking practises. First, there is the ability to diversify services and effectively adapt to the ever-changing demands of the market. Second, there is the capacity to promptly address the needs that arise as a result of market dynamics (Deloitte, 2012).

One example is the banking sector in India. In the context of South Africa, the utilization of BLB facilitated by micro-agents is exclusively authorized for financial institutions that have obtained official approval. Amalgamated Banks of South Africa Limited (ABSA) and Medium Term Note (MTN) banks can be regarded as exemplars of this particular banking model. In the Philippines, mobile telecommunications operators and smartphones have been providing BlackBerry services since 2000. Safaricom, a telecommunications company based in Kenya, operates as a fully owned subsidiary of Vodafone and is recognized as an innovative industry player. The company provides its customers with access to M-Pesa accounts, which enable them to deposit or withdraw funds in a manner akin to mobile electronic money transactions.

GoBank, launched exclusively for American customers, serves as a notable and pragmatic illustration of offshore banking (GoBank, 2016). GoBank is a bona fide financial institution that operates exclusively through mobile platforms.

There exist five significant reasons that lure customers toward this type of banking: quick inventory checking, online check-in, money transfer, extensive ATM network, and security (Mehdiabadi, Tabatabeinasab, Spulbar, Karbassi Yazdi, & Birau, 2020).

11.3.2.7 Successfully Integrating Completely Novel Concepts Such as Interest-free Lending, Cryptocurrencies, and Crowdfunding into Daily Operations

Fintech and resultant disruptions have left traditional bankers wondering about the scope of banking. Hitherto unheard-of concepts such as "Islamic banking" or "crowdfunding" and new age assets such as "cryptocurrencies" and "non-fungible token" (NFT).

However, if banks want to ensure that in the future they are not chasing the disruptions and scrambling to adapt to them in time, then they have to become comfortable with these concepts and asset classes. The new age customers are getting interested in interest-free lending and will surely demand such products in the future. The younger generation is already considerably comfortable investing in cryptocurrencies (Auer, Farag, Lewrick, Orazem, & Zoss, 2023) and will surely expect bankers and wealth managers to cater to their investment and speculation-induced activities through new financial instruments such as hedge funds, exchange traded funds, etc.

The banks of the future will have to be ready to cater to these needs before they come to the forefront.

11.3.2.8 Ensuring Data Integrity and Cybersecurity for All Stakeholders

Banks have already tasted the effects of cybersecurity and data-integrity-related attacks in the past. However, with progress toward Banking 5.0, in which banks will find themselves in a position to have access to a large amount of data, this issue becomes paramount.

The significance of cybersecurity in the context of the Fourth Industrial Revolution is substantial due to the pervasive nature of cyber-threats, which pose a risk to all types of organizations. One notable threat that has emerged in recent years is the Stuxnet malware. The proliferation of malware has posed a significant risk to the operational integrity of nuclear power plants through the deliberate manipulation of centrifuge speed, resulting in detrimental consequences. Undoubtedly, the Fourth Industrial Revolution presents a formidable challenge in terms of cybersecurity and privacy for both organizations and individuals (Thames & Schaefer, 2017).

11.3.2.9 Dealing with Costly Legacy Systems

All existing banks have their fair share of legacy systems. The term "legacy systems" pertains to pre-existing information systems that were implemented in the past and are currently operating essential business processes within an enterprise's present IT architecture. Due to their crucial function, legacy systems are regarded as the cornerstone of a company's operational profitability, thus holding substantial business value for the organization. Hence, IT architects have duly recognized the significance of leveraging the potential of these pre-existing assets in the implementation of service-oriented architecture. Consequently, they have undertaken extensive research on various approaches and considerations for seamlessly transitioning legacy investments into the new architectural framework, thereby capitalizing on their inherent business value. Nevertheless, the successful migration of legacy systems into service-oriented architecture (SOA) has not been universally achieved in all instances. The degree of success in integrating legacy systems into a company's new SOA is contingent upon various factors that differ across different legacy infrastructures and sets of business processes. The transformation of existing legacy assets does not have a quick solution, emphasizing the importance of carefully considering the relevant factors for achieving successful legacy system migration in a particular company (Galinium & Shahbaz, 2009).

The inquiry arises regarding the determinants of success that contribute to the effective transition from legacy systems to SOA. The factors encompassed in this context comprise the potential for migration of legacy systems, the strategy employed for migration, the governance of SOA, the business processes of the organization, budgetary considerations and resource allocation, the architecture of legacy systems, diligent monitoring practises, reliance on commercial products, information architecture, testing procedures, and the technical proficiency of personnel (Galinium & Shahbaz, 2009).

11.4 Conclusion

This chapter raises the question of whether banks should limit themselves to integrating with Industry 4.0 or if they should adopt a proactive approach and consider future developments that are rapidly approaching. The chapter elucidates the numerous challenges that conventional banks must confront in order to attain a state in which disruptions are compelled to keep pace with them rather than vice versa. It becomes evident that attaining this highly desired objective necessitates adopting a shift in mindset and directing one's focus toward the forthcoming challenges and opportunities. It has been observed that banks are required to implement new strategies in order to effectively address their customers, employees, and leadership. This chapter examined the demographic and attitudinal shifts that a bank must consider when formulating its strategic plans to effectively navigate the existing challenges as well as to attract and retain future talent. Additionally, it was observed that the development of novel financial concepts and asset classes will persist, requiring the introduction of new financial instruments to effectively attract prospective customers. Furthermore, the adoption of an OC approach to customer engagement is anticipated to enhance the profitability of customer acquisition and retention. In order to effectively capitalize on the vast opportunities and effectively mitigate potential risks, stakeholders within the financial sector must maintain a proactive and adaptable approach as the new landscape of banking continues to evolve.

References

Asadi, S., Nilashi, M., Husin, A. R., & Yadegaridehkordi, E. (2017). Customers perspectives on adoption of cloud computing in banking sector. *Information Technology Management, 18*(4), 305–330.

Aslam, F., Aimin, W., Li, M., & Ur Rehman, K. (2020). Innovation in the era of IoT and Industry 5.0: Absolute Innovation Management (AIM) framework. *Information, 11*(2), 124. https://doi.org/10.3390/info11020124

Auer, R., Farag, M., Lewrick, U., Orazem, L., & Zoss, M. (2023). Banking in the shadow of Bitcoin? The institutional adoption of cryptocurrencies.

Awadallah, N. (2016). Usage of cloud computing in banking system. *IJCSI International Journal of Computer Science Issues, 13*(1), 49–52.

Aymerich, F. M., Fenu, G., & Surcis, S. (2008). An approach to a cloud computing network. *First International Conference on the Applications of Digital Information and Web Technologies.* ICADIWT.

Azmi, S., Akhtar, S., & Nadeem, M. (2020). Impact of digitalisation on bank performance: A study of Indian Banks. *Test Engineering and Management,* 23678–23691.

Baldwin, R., & Forslid, R. (2020). *Globotics and Development: When Manufacturing Is Jobless and Services Are Tradable.* National Bureau of Economic Research.

Bassett, G. (2018). *How Insurers Can Appeal to Millennials in 2018.* Retrieved from Insurance Business. https://www.insurancebusinessmag.com/au/news/break ing-news/how-insurers-can-appeal-to-millennials-in-2018-86282.aspx

Breque, M., De Nul, L., & Petridis, A. (2021). *Industry 5.0: Towards a Sustainable, Human-Centric and Resilient European Industry.* Publications Office of European Commission.

Brettel, M., Friederichsen, N., Keller, M., & Rosenberg, M. (2014). How virtualization, decentralization and network building change the manufacturing landscape. *International Journal of Information and Communication Engineering,* 8(1), 37–44.

CGAP. (2011). *CGAP 2011 Bank Agents: Risk Management, Mitigation, and Supervision.* Retrieved from https://www.cgap.org/

Chowdhury, M. U., Suchana, K., Alam, S. M. E., & Khan, M. M. (2021). Blockchain application in banking system. *Journal of Software Engineering and Applications* 14(7), 298–311.

Deloitte. (2012). *Are We Headed towards Branchless Banking?* Retrieved from Deloitte.

Deshpande, R. S. (2020). A study of adoption of artificial intelligence in banking sector. *UGC Care Journal, 31*(13), 61–67.

Donepudi, P. K. (2017). Machine learning and artificial intelligence in banking. *Engineering International, 5*(2), 83–86.

Dzombo, G. K., Kilika, J. M., & Maingi, J. (2017). The effect of branchless banking strategy on the financial performance of commercial banks in Kenya. *International Journal of Financial Research, 8*(4), 167–183.

Fueled. (2017). *How Blockchain Is Solving the Finance Industry's Biggest Problems?* Retrieved from Fueled .co m. https://fueled .com /blog /how-blockchain-is-solving-the-finance-industrys-biggest-prob-lems/?fbclid=IwAR1rmdXdLKdKffm-Myu9jT1yKQ OavXwwnVtq4KDXlHpz8tVXrlvdRd1OgEAA

Galinium, M., & Shahbaz, N. (2009). *Factors Affecting Success in Migration of Legacy Systems to Service-Oriented Architecture (SOA).* School of Economic and Management, Lund University.

Gianderico, P., & Di Gilio, A. (2018, March 28). *National Focus MECSPE Observatory.* Retrieved from MECSPE. http://www.mecspe.com/en/comunicati -stampa-en/osservatorio-mecspe-focus-nazionale/

GoBank. (2016). Green dot's Gobank opens its us-only branchless mobile bank to the public, available today. *Green Dot's GoBank Opens Its US-Only Branchless Mobile Bank to the Public, Available Today.* thenextweb.com

Heng, S., Hörster, A. K., Karollus, A., Slomka, L., AG, D. B., & Hoffmann, R. (2015). *Augmented Reality.* Publication of the German Original.

Hermann, M., Pentek, T., & Otto, B. (2016). Design principles for Industry 4.0 scenarios. *49th Hawaii International Conference on System Sciences (HICSS)* (pp. 3928–3937). Koloa, HI.

Jiang, J., & Yang, D. (2011). A research on commercial bank information systems based on cloud computing. *3rd International Conference on Communication Software and Networks* (pp. 363–399). IEEE.

Kagermann, H. (2015). Change through digitization—Value creation in the age of industry 4.0. In *Management of Permanent Change*, 23–45, Wiesbaden: Springer Fachmedien Wiesbaden.

Kaya, O., Schildbach, J., AG, D. B., & Schneider, S. (2019). Artificial intelligence in banking. *Artificial Intelligence.*

King, B. (2018). *Bank 4.0: Banking Everywhere, Never at a Bank.* John Wiley & Sons.

Krivkovich, A., White, O., Townsend, Z., & Euart, J. (2020). How US customers' attitudes to fintech are shifting during the pandemic. McKinsey Paper.

Lu, L. (2018). How a little ant challenges giant banks? The rise of ant financial (Alipay)'s fintech empire and relevant regulatory concerns. *International Company and Commercial Law Review*, 0958-5214.

Maddikunta, P. K. R., Pham, Q. V., Prabadevi, B., Deepa, N., Dev, K., Gadekallu, T. R., ... & Liyanage, M. (2021). Industry 5.0: A survey on enabling technologies and potential applications. *Journal of Industrial Information Integration*, 26, 100257.

Malini, A., & Menon, D. G. (2017). Technological innovations in the banking sector in India: An analysis. *International Conference on Technological Advancements in Power and Energy (TAP Energy)* (pp. 1–5). IEEE.

Mehdiabadi, A., Shahabi, V., Shamsinejad, S., Amiri, M., Spulbar, C., & Birau, R. (2022). Investigating Industry 5.0 and its impact on the banking industry: Requirements, approaches and communications. *Applied Sciences*, *12*(10), 5126.

Mehdiabadi, A., Tabatabeinasab, M., Spulbar, C., Karbassi Yazdi, A., & Birau, R. (2020). Are we ready for the challenge of banks 4.0? Designing a roadmap for banking systems in Industry 4.0. *International Journal of Financial Studies*, *8*(2), 32.

Metcalfe, W. (2020). Ethereum, smart contracts, DApps. In W. Metcalfe (Ed.), *Blockchain and Crypt Currency*, 77, 77–93.

More, R., & Moily, Y. (2021). Big data analysis in banking sector. *International Journal of Engineering Research and Applications*, *11*(4), 1–5.

Motienko, A. (2020). Integration of information and communication system for public health data collection and intelligent transportation. *Transportation Research Procedia*, *50*, 466–472.

Muaz, A., Jayabalan, M., & Thiruchelvam, V. (2020). A comparison of data sampling techniques for credit card fraud detection. *International Journal of Advanced Computer Science and Applications*, *11*(6).

Nair, V. M., & Menon, D. G. (2017). Fin Tech firms-A new challenge to traditional banks: A review. *International Journal of Applied Business and Economic Research*, *15*, 173–184.

Nethravathi, R., Sathyanarayana, P., Vidya Bai, G., Spulbar, C., Suhan, M., Birau, R., ... Ejaz, A. (2020). Business intelligence appraisal based on customer behaviour profile by using hobby based opinion mining in India: A case study *Economic Research-Ekonomska istraživanja*, *33*(1), 1889–1908.

Nicoletti, B. (2017). *Agile Insurance. Volume I: Adding Value with Lean Processes.* Springer International Publishing.

Nicoletti, B. (2021). *Banking 5.0 How Fintech Will Change Traditional Banks in the 'New Normal' Post Pandemic.* Palgrave Studies in Financial Services Technology.

Nobanee, H., Dilshad, M. N., Al Dhanhani, M., Al Neyadi, M., Al Qubaisi, S., & Al Shamsi, S. (2021). Big data applications the banking sector: A bibliometric analysis approach. *Sage Open, 11*(4), 21582440211067234.

Normann, R., & Ramirez, R. (1993). From value chain to value constellation:Designing interactive strategy. *Harvard Business Review, 71*(4), 65–77.

Perera, C., Liu, C. H., Jayawardena, S., & Chen, M. (2014). A survey on internet of things from industrial market perspective. *IEEE Access, 2*, 1660–1679.

Petracek, N. (2018). *Is Blockchain the Way to Save IoT?* Retrieved from FORBES [Online]. https://www.forbes.com/sites/forbestechcouncil/2018/07/18/is-block-chain-the-way-to-save-iot/#65d086d25a74.

Rana, D. M., & Ji, M. L. (2023). The role and potential applications of cloud computing in the banking industry. *15th International Conference on Developments in eSystems Engineering (DeSE)* (pp. 293–298). IEEE.

Rao, S., Pan, Y., He, J., & Shangguan, X. (2022). Digital finance and corporate green innovation: Quantity or quality?. *Environmental Science and Pollution Research, 29*(37), 56772–56791.

Rose, J. T. (1993). Commercial banks as financial intermediaries and current trends in banking: A pedagogical framework. *Financial Practice and Education, 3*, 113–118.

Rundle, E. (2017). The 5th industrial revolution: When it will happen and how. *The 5th Industrial Revolution: When It Will Happen and How*. Published on, 27, 2017.

Sachs, G. (2015). *The Asian Consumer: Chinese Millennials*. Goldman Sachs.

Saravanan, K., & Lakshmi, K. M. (2016). A study on banking services of new generation banking in the Indian banking sector. *Purakala*, 31, 552–61.

Shelzer, R. (2017). *What Is Industry 5.0 and How Will It Affect Manufacturers?* Retrieved from https://blog.gesrepair.com/industry-5-0-will-affect -manufacturers/

Shivdas, A., & Chandrasekhar, J. (2016). Sustainability through frugal innovations: An application of Indian spiritual wisdom. *Prabandhan: Indian Journal of Management, 9*(5), 7–23.

Shook, E., Knickrehm, M., Mcintyre, A., Woolf, A., Browne, Y., & Lavelle, K. (2022). *Realizing the Full Value of AI*. Accenture.

Soomro, Z. A., Ali, Q., & Parveen, S. (2022). Diffusion of Industry 5.0 in the financial sector: A developmental study. *Proceedings of the BAM*.

Srivastava, U., & Gopalkrishnan, S. (2015). Impact of big data analytics on banking sector: Learning for Indian banks. *Procedia Computer Science, 50*, 643–652.

Sundmaeker, H., Guillemin, P., Friess, P., & Woelfflé, S. (2010). Vision and challenges for realising the Internet of Things. *Cluster of European Research Projects on the Internet of Things, European Commission, 3*(3), 34–36.

Thames, L., & Schaefer, D. (2017). Industry 4.0: An overview of key benefits, technologies, and challenges. *Cybersecurity for Industry 4.0: Analysis for Design and Manufacturing*, 1–33.

Xu, X., Lu, Y., Vogel-Heuser, B., & Wang, L. (2021). Industry 4.0 and Industry 5.0—Inception, conception and perception. *Journal of Manufacturing Systems, 61*, 530–535.

Zambon, I., Cecchini, M., Egidi, G., Saporito, M. G., & Colantoni, A. (2019). Revolution 4.0: Industry vs. agriculture in a future development for SMEs. *Processes, 7*(1), 36.

Chapter 12

Role of Cryptocurrency in Fintech: Hope and Hype

Somnath Roy and Chandan Dasgupta

12.1 Introduction

The phenomenon of cryptocurrency started with a white paper published October 31, 2008, that envisioned a peer-to-peer (P2P) electronic cash system, demonstrating the challenge of decentralizing digital currencies for central banks. The technology that powered the new age application was called blockchain (Ammous, 2018).

Cryptocurrencies or digital currencies can be thought of as alternatives to traditional paper money issued by governments. As well as protecting transactions from fraud, cryptography also controls the amount of digital currency in circulation and prevents users from reusing existing balances (avoidance of double spending). Due to the decentralization of some cryptocurrencies, it is possible to conduct almost anonymous transactions, making it difficult for governments to regulate them. Furthermore, cryptocurrencies can be easily used across international borders because they are in electronic form (Hughes et al., 2019; Luther, 2016).

Various applications of cryptocurrency exist, including online payments, remittances, P2P lending, crowdfunding, and more. Cryptocurrencies are also being invested in by some people in the hope that their value will increase over time. Each cryptocurrency has its own features and functions, and there are thousands of them available. Dogecoin, Ethereum, Litecoin, Ripple, and Bitcoin are among the most popular (Rosati & Čuk, 2019).

 DOI: 10.4324/9781032644165-12

By 2023, cryptocurrency revenue is expected to reach 37.87 billion US dollars. In 2027, the projected total revenue amount of 64.87 billion US dollars is expected to reflect a compound annual growth rate (CAGR) of 14.40%. In 2023, the cryptocurrencies market is expected to generate an average of 56.19 US dollars per user. Throughout the world, the United States will generate the highest revenues in 2023 (17,960.00 million US dollars). It is anticipated that 994.30 million users will be involved in the cryptocurrency market by 2027. A user penetration rate of 8.8% is expected in 2023, rising to 12.5% by 2027 (Statista, 2023).

A digital ledger paired with strong cryptography secures cryptocurrency transactions online. In blockchain technology, individual transactions are recorded across decentralized computers without a central authority via a distributed ledger system. Blockchain technology is at the heart of cryptocurrency networks (Statista, 2023).

Globally, the valuation of the blockchain technology market stood at 5.85 billion US dollars (2021), and it is expected to grow at an annualized CAGR of 82.8% in the period 2022–2030. Due to blockchain technology's inherent advantages, such as less infrastructure costs for reconciling accounts, managing information, and making payments, organizations are increasingly adopting it. Furthermore, it promotes efficiency in operations by eliminating the role of an intermediary. The rising end-use applications of blockchain technology in conjunction with increasing awareness of its benefits should increase the market growth for blockchain technology (Polaris, 2022).

Cryptocurrencies have attracted attention from various sectors, such as finance, technology, media, and social movements. Cryptocurrencies provide multiple benefits. Fast, cost-effective, global transaction processing without intermediaries and associated fees can be made possible through cryptocurrencies. They also provide privacy and anonymity for users, as transactions do not require personal information or identification. People who are discriminated against or censored in society are empowered with the ability to participate in the financial system through cryptocurrency. Blockchain-based applications and platforms foster innovation and creativity (Hughes et al., 2019; Jaoude & Saade, 2019; Ozili, 2022; Rejeb et al., 2021).

In addition to their many benefits, cryptocurrencies also present a number of challenges and risks. As their prices can fluctuate significantly due to market forces, speculation, or external events, they have a major drawback of being volatile and unpredictable. Because users are responsible for securing their own funds and private keys, cryptocurrency is also vulnerable to cyberattacks, hacking, fraud, theft, or loss. Moreover, different countries

have different laws and policies regarding cryptocurrencies and their taxation, which leads to regulatory uncertainty and legal disputes. Several
cryptocurrencies also pose environmental and social concerns due to
their high energy and resource consumption in order to operate their networks and generate new coins (Ashta, 2021; Harrast et al., 2022; Tarr, 2018;
Voskobojnikov et al., 2020).

12.2 Cryptocurrencies: Benefits and Positive Aspects

Through their technological underpinnings – blockchain and cryptography – cryptocurrencies implement a decentralized, high-availability, persistent, consistent, transparent, anonymous, auditable, secure, efficient,
accountable, and inclusive system of value exchange that can be leveraged
in different domains beyond digital currency and financial services to the
Internet of Things (IoT), sharing economic, public, and social services that
cover abstract entities such as reputation, thereby offering many benefits
for its users (Azmi & Akhtar, 2023; Jafar et al., 2023; Li et al., 2018; Wajid et
al., 2022).

Unlike traditional financial systems, cryptocurrencies are decentralized applications. Decentralization is not a binary concept but a spectrum. Different cryptocurrencies have different degrees of decentralization,
depending on various factors such as the number and distribution of nodes,
the consensus mechanism, the governance model, and the ownership structure. Decentralization implies that there is no controlling authority at a
central level, such as a bank or a government, that regulates the transactions
on the network. Instead, transactions are validated and confirmed by a distributed network of participants (nodes) who maintain a shared ledger called
the blockchain. By removing the need for intermediaries, decentralization
legitimizes more power to the users to have sway over their own money
and financial decisions. Users can transact directly with each other in a P2P
fashion, without having to pay fees or wait for approvals from any authority. They can also vote on proposals pertaining to the rules associated with
the cryptocurrency or contributing to its code, thereby participating in the
governance and development of the network (Bitsgap, 2023; Jefferson, 2023;
StormGain, 2023).

Cryptocurrencies depend on cryptography and consensus algorithms to
ensure a collaborative working toward goals, thereby overcoming censorship
and corruption. The network cannot be controlled (manipulated to perform

in a specific manner) or shut down by a single powerful entity, as being a decentralized system, it would require the majority of the participant nodes to agree. This implies that the cryptocurrency application can continue to operate even when some of the participating nodes are out of circulation (Bitsgap, 2023; StormGain, 2023).

Cryptocurrencies are known for their transparency. They host their entire transaction repository (since inception) on their blockchains that is accessible to anyone for viewing and verifying the transactions, thereby having the ability to work out the balances of the network participants. The transaction repository is continuously updated and synchronized between all nodes participating in the operations of the cryptocurrency in real time. The blockchain ensures the validity and authenticity of transactions and also prevents them from being modified in any way after they have been confirmed (immutability) by using cryptographic mechanisms, leading to several advantages. The system renders itself open to audits at the individual node level (preventing the possibility of collusion amongst nodes) to check for errors or fraudulent transactions, tracking the flow of funds, and validating the authenticity of transactions. This enables users to avoid scams, disputes, and resultant losses and establishes accountability for parties that attempt to manipulate the system. The strength of cryptographic primitives results in the absence of corruption or interference by any minority parties and ensures that it can operate in a trustless environment (nodes need not know each other, in a modern-day replication of the Byzantine General's Problem). By using the network of their own accord and efforts, users can control the application and verify its transactions without the involvement of third parties such as banks, governments, or large corporations. As an added benefit, users get more control and choice over their finances, as they can choose how to use their funds and who to transact with (Hasan & Salah, 2018; Nadeem et al., 2021; Nawari & Ravindran, 2019; Nguyen, 2016; Pal et al., 2021).

The security of cryptocurrencies is rooted in multiple factors, such as cryptographic algorithms, consensus mechanisms, network protocols, and user behaviour. Cryptocurrencies also require their users to be vigilant and responsible for their own funds and transactions. The anonymity and pseudonymity associated with cryptocurrencies also adds to their security. While transactions are transparent and can be observed on the blockchain, the identities of the participants remain private. This protects users from privacy breaches, reducing the risk of identity theft (Ali et al., 2019; Fernández-Caramés & Fraga-Lamas, 2018; Xiao et al., 2020; Yli-Huumo et al., 2016; Zhang et al., 2019).

Cryptocurrency usage leads to an efficiency improvement in the financial services sector (performing the intended function with minimal waste of resources) in various ways. They can facilitate cost-effective and faster money transfers, especially across borders, without intermediaries or fees. Cryptocurrencies can also enable micropayments and P2P lending, which can increase financial inclusivity and access for underserved and unserved populations. Cryptocurrencies also provide a clear and immutable record of all transactions on a distributed ledger, which can be certified by anyone on the network. This prevents corruption, fraud, or manipulation of the data as well as improve confidence among the participants (Apopo & Phiri, 2021; Frankenfield, 2023; López-Martín et al., 2021; Perkins, 2020; Yu et al., 2022).

12.3 Cryptocurrencies: Ethical and Social Implications

While cryptocurrencies have the capability to transform the world of money and finance, they also have various ethical and social implications that need to be considered.

Cryptocurrency design fundamentals allow for a variety of cryptocurrencies to coexist and flourish, each with its own unique feature sets and use cases. Users can choose to join the cryptocurrency ecosystem that best suits their needs, ideals, and preferences. This facility encourages experimentation and creativity, as anyone can build applications or services on top of an existing non-proprietary cryptocurrency network without needing any permission or approval from any central authority, as is usually the case with standard applications (Bitsgap, 2023).

Cryptocurrency enables financial inclusion and empowers the underserved and unserved populace. This is equally effective for those who face discrimination or censorship in society. These otherwise marginalized sections of the society can utilize the privacy and anonymity of cryptocurrencies to engage in financial transactions, safe in the knowledge that their identities will not be revealed. Cryptocurrencies can also be used in the opposite manner to violate human rights, with the same anonymity protecting those who are engaged in financing terrorism, organized crimes, or wars. Because the end users are solely responsible for managing their own funds and private keys, cryptocurrencies can also expose them to cyberattacks, hacking, fraud, theft, or loss (Al-Shdaifat, 2023; Anthony, 2022; Chow et al., 2021).

Cryptocurrencies encourage democracy and decentralization, as they operate on networks that are outside the sphere of control of any central intermediary or authority. They can also enable participatory governance and voting mechanisms through smart contracts or decentralized autonomous organizations (DAOs). Cryptocurrencies can also do the opposite – undermine democracy and accountability – as they can be used to elude taxes, regulations, or sanctions. They can also create power imbalances and conflicts among different stakeholders, such as miners, developers, users, or regulators (Berg, 2017; Bhimani et al., 2022; Calhoun, 2022; Garrett, 2004; Johnson, 2022; Kousser & McCubbins, 2004; Shapiro, 2018; Torregrosa & Fontrodona, 2022).

Cryptocurrencies, in their permissionless forms, can foster equality and diversity, as they can be accessed by anyone with an internet connectivity through a regular device. They also reduce socio-economic inequalities, as they can offer more opportunities and innovation for people in developing countries or marginalized communities. However, the required digital literacy and resources that are not equally distributed, also amongst genders, can also exacerbate inequality and exclusion. Wealth disparities and concentration can also be linked to cryptocurrencies, as they are subject to high volatility and speculation (Boateng, 2023; Chohan, 2021; De Jong, 2022; McKay & Peters, 2018; Stoker, 2023). Cryptocurrencies can be associated with a positive environmental impact, as they can enable green initiatives and solutions, such as carbon credits, renewable energy sources, or environmental conservation. They can also reduce the environmental footprint of the traditional financial system, which tend to rely on non-digital means. However, cryptocurrencies driven by proof-of-work blockchains can also have an adverse effect on the environment, as they tend to consume a lot of energy and resources to operate their networks and mine new coins. This can contribute to global warming and climate change (Egiyi & Ofoegbu, 2020; Mohsin, 2021; Wang et al., 2022; Wendl et al., 2023).

12.4 Cryptocurrencies: Issues and Challenges

The prices of cryptocurrencies tend to fluctuate dramatically in a short period of time due to their volatility. While creating opportunities and risks in equal measure for the investing community, this also causes challenges and uncertainties for the crypto industry and society at large.

Cryptocurrency prices and its supply and demand are influenced by a variety of factors. Market sentiment, speculation, innovation, adoption, regulation, or external events can, in some way, contribute to the fluctuations. Cryptocurrencies are also subject to non-standardized (widely differing) regulation and legal issues, as different countries deal with cryptocurrencies differently, having different laws and policies regarding their status, taxation, or usage. Regulation has the ability to create uncertainty or generate clarity for the market participants and can, therefore, affect the prices of cryptocurrencies and their volatility (Lapin, 2021; Palomo, 2022; Statista, 2022).

Cryptocurrencies face issues around the scalability of their operations that can affect their usability and adoption. Their basic design elements – the cryptographic algorithms, the consensus mechanisms, the network protocols – apart from the user behaviour, are the key factors that determine the speed, capacity, and cost of transactions for a cryptocurrency. Decentralization, security, and scalability are the three main outcomes that cryptocurrencies aim to achieve, but those often conflict with each other. For instance, increasing the size of a block or reducing the time taken to mine a block (in the blockchain) can improve the scalability, but it can also reduce the extent of decentralization and, thereby, the security, as it can lead to more centralization of power among large miners or nodes or more vulnerability to attacks or possibility of forks. Scalability issues can be attempted to be solved by Layer 1 solutions that modify the base layer of the blockchain, such as changing the consensus mechanism, increasing the block size or frequency, or using sharding or sidechains. Layer 2 solutions that build atop the underlying base layer of the blockchain can also be considered, such as using payment channels or state channels (CryptoCompare, 2018; Gondek, 2022; Khan et al., 2021; Zhou et al., 2020).

Cryptocurrencies are facing an uncertain regulatory environment with the different country jurisdictions grappling with how to best control the fast-paced and dynamic nature of the cryptocurrency ecosystem. Regulation can stifle the blossoming of the crypto industry in terms of its spread and development, as it can impose excessive restrictions or requirements on the creation and operation of cryptocurrencies and their platforms. Regulation can also discourage new entrants and investors from joining the crypto space, as it can increase the costs and risks of doing business. Regulation can also hamper the adoption and usage of cryptocurrencies, as it can limit their accessibility and functionality for the users. Regulation can undermine the core principles and values of cryptocurrencies, such as decentralization, security, and privacy (Hancock, 2021; Newbery, 2021; Reiff, 2023; Silva & Mira da Silva, 2022).

Cryptocurrencies also have an adverse environmental impact, as they consume a lot of energy and resources to operate their networks and generate new coins. They produce a large amount of electronic waste, as they require constant upgrading and replacing of the hardware and equipment used for their mining and transaction processes. This needs to be addressed and reduced (Bandera, 2022; Bogna, 2022; Reiff, 2022; Whitt, 2019).

12.5 Cryptocurrencies: Future Prospects

Cryptocurrency has exhibited the capacity to transform and innovate the world of money and finance, but it also faces many challenges and uncertainties that could affect its development and adoption in the near and long term. In the best-case future scenario, cryptocurrency becomes widely accepted and adopted as a mainstream form of payment, investment, and value transfer. Cryptocurrency benefits from technological innovation, market demand, public perception, and government support. Technological innovation enables more scalability, security, and functionality for cryptocurrency and its platforms. Market demand increases as more users, businesses, and institutions adopt cryptocurrency for various purposes and use cases. In this context, public perception improves with more people becoming aware of the benefits and advantages of cryptocurrency over traditional fiat currencies. Government support facilitates the regulation and integration of cryptocurrency into the legal and financial systems as well as the promotion of innovation and healthy competition in the crypto industry.

In a scenario that would describe other extremes, cryptocurrencies would become isolated as a societal ill and rejected as a fringe activity, representing illicit forms of money, akin to other vices such as gambling. Cryptocurrency, in that context, would suffer from technological stagnation, market decline, public distrust, and adverse government intervention. Market decline occurs as fewer users, businesses, and institutions adopt or use cryptocurrency for reasons such as volatility, complexity, or risk. Public distrust worsens as more people become sceptical or hostile toward cryptocurrency due to misinformation, fraud, or associated crimes. Government intervention restricts or bans the use of cryptocurrency in the legal and financial systems as well as leads to the suppression of innovation and competition in the crypto industry.

In a realistic, more middle ground, scenario, cryptocurrency coexists and competes with traditional currencies as a viable and credible alternative or complementary form of money. Cryptocurrency experiences a mix of technological progress, market fluctuation, public awareness, and government regulation. Technological progress enables some improvements and innovations for cryptocurrency and its platforms but also surfaces some challenges and limitations. Market fluctuation occurs as the demand and supply of cryptocurrency vary depending on various factors, such as sentiment, speculation, adoption, or regulation. Public awareness increases as more people become familiar with the concept and potential of cryptocurrency as well as some concerns and issues. Government regulation varies depending on the country and the policy stance toward cryptocurrency, ranging from supportive to restrictive to neutral (Barone, 2019; Bylund, 2023; CoinTree, 2022; Disparte, 2023).

Therefore, the future of cryptocurrency is uncertain and unpredictable, as it depends on many factors that could influence its growth or decline in the near and long term.

12.6 Conclusion

For all their shortcomings, it is unlikely that cryptocurrencies will disappear anytime soon. The evolution of the emerging technology that is cryptocurrency holds the key to the future of money that is expected to benefit mankind as a whole. There is no doubt that cryptocurrency users and industry players can assess whether it can help or harm them according to their own ideas, aims, and standpoints. This chapter reviews cryptocurrency's various aspects. A deeper study of several aspects of cryptocurrency is needed, considering the favourable outlook of blockchain technology and the prospects of impending legislation. Blockchain technology and cryptocurrency offer researchers opportunities to benefit from the disruptive technology that can dramatically improve human lives. Cryptocurrency is a fascinating and complex phenomenon that can profoundly transform the world of money and finance. However, it also involves many challenges and uncertainties that require careful research and evaluation before engaging in any activity involving cryptocurrencies.

References

Ali, M. S., Vecchio, M., Pincheira, M., Dolui, K., Antonelli, F., & Rehmani, M. H. (2019). Applications of blockchains in the internet of things: A comprehensive survey. *IEEE Communications Surveys and Tutorials, 21*(2), 1676–1717. Scopus. https://doi.org/10.1109/COMST.2018.2886932

Al-Shdaifat, S. M. (2023). The criminal confrontation of the cryptocurrency (Bitcoin) and its illegal use. *International Journal of Electronic Security and Digital Forensics, 15*(2), 114–123. https://doi.org/10.1504/IJESDF.2023.129280

Ammous, S. (2018). Can cryptocurrencies fulfil the functions of money? *The Quarterly Review of Economics and Finance, 70*, 38–51. https://doi.org/10.1016/j.qref.2018.05.010

Anthony, N. (2022). *How Canada Made the Case for Cryptocurrency, Not CBDCs.* https://policycommons.net/artifacts/2269595/how-canada-made-the-case-for-cryptocurrency-not-cbdcs/3029404/

Apopo, N., & Phiri, A. (2021). On the (in)efficiency of cryptocurrencies: Have they taken daily or weekly random walks? *Heliyon, 7*(4), e06685. https://doi.org/10.1016/j.heliyon.2021.e06685

Ashta, A. (2021). Fintech – Technology in finance: Strategic risks and challenges. In D. Uzunidis, F. Kasmi, & L. Adatto (Eds.), *Innovation Economics, Engineering and Management Handbook 2* (1st ed., pp. 137–143). Wiley. https://doi.org/10.1002/9781119832522.ch15

Azmi, S. N., & Akhtar, S. (2023). Interactions of services export, financial development and growth: Evidence from India. *Quality & Quantity, 57*(5), 4709–4724. https://doi.org/10.1007/s11135-022-01566-8

Bandera, G. (2022, January 27). *The Hidden Costs: Understanding the Environmental Footprint of Crypto Currency.* FairPlanet. https://www.fairplanet.org/story/is-cryptocurrency-bad-for-the-environment/

Barone, A. (2019, June 25). *The Future of Cryptocurrency.* Investopedia. https://www.investopedia.com/articles/forex/091013/future-cryptocurrency.asp

Berg, C. (2017). *Delegation and Unbundling in a Crypto-Democracy* (SSRN Scholarly Paper 3001585). https://doi.org/10.2139/ssrn.3001585

Bhimani, A., Hausken, K., & Arif, S. (2022). Do national development factors affect cryptocurrency adoption? *Technological Forecasting and Social Change, 181*, 121739. https://doi.org/10.1016/j.techfore.2022.121739

Bitsgap. (2023, June 19). *Breaking the Chains: Understanding Crypto Decentralization.* https://bitsgap.com/blog/cryptocurrency-decentralization-explained-what-are-the-pros-and-cons

Boateng, S. L. (2023). Gender disparities in cryptocurrencies: Perspectives from developing and emerging economies. In *Empowering Women in the Digital Economy,* (pp. 119–130). Productivity Press.

Bogna, J. (2022, January 8). *What Is the Environmental Impact of Cryptocurrency?* PCMAG. https://www.pcmag.com/how-to/what-is-the-environmental-impact-of-cryptocurrency

Bylund, A. (2023, September 22). *The Future of Cryptocurrency in 2023 and Beyond*. The Motley Fool. https://www.fool.com/investing/stock-market/market-sectors/financials/cryptocurrency-stocks/future-of-cryptocurrency/

Calhoun, G. (2022, October 11). *The Ethics of Crypto: Good Intentions and Bad Actors*. Forbes. https://www.forbes.com/sites/georgecalhoun/2022/10/11/the-ethics-of-crypto-sorting-out-good-intentions-and-bad-actors/

Chohan, U. W. (2021). Cryptocurrencies and inequality. In *Cryptofinance* (pp. 49–62). World Scientific. https://doi.org/10.1142/9789811239670_0003

Chow, S. S. M., Choo, K.-K. R., & Han, J. (2021). Editorial for accountability and privacy issues in blockchain and cryptocurrency. *Future Generation Computer Systems, 114*, 647–648. https://doi.org/10.1016/j.future.2020.08.039

CoinTree. (2022). *13 Expert Predictions on the Future of Cryptocurrency*. https://www.cointree.com/learn/cryptocurrency-future/

CryptoCompare. (2018, January 21). *Scalability and the Future of Cryptocurrency*. CryptoCompare. https://www.cryptocompare.com/coins/guides/scalability-and-the-future-of-cryptocurrency/

De Jong, J. (2022). *Here be Dragons: Squid Game and Wealth Disparity*. https://digitalcollections.dordt.edu/cgi/viewcontent.cgi?article=1076&context=student_work

Disparte, D. (2023, January 2). *What the Future Holds for Cryptocurrencies*. World Economic Forum. https://www.weforum.org/agenda/2023/01/future-of-cryptocurrencies-davos2023/

Egiyi, M. A., & Ofoegbu, G. N. (2020). Cryptocurrency and climate change: An overview. *International Journal of Mechanical Engineering and Technology (IJMET), 11*(3), 15–22.

Fernández-Caramés, T. M., & Fraga-Lamas, P. (2018). A review on the use of blockchain for the internet of things. *IEEE Access, 6*, 32979–33001. https://doi.org/10.1109/ACCESS.2018.2842685

Frankenfield, J. (2023, August 29). *Cryptocurrency Explained With Pros and Cons for Investment*. Investopedia. https://www.investopedia.com/terms/c/cryptocurrency.asp

Garrett, E. (2004). Crypto-initiatives in hybrid democracy. Southern California Law Review, 78, 985.

Gondek, C. (2022). *10 Main Challenges of Crypto Adoption*. https://originstamp.com/blog/10-main-challenges-of-crypto-adoption/

Hancock, D. (2021, November 16). *Is Regulation Bad For Cryptocurrency?* Benzinga. https://www.benzinga.com/money/is-crypto-regulation-bad

Harrast, S. A., McGilsky, D., & Sun, Y. T. (2022). Determining the inherent risks of cryptocurrency: A survey analysis. *Current Issues in Auditing, 16*(2), A10–A17.

Hasan, H. R., & Salah, K. (2018). Proof of delivery of digital assets using blockchain and smart contracts. *IEEE Access, 6*, 65439–65448. https://doi.org/10.1109/ACCESS.2018.2876971

Hughes, A., Park, A., Kietzmann, J., & Archer-Brown, C. (2019). Beyond bitcoin: What blockchain and distributed ledger technologies mean for firms. *Business Horizons, 62*(3), 273–281. https://doi.org/10.1016/j.bushor.2019.01.002

Jafar, S. H., Akhtar, S., El-Chaarani, H., Khan, P. A., & Binsaddig, R. (2023). Forecasting of NIFTY 50 index price by using backward elimination with an LSTM model. *Journal of Risk and Financial Management, 16*(10), Article 10. https://doi.org/10.3390/jrfm16100423

Jaoude, J. A., & Saade, R. G. (2019). Blockchain applications – Usage in different domains. *IEEE Access, 7,* 45360–45381. https://doi.org/10.1109/ACCESS.2019 .2902501

Jefferson, F. (2023, September 21). What is decentralized in cryptocurrency. *Robots. Net.* https://robots.net/ai/what-is-decentralized-in-cryptocurrency/

Johnson, D. (2022). *Cryptocurrency and Public Policy: Implications for Democracy and Governance.* Taylor & Francis. https://books.google.com/books?hl=en&lr= &id=LGWFEAAAQBAJ&oi=fnd&pg=PT7&dq=cryptocurrency+democracy&ots =inUEVsS3NB&sig=OJwQyZ8tX-fcLFvNJZLUHMLbD4I

Khan, D., Jung, L. T., & Hashmani, M. A. (2021). Systematic literature review of challenges in blockchain scalability. *Applied Sciences, 11*(20), Article 20. https:// doi.org/10.3390/app11209372

Kousser, T., & McCubbins, M. D. (2004). Social choice, crypto-initiatives, and poli-cymaking by direct democracy. *Southern California Law Review, 78,* 949.

Lapin, N. (2021, December 23). Explaining Crypto's Volatility. *Forbes.* https://www .forbes.com/sites/nicolelapin/2021/12/23/explaining-cryptos-volatility/

Li, Q.-L., Ma, J.-Y., & Chang, Y.-X. (2018). Blockchain queue theory. In M. T. Thai, X. Chen, W. W. Li, & A. Sen (Eds.), *Lecture Notes in Computer Science Vol. 11280 LNCS* (pp. 25–40). Springer Verlag; Scopus. https://doi.org/10.1007/978-3-030 -04648-4_3

López-Martín, C., Benito Muela, S., & Arguedas, R. (2021). Efficiency in cryptocur-rency markets: New evidence. *Eurasian Economic Review, 11*(3), 403–431. https://doi.org/10.1007/s40822-021-00182-5

Luther, W. J. (2016). Cryptocurrencies, network effects, and switching costs. *Contemporary Economic Policy, 34*(3), 553–571. https://doi.org/10.1111/coep .12151

McKay, D. R., & Peters, D. A. (2018). Digital gold: A primer on cryptocurrency. *Plastic Surgery, 26*(2), 137.

Mohsin, K. (2021). Cryptocurrency & its impact on environment. *International Journal of Cryptocurrency Research ISSN,* 2790–1386.

Nadeem, M. A., Liu, Z., Pitafi, A. H., Younis, A., & Xu, Y. (2021). Investigating the adoption factors of cryptocurrencies—A case of bitcoin: Empirical evidence from China. *SAGE Open, 11*(1). https://doi.org/10.1177/2158244021998704

Nawari, N. O., & Ravindran, S. (2019). Blockchain and Building Information Modeling (BIM): Review and applications in post-disaster recovery. *Buildings, 9*(6). https://doi.org/10.3390/BUILDINGS9060149

Newbery, E. (2021, October 21). *Do We Need More Crypto Regulation? Two Sides of the Story.* https://www.fool.com/the-ascent/cryptocurrency/articles/do-we-need -more-crypto-regulation-two-sides-of-the-story/

Nguyen, Q. K. (2016). Blockchain-a financial technology for future sustainable development. *Proceedings of International Conference on Green Technology and Sustainable Development, GTSD,* 51–54. https://doi.org/10.1109/GTSD.2016.22

Ozili, P. K. (2022). CBDC, fintech and cryptocurrency for financial inclusion and financial stability. *Digital Policy, Regulation and Governance, 25*(1), 40–57. https://doi.org/10.1108/DPRG-04-2022-0033

Pal, A., Tiwari, C. K., & Behl, A. (2021). Blockchain technology in financial services: A comprehensive review of the literature. *Journal of Global Operations and Strategic Sourcing, 14*(1), 61–80. https://doi.org/10.1108/JGOSS-07-2020-0039

Palomo, K. (2022, August 17). *What Makes the Crypto Currency Market Volatile? 6 Key Reasons.* MUO. https://www.makeuseof.com/what-makes-the-crypto-currency-market-volatile/

Perkins, D. W. (2020). *Cryptocurrency: The Economics of Money and Selected Policy Issues,* (pp. 1–27). Congressional Research Service, 1–27.

Polaris. (2022). *Blockchain Technology Market Size Report, 2022–2030.* Polaris. https://www.polarismarketresearch.com/index.php/industry-analysis/blockchain-technology-market

Reiff, N. (2022, September 28). *What's the Environmental Impact of Cryptocurrency?* Investopedia. https://www.investopedia.com/tech/whats-environmental-impact-cryptocurrency/

Reiff, N. (2023, August 18). *What Are the Legal Risks to Cryptocurrency Investors?* Investopedia. https://www.investopedia.com/tech/what-are-legal-risks-cryptocurrency-investors/

Rejeb, A., Rejeb, K., & Keogh, J. G. (2021). Cryptocurrencies in modern finance: A literature review. *Etikonomi, 20*(1), 93–118.

Rosati, P., & Čuk, T. (2019). Blockchain beyond cryptocurrencies. *Disrupting Finance,* 149.

Shapiro, E. (2018). Point: Foundations of e-democracy. *Communications of the ACM, 61*(8), 31–34. https://doi.org/10.1145/3213766

Silva, E. C., & Mira da Silva, M. (2022). Research contributions and challenges in DLT-based cryptocurrency regulation: A systematic mapping study. *Journal of Banking and Financial Technology, 6*(1), 63–82. https://doi.org/10.1007/s42786-021-00037-2

Statista. (2022, June 7). *The Varying Volatility of Cryptocurrencies.* Statista Daily Data. https://www.statista.com/chart/27577/cryptocurrency-volatility-dmo

Statista. (2023). *Cryptocurrencies—Worldwide Market Forecast.* Statista. https://www.statista.com/outlook/dmo/fintech/digital-assets/cryptocurrencies/worldwide

Stoker, S. (2023, September 20). What are the ethical implications of cryptocurrency? *Robots.Net.* https://robots.net/ai/what-are-the-ethical-implications-of-cryptocurrency/

StormGain. (2023, February 1). *Most Decentralised Coin List.* StormGain. https://stormgain.com/blog/most-decentralised-crypto-list

Tarr, J.-A. (2018). Distributed ledger technology, blockchain and insurance: Opportunities, risks and challenges. *Insurance Law Journal, 29*(3), 254–268.

Torregrosa, J. P., & Fontrodona, J. (2022, December 16). *The Ethical Concerns of Cryptocurrencies.* IESE Insight. https://www.iese.edu/insight/articles/cryptocu rrencies-blockchain-crypto-assets-ethics/

Voskobojnikov, A., Obada-Obieh, B., Huang, Y., & Beznosov, K. (2020). Surviving the Cryptojungle: Perception and management of risk among North American cryptocurrency (non)users. In J. Bonneau, & N. Heninger (Eds.), *Financial Cryptography and Data Security* (Vol. 12059, pp. 595–614). Springer International Publishing. https://doi.org/10.1007/978-3-030-51280-4_32

Wajid, A., Sabiha, A., Akhtar, S., Tabash, M. I., & Daniel, L. N. (2022). Cross-border acquisitions and shareholders' wealth: The case of the Indian pharmaceutical sector. *Journal of Risk and Financial Management, 15*(10), Article 10. https://doi.org/10.3390/jrfm15100437

Wang, Y., Lucey, B., Vigne, S. A., & Yarovaya, L. (2022). An index of cryptocurrency environmental attention (ICEA). *China Finance Review International, 12*(3), 378–414. https://doi.org/10.1108/CFRI-09-2021-0191

Wendl, M., Doan, M. H., & Sassen, R. (2023). The environmental impact of cryptocurrencies using proof of work and proof of stake consensus algorithms: A systematic review. *Journal of Environmental Management, 326,* 116530. https://doi.org/10.1016/j.jenvman.2022.116530

Whitt, R. (2019, November 13). Environmental cost of cryptocurrency mines. *ScienceDaily.* https://www.sciencedaily.com/releases/2019/11/191113092600.htm

Xiao, Y., Zhang, N., Lou, W., & Hou, Y. T. (2020). A survey of distributed consensus protocols for blockchain networks. *IEEE Communications Surveys & Tutorials, 22*(2), 1432–1465. https://doi.org/10.1109/COMST.2020.2969706

Yli-Huumo, J., Ko, D., Choi, S., Park, S., & Smolander, K. (2016). Where is current research on Blockchain technology? - A systematic review. *PLoS One, 11*(10). https://doi.org/10.1371/journal.pone.0163477

Yu, C., Yang, W., Xie, F., & He, J. (2022). Technology and security analysis of cryptocurrency based on blockchain. *Complexity,* e5835457. https://doi.org/10.1155/2022/5835457

Zhang, R., Xue, R., & Liu, L. (2019). Security and privacy on blockchain. *ACM Computing Surveys, 52*(3). https://doi.org/10.1145/3316481

Zhou, Q., Huang, H., Zheng, Z., & Bian, J. (2020). Solutions to scalability of blockchain: A survey. *IEEE Access, 8,* 16440–16455. https://doi.org/10.1109/ACCESS.2020.2967218

Chapter 13

Machine Learning in Fintech

David Campbell, Aleem Ansari, and Vikrant Vikram Singh

13.1 Machine Learning and Financial Technology: A Growing Intersection

A fascinating new area of research in the field of finance is the convergence of Fintech and machine learning (ML). Fintech aims to improve and streamline the delivery of financial services, and ML, a crucial aspect of artificial intelligence (AI), enables Fintech systems to learn from the past rather than relying solely on human expertise. There is enormous room for innovation when ML and Fintech are combined because ML allows Fintech companies to mine vast financial datasets for insightful data that can improve efficiency and decision-making. Due to their predictive abilities, a variety of ML techniques are widely utilized in the finance sector to manage complex and large amounts of data. These methods include deep learning, reinforcement learning, unsupervised learning, and supervised learning (Janiesch et al., 2021; Jafar et al., 2023).

13.2 Fintech

A technology-driven strategy called Fintech is used to improve financial services and systems. To address persistent financial challenges while enhancing the effectiveness, accessibility, and convenience of financial services, it integrates cutting-edge technologies such as AI, ML, big data,

DOI: 10.4324/9781032644165-13

blockchain, and more (Gomber et al., 2018). Fintech transforms the financial sector by integrating cutting-edge technologies to improve operational effectiveness, security, and capabilities (Chaklader et al., 2023). Traditional in-person financial transactions have been replaced by digital platforms, which has fuelled the growth of online banking, payments, lending, and other services. Fintech also excels at automating processes, which lowers the need for human intervention, increases productivity, reduces errors, and lowers operating costs. Examples of this include automated customer support bots and algorithmic trading. Fintech platforms also provide personalized services catered to the preferences and actions of each user. Fintech platforms can provide insightful financial guidance, make accurate product recommendations, and better assess risks by looking at each user's financial goals and patterns (Chaklader et al., 2023). Last but not least, Fintech plays a crucial role in financial inclusion because it ensures that everyone has access to financial services regardless of their financial situation (Akhtar et al., 2020; Awotunde et al., 2021). Microfinance platforms and mobile payment technologies are two examples of innovations that have greatly increased access to financial services and ensured financial inclusivity (Azmi et al., 2020).

13.3 Machine Learning

The concept of ML states that systems can learn from data, recognize patterns, and make decisions with little human intervention (Al-Sahaf et al., 2019). This learning process is accomplished through algorithms, which are sets of rules or instructions for machines to solve problems. There are three primary types of ML algorithms. Supervised learning involves a model learning from labelled data to predict outcomes. Unsupervised learning allows a model to find patterns and structures in unlabelled data. Lastly, reinforcement learning enables an agent to learn decision-making through rewards for good choices and penalties for bad ones. When using ML, it's important to keep both overfitting and underfitting in check. Overfitting is when a model performs inadequately on new, untested data because it fits the training data too closely (Lawrence & Giles, 2000). When a model does not adequately learn from the training data, underfitting occurs. To determine how well the system predicts, the accuracy of the model is assessed using the appropriate metrics.

13.4 The Synergy between Fintech and Machine Learning

The impact of ML on decision-making, risk management, and customer service is increasingly advantageous to the Fintech industry. Its potential to revolutionize many industries is illustrated by ML's capacity to analyze massive amounts of data, which is especially helpful in fields such as credit scoring, algorithmic trading, and fraud detection. Because rich data sets are crucial for efficient ML algorithms, ML and Fintech complement each other well. Automation follows, which lowers human error, improves accuracy, and saves a lot of money. Additionally, ML can accommodate unique preferences and behaviours, enabling personalized financial services to enhance the user experience. Clients can now receive proactive, data-driven financial advice thanks to the predictive power of ML in Fintech (Bachmann et al., 2022). The combination of Fintech and ML is reshaping the financial sector to be more digital, efficient, and consumer-centric (Sadman et al., 2022). ML has transformed several Fintech areas including fraud detection, risk management, algorithmic trading, robo-consulting, customer service, personalized services, credit scoring, regulatory compliance (Regtech), Insurtech, anti-money laundering (AML) and invoice management. By exploring these areas, one can gain a deeper understanding of the intersection between Fintech and ML.

13.5 Credit Scoring

Fintech platforms provide tailored offerings catered to the individual needs and acts of each user. Fintech platforms can provide insightful financial advice, make accurate product recommendations, and better assess risks by looking at each user's financial goals and patterns (Chaklader et al., 2023). Last but not least, Fintech plays a crucial role in financial inclusion because it ensures that all individuals can have access to financial services regardless of their financial situation (Awotunde et al., 2021). Micro-finance platforms and mobile payment technologies are two examples of innovations that have greatly increased access to financial services and ensured financial inclusivity. The ML models can reveal intricate non-linear interactions between variables that traditional models might miss, thereby enhancing credit score accuracy and default probability prediction (Barboza et al., 2017). Additionally, ML's automation capabilities speed up the credit scoring process, enabling real-time credit decisions and improving customer experience.

Furthermore, ML's potential to democratize credit access by using broader datasets to evaluate the creditworthiness of individuals who were previously overlooked due to a lack of credit history is notable, promoting financial inclusion (Allen et al., 2020). Commonly used ML algorithms in credit scoring models include logistic regression, decision trees, support vector machines (SVMs), and neural networks (Golbayani et al., 2020). The extreme gradient boosting (XGBoost) algorithm, known for its speed, performance, and adaptability to specific problems such as credit scoring, has shown high efficiency and accuracy. Another popular gradient-boosting framework using tree-based learning algorithms, LightGBM, has gained popularity, especially with large datasets due to its speed and accuracy (Golbayani et al., 2020; Huang et al., 2023).

13.6 Risk Assessments

With the adoption of ML technologies for risk assessment, the Fintech sector has significantly sped up innovation in the financial services sector. Financial risk assessment has historically been largely manual and reliant on pre-established rule sets and human intuition. ML, on the other hand, is revolutionizing this field and has many advantages over conventional approaches. The strength of ML lies in its ability to sift through large troves of data, revealing nuanced patterns needed to understand risk (Albreiki et al., 2021; Ka et al., 2021). From flagging potential risks to quantifying their severity and developing strategies to mitigate risk, the power of ML is visible across the entire scope of risk management. Its ability to generate both structured and chaotic data ensures that often-overlooked aspects of risk are highlighted. Based on historical records, ML predicts the probability and ramifications of risk events, allowing financial institutions to map their paths with greater caution and effectively deploy power. In the risk domain, the choice of the ML algorithm depends on the nature of the target risk:

- **Credit Risk**: Here, logistic regression, decision-tree, and SVM are the pillars. However, deep learning models are gaining momentum due to their unparalleled pattern discrimination capabilities.
- **Market Risks**: To evaluate this, time-limited models such as autoregressive integrated moving average (ARIMA) and Generalized AutoRegressive Conditional Heteroskedasticity (GARCH) are often paired with ML giants like long short-term memory (LSTM).

■ **Operational Risks**: Covering areas such as fraud detection, the focus is on clustering methods and outlier recognition techniques for anomaly detection.

It is noteworthy that models such as XGBoost and LightGBM are gaining popularity, mainly due to their exceptional efficiency and accuracy, especially in the face of data of a biased nature.

13.7 Algorithmic Trading

Algorithmic trading, also known as algo or black box trading, has greatly benefited from the advent of ML. This process involves the use of advanced algorithms to automate trading, which has become more popular with the rise of high-frequency trading and increased data availability. There are several key stages to algorithmic trading, including formulating strategies, back testing them, implementing them, and executing trades. ML models are crucial in optimizing each of these stages (Jansen, 2020). Trading strategies are developed through careful consideration of market indices, financial indicators, and ancillary sources such as news feeds. ML models, including linear regression, neural profiles, and sophisticated LSTM architectures, are adept at deciphering hidden patterns in these datasets. Once a strategy is created, its guts are tested against past data – a process known as back testing. Here, ML methods, such as cross-validation, play a central role, providing a reliable measure of a strategy's true potential. Once validated, as we move into strategy implementation, ML shines with its ability to shape and modify strategy as new data becomes available. In ML, reinforcement learning – emphasizing the accumulation of maximum rewards over a series of decisions – becomes instrumental. Specific algorithms such as Q-learning and deep Q networks (DQN) prove their worth by refining strategies and optimizing iterative decisions (Park et al., 2020). When a business strategy is implemented, ML helps to reduce costs and protect against market fluctuations. Approaches such as Bayesian refinement and multibranch bandit frameworks become invaluable, optimizing transaction execution and tuning model hyperparameters for optimal performance (Pearce & Branke, 2018).

13.8 Fraud Detection and Prevention

The Fintech landscape has seen a surge in fraud detection efficiency thanks to the introduction of ML. Unlike conventional rule-based systems, which often fall short in recognizing constantly changing fraudulent behaviours, ML offers a dynamic defence mechanism. The process of employing ML for fraud detection is methodical, encompassing stages such as data gathering and refining, feature crafting, model formulation, addressing data skewness, and the final stages of model evaluation, validation, and implementation (Franco et al., 2021; Hemachandran et al., 2024). During the pivotal model formulation step, a myriad of algorithms come into play. There's a draw toward anomaly detection techniques such as isolated forests and one-class SVMs. Simultaneously, supervised methodologies such as logistic regression, decision-tree structures, random forests, and neural frameworks are employed based on the nature and specifics of the dataset. One of the critical challenges in fraud detection is the inherent data imbalance, in which legitimate transactions heavily outnumber fraudulent ones. To balance this scale, strategies such as synthetic minority oversampling technique (SMOTE) and adaptive synthetic sampling (ADASYN) are employed (He et al., 2008). Upon model optimization, its efficacy is gauged using measures specially curated for skewed datasets. In the culmination phase, the refined model is activated for real-time transactional scrutiny, primed to adapt and respond to the shifting nuances of fraudulent activities.

13.9 Regulatory Compliance

The financial sector is gravitating toward ML solutions in their quest to address regulatory concerns with precision and efficacy. ML has the potential to streamline and make autonomous integral facets such as the know your customer (KYC) verifications, anti-money laundering (AML) protocols, and on-the-go transactional scrutiny. One of ML's fortes is its capability to seamlessly pull data from KYC dossiers and spot inconsistencies. Convolutional neural networks (CNNs) stand out as optimal choices when it comes to automating the review of KYC submissions. Furthermore, natural language processing (NLP), an ML offshoot, is adept at sifting through textual datasets to garner significant insights (Hemachandran et al., 2022; Dash et al., 2023). Diving into the AML sphere, ML's prowess in dissecting transactional data for anomalies that could be red flags for fraudulent activity is noteworthy (Huang et al., 2009). Algorithms from the unsupervised learning domain can pinpoint data anomalies and distinct patterns, whereas supervised counterparts categorize transactions into benign or suspicious buckets by leveraging historical records. For serial transactional data analysis, recurrent neural networks (RNNs) are apt given their ability to recall past events. On the regulatory reporting front, ML emerges as a time-saver, automating data collation and its subsequent report-age. Moreover, predictive analytics, an ML derivative, can foresee regulatory shifts by gauging ongoing trends and empowering financial entities to be a step ahead. Nevertheless, a crucial caveat is that these algorithms' effectiveness is intertwined with the calibre and pertinence of the data they're trained on. To encapsulate, the potential of ML in ensuring regulatory adherence within the Fintech realm is noteworthy. It offers a gamut of tools, from automating data handling and report generation, refining KYC checks, to bolstering AML steps and offering real-time transactional surveillance.

13.10 Anti-Money Laundering

The integration of ML into the Fintech sector offers a potent solution to coun-tering financial misdeeds, especially in the realm of anti-money laundering (AML). Conventional systems, anchored in predefined rules, often falter when encountering sophisticated and concealed money laundering schemes, result-ing in a high rate of false alarms. In contrast, ML's knack for discerning data patterns and autonomously drawing conclusions has given a boost to AML strategies. It enables the pinpointing of anomalous patterns amidst extensive transaction records, thereby refining the precision and speed of identifying potential laundering activities. The incorporation of ML in AML usually unfolds in stages. At the outset, techniques of unsupervised learning, such as clustering algorithms, cluster similar transactions, paving the way to spot dubious move-ments (Liu et al., 2008; Hemachandran et al., 2021). Following this, supervised learning techniques such as random forest, SVMs, and neural architectures are fine-tuned with annotated data to detect these peculiar patterns. Among neural frameworks, autoencoders have shown promise in anomaly spotting, vital for AML efforts. These models are tailored to mirror their input, mastering concise data representations that aid in unearthing irregularities. Notwithstanding the potency of deep learning in grasping intricate patterns, it demands a substantial dataset with annotations and may not offer straightforward interpretability.

13.11 Personal Financial Management

The realm of Fintech has witnessed a remarkable evolution in personal financial planning (PFP) thanks to ML. By scrutinizing an individual's financial activity, ML discerns behavioural tendencies, pinpoints patterns, and foresees forthcoming trends, thus guiding toward more personalized, pre-emptive, and automated financial choices. Within the PFP domain, ML aids in understanding expenditure tendencies, spotlighting areas for potential savings and forecasting earnings and outlays. This empowers individuals to devise more precise fiscal strategies (Mulvey, 2017). Additionally, the world of automated trading taps into ML to handle enormous chunks of live market information, anticipate prospective price shifts, and autonomously carry out trades. A variety of ML techniques find their applications at distinct phases of PFP and automated trading. For instance, methods of unsupervised learning come into play during the data accumulation and cleaning stages, while supervised techniques, encompassing regression, decision trees, and neural networks, are pivotal during feature delineation and model calibration stages. Deep Q-learning, a subset of reinforcement learning, stands out for back testing given its adeptness at managing intricate data structures and multifaceted scenarios. Finally, techniques like LSTM and associated recurrent neural algorithms become indispensable for split-second trading decisions, owing to their prowess in handling time-series data. Consequently, ML's merger with PFP has heralded a new era in astute financial judgment.

13.12 Limitations of Using Machine Learning in Fintech

With the incorporation of ML, the Fintech industry has undergone significant transformation. This technology improves efficiency and personalization, as well as predictability. However, there are some difficulties associated with this transformation. Data privacy is one of the major concerns. ML necessitates access to large amounts of sensitive financial data, which can be difficult to achieve while adhering to privacy laws such as the General Data Protection Regulation (GDPR). Another issue that must be addressed is algorithmic bias. If trained on biased data, ML models can perpetuate discrimination, resulting in unfair outcomes. To avoid this issue, careful data collection and model training are required. The Fintech sector's highly regulated nature presents regulatory challenges. The regulatory framework for newer technologies, such as ML, is still evolving, which creates uncertainty and can limit the flexibility of Fintech companies, potentially stifling innovation. Technical constraints also pose difficulties. Implementing ML requires specialized skills as well as significant computational resources. The interpretability issue is also significant, especially with complex models such as deep learning networks. Despite these challenges, ML continues to be a game changer in Fintech. Strategies for addressing these issues and ensuring that ML can be used effectively and ethically in the financial industry are being developed (Boot et al., 2021).

13.13 Ethical Implications of ML Decisions in Fintech

The use of ML in the Fintech industry raises ethical concerns, such as job loss and discrimination due to algorithmic bias. While ML can make mundane financial tasks more efficient and cost-effective, it also poses a threat to job security and may exacerbate income inequality. This emphasizes the importance of investing in worker retraining and upskilling. Furthermore, there are concerns about discrimination in financial services as a result of biased ML models. Biased data, for example, could result in unfair credit scoring and the denial of loans to certain demographic groups. To address these issues, ML models should be trained on unbiased and representative data with the help of robust auditing and bias mitigation techniques. It is also crucial to maintain transparency and explainability in ML algorithms to ensure customer trust and regulatory compliance (Bibal et al., 2021).

13.14 The Transformative Potential of ML and Fintech

The use of ML in the financial sector has numerous advantages for managing finances and executing transactions. ML can automate time-consuming tasks, freeing up humans to focus on more strategic tasks and increasing overall efficiency. ML improves prediction accuracy in credit scoring and risk analysis, promoting financial resilience. The pattern recognition abilities of ML can also provide personalized advice for managing personal finances and improving financial health. Furthermore, by using non-traditional data and advanced algorithms, ML can help serve underserved populations, promoting financial inclusion. While mastering ML can benefit Fintech practitioners by improving customer experiences, product offerings, and operational efficiency, they must consider data privacy, algorithmic bias, and regulatory compliance. Researchers can also investigate intriguing areas at the intersection of ML and Fintech, such as algorithm development, novel application identification, and ethical and societal implications. Finally, understanding the role of ML in Fintech is becoming increasingly important for students of both technology and finance.

References

Akhtar, S., Niazi, M. H., & Khan, M. M. (2020). Cascading effect of COVID 19 on Indian economy. *International Journal of Advanced Science and Technology, 29*(9), 4563–4573.

Al-Sahaf, H., Bi, Y., Chen, Q., Lensen, A., Mei, Y., Sun, Y., Tran, B., Xue, B., & Zhang, M. (2019). A survey on evolutionary machine learning. *Journal of the Royal Society of New Zealand, 49*(2), 205–228. https://doi.org/10.1080/03036758 .2019.1609052

Albreiki, B., Zaki, N., & Alashwal, H. (2021). A systematic literature review of student' performance prediction using machine learning techniques. *Education Sciences, 11*(9). https://doi.org/10.3390/educsci11090552

Allen, F., Gu, X., & Jagtiani, J. (2020). *A Survey of Fintech Research and Policy Discussion* (Current dr). Philadelphia, PA: Research Department, Federal Reserve Bank of Philadelphia. https://doi.org/10.21799/frbp.wp.2020.21 LK-https://worldcat.org/title/1227087869

Awotunde, J. B., Adeniyi, E. A., Ogundokun, R. O., & Ayo, F. E. (2021). *Application of Big Data with Fintech in Financial Services BT - Fintech with Artificial Intelligence, Big Data, and Blockchain* (P. M. S. Choi, & S. H. Huang (Eds.); pp. 107–132). Singapore: Springer. https://doi.org/10.1007/978-981-33-6137-9_3

Azmi, S., Akhtar, S., & Nadeem, M. (2020). Impact of digitalisation on bank performance: A study of Indian Banks. *Test Engineering and Management, 83,* 23678–23691.

Bachmann, N., Tripathi, S., Brunner, M., & Jodlbauer, H. (2022). The contribution of data-driven technologies in achieving the sustainable development goals. *Sustainability, 14*(5). https://doi.org/10.3390/su14052497

Barboza, F., Kimura, H., & Altman, E. (2017). Machine learning models and bankruptcy prediction. *Expert Systems with Applications, 83,* 405–417. https://doi .org/10.1016/j.eswa.2017.04.006

Bibal, A., Lognoul, M., de Streel, A., & Frénay, B. (2021). Legal requirements on explainability in machine learning. *Artificial Intelligence and Law, 29*(2), 149–169. https://doi.org/10.1007/s10506-020-09270-4

Boot, A., Hoffmann, P., Laeven, L., & Ratnovski, L. (2021). Fintech: What's old, what's new? *Journal of Financial Stability, 53,* 100836. https://doi.org/10.1016/j .jfs.2020.100836

Chaklader, B., Gupta, B. B., & Panigrahi, P. K. (2023). Analyzing the progress of FINTECH-companies and their integration with new technologies for innovation and entrepreneurship. *Journal of Business Research, 161,* 113847. https:// doi.org/10.1016/j.jbusres.2023.113847

Dash, B., Swayamsiddha, S., & Ali, A. I. (2023). *Evolving of Smart Banking with NLP and Deep Learning BT - Enabling Technologies for Effective Planning and Management in Sustainable Smart Cities* (M. A. Ahad, G. Casalino, & B. Bhushan (Eds.); pp. 151–172). Springer International Publishing. https://doi.org /10.1007/978-3-031-22922-0_6

Franco, P., Martínez, J. M., Kim, Y.-C., & Ahmed, M. A. (2021). A framework for IoT based appliance recognition in smart homes. *IEEE Access, 9*, 133940–133960. https://doi.org/10.1109/ACCESS.2021.3116148

Golbayani, P., Florescu, I., & Chatterjee, R. (2020). A comparative study of forecasting corporate credit ratings using neural networks, support vector machines, and decision trees. *The North American Journal of Economics and Finance, 54*, 101251. https://doi.org/10.1016/j.najef.2020.101251

Gomber, P., Kauffman, R. J., Parker, C., & Weber, B. W. (2018). On the fintech revolution: Interpreting the forces of innovation, disruption, and transformation in financial services. *Journal of Management Information Systems, 35*(1), 220–265. https://doi.org/10.1080/07421222.2018.1440766

He, H., Bai, Y., Garcia, E. A., & Li, S. (2008). ADASYN: Adaptive synthetic sampling approach for imbalanced learning. *2008 IEEE International Joint Conference on Neural Networks (IEEE World Congress on Computational Intelligence)*, 1322–1328.

Hemachandran, K., Khanra, S., Rodriguez, R. V., & Jaramillo, J. (Eds.). (2022). *Machine Learning for Business Analytics: Real-Time Data Analysis for Decision-Making.* CRC Press.

Hemachandran, K., Rodriguez, R. V., Toshniwal, R., Junaid, M., & Shaw, L. (2021). Performance analysis of different classification algorithms for bank loan sectors. In *Intelligent Sustainable Systems: Proceedings of ICISS 2021* (pp. 191–202). Singapore: Springer Singapore.

Hemachandran, K., Rodriguez, R. V., Subramaniam, U., & Balas, V. E. (Eds.). (2024). *Artificial Intelligence and Knowledge Processing: Improved Decision-Making and Prediction.*

Huang, M. L., Liang, J., & Nguyen, Q. V. (2009). A visualization approach for frauds detection in financial Market. *2009 13th International Conference Information Visualisation*, 197–202. https://doi.org/10.1109/IV.2009.23

Huang, Y., Li, J., Zheng, T., Ji, D., Wong, Y. J., You, H., Gu, Y., Li, M., Zhao, L., Li, S., Geng, S., Yang, N., Chen, G., Wang, Y., Kumar, M., Jindal, A., Qin, W., Chen, Z., Xin, Y., ... Qi, X. (2023). Development and validation of a machine learning–based model for varices screening in compensated cirrhosis (CHESS2001): An international multicenter study. *Gastrointestinal Endoscopy, 97*(3), 435-444. e2. https://doi.org/10.1016/j.gie.2022.10.018

Jafar, S. H., Akhtar, S., El-Chaarani, H., Khan, P. A., & Binsaddig, R. (2023). Forecasting of NIFTY 50 index price by using backward elimination with an LSTM model. *Journal of Risk and Financial Management, 16*(10):423. https://doi.org/10.3390/jrfm16100423

Janiesch, C., Zschech, P., & Heinrich, K. (2021). Machine learning and deep learning. *Electronic Markets, 31*(3), 685–695. https://doi.org/10.1007/s12525-021-00475-2

Jansen, S. (2020). *Machine Learning for Algorithmic Trading: Predictive models to extract signals from market and alternative data for systematic trading strategies with Python* (C. Nelson (Ed.); Second). Packt Publishing Ltd.

Ka, H., Georgeb, P. M., Rodriguezc, R. V., Kulkarnid, R. M., & Roye, S. (2021). Performance analysis of KN earest neighbor classification algorithms for bank loan sectors. *Smart Intelligent Computing and Communication Technology, 38*(9).

Lawrence, S., & Giles, C. L. (2000). Overfitting and neural networks: Conjugate gradient and backpropagation. *Proceedings of the IEEE-INNS-ENNS International Joint Conference on Neural Networks. IJCNN 2000. Neural Computing: New Challenges and Perspectives for the New Millennium, 1,* 114–119. https://doi.org/10.1109/IJCNN.2000.857823

Liu, X., Zhang, P., & Zeng, D. (2008). *Sequence Matching for Suspicious Activity Detection in Anti-Money Laundering BT - Intelligence and Security Informatics* (C. C. Yang, H. Chen, M. Chau, K. Chang, S.-D. Lang, P. S. Chen, R. Hsieh, D. Zeng, F.-Y. Wang, K. Carley, W. Mao, & J. Zhan (Eds.); pp. 50–61). Berlin Heidelberg: Springer.

Mulvey, J. M. (2017). Machine learning and financial planning. *IEEE Potentials, 36*(6), 8–13. https://doi.org/10.1109/MPOT.2017.2737200

Park, H., Sim, M. K., & Choi, D. G. (2020). An intelligent financial portfolio trading strategy using deep Q-learning. *Expert Systems with Applications, 158,* 113573. https://doi.org/10.1016/j.eswa.2020.113573

Pearce, M., & Branke, J. (2018). Continuous multi-task Bayesian optimisation with correlation. *European Journal of Operational Research, 270*(3), 1074–1085. https://doi.org/10.1016/j.ejor.2018.03.017

Sadman, N., Ahsan, M. M., Rahman, A., Siddique, Z., & Gupta, K. D. (2022). Promise of AI in DeFi, a systematic review. *Digital, 2*(1), 88–103. https://doi.org/10.3390/digital2010006

Chapter 14

Navigating Fintech's Mechanism toward Trading and Hedging

Humaira Fatima, Mohsin Khan, and Nomani Abuzar

14.1 Introduction

To address these developments, there is a need for a broader understanding of the new technologies and players that are driving the Fintech revolution in the financial services sector. This chapter provides new insights into the variety of emerging ideas and technologies that are revolutionizing the global financial services market. Additionally, it seeks to explore the impact of Fintech on trading and hedging mechanisms and investigate the new hedging opportunities offered by Fintech, such as decentralized finance (DeFi) and embedded finance.

In a nutshell, the purpose of this chapter is to contribute to the current body of knowledge by delivering new insights into the shifting terrain of the financial services industry. By examining the impact of Fintech on trading and hedging mechanisms, this chapter endeavours to bridge the gap in current scholastic articles and shed light on the opportunities and challenges associated with these technological advancements. A more profound comprehension of the prospective advantages and disadvantages of Fintech in the financial services industry can be attained via this research, thereby providing direction for subsequent policy formulations and business choices.

DOI: 10.4324/9781032644165-14

14.2 Transitioning from Pipeline Banking to Open Banking

In recent years, the banking industry has undergone a significant transformation, shifting away from the traditional pipeline and vertical paradigm toward more open banking business models (Accenture, 2021). This transition is driven not only by technological advancements but also by the need to meet evolving customer demands and remain competitive in a changing landscape (EY, 2022).

14.3 How Fintech is Reshaping Trading and Hedging Mechanisms

The emergence of Fintech has had a profound impact on trading and hedging mechanisms within the financial services sector, revolutionizing traditional approaches (Arner et al., 2017). Traditional banking relied heavily on proprietary systems and limited partnerships, while Fintech has introduced innovation, automation, transparency, and accessibility into these mechanisms (Iqbal et al., 2020).

- **Automation and Efficiency**: Fintech solutions, such as algorithmic trading platforms and robo-advisors, have streamlined the trading process. According to a report by McKinsey, algorithmic trading accounted for approximately 35% of all trading in 2021, up from 25% in 2019, indicating a growing reliance on technology for efficient trade execution (McKinsey, 2022).
- **Decentralized Finance (DeFi)**: DeFi, a subset of Fintech, is disrupting traditional hedging mechanisms. DeFi platforms, built on blockchain technology, enable peer-to-peer lending, borrowing, and trading of financial instruments. In 2021, the total value locked in DeFi smart contracts exceeded $80 billion (DeFi Pulse).
- **Real-time Data Analysis**: Advanced analytics and artificial intelligence-driven tools provided by Fintech companies offer real-time market insights, empowering banks to make informed trading and hedging decisions. These tools have significantly reduced the time required for market data analysis, ensuring timely trade execution (Gartner, 2023).

14.4 Regulatory Compliance and Security

The shift to open banking models introduces new challenges and responsibilities regarding regulatory compliance and security.

- **Regulatory Frameworks**: Banks must adapt to evolving regulatory frameworks, such as Payment Services Directive TwoPSD2 in Europe, which mandate secure customer data sharing with authorized third-party providers. Non-compliance can result in substantial fines, as evidenced by the European Commission's 344 million euros in fines to financial institutions for anti-trust violations in 2020 (European Commission, 2020).
- **Cybersecurity**: Collaboration with Fintech firms and the opening of application programming interfaces (APIs) expose banks to increased cyberthreats. A report by Cybersecurity Ventures predicts global cybercrime costs of 6 trillion US dollars annually by 2021, emphasizing the need for robust security measures (Cybersecurity Ventures, 2021).

14.5 Measuring Success

Measuring the success of the transition from pipeline banking to open banking models relies on key performance indicators (KPIs).

- **User Adoption**: The number of users and transactions on open banking platforms serves as a clear indicator of success. By 2021, over 500 million Europeans had access to open banking services, showcasing its growing adoption (European Central Bank, 2022).
- **Revenue Growth**: Banks need to track revenue generated from new services and partnerships facilitated by open banking. PricewaterhouseCoopers (PwC) projects that by 2025, open banking could generate 1 trillion US dollars in new revenue for banks globally (PwC, 2023).
- **Customer Satisfaction**: Customer feedback and net promoter scores (NPS) help gauge the success of open banking initiatives. A study by J.D. Power found that banks with higher NPS scores tend to have a larger market share (Power, 2022).

14.6 Objectives of the Study

- Identify the key trends in Fintech that are reshaping trading and hedging mechanisms.
- Analyze the impact of Fintech on the case study of Robinhood.
- Assess the new opportunities and challenges presented by Fintech in the trading and hedging landscape.
- Develop recommendations for how policymakers and financial institutions can navigate the Fintech revolution in the financial services sector.

14.6.1 Objective 1: Identify the Key Trends in Fintech that Are Reshaping Trading and Hedging Mechanisms

Fintech is swiftly transforming the financial services sector, including trading and hedging mechanisms (Arner et al., 2017; Iqbal et al., 2020). Algorithmic trading is one of the key trends in Fintech that is modifying trading and hedging mechanisms (Investopedia, 2023). Algorithmic trading platforms use algorithms to automate the trading process, resulting in faster and more methodical trade execution (Investopedia, 2023; Maan, 2023). DeFi is another trend in Fintech that is gaining admiration and sanctioning new hedging strategies (Iqbal et al., 2020). DeFi platforms are built on blockchain technology and permit peer-to-peer lending, borrowing, and trading of financial instruments (Iqbal et al., 2020). DeFi has several advantages over traditional trading markets, such as higher transparency, lower transaction costs, and 24/7 access (Iqbal et al., 2020; Cointelegraph, 2022). Additionally, real-time data analytics and artificial intelligence-driven tools provided by Fintech companies offer real-time market insights, empowering banks to make informed trading and hedging decisions (Iqbal et al., 2020). Open banking is another trend in Fintech that is reshaping trading and hedging mechanisms (Iqbal et al., 2020). Open banking is a framework that allows banks and other financial institutions to share customer data with authorized third-party providers (Iqbal et al., 2020).

Fintech is considerably transforming how hedging and trading are implemented. For example, algorithmic trading is now widely used by both institutional and retail investors (Investopedia, 2023; Maan, 2023). DeFi is also gaining popularity, particularly among cryptocurrency traders (Iqbal et al., 2020; Cointelegraph, 2022). Additionally, real-time data analytics and open banking are enabling banks to offer more sophisticated trading and hedging products and services to their customers (Iqbal et al., 2020).

14.6.2 Objective 2: Analyze the Impact of Fintech on the Case Study of Robinhood

The Fintech industry is rapidly evolving, transforming the way financial services are delivered and consumed (Investopedia, 2023). Fintech enterprises are capitalizing on emerging technologies in order to provide inventive offerings and services that surpass the efficiency, accessibility, and cost-effectiveness of conventional financial establishments (Investopedia, 2023).

One of the most significant impacts of Fintech has been on the trading and hedging landscape (Investopedia, 2023). Fintech companies have developed new trading platforms and tools that make it easier and more affordable for individuals and businesses to trade financial instruments (Investopedia, 2023). They have also introduced new hedging products and strategies that help investors to manage their risk (Investopedia, 2023).

One of the most well-known examples of a Fintech company that is ruling the trading and hedge landscape is Robinhood (Robinhood, 2023). Robinhood is an investment firm that prioritizes mobile platforms and provides commission-free trading for equities, exchange-traded funds (ETFs), and options (Robinhood, 2023). Robinhood has made trading more affordable and within reach for millions of people.

Table 14.1 Estimated Market Size of Fintech Segments

Segment	2022 Market Size (USD billion)	2027 Projected Market Size (USD billion)	Compound Annual Growth Rate (CAGR)
Mobile Wallets	1.9	4.5	20.9%
Digital Payments	80.3	141.7	12.8%
Lending	1.5	4.5	29.6%
Insurance	1.6	3.4	17.6%
Wealth Management	0.8	2.5	27.7%
Other	5.8	13.5	18.2%

Table 14.2 Key Fintech Trends that Are Reshaping Trading and Hedging Mechanisms

Trend	Description
Algorithmic Trading	The use of algorithms to automate the trading process.
Decentralized Finance (DeFi)	Peer-to-peer lending, borrowing, and trading of financial instruments on blockchain technology.
Real-time Data Analytics	The use of advanced analytics and artificial intelligence-driven tools to gain real-time market insights.
Open Banking	A framework that allows banks and other financial institutions to share customer data with authorized third-party providers.

14.6.2.1 Impact of Robinhood on the Trading and Hedging Landscape

Robinhood has had a significant influence on the trading and hedging landscape in several ways.

- **Obtain Access to Trading**: Robinhood has made trading more available to millions of people by offering a commission-free and user-friendly interface (Robinhood, 2023). This has democratized trading to people of all income levels.
- **Reduced Trading Costs**: Robinhood's commission-free trading has significantly reduced the costs associated with trading (Robinhood, 2023). This has made trading more affordable for small investors.
- **Increased Trading Activity**: Essential growth in trading activity has resulted from Robinhood's eminence (Robinhood, 2023). This has led to increased liquidity in the markets and made it easier for people to buy and sell financial instruments.
- **New Trading Products**: Robinhood has introduced new trading products, such as fractional shares and options on stocks and ETFs (Robinhood, 2023). This made it possible for people to invest in the markets with smaller amounts of money.
- **New Trading Strategies**: Robinhood has also introduced new trading strategies, such as social trading and copy trading (Robinhood, 2023). This has made it possible for people to learn and follow other traders and to copy their trades.

14.6.2.2 Case Study: Robinhood and the GameStop Short Squeeze

In January 2021, Robinhood played a major role in the GameStop short squeeze (Securities and Exchange Commission, 2021). The GameStop short squeeze was a prime event in the financial markets that saw the share price of GameStop, a video game retailer, increase by more than 1,600% in a matter of weeks (Securities and Exchange Commission, 2021).

The GameStop short squeeze was driven by a group of retail investors on Reddit who banded together to buy GameStop stock and drive up the price (Securities and Exchange Commission, 2021). The retail investors were persuaded by several factors, including a desire to punish hedge funds that were shorting GameStop stock, and a belief that the company was undervalued (Securities and Exchange Commission, 2021).

Robinhood played a major role in the GameStop short squeeze by providing retail investors with a platform to trade GameStop stock (Securities and Exchange Commission, 2021) is shown in figure 14.1. Robinhood also restricted trading in GameStop stock at a critical point in the short squeeze, which angered retail investors and led to the attribution that Robinhood was protecting the interests of hedge funds over its customers (Securities and Exchange Commission, 2021).

The GameStop short squeeze highlighted the power of social media and retail investors to move markets (Securities and Exchange Commission, 2021). It also raised questions about the role of Fintech companies in the financial system and their obligations to their customers (Securities and Exchange Commission, 2021).

Table 14.3   Robinhood's Trading Volume

Year	Trading Volume (USD billions)
2019	174
2020	667
2021	3.2 trillion
2022	1.6 trillion

Source: Robinhood (2023)

Table 14.4   Robinhood's Customers by Age Group

Age Group	Percentage of Robinhood Customers
18–24	35%
25–34	40%
35–44	15%
45–54	5%
55–older	5%

Source: Robinhood (2023)

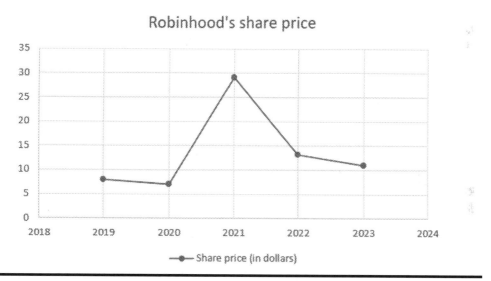

Figure 14.1   Robinhood's share price

14.6.3 Objective 3: Assess the New Opportunities and Challenges Presented by Fintech in the Trading and Hedging Landscape

Recent years have witnessed a profound transformation in the financial services industry because of the emergence of new technologies and competitors, including Fintechs and Techfins (Kshetri, 2020). To satiate their financial requirements, these new entrants have altered the manner in which consumers interact and enabled the introduction of new services (Mohammed, 2022). The Fintech space has gained significant traction in recent years, and diverse

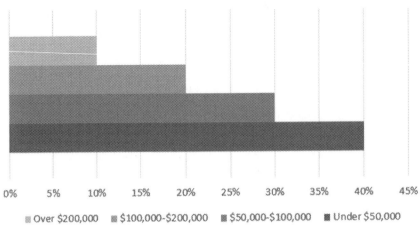

Figure 14.2 Robinhood's customers by income level

entrepreneurial efforts are being made to achieve this (PwC, 2022). In fact, there is a high tendency for complexity, spanning a variety of financial services, markets, innovations, business players, infrastructures, and technology (Ernst & Young, 2023) is shown in figure 14.2. This chapter aims to assess the new opportunities and challenges presented by Fintech in the trading and hedging landscape.

14.6.3.1 Opportunities

- **Improved User Experience**: Fintech companies integrate technological innovations such as big data, artificial intelligence (AI), and machine learning to improve user experience in financial services, including trading and hedging (Mohammed, 2022; PwC, 2022).
- **Time-to-market Framework**: Fintechs enable banks to innovate their products, processes, and channels within a streamlined time-to-market framework, thereby enhancing cost efficiency (Mohammed, 2022; PwC, 2022).
- **Partnering on Order**: Fintechs can assist banks in reducing regulatory burdens through order-specific partnerships.
- **Open Banking Business Models**: The banking industry is undergoing a significant shift from a vertical, pipeline-based paradigm to open banking business models, in which modularity, open innovation, and ecosystem-based business models may emerge as the new norm and paradigm for further development (Ernst & Young, 2023).

- **Wholesale Digital Solutions**: Fintech solutions are progressively materializing as comprehensive digital solutions that leverage cutting-edge technologies, including distributed ledgers, cloud computing, AI, and robotic process automation (RPA). These solutions enable the provision of innovation that was hitherto unattainable (PwC, 2022).

14.6.3.2 Challenges

- **Regulatory Challenges**: Fintechs encounter regulatory obstacles within the realm of trading and hedging, encompassing the need to adhere to stringent know-your-customer (KYC) and anti-money laundering (AML) protocols.
- **Cybersecurity Risks**: The use of technology in trading and hedging increases the risk of cybersecurity breaches, which can lead to financial losses and reputational damage.
- **Lack of Standardization**: Interoperability problems, caused by the Fintech industry's lack of standardization, might slow the widespread adoption of innovative technology.
- **Data Privacy Concerns**: The utilization of customer information for hedging and trading raises privacy and security concerns.
- **Avoid Changes**: Traditional financial institutions avoid the adoption of new technologies because they are worried about the consequences on their current business models.

The introduction of Fintech in the trading and hedging landscape contains both opportunities and challenges. They provide better user experience, time-to-market framework, partnering on order, open banking business models, and wholesale digital solutions. However, they also face regulatory challenges, cybersecurity risks, lack of standardization, data privacy concerns, and change avoidance. To fully realize the power of Fintech in the trading and hedging landscape, it is important to address these challenges and risks to create an environment that includes innovation and collaboration between traditional financial institutions and Fintechs.

14.6.4 Objective 4: Expand Recommendations for How Policymakers and Financial Institutions Can Steer the Fintech Revolution in the Financial Services Sector

The Fintech revolution has brought remarkable changes in the financial services sector, with new technologies and players such as Fintechs and

Techfins introducing new services and changing the way customers interact to fulfil their financial needs. This has led to a high level of convolution that is extended across a variety of financial services, markets, innovations, business players, infrastructures, and technology. Policymakers and financial institutions need to navigate this revolution to make sure they can take advantage of the opportunities it presents while coping with the risks.

14.6.4.1 Trading and Hedging Mechanisms in Fintech

One area in which Fintech is having a notable impact is in trading and hedging mechanisms. Fintech is enabling the growth of new trading platforms and tools that are more pellucid, systematic, and accessible than traditional trading mechanisms. For example, with the use of blockchain technology, decentralized trading platforms are increasingly making direct transactions between buyers and sellers smoother. This may lower transaction cost and increase transaction speed.

Furthermore, Fintech is easing the advancement of novel hedging mechanisms that have the potential to improve the risk management capabilities of financial institutions. For example, machine learning algorithms can be used to analyze large amounts of data and identify patterns that can be used to predict market movements and manage risk. This can help financial institutions to hold their positions more effectively and reduce their risk.

14.6.4.2 Recommendations for Policymakers and Financial Institutions

To navigate the Fintech revolution in the financial services sector, policymakers and financial institutions should consider the following advice.

■ **Embrace Open Banking Business Models**: The banking industry is undergoing a shift from a vertical, pipeline-based paradigm to open banking business models, which emphasize modularity, open innovation, and ecosystem-based business models. These approaches can bud as the prevailing standard and paradigm that further develops the industry. Policymakers and financial institutions should welcome this shift and work to create an environment that supports open banking business models.

- **Promote Collaborations**: Policymakers and financial institutions should promote collaboration between traditional financial institutions and Fintechs to create new value propositions that benefit customers.
- **Advance Regulatory Frameworks**: Policymakers should advance regulatory frameworks that support changes while managing risks. This can include creating sandboxes in which Fintechs can test their products and services in a controlled environment and develop advanced regulatory systems that can keep up the pace with the rapid changes in the Fintech industry.
- **Infuse Talent and Technology**: Policymakers and financial institutions should infuse talent and technology to ensure that they have the skills and resources needed for the Fintech revolution. This can include investing in training programs for employees and developing affiliations with universities and financial services that are undergoing a paradigm shift due to the Fintech revolution; policymakers and financial institutions must navigate this revolution in order to capitalize on the opportunities it offers while mitigating the associated risks.

References

Accenture. (2021). *Banking in the new: Decoding the digital playbook*. Accenture.

Accenture. (2021). Open banking: The future of banking is here. Retrieved from https://www.accenture.com/us-en/insights/banking/open-banking

Arner, D. W., Barberis, J. N., & Buckley, R. P. (2017). The evolution of Fintech: A new post-crisis paradigm? University of Hong Kong Faculty of Law Research Paper (2017/018).

Arner, D. W., Barberis, J. N., & Buckley, R. P. (2017). The evolution of fintech: A new post-crisis paradigm? *Georgetown Journal of International Law*, 48(4), 1271–1319.

Arner, D. V., Frost, J., & Gandy, D. R. (2017). *The fintech revolution: How new technology is transforming the financial services industry*. Routledge.

Bank for International Settlements. (2020, January). Policy responses to fintech: A cross-country overview. Retrieved from https://www.bis.org/fsi/publ/insights23.pdf

Built In. (2023, September 21). What is fintech? Financial technology definition. Retrieved from https://builtin.com/fintech

Cointelegraph. (2022). How does high-frequency trading work on decentralized exchanges? Retrieved from https://cointelegraph.com/news/how-does-high-frequency-trading-work-on-decentralized-exchanges

Columbia Engineering Boot Camps. (2023, September 20). What is financial technology (Fintech)? A beginner's guide for 2023. Retrieved from https://bootcamp.cvn.columbia.edu/blog/what-is-fintech/

Cybersecurity Ventures. (2021). Cybersecurity statistics 2021. Retrieved from https://cybersecurityventures.com/top-5-cybersecurity-facts-figures-predictions-and-statistics-for-2019-to-2021/

DeFi Pulse. (2023). Total value locked. Retrieved from https://docs.defipulse.com/methodology/tvl

Ernst & Young. (2023). The future of banking: Open banking, Fintech, and the rise of ecosystems. Retrieved from https://www.ey.com/en_in/banking-capital-markets/fintech-ecosystems

European Central Bank. (2022). Open banking in Europe. Retrieved from https://www.openbankingeurope.eu/

European Commission. (2020). Antitrust: Commission fines financial institutions €344 million for cartels on government bonds. Retrieved from https://www.reuters.com/business/finance/eu-fines-bank-america-merrill-lynch-c-agricole-credit-suisse-285-mln-euros-2021-04-28/

EY. (2022). *Global fintech adoption index 2022*. EY.

EY. (2022). Open banking: The next chapter. Retrieved from https://www.ey.com/en_gl/open-banking

Gartner. (2023). Top 10 strategic technology trends for 2023. Retrieved from https://www.gartner.com/en/articles/gartner-top-10-strategic-technology-trends-for-2023

Gartner. (2023). *Top strategic predictions for 2023 and Beyond: Digital business acceleration*. Gartner.

Investopedia. (2023). Basics of algorithmic trading: Concepts and examples. Retrieved from https://www.investopedia.com/articles/active-trading/101014/basics-algorithmic-trading-concepts-and-examples.asp

Investopedia. (2023, September 23). Financial technology (Fintech): Its uses and impact on our lives. Retrieved from https://www.investopedia.com/terms/f/fintech.asp

Iqbal, M. J., Akhtar, M. F., & Hussain, M. (2020). Fintech and financial services: A systematic review of the literature. *Journal of Financial Services Marketing*, 25(3), 109–123.

Iqbal, M., Akhtar, N., & Khan, M. A. (2020). Fintech and its impact on financial services: A review of the literature. *Journal of Financial Services Marketing*, 25(2), 67–79.

Iqbal, Z., Usman, M., Farooq, M. U., & Khan, M. A. (2020). The impact of fintech on trading and hedging mechanisms in the financial services sector: A systematic review. *Risks*, 8(3), 53.

J.D. Power. (2022). 2022 US retail banking customer satisfaction study. Retrieved from https://www.jdpower.com/business/press-releases/2022-us-retail-banking-satisfaction-study

Kshetri, N. (2020). Fintech disruption in the global financial services industry: A review of literature. *Financial Innovation*, 6(1), 1–30.

Maan, B. (2023). Fintech & AI: Hedge funds innovation - Unleashing the power of multi-strategy hedge funds. Retrieved from https://www.linkedin.com/pulse/fintech-ai-hedge-funds-innovation-unleashing-power-bally-maan

McKinsey. (2022). Global trading report 2022. Retrieved from https://www.mckinsey .com/~/media/mckinsey/industries/financial%20services/our%20insights/the %202022%20mckinsey%20global%20payments%20report/the-2022-mckinsey -global-payments-report.pdf

Mohammed, T. B. (2022). Fintech and its impact on the financial services sector: A review of literature. *Journal of Financial Regulation and Compliance*, 30(2), 241–262.

Plaid. (2023, August 9). What is fintech? 6 main types of fintech and how they work. Retrieved from https://plaid.com/resources/fintech/what-is-fintech/

PwC. (2022). Global Fintech investment trends and growth opportunities. Retrieved from https://www.pwc.com/jg/en/publications/fintech-growing-influence-financial-services.html.

PwC. (2023). Open banking: The future of financial services. Retrieved from https://www.pwc.co.uk/industries/financial-services/insights/seize-open-banking-opportunity.html

Robinhood. (2023, November 07). Robinhood reports. Third quarter 2023 results. Retrieved from https://investors.robinhood.com/news/news-details/2023/Robinhood-Reports-Third-Quarter-2023-Results/default.aspx

Securities and Exchange Commission. (2021, September 24). Advocate for small business capital formation. Retrieved from https://www.sec.gov/files/2021_oasb_annual_forum_report_final_508.pdf

World Bank. (2023, September 19). Fintech and the future of finance. Retrieved from https://www.worldbank.org/en/publication/fintech-and-the-future-of-finance

Chapter 15

Insurtech: Powering Fintech's Evolution

Muneer Shaik and Medhansh Bairaria

15.1 Introduction

In the ever-changing world of finance, the merging of technology and financial services has sparked the Fintech revolution, as noted by Puschmann (2017) and Mention (2019), and the collision of insurance and technology, known as Insurtech, has emerged as a focal point of both interest and disruption in this dynamic landscape, as highlighted by Mueller (2018), Ma and Ren (2023), and Yan et al. (2018). This chapter explores the revolutionary influence of Insurtech, the amalgamation of insurance technology, in the global transformation of the Fintech arena. We endeavour to offer a comprehensive view of the impact and potential of Insurtech, drawing insights from a diverse array of credible sources, encompassing industry publications, scholarly research, and expert interviews.

This chapter will delve into the profound consequences of disruptive technologies such as artificial intelligence (AI), big data analytics, and the Internet of Things (IoT) on conventional insurance practices. Throughout the exploration, we will focus on how Insurtech improves client experiences, creates operational efficiencies, increases insurance access, and changes the global insurance environment. Some of the areas that will be addressed show how personalized insurance solutions, faster claims procedures, and cutting-edge distribution channels may alter the insurance industry. The

 DOI: 10.4324/9781032644165-15

ethical, legal, and regulatory ramifications of the use of Insurtech must be addressed. We'll look closely at privacy issues, cybersecurity dangers, and the need for strong regulatory frameworks that support innovation while safeguarding consumers. By doing this, we hope to encourage a fair understanding of the difficulties and obligations posed by the integration of Insurtech.

As we conclude this chapter, readers will gain a deeper understanding of how Insurtech is driving transformation in the broader Fintech revolution. Our discovery is intended to encourage insightful discussions and inspire future research into the evolving insurance landscape.

15.2 Literature Review

In the realm of insurance, Insurtech has risen as a powerful disruptor in recent times, commanding considerable attention for its fusion of technology and economics. Renowned scholars and industry stalwarts underscore how Insurtech's rapid proliferation, coupled with its embrace of cutting-edge technologies such as AI, big data, and blockchain, has ushered in a profound transformation in traditional insurance practices. The academic discourse delves into how Insurtech has reshaped the very fabric of the insurance value chain, redefined customer interactions, and reimagined the fundamental architecture of the industry itself (Stoeckli et al., 2018; Lin et al., 2020).

The literature delves into the field of operational efficiency and cost reductions in Insurtech. Using superior technologies, Insurtech has automated numerous insurance activities such as underwriting, claims handling, and risk assessment.

Research highlights the role of Insurtech in expanding insurance access to underserved populations. The literature examines the impact of Insurtech on microinsurance, parametric insurance, and reaching remote areas with limited access to traditional insurance services.

The present literature readily acknowledges the challenges and regulatory elements associated with the embrace of Insurtech. Concerns about privacy, data security, adherence to regulatory standards, and the ethical complexities involved in exploiting customer data emerge as important focal points.

15.3 The Evolution of Insurtech

15.3.1 The Emergence of Insurtech

The remarkable development trajectory of the Insurtech sector is demonstrated by the record-breaking 15.4 billion US dollars in capital raised in 2021.[1] It is projected that this upward tendency will continue as the demand for insurance-related products and services increases in a complex and interconnected world. Insurtech firms now have the opportunity to maximize productivity, leveraging the IoT, sophisticated analytics, AI, and automation to improve operations and use data-driven insights for better risk assessment and pricing (Sharma et al., 2022; Cortis et al., 2019; Nicoletti et al., 2017). As Insurtech start-ups continue to threaten established insurance practices, incumbents are being driven to investigate digital transformation and embrace technological advancements.[2]

15.3.2 Enhancing Customer Experience

The successful integration of AI chatbots and virtual assistants into Insurtech is a tremendous achievement. These clever solutions have ushered in a new era of timely and seamless customer service, dramatically cutting wait times and delivering assistance 24/7. According to Accenture research, AI-powered

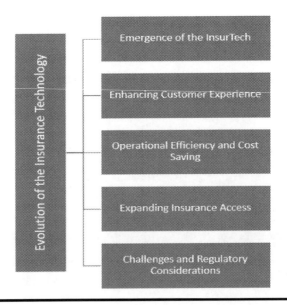

Figure 15.1   The evolution of Insurtech and its main functions

chatbots can handle an amazing 80% of customer inquiries, leaving human agents to focus on more complex issues.[3]

Moreover, Insurtech has played a pivotal role in crafting user-friendly mobile applications and internet platforms, granting clients effortless access to an extensive array of insurance offerings. These modern digital hubs present customers with a seamless, user-friendly interface, allowing them to effortlessly navigate through a diverse spectrum of insurance options as shown in figure 15.1.[4]

The infusion of advanced analytics and machine learning within Insurtech has yielded profound insights into customer preferences and risk profiles.[5] According to PricewaterhouseCoopers (PwC), Insurtech adoption has the potential to save insurance firms and their consumers between 30% and 40% on claim-processing costs. With fewer manual chores to manage, insurers can focus more on providing efficient and timely services to their clients, while customers benefit from faster and less complicated claims processing.[6]

15.3.3 Operational Efficiency and Cost Savings in Insurtech

This section digs into Insurtech's substantial impact on operational efficiency, shining light on its potential to generate large financial gains.

15.3.3.1 Streamlined Underwriting Processes

Insurtech organizations have adopted automated underwriting procedures by integrating cutting-edge technologies leading to a significant rise in workflow efficiency. This digital transformation not only speeds up underwriting operations but also improves accuracy, resulting in higher revenue for insurance firms (Liu et al., 2023). According to research, integrating Insurtech might potentially reduce costs by 25% to 35% due to savings brought about by automation and digitization.[7]

15.3.3.2 Efficient Claims Handling

The landscape of claims handling has been profoundly transformed by Insurtech, owing to the integration of AI and machine learning (ML). This improved automation of claims processing has the potential to save costs by 30% to 40%, allowing insurers to better deploy their resources and focus their efforts on providing excellent service.[8]

15.3.3.3 Enhanced Risk Assessment

Data-driven strategy enables insurers to make better-informed decisions, fine-tune their risk portfolios, and price their offers more correctly. Incorporating sophisticated analytics into Insurtech can improve loss ratios by up to 20%, providing a mutual benefit to insurers and policyholders.[9]

15.3.3.4 Cost Savings for Insurers and Customers

The operational improvements brought about by Insurtech have a direct influence on cost savings for both insurers and customers. Process simplification decreases administrative costs, and automated claims processing enables insurers to offer more competitive rates (Njegomir et al., 2023). This not only means possible financial benefits for customers but also means faster and more precise services.[10]

15.3.4 Microinsurance and Inclusive Coverage: The Case of BIMA

BIMA, a pioneering Insurtech start-up, uses mobile technology to provide microinsurance coverage to underprivileged areas in emerging nations. BIMA has accomplished a remarkable feat by simplifying the difficult process of underwriting and digitizing the claims system, reaching out to about 37 million people who were previously uninsured. This outstanding achievement not only promotes financial inclusion but also strengthens their ability to face unexpected problems.[11]

15.3.4.1 Parametric Insurance and Risk Mitigation: The Case of Hurricane-linked Insurance

A remarkable example of this can be found in the field of hurricane-related insurance. The traditional technique of insuring against hurricane-related losses can be complicated and time-consuming. However, by exploiting the possibilities of insurance-powered parametric insurance, firms such as Swiss Re have cleverly constructed plans that are linked to specific weather indications. For example, if wind speeds exceed a certain threshold during a storm, policyholders are automatically compensated.

15.3.4.2 Reaching Remote Areas and Digital Distribution: The Case of BIMA in Ghana

A remarkable instance of this is seen in Ghana, where BIMA formed a partnership with MTN, a prominent telecommunications entity, to extend insurance services to communities that were previously unreached. By capitalizing on the expansive network of mobile operators, BIMA introduced tailor-made micro-insurance policies tailored specifically to the needs of Ghanaians, covering aspects such as life, health, and accidents. Leveraging the wide reach of MTN and the power of mobile technology, BIMA managed to successfully extend its services to remote locales where traditional insurance providers had struggled to establish a foothold. This noteworthy collaboration stands as a testament to how Insurtech has the potential to erase geographical limitations and offer insurance coverage to populations that were once isolated from such services.

15.3.5 Privacy Concerns and Data Protection

One of the foremost challenges in the realm of Insurtech revolves around privacy concerns and data protection. Insurtech companies, driven by the need to personalize insurance offerings, collect substantial amounts of personal data. However, appropriate data processing is critical for addressing privacy concerns and complying with severe data protection rules.

15.3.5.1 Data Security and Cybersecurity Risks

The insurance industry's increasing reliance on technology and digital procedures poses substantial vulnerabilities in terms of data protection and cybersecurity. Protecting client data from unauthorized access, breaches, and cyberinvasions has emerged as a critical problem for Insurtech businesses. To best combat these threats, robust cybersecurity measures, such as advanced encryption techniques, regular security audits, and thorough personnel training efforts, must be proactively implemented.

15.3.5.2 Regulatory Compliance and Supervision

As Insurtech innovations continue to reshape the industry, comprehensive regulations are necessary to address the specific challenges posed by technological advancements. These regulations encompass areas such as data privacy, consumer protection, risk management, and fair competition (Chatzara, 2020; Marano et al., 2020). Collaborative efforts between regulatory bodies and Insurtech stakeholders are essential in developing regulatory frameworks that foster innovation while upholding the best interests of policyholders.

15.3.5.3 Ethical Implications of Customer Data Usage

The ethical implications associated with customer data usage in the Insurtech realm require thoughtful consideration. Insurtech companies have access to a wealth of customer data, and responsible and ethical utilization of this information is paramount (Derradji et al., 2023). Transparency in data usage practices, clear communication with policyholders regarding data collection and utilization, and adherence to ethical guidelines and standards are critical aspects.

15.3.5.4 Building Robust Regulatory Frameworks

The literature underscores the significance of regulatory bodies collaborating closely with industry stakeholders to develop clear guidelines and standards (Sharan, 2023). By striking the right balance, regulatory frameworks can create an environment that fosters Insurtech innovation, protects the interests of policyholders, and promotes fair competition within the industry.[12]

15.4 Advantages of Insurtech

15.4.1 Enhanced Customer Experience

According to a significant survey performed by Accenture Research (2021)[13], 80% of insurance executives believe that customer experience would determine market differences. Insurtech firms have effectively developed insurance products that are not only personalized but also readily available depending on consumer requirements by strategically utilizing cutting-edge technology such as AI, big data analytics, and mobile applications (Azmi et al., 2020; Eling et al., 2021). As a result, this paradigm change has resulted in a tremendous increase in customer satisfaction, building strong bonds between insurers and policyholders.[14]

15.4.2 *Improved Operational Efficiency*

Insurtech acts as a catalyst for optimizing complex insurance procedures, ushering in a new era of increased operational efficiency. The use of automation in critical processes including underwriting, claims processing, and risk assessment streamlines complex workflows, decreasing the need for considerable manual intervention and, as a result, administrative costs. This improved efficiency not only saves insurers money, with potential savings of up to 30%, but it also improves the overall quality and speed of service delivery to clients. Along with this, new revenue-generating opportunities develop. The traditional notion of insurance as a low-engagement, disintermediated business where customer interactions are mostly facilitated by agents and brokers is rapidly becoming obsolete. The digital landscape, together with the important insights produced from data analysis, provides insurers with unprecedented chances to better understand their clients.

15.4.3 *Expanded Insurance Access*

According to a report by PwC (2022), the digital distribution channels offered by Insurtech companies have made it easier for individuals in remote or inaccessible areas to access insurance products and services.[15] This has contributed to greater financial inclusion, bringing insurance coverage to those who were previously excluded from traditional insurance offerings. For example, microinsurance products offered by Insurtech firms have provided affordable insurance solutions to low-income individuals in emerging markets, increasing their financial resilience.

15.5 Disadvantages of Insurtech

15.5.1 *Regulatory and Compliance Challenges*

Insurtech operates within a complex regulatory environment, necessitating compliance with insurance laws, consumer protection regulations, and data privacy requirements. Keeping up with evolving regulations and ensuring compliance can be challenging, particularly for start-ups and innovative Insurtech firms.

15.5.2 Technological Dependencies and Risks

Insurtech heavily relies on advanced technologies, making it vulnerable to technological risks and dependencies. System failures, cyberattacks, or technological glitches can disrupt operations, leading to service disruptions, financial losses, and reputational damage.

15.5.3 Resistance to Change and Industry Disruption

Disruptive innovations and new business models introduced by Insurtech start-ups can challenge existing industry practices and disrupt established market players. Overcoming resistance and navigating industry dynamics require strong leadership, effective change management strategies, and collaboration between incumbents and Insurtech firms.[16]

15.6 Challenges of Insurtech

15.6.1 Regulatory Complexity

The Insurtech industry operates within a complex regulatory landscape, with different jurisdictions imposing varying insurance laws, consumer protection regulations, and data privacy requirements. According to a survey conducted by Deloitte, 87% of Insurtech executives consider regulatory compliance as a significant hurdle in their operations, highlighting the urgency for regulatory clarity and streamlined processes.

15.6.2 Data Privacy and Security

The rise of Insurtech has resulted in massive amounts of personal and sensitive data being collected, stored, and analyzed, raising the importance of data privacy and security to new heights. To safeguard clients from potential cyber-risks and unauthorized access, the sector must put in place strong data protection measures such as encryption, secure storage technology, and tight access controls. According to an informative survey by One Inc., a remarkable 86% of consumers are concerned about the privacy of their data.[17]

15.6.3 Customer Trust and Adoption

Building trust and encouraging the widespread use of Insurtech solutions emerge as critical considerations in assuring the sector's long-term existence

(Dekkal et al., 2023). To handle this hurdle, Insurtech companies must engage in proactive consumer education programs. An important poll done by Capgemini emphasizes this point, finding that a considerable 59% of consumers see personalized services provided by Insurtech enterprises as a critical incentive for their adoption.

15.7 Implications of Insurtech

15.7.1 Personalization

The rise of Insurtech has caused a significant shift in the insurance sector toward customer-centricity. This change is supported by Insurtech businesses' skilful use of cutting-edge technology such as AI and sophisticated data analytics. These technologies enable the analysis of consumer data, allowing for the implementation of tailored insurance solutions and customer experiences.

15.7.2 Industry Disruption and Collaboration

Insurtech has presented a significant challenge to the industry's main participants, drastically altering the landscape of traditional insurance practices. Fostering strategic relationships, making investments, and even organizing acquisitions between these incumbent corporations and the growing Insurtech firms are all part of this.

15.7.3 Enhanced Efficiency and Cost Reduction

Insurtech solutions are critical in the areas of process automation, operational efficiencies, and cost reduction. The use of AI-powered chatbots for customer service, combined with the automation of underwriting and claims processing, results in increased efficiency and lower operational costs. Insurtech can transform the underlying structure of traditional insurance business models, which goes beyond immediate efficiency improvements.

15.8 Future Trends in Insurtech

15.8.1 Expansion of the Insurtech Ecosystem

The Insurtech arena is ready to witness the introduction of fresh solutions and innovative business models, precisely crafted to correspond with the ever-changing expectations of consumers and the market at large, propelled by the continual growth of technology (Puschmann, 2017).

15.8.2 Embracing AI and ML

The intersection of AI and ML is poised to shape the future of insurance technology. These technologies, which rely on sophisticated algorithms, can improve a wide range of critical operations, from refined risk assessment and adept claims management to smart fraud detection and enhanced customer relations such as the growth of crowdfunding and peer-to-peer (P2P) lending (Balasubramanian et al., 2018; Rabbani et al., 2022).

15.8.3 Focus on Customer Experience and Engagement

Utilizing customer data, digital platforms, and mobile apps, insurers will offer tailored insurance options and convenient self-service, aiming to foster strong and lasting customer relationships.

15.8.4 Addressing Emerging Risks

Cybersecurity threats, data breaches, and ethical concerns surrounding AI and automation will require ongoing attention and proactive risk management. Collaboration between industry stakeholders, regulators, and policymakers will be crucial in navigating these risks effectively. It is also critical to understand how shocks like COVID-19 would impact the Insurtech industry like other industries and the economy (Singh et al., 2021; Shaik et al., 2023; Akhtar et al., 2020).

15.9 Conclusion

Insurtech, or the use of sophisticated technologies in the insurance industry, has brought both advantages and disadvantages. On the plus side, Insurtech has changed the delivery of insurance services, increasing client satisfaction through tailored and on-demand alternatives. It has also improved operational efficiency by automating processes, reducing the need for manual intervention, and enabling faster and more accurate decision-making. Insurtech has also expanded insurance access to underprivileged groups, bridging the coverage gap and increasing financial inclusion.

However, Insurtech faces some challenges that must be overcome. Concerns regarding data privacy and security have risen in response to increased reliance on technology and the collection of massive amounts of personal information. Another significant issue is balancing innovation and regulatory compliance, as Insurtech operates in a complex regulatory environment. System outages and cyberattacks are instances of technology dependencies and threats that jeopardize operations and reputation.

Moving forward, it is important to consider the implications of Insurtech. Customer-centricity and personalization will continue to be prioritized, leading to tailored insurance offerings and improved customer engagement. Collaboration between traditional insurers and Insurtech firms is essential to drive industry-wide transformation and stay competitive. Enhanced efficiency and cost reduction will reshape traditional insurance models, making operations more streamlined and profitable.

Notes

1. Ernst & Young LLP. Insurtech: Transforming insurance through technology. Retrieved from https://www.ey.com/en_us/insurance/Insurtech-trends-and -investment-landscape?WT.mc_id=10818314&AA.tsrc=paidsearch&gad=1
2. Deloitte. (2021). Insurtech: Innovating to stay ahead. Retrieved from https:// www2.deloitte.com/global/en/pages/financial-services/articles/Insurtech.html
3. Accenture. (2021). The Future of Insurance: Three Key Insurtech Trends. Retrieved from https://www.accenture.com/us-en/insights/insurance/future -insurance-Insurtech-trends
4. McKinsey & Company. (2018). Insurance 2030 - The impact of AI on the future of insurance. Retrieved from https://www.mckinsey.com/industries/ financial-services/our-insights/insurance-2030-the-impact-of-ai-on-the-future-of -insurance
5. KPMG. (2020). Insurtech: Innovating to Win. Retrieved from https://assets .kpmg/content/dam/kpmg/us/pdf/2020/04/us-Insurtech-innovating-to-win .pdf
6. PwC. (2021). Insurance 2025: Redefining the Customer Experience. Retrieved from https://www.pwc.com/gx/en/industries/insurance/library/insurance-2025/ customer-experience.html
7. McKinsey & Company. (2018). Insurance 2030 - The impact of AI on the future of insurance. Retrieved from https://www.mckinsey.com/industries/ financial-services/our-insights/insurance-2030-the-impact-of-ai-on-the-future-of -insurance
8. Capgemini. (2018). World Insurtech Report 2018. Retrieved from https://www .assiteca.it/wp-content/uploads/2018/10/WITR_2018_Final_Web-1.pdf

9. Deloitte. (2021). The Future of Insurtech: Redefining the Insurance Value Proposition. Retrieved from https://www2.deloitte.com/content/dam/Deloitte/global/Documents/Financial-Services/dttl-fsi-Insurtech-trends.pdf

10. Insurtech: Infrastructure for New Insurance - KPMG. (n.d.). Retrieved from https://assets.kpmg.com/content/dam/kpmg/cn/pdf/en/2019/07/insurance-technology.pdf

11. Microinsurance and Inclusive Coverage: The Case of BIMA. Retrieved from https://www.digitalinsuranceagenda.com/featured-Insurtechs/bima-brings-micro-insurance-to-underserved-families-in-emerging-markets/

12. Data Protection Compliance for Insurance Companies - Ekran System. (2023, April 12). Retrieved from https://www.ekransystem.com/en/blog/data-protection-compliance-insurance-industry

13. Accenture Research. (2021). Business Futures 2021: Signals of Change. Retrieved from https://www.accenture.com/content/dam/accenture/final/a-com-migration/manual/r3/pdf/pdf-5/Accenture-Signals-Of-Change-Business-Futures-2021-Report.pdf

14. Deloitte. (2021). Insurtech: Innovating to stay ahead. Retrieved from https://www2.deloitte.com/global/en/pages/financial-services/articles/Insurtech.html

15. PwC. (2022). How Insurtechs are transforming (re)insurers. Retrieved from https://www.pwc.com/gx/en/insurance/pdf/pwc-Insurtechs-transforming-reinsurers.pdf

16. PwC. (2021). How Insurtechs can ease growing pains. Retrieved from https://www.pwc.com/us/en/industries/financial-services/library/Insurtechs-challenges.html

17. One Inc. (2022). Data Privacy: The Insurance Industry's Next Obstacle. Retrieved from https://www.oneinc.com/resources/blog/data-privacy-the-insurance-industrys-next-obstacle

References

Akhtar, S., Niazi, M. H., & Khan, M. M. (2020). The cascading effect of COVID-19 on Indian economy. *International Journal of Advanced Science and Technology, 29*(9), 4563–4573.

Azmi, S., Akhtar, S., & Nadeem, M. (2020). Impact of digitalisation on bank performance: A study of Indian Banks. *Test Engineering and Management, 83,* 23678–23691.

Balasubramanian, R., Libarikian, A., & McElhaney, D. (2018). *Insurance 2030—The Impact of AI on the Future of Insurance.* McKinsey & Company.

Chatzara, V. (2020). Fintech, Insurtech, and the regulators. In *Insurtech: A Legal and Regulatory View,* 3–25.

Cortis, D., Debattista, J., Debono, J., & Farrell, M. (2019). Insurtech. In *Disrupting Finance: Fintech and Strategy in the 21st Century,* 71–84.

Dekkal, M., Arcand, M., Prom Tep, S., Rajaobelina, L., & Ricard, L. (2023). Factors affecting user trust and intention in adopting chatbots: The moderating role of technology anxiety in Insurtech. *Journal of Financial Services Marketing*, 1–30.

Derradji, A., & Aouatef, M. (2023). The impact of the financial position elements changes on the market capitalization of Insurtech companies: A standard study on a sample of companies operating in the US insurance market using panel models. *Economic Perspectives*, 8(2), 39–52.

Eling, M., Nuessle, D., & Staubli, J. (2021). The impact of artificial intelligence along the insurance value chain and on the insurability of risks. In *The Geneva Papers on Risk and Insurance-Issues and Practice*, 47(2), 205–241.

Lin, L., & Chen, C. (2020, March). The promise and perils of Insurtech. *Singapore Journal of Legal Studies*, 115–142.

Liu, J., Ye, S., Zhang, Y., & Zhang, L. (2023). Research on Insurtech and the technology innovation level of Insurance enterprises. *Sustainability*, 15(11), 8617.

Ma, Y. L., & Ren, Y. (2023). Insurtech—Promise, threat or hype? Insights from stock market reaction to Insurtech innovation. *Pacific-Basin Finance Journal*, 80, 102059.

Marano, P., & Noussia, K. (Eds.). (2020). *Insurtech: A Legal and Regulatory View*. Springer International Publishing.

Mention, A. L. (2019). The future of fintech. *Research-Technology Management*, 62(4), 59–63.

Mueller, J. (2018). *Insurtech Rising: A Profile of the Insurtech Landscape*. Milken Institute, 10.

Nicoletti, B., & Nicoletti, B. (2017). A business model for Insurtech initiatives. In *The Future of Fintech: Integrating Finance and Technology in Financial Services*, 211–249.

Njegomir, V., & Demko-Rihter, J. (2023). Insurtech: New competition to traditional insurers and impact on the economic growth. In *Digital Transformation of the Financial Industry: Approaches and Applications* (pp. 133–150). Springer International Publishing.

Puschmann, T. (2017). Fintech. *Business & Information Systems Engineering*, 59, 69–76.

Rabbani, M. R., Bashar, A., Hawaldar, I. T., Shaik, M., & Selim, M. (2022). What do we know about crowdfunding and P2P lending research? A bibliometric review and meta-analysis. *Journal of Risk and Financial Management*, 15(10), 451.

Shaik, M., Jamil, S. A., Hawaldar, I. T., Sahabuddin, M., Rabbani, M. R., & Atif, M. (2023). Impact of geo-political risk on stocks, oil, and gold returns during GFC, COVID-19, and Russian–Ukraine War. *Cogent Economics & Finance*, 11(1), 2190213.

Sharan, B. (2023). A discussion of the impact of technology on insurance law. *Indian Journal of Law and Legal Research*, 5(2), 1.

Sharma, V., & Sood, D. (2022). Adoption of internet of things and services in the Indian insurance industry. In *Big Data: A Game Changer for Insurance Industry* (pp. 35–42). Emerald Publishing Limited.

Singh, G., & Shaik, M. (2021). The short-term impact of COVID-19 on global stock market indices. *Contemporary Economics*, 1–18.

Stoeckli, E., Dremel, C., & Uebernickel, F. (2018). Exploring characteristics and transformational capabilities of Insurtech innovations to understand insurance value creation in a digital world. *Electronic Markets*, *28*, 287–305.

Yan, T. C., Schulte, P., & Chuen, D. L. K. (2018). Insurtech and Fintech: Banking and insurance enablement. *Handbook of Blockchain, Digital Finance, and Inclusion*, *1*, 249–281.

Chapter 16

Insurtech Disruption: Reshaping the Future of Insurance in the Fintech Era

K Balaji and Ezendu Ariwa

16.1 Introduction: Background

Insurtech has become an influential player in the world of conventional insurance, reversing accepted practices and changing how insurance offerings are developed, sold, and handled. The whole insurance value chain, from underwriting and handling claims to customer interaction and risk evaluation, is being reimagined by Insurtech start-ups and traditional insurers alike through the use of technology. A new generation of clear, readily available, and increasingly personalized operations, goods, and services have emerged as a result of the use of Insurtech products. Because of this, insurance is now readily available to a wider spectrum of clients, particularly individuals who had been once underserved. Insurtech innovations encompass a variety of areas.

The fusion of data analytics and artificial intelligence (AI) is reshaping the insurance sector. Insurers are able to improve risk evaluations, hone underwriting procedures, and strengthen identification of fraud through the utilization of vast data. The emergence of digital distribution networks, which have made it easier for clients to assess and select coverage alternatives with ease via websites and mobile applications, is comparable to this. Blockchain

DOI: 10.4324/9781032644165-16

technology has become a crucial factor, bringing greater safety and openness to insurance operations. This invention has simplified the claims filing procedure and reduced fraudulent occurrences. Telemetry uses monitoring devices to assess driving behaviour, especially in the auto insurance industry. This data-driven methodology enables insurers to develop usage-based policies that accurately represent unique driving preferences.

With the development of Insurtech, new ideas such as peer-to-peer (P2P) insurance have taken off, allowing a group of people to pool their money in order to jointly reduce certain risks. Micro-insurance serves underserved and lower-income people and is made possible by online services and mobile applications. On-demand insurance, which is represented by single-trip travel insurance, allows policy activation or deactivation according to specific events or needs, thus propelling the change. Utilizing blockchain technology, smart contracts speed up the review of complaints and reimbursements by automatically carrying out predetermined criteria. Additionally, AI permeates the claims domain, as AI-powered chatbots and algorithms speed up claims processing and increase the effectiveness of customer support. These revolutionary developments come together to transform the insurance industry into one that is not only secure and data-informed but also incredibly customer-centric.

Besides improving the client experience, Insurtech also helps insurers by streamlining risk analysis, lowering operating expenses, and minimizing false claims. To remain competitive and inventive as the Insurtech environment changes, established insurance firms have been collaborating or acquiring Insurtech start-ups. Insurtech, which uses technologies to build an improved customer-focused, effective, and readily available environment for insurance goods and services, is essentially an evolutionary change in the insurance industry.

16.2 Objectives of the Chapter

This chapter aims to achieve the following objectives.

1. Examine the historical evolution of insurance technology under the context of financial technology.
2. Investigate the way innovations in areas such as risk evaluation, customer engagement, and handling claims has been made possible by Insurtech, which has upended conventional insurance structures.

3. Analyze customer views and actions regarding technologically driven insurance offerings while determining how credibility influences acceptance and promotes ongoing relationships with customers.
4. Examine the legal concerns raised by the inclusion of Insurtech, looking at how legal compliance, security of data, and ethical concerns are handled in this dynamic environment.

16.3 Theoretical Background

16.3.1 History of Insurtech

The development of Insurtech charts the revolutionary path of technology's enormous impact on the insurance sector. This story highlights significant turning points which have affected its development, covering from the beginning to its current position as a potent disruptor. Computers sparked an operational renaissance throughout the 1960s to the 1990s, speeding underwriting, policy management, and claims handling. Online insurance portals and price comparison sites emerged in the 2000s, easing the procedure of comparing policies and making purchases. Telematics gained popularity for detailed risk assessments in auto insurance by utilizing GPS and sensors. The 2010s saw the emergence of Insurtech, which was characterized by start-ups adopting technologically advanced solutions for insurance. P2P platforms arose, changing the pattern of risk-sharing, and insurance based on usage prospered thanks to the incorporation of telematics and the Internet of Things (IoT). Smoothly purchasing insurance and submitting claims was made possible by digital platforms and user-friendly apps. In parallel, AI and machine learning transformed the underwriting and claims procedures, while blockchain technology brought transparent improvements and the ability to reduce fraud. Particularly focused start-ups have emerged, such as those offering micro-insurance and parametric insurance.

The early 2020s saw the growth of Insurtech, which was characterized by joint initiatives between established insurers and start-ups. This convergence combined cutting-edge innovation with expert industrial understanding. Data analytics, AI, and machine learning were integrated to develop techniques for risk assessment and improve customer service. The development of fresh insurance products and creative pricing methods was influenced by the IoT, wearables, and sensor technology. As Insurtech developed, personalized, on-demand coverage became more popular. Despite the advancements, problems such as legislative complexities and privacy issues continued, necessitating constant monitoring. The background of Insurtech describes how the technology's revolutionary impact led to the development of insurance into a customer-centric, efficiency-focused industry. Insurtech, which encompasses innovation, distribution of wealth, and interaction with customers, is positioned to continue to transform the field of insurance as advances in technology occur.

16.3.2 Major Components of Insurtech

Insurtech encompasses a range of technological innovations that impact various components of the insurance industry, from customer engagement to risk assessment and claims processing. The following sections discuss the major components of Insurtech.

16.3.2.1 Technology-Related Elements

Some of the technologies that these businesses employ include the following.

1. **AI**: This is the term for computer programmes that mimic human abilities. Chatbots are one type of AI-based tool that insurance companies utilize to answer consumer questions.
2. **Advanced Analytics**: By utilizing data analytics, insurance businesses can gain a deeper understanding of consumer needs. It enables businesses to put into practise a distinctive strategy for marketing. They are then able to maintain an advantage over their rivals as a result.
3. **IoT**: Using gadgets that link to the internet, the IoT enables businesses to gather information for risk analysis. IoT includes electronic gadgets such as GPS devices used in automobiles. These devices collect data, such as the vehicle's speed and location, and then communicate it through the network. Such information can be used by commercial auto insurance providers for accident analysis, discounting, etc., which is similar to how smartwatch data can aid in the identification of health risks.
4. **Drones**: A number of insurers, particularly property insurance firms, use drones to survey homes in risky areas, such as homes in regions vulnerable to earthquakes or hurricane damage. Drones can also be used by casualty insurance firms to survey the scene of auto accidents.

5. **Applications for Mobile Devices**: For both clients and providers of insurance, firms can create applications for smartphones. As was already said, these apps have been crucial in simplifying the back-office activities of insurers and enhancing the customer experience.

6. **Machine Learning**: As the term implies, machine learning (ML), a branch of AI, enables machines and tools to acquire new skills as time passes. It entails creating algorithms that mimic the neural networks seen in the human brain. By recognizing and extracting trends from raw data, it allows machines to gather helpful data about clients. By considering these trends, insurers may forecast client requirements and determine premium costs.

A last benefit of using blockchain technology is improved security of information. As a result, it increases customer and insurance company trust. At the same time, it reduces transaction fees, makes it easier to collect better data, and speeds up the processing of insurance claims.

16.3.2.2 Solution-Based Components

The elements that constitute solution-based components include the following.

1. **Data Solutions**: Data is a major driving force in the insurance sector. As a result, businesses need to use it as effectively as they can. Users can get useful data through interconnected networks with the aid of data services.

2. **Appetite Solutions**: These tools assist brokers and agents in narrowing down the market's possibilities to a specific policy for a client. The brokers' effectiveness consequently rises. Additionally, it offers a variety of underwriting possibilities for insurers to think about.

3. **Price Solutions**: With the help of these solutions, brokers and agents can enter information into the system to receive a preapproved price. Both brokers and consumers benefit from this time savings.

4. **Payment Solutions**: By digitizing the systems, payment solutions make it simple for customers to make payments. These components collectively reshape the insurance industry, making it more responsive, efficient, and customer-centric. Insurtech's transformative impact continues to evolve as technology advances and innovative solutions emerge.

16.3.3 Theoretical Foundation

The theoretical foundations of many fields, including insurance, technology, economics, and creativity, are combined to form the basis of Insurtech. The theoretical basis and fundamental values for the creation and application of technical advancements in the insurance sector are provided by this foundation. The following are a few important Insurtech conceptual pillars.

16.3.3.1 Insurance Theory

Insurance theory, which focuses on analyzing and managing risks, is a major source of inspiration for Insurtech. The core idea of protecting against unforeseen disasters serves as the foundation for cutting-edge risk assessment methods and fresh insurance coverage. Risk estimation as well as the price of insurance policies are all governed by actuarial principles. To improve actuarial procedures, Insurtech makes use of cutting-edge data analytics and AI.

16.3.3.2 Technology and Innovation Theory

Disruptive innovation is a theory that Clayton Christensen developed to describe why new technology upends established businesses and sectors. By challenging conventional insurance models and changing industry behaviour, Insurtech works as an innovator in the insurance industry. Everett Rogers's theory explains how various societal groups acquire new technologies. Adoption of Insurtech follows the diffusion curve, starting with innovators, moving via early adopters, and finally reaching the mass market.

16.3.3.3 Information Technology and Data Science

Data Analytics: To analyze enormous volumes of data and glean insightful information for risk evaluation, underwriting, and handling claims, Insurtech uses data science concepts.
ML and AI: Algorithms that automate making choices, improve customer service, and optimize procedures for insurance are developed using mathematical concepts from ML and AI.

16.3.3.4 Behavioural Economics

The field of behavioural economics studies whether psychological variables affect financial choices. By implementing wellness initiatives that are connected to insurance benefits, Insurtech uses these concepts to promote positive behaviours such as developing beneficial behaviours.

16.3.3.5 Economic and Business Models

16.3.3.5.1 Peer-to-Peer (P2P) and Sharing Economy

With the use of technological systems, Insurtech enables people to jointly cover other people's risks by incorporating ideas of the sharing economy and P2P systems. These business models, which are frequently employed by digital start-ups, have an impact on the way Insurtech businesses provide additional services or interact with clients via subscriber-based insurance services.

16.3.3.6 Digital Transformation and Ecosystem Theory

Insurtech makes use of the economy of platforms to build environments that connect clients, agents, insurance companies, and technology companies with unified solutions and value propositions. Insurtech is a great illustration of how technology is profoundly altering how insurance is thought about, offered for sale, and provided to customers.

16.3.4 Models for Insurtech

The insurance sector is driven by innovation, efficiency, and client involvement through the use of diverse Insurtech models. These frameworks cover several methods for creating products, distribution, risk analysis, and client engagement. The following are a few major approaches that Insurtech companies have used.

1. **P2P Insurance**: P2P insurance solutions combine the assets of a number of people to safeguard against their mutual risks. Users of the organization split the expenses of claims, but any money that is left over may be refunded as dividends or donated to charity. Members in this paradigm are encouraged to experience a feeling of shared accountability and togetherness.
2. **Usage-Based Insurance (UBI)**: UBI entails adjusting insurance rates in accordance with actual usage and behaviour trends. Insurance companies may provide individualized rates and rewards for safe behaviour thanks to telematics devices, IoT sensors, and data analytics, which track behaviours such as driving patterns.

3. **Parametric Insurance**: A predetermined sum is paid out by parametric insurance in response to certain causes, such as climate change or earthquakes. It does away with the requirement for conventional claims processing and offers quicker payments when a triggering event occurs.

4. **Micro-Insurance**: Low-income and marginalized communities can choose from a limited selection of economical micro-insurance policies. Thanks to Insurtech, which makes use of online platforms and mobile applications, micro-insurance is now available to folks who had no alternative choices for insurance.

5. **Digital Insurance**: Clients may easily research, evaluate, and buy insurance products online thanks to online platforms. These marketplaces on the internet make it easier for users to shop by providing a variety of insurance services from various suppliers.

6. **Bundled Insurance Services**: To provide insurance as a component of a bundled service, Insurtech businesses collaborate with non-insurance organizations such as merchants or travel agencies. This strategy reaches clients throughout pertinent activities and improves insurance exposure and ease.

These various examples show how Insurtech is changing the insurance industry by utilizing technology to develop cutting-edge products, improving customer service, and increasing operational effectiveness.

16.3.5 Global Insurtech Market Size

The size of the worldwide Insurtech industry was estimated at 5.45 billion US dollars in 2022 and is anticipated to increase at a compound annual growth rate (CAGR) of 52.7% from 2023 to 2030. One of the key drivers of the industry's expansion is the rise in claims for insurance across the globe. The three types of claims for insurance that individuals most frequently obtain are auto, life, and house. In response Insurance Barometer research from 2021, 36% of Americans said they intended to buy life insurance that year. In order to cut operating expenses, increase efficiency in operations, and enhance every aspect of the customer journey, insurers are making investments more and more in technological innovations. The size of the worldwide Insurtech industry is depicted in Figure 16.1.

Figure 16.1 shows the size of the worldwide Insurtech industry. According to Grandview research, the size of the worldwide Insurtech industry was estimated at 5.45 billion US dollars in 2022 and is anticipated to increase at a CAGR of 52.7% from 2023 to 2030.

16.3.6 India Insurtech Market Size

The expansion of the Insurtech industry is being propelled by a change in customer preference for healthcare products and a staggering 167% rise in financing. The size of the India Insurtech market is depicted in Figure 16.2.

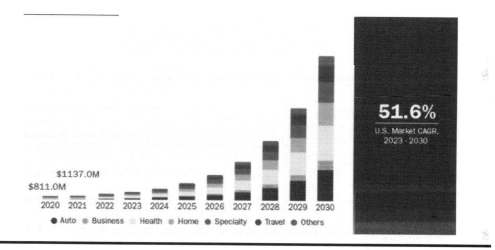

Figure 16.1   Global Insurtech market size (Based on Grandview research.com)

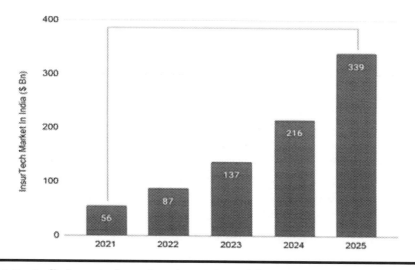

Figure 16.2   India Insurtech market size (Adapted from INC 42)

Figure 16.2 shows that Insurtech in India has a revenue potential of 339 billion US dollars by 2025, with a 57% CAGR, based on Inc42's latest "Status of Indian Fintech Survey Q2 2022."

16.3.7 Key Players in Insurtech in India and the Globe

The Insurtech landscape is dynamic and evolving, with various players making an impact in India and globally. While the landscape may have changed since then, the following are some key players in Insurtech from both India and the global stage.

16.3.7.1 Insurtech Players in India

The Policy Bazaar, a top online healthcare aggregator that makes it easy to compare and buy a variety of insurance policies, and Coverfox, a digital insurance brokerage platform that offers a range of online insurance services, are major players in the Indian Insurtech sector. While Digit Insurance pursues a tech-driven strategy to expedite insurance offerings and claims procedures, Acko stands out as a digital insurance provider that offers innovative offerings such as micro-insurance and usage-based coverage. Individualized insurance suggestions are offered by Turtlemint's digital platform, ease of use is prioritized by Go Digit in its range of insurance choices, and technologically enabled insurance products are provided by Symbo using data analytics and AI. With comparing and buying services, Renew Buy streamlines the insurance purchasing process. Easy policy functions in an online insurance market enable policy evaluations and purchases.

16.3.7.2 Global Insurtech Players

Lemonade, an AI-driven insurance company that prioritizes homeowners and renters' insurance with a clear and straightforward approach, is one of the most well-known international Insurtech businesses. Based on your driving patterns, Root Insurance customizes auto insurance using telematics. Data analytics are used by Hippo, a company with an online focus, to provide correct homeowner insurance coverage. Leading Chinese online insurer ZhongAn provides a wide selection of digital insurance products. Wefox is a German digital platform that connects insurance agents, clients, and insurers for improved service and distribution. Blockchain is used by the UK company Globacap to issue and manage insurance-linked securities effectively.

For pay-per-mile auto insurance, Metro mile uses telematics and a digital-first strategy. Applications for term life insurance are made simple by Haven Life. UK-based Neos combines house insurance with smart home technology for proactive risk management. The data used by various Insurtech players in India and the globe are depicted Table 16.1.

Table 16.1 depicts the key Insurtech players in India and the globe that support Insurtech industry growth and development.

16.4 SWOT Analysis of the Insurtech Industry

A SWOT analysis examines the strengths, weaknesses, opportunities, and threats of an industry or organization. A SWOT analysis of the Insurtech industry is shown in Figure 16.3.

Figure 16.3 highlights the analysis of strengths (new products are being introduced, room for corporate expansion, rising per capita income, and middle-class expansion), weaknesses (inadequate funding, hegemony of government-owned businesses, and barriers to advertising), opportunities (rising demand, strong growth potential, rising consumer income and consciousness, and expanded health coverage), and threats (need to manage different risks, including exposure to natural disasters and financial risks) of an Insurtech industry.

Table 16.1   Insurtech Players in India and the Globe (Data from Google)

S.NO	Insurtech Players in India	Global Insurtech Players
1	Policy Bazaar	Lemonade (USA)
2	Coverfox	Root Insurance (USA)
3	Acko	Hippo (USA)
4	Digit Insurance	ZhongAn (China)
5	Turtlemint	Wefox (Germany)
6	Go Digit	Globacap (UK)
7	Symbo	Haven Life (USA)
8	Renew Buy	Neos (UK)
9	Easypolicy	Clark (Germany)
10	Health Kart Plus	

Figure 16.3   SWOT analysis of the Insurtech industry (Data from review of literature)

16.4.1 Strengths

1. **New Product**: A variety of novel goods were introduced to meet the needs of different customer groups, and conventional dealers were augmented by fresh avenues such as internet-based platforms and branch offices.
2. **Business Growth**: From 1999 to 2003, there was a genuine increase in life insurance of 19% and non-life insurance of 11% thanks to these advances.
3. **Increased Per Capita Income**: India's per capita income has increased despite the country's massive population.
4. **Middle-Class Expansion**

16.4.2 Weaknesses

1. **Insufficient Investments**: India spends less on insurance than any other country in Asia (China contributed 36.3 US dollars on insurance services for each person, while Indians paid 16.4 US dollars)
2. **Government-owned Supremacy**: Government sector insurers have maintained a dominant position in the market for insurance despite the fact that the insurance industry was liberalized.
3. **Advertising as an Obstacle**: Over time, intense advertising battles and other non-price rivalries will probably drive up prices and ulti-mately hurt customers' interests.
4. **Outdated Tariffs Architecture**: Reforming the current rate system would be a major task for India's non-life insurance industry. The Indian non-life market remains highly controlled in terms of pricing.
5. **Minimal Services**: GIC is the sole company that offers reinsurance. Thus, coverage amenities are insufficient.

16.4.3 Opportunities

1. **Increasing the Level of Demand**: India's economy is going to expand more quickly because to better foundations.in the years ahead, this would result in a higher need for insurance services. Income per capita.
2. **Robust Prospective Growth**: Until the marketplace becomes satu-rated, robust expansion can take place for 30–40 years. Professional, accident, wellness, and other liability classes have a lot of space to develop.
3. **Increase in Wealth and Consciousness**: The main drivers of antici-pated demand for these sectors are expected to increase disposable income and increased risk consciousness.
4. **Health Coverage**: Medical coverage may play an important part in advancing the growth of the insurance industry.

16.4.4 Threats

1. **Financial Threats**: From 1985 to 2003, catastrophic disaster-related revenue losses in the country amounted to an average of 1.2 billion US dollars, representing 0.4% of the gross domestic product (GDP) annually.

2. **Natural Hazards**: Hurricanes (35%) and earthquakes (20%) caused the majority of the total damages during the period, with floods causing 40% of those losses.

3. **Pressure to Control Perils**: The sector and the financial system as a whole are under demand to more effectively handle the vulnerability to hazards from nature due to the sector's significant growth potential.

16.5 Review of Literature

Studying the literature has provided a thorough grasp of Insurtech's effects on the financial industry, which has a focus on change, trust, and consumer behaviour. In their investigation of how Fintech transforms the financial sector, Alt et al. (2018) place a strong emphasis on the necessity of adaptability. In order to provide guidance for fostering confidence in Insurtech uses, Aoki (2020) investigates public perceptions of AI chatbots. The financial worth of trust is quantified by Bapna et al. (2017), which is important for fostering client confidence in Insurtech engagements. Catlin et al. (2017) argue for cooperation as a means of growth while discussing the revolutionary potential of Insurtech. Using evidence from a variety of fields, such as adoption of technology, scientific investigations, and regulatory concerns, as a whole, the articles emphasize the importance of trust.

Johnson (2017) emphasizes that despite technology developments, human engagement in customer service is crucial. In their 2019 study, Kerényi and Müller look at the influence of financial technology on the dynamics of information power. A methodology for managing the digital age through organizational competencies is put forth by Konopik et al. in 2021. The probable impact of cutting-edge technological advancements on the insurance sector is covered by Krishnakanthan et al. in their study from 2021. In their 2015 study, Lankton et al. explore the interplay between technology, humanity, and trust. Lee and Shin (2018) examine the obstacles, business strategies, and choices for investment in the Fintech industry. The human component in technology adoption, the changing financial technology landscape, and the complex interactions are the overriding themes.

Insurtech's function in the banking sector offer useful information about consumer behaviour, trust, and technology adoption. In order to better understand whether customers will adopt technology-driven insurance choices, Möhlmann (2015) investigates the factors that influence satisfaction and repurchase behaviour in shared consumption. Customer trust in

Insurtech platforms is addressed by Mou et al. (2017) in their discussion of risk and confidence in electronic services adoption. Olivia and Smolnik's (2021) investigation of unfavourable feelings associated with AI use at work is pertinent to AI-based client interactions in the insurance industry. The significance of business intelligence in digital transformation is discussed by Park et al. (2020), which may be relevant to improving the client experience in Insurtech. Customer trust, technology acceptability, and the effects of digitization are some of the bigger themes.

16.6 Challenges for Insurtech Industry

According to the McKinsey study, five quickly developing technologies will fundamentally alter how insurance is used in the future. These involve trust architecture, next-level robotics, networked infrastructures, and integrated AI. Insurtech players can bolster their operations and broaden their product line by applying all their technological advantages in this area.

16.6.1 Using AI to Boost Essential Procedures

To speed up the insurance application process during the pandemic, at least a quarter of US life insurance companies have increased their use of computerized underwriting. AI and automation are proven to be beneficial in a number of ways, including lowering the time and cost associated with handling claims and enhancing the processes for identifying false claims and claim adjustments.

According to studies, research indicates that AI is poised to enable interactions with clients that closely mimic human engagement across a wide range of client interactions, potentially disrupting key activities like underwriting, claims processing, marketing, distribution, and others. There are numerous possibilities which may be taken advantage of. For instance, connected client information may be utilized for prediction and forecasting, which may then help with the creation of novel lines of products and services.

16.6.2 Enabling Intelligent Insurance with Distributed Infrastructure on the Cloud

A lot of fundamental insurance procedures that have been hampered by outdated technology are now being modernized. Insurers may take use of cloud-native architecture in this way, scale up to handle loads with degrading client experience, and accelerate their innovation efforts.

Traditional insurers have an opportunity to work with Insurtech to create alliances that make the most of each party's advantages and swiftly allow plug-ins, distribution channels, and other value-adds. For example, Insurtech can provide electronic tools to effectively sift through large amounts of past information from well-established insurers, find and understand customer trends and insights, and choose the type of novel product/service line that should be produced. In fact, a Capgemini survey indicated that a minimum of 75% of insurers are looking for Insurtech partnership to enhance their client relations.

16.6.3 *Developing Insurance Products Using Telematics*

More and more, consumer behaviour is being tracked, deciphered, and even influenced via telematics technologies. For instance, IoT innovation is being used in linked homes to track temperature, humidity, and other elements that may lead to property damage. The data produced by these gadgets can be used by insurers to calculate risk over a period of time. Similar technologies have been investigated in the fields of life, health, auto, manufacturing, and commerce insurance among others. Real-time data sharing and quicker service turnaround times will be made feasible by the introduction of 5G.

16.6.4 *Enabling Human Decisions via Bots*

Although robotic process automation (RPA) has shown its value in the automation of back-office tasks in the insurance industry, there is much it can accomplish in terms of next-level process automation which will influence insurance in the years to come. For instance, IoT-enabled continuous surveillance of production equipment can forecast the requirement for maintenance and stop damage or repairs that could result in claims to insurance companies.

RPA has a special place of its own for assisting human choices in a timely and cost-effective manner. For instance, it can speed up claims handling when pictures of a vehicle's damage are digitally evaluated and validated for legitimacy without necessitating a claims adjuster's physical visit to the damage location.

16.6.5 *Laying the Foundations for Trust with Blockchain*

Because of the highly confidential nature of the consumer data that is transmitted throughout the insurance environment, there are growing security risks as insurance becomes more digital. Companies in the insurance industry will prioritize establishing confidence among consumers, which is where blockchain may help.

In addition to its benefits for speed and openness, blockchain will be crucial in assisting carriers to protect client data from hacks and data leaks. Additionally, it will make the processes for managing identities, detecting fraudulent claims, and other processes simpler. Policies can be transformed into decentralized lines of code using blockchain-based smart contracts, making customer data immutable and readily accessible for instant confirmation in the case that an insurer receives a claim.

16.7 Opportunities for Insurtech Industry

According to the McKinsey study, Insurtech has seen explosive development and rising values for almost a decade. However, in 2022, investors' euphoria was muted by mounting inflationary pressures, higher interest rates, and budgetary and international instability. Shareholders are increasingly concentrating on sustainability operational advantages, which is in sharp contrast to the earlier "development at all costs" emphasis. As a consequence, Insurtech companies have grown quickly and seen their valuations soar for almost a decade now. However, the increasing pressures from price increases, increasing interest rates, and socio-economic and political instability in 2022 has dampened buyers' confidence. Far removed from the "development at all costs" approach of the past few decades, buyers are now seeking a sustainable business model. Most publicly listed Insurtech firms have experienced a sharp decline in value since their record highs as a consequence. The Insurtech industry has been shocked by this cooling, which has served as a reminder to participants to reconcile their desire for development with sustainable profitability.

Many possibilities are presented by the Insurtech sector as a result of the use of technology to alter the traditional insurance landscape. These positions cover a range of insurance operations, including risk evaluation, client involvement, and more. Several significant chances for the insurance technology sector include the following.

- Thanks to easy-to-use platforms and mobile apps, Insurtech enables personalized, digital-first client interactions that make it simple for customers to buy insurance, submit claims, and communicate with insurers.
- Insurtech allows the development of fresh, cutting-edge insurance offerings that address particular client requirements and developing dangers, such as P2P insurance, usage-based plans, and cyberinsurance.
- Insurtech firms may arrive at superior underwriting and claims judgements thanks to their access to large amounts of data and cutting-edge analytics, which improves risk evaluation and pricing.
- Real-time data from IoT and telematics devices may be used for risk assessment and prevention, which encourages safer behaviour and lower insurance claims.
- Automation, AI, and digitization speed insurance operations, cut expenses associated with administration, and boost operational effectiveness.
- Insurtech platforms make it possible for underprivileged communities and developing nations to obtain coverage for insurance, improving their access to finance.

Insurtech firms can provide insurance coverage and solutions for cybersecurity to safeguard individuals and companies from online dangers and data intrusions. These opportunities highlight the potential for Insurtech to revolutionize the insurance industry by offering tailored products, improving customer experiences, increasing efficiency, and addressing previously unmet needs. As Insurtech continues to evolve, it will likely uncover new avenues for innovation and growth.

16.8 Future of Insurtech

The continuous fusion of technology and insurance has opened up a world of fascinating new opportunities for Insurtech. Risk evaluation will become more precise as data analytics, AI, and ML continue to develop, producing more specialized insurance options. With chatbots, virtual assistants, and automated claims, customer relations will advance, ensuring prompt responses and improved experiences. Blockchain technology will be used to improve security, deter fraud, and facilitate fair operations, whereas on-demand insurance, which provides flexible coverage for particular situations, will become increasingly popular. Innovative insurance products that pro-actively handle risks will emerge from the combination of IoT devices, wearables, and real-time data. The partnership between traditional insur-ers and Insurtech companies will grow, merging proven experience with game-changing innovation. Aiming for standardized procedures across the industry, initiatives will address regulatory difficulties and data protection issues. In conclusion, the future of Insurtech sees a landscape characterized by seamless digital interactions, tailored coverage, efficient processes, and transformative alliances, changing the insurance industry into an active and client-focused space.

16.9 Conclusion

Insurtech undoubtedly has a transformational impact on the overall Fintech industry. By incorporating innovative technology in the insurance industry, or "Insurtech," old models have been changed, resulting in enhanced client experiences, successful operations, and better risk analysis. The literature emphasizes the development of consumer behaviour while highlighting the value of trust and fulfilment driven by technology insurance exchanges. Instead of seeing Insurtech only as a threat, cooperation and adaption have become crucial methods for conventional insurance companies to capitalize on the opportunity it presents. The emerging convergence of Insurtech and Fintech is expected to continue driving innovation in the industry, trans-forming how insurance services are produced, distributed, and experienced by consumers. However, hurdles still exist, such as regulatory adaption and tackling data privacy issues.

References

Alt, R., et al. (2018). Fintech and the transformation of the financial industry. *Electron Mark*, 28(3), 235–243.

Aoki, N. (2020). An experimental study of public trust in AI chatbots in the public sector. *Gov. Inf. Q*, 37(4), 101490.

Bapna, R., et al. (2017). Repeated interactions versus social ties: Quantifying the economic value of trust, forgiveness, and reputation using a field experiment. *MIS Q*, 41(3), 841–866.

Catlin, T., et al. (2017). Insurtech the threat that inspires. *McKinsey & Company*, 3(12), 22–26.

Chin, W. (1998). The partial least squares approach to structural equation modelling. Marcoulides, G.A. (Ed.) *Modern Methods for Business Research*, 1(98), 295–336.

Grandview Research. (2023). Market research reports. Retrieved from https://www.grandviewresearch.com/services/market-research-reports

Johnson, G. (2017). Your customers still want to talk to a human being. *Harv. Bus. Rev*, 1(1), 1–12.

Kerényi, Á., & Müller, J. (2019). Brave new digital world? – Financial technology and the power of information. *Financial Econ. Rev*, 18(1), 5–32.

Konopik, J., et al. (2021). Mastering the digital transformation through organizational capabilities: A conceptual framework. *Digit. Bus*, 2(12), 1–13.

Krishnakanthan, K., et al. (2021). How top tech trends will transform insurance. *McKinsey & Company*, 9(1), 24–26.

Lankton, N., et al. (2015). Technology, humanness, and trust: Rethinking trust in technology. *J. Assoc. Inf. Technology*, 16(10), 880–918.

Lee, I., Shin, Y.J. (2018). Fintech: Ecosystem, business models, investment decisions, and challenges. *J. Bus. Horizons*, 61(1), 35–46.

Möhlmann, M. (2015). Collaborative consumption: Determinants of satisfaction and the likelihood of using a sharing economy option again. *J. Consum. Behav*, 14(3), 193–207.

Mou, J., Shin, D.H., et al. (2017). Trust and risk in consumer acceptance of e-services. *J. Electron. Commer*, 17(2), 255–288.

Olivia, H., & Smolnik, S. (2021). AI invading the workplace: Negative emotions towards the organizational use of personal virtual assistants. *Electronic Marketing*, 7(3), 101–134.

Park, Y., et al. (2020). Digital transformation to real-time enterprise to sustain competitive advantage in the digitized world: The role of business intelligence and communication systems. *Korea Bus. Rev*, 24(1), 105–130.

Chapter 17

Future of Fintech

Harendra Singh, Aleem Ansari, and Vikrant Vikram Singh

17.1 Introduction

The fast development of technology has ushered in a new age for the financial sector. How we handle our money, do business, and access financial services has changed dramatically thanks to financial technology (Fintech). In this chapter, we will look at the significant technological advancements and their potential effects on various financial sectors. We'll also look at game-changing developments in open banking, wealth management, alternative financing, Insurtech, and digital payments. We will also discuss Fintech's regulatory framework and policy implications, shining light on both the difficulties and opportunities that lie ahead. The discussion of future trends that will conclude this chapter will cover topics including the fusion of Fintech with other industries, the emergence of decentralized finance (DeFi), customized financial experiences, and improved cybersecurity measures. As we help to build the financial future, we will also stress the value of cooperation between Fintech start-ups and established players. We will also reflect on the revolutionary potential of Fintech and examine the possibilities and difficulties that lie ahead.

Several key technical advancements that are currently changing the financial landscape are propelling the Fintech sector toward a transformational future. Artificial intelligence (AI) and machine learning (ML), which are important among these trends, are expected to continue playing a crucial role in transforming numerous facets of the financial industry. A new era of more accurate and efficient decision-making in financial transactions is

DOI: 10.4324/9781032644165-17

expected to be ushered in by AI and ML technologies, which are anticipated to significantly contribute to the automation of processes, delivery of personalized financial guidance, and enhancement of fraud detection and risk management (Wilson, 2019).

In parallel, the integration of blockchain and distributed ledger technology is poised to revolutionize the realm of financial services. These innovations are on track to establish a framework for secure, transparent, and tamper-proof transactions, potentially eliminating intermediaries and streamlining processes across the financial ecosystem (Petrov, 2019). The robust cryptographic features of blockchain enhance data integrity and security, creating an environment in which trust is inherently embedded in transactions, which is expected to bolster confidence and facilitate the widespread adoption of these technologies in the financial sector.

Furthermore, the ongoing development of cryptocurrencies has become a powerful force that challenges accepted beliefs about money and finance. It is anticipated that this trend will continue, possibly resulting in significant changes to the world's monetary system. By enabling underprivileged communities to access financial services and enabling borderless transactions with minimal costs and friction, cryptocurrencies have the potential to promote broader financial inclusion (Noguer, 2018; Hemachandran et al., 2021). The decentralized nature of cryptocurrencies and the technology that powers them has the power to reinvent the traditional idea of money as well as cross-border transactions.

17.2 Disruptive Innovations in Fintech

Due to technical breakthroughs and shifting customer demands, the Fintech business has undergone a remarkable evolution in recent years. This chapter explores the major disruptive Fintech breakthroughs that are about to change the financial sector. We can learn a lot about the future of financial services by investigating digital payments, alternative lending, wealth management, Insurtech, and open banking.

17.2.1 Digital Payments

The proliferation of digital payment solutions is poised to continue its upward trajectory, fuelled by the inherent advantages of convenience, speed, and security that they offer. In addition to revolutionizing the way transactions are carried out, digital payments have also entered both consumers' and enterprises' daily lives. Recent research (Al-Sabaawi et al. 2021; Hemachandran et al., 2024) predicts that as more people prefer the convenience of contactless transactions, the usage of digital payment systems will continue to soar.

Additionally, the incorporation of biometrics, near-field communication (NFC), and contactless payment systems is imminent. The seamless character of transactions is expected to be improved by this technological convergence, which will also cut down on processing times and the necessity for physical touch (Sadiku, 2019; Ka et al., 2021). Consumers might see a time when financial transactions are simple and secure thanks to the widespread adoption of biometric authentication and NFC-enabled devices.

17.2.2 Alternative Lending

Alternative lending platforms driven by Fintech are gaining a lot of traction and are transforming the loan industry by providing flexible and accessible funding solutions. To speed up loan processing timelines and enhance credit risk assessment, these platforms use data-driven lending models (Byanjankar et al., 2021). Due to this, people and companies can obtain funds more rapidly and effectively than they could through conventional lending institutions.

Research by Agarwal et al. (2020) emphasizes the significant influence alternative financing has had on financial inclusion. The study emphasizes how Fintech-driven lending platforms have widened access to capital for underprivileged people and small enterprises that previously had difficulty getting loans. In addition to promoting economic growth, this democratization of financing also encourages financial sector innovation.

17.2.3 Wealth Management

The democratization of wealth management is a pivotal trend facilitated by Fintech, which enables a broader range of investors to access investment advice and portfolio management services. Robo-advisors, in particular, are anticipated to undergo substantial enhancements, offering personalized investment strategies tailored to individual goals and risk preferences (Chaturvedi et al., 2021; Severino & Thierry, 2022).

Recent research (Hong et al., 2023; Capponi et al., 2022) shows that robo-advisors can provide highly specialized investment recommendations thanks to the incorporation of AI and ML algorithms. This change from a one-size-fits-all strategy to customized investing plans guarantees that investors, regardless of their level of financial intelligence, can make educated decisions in line with their particular objectives.

17.2.4 Insurtech

By utilizing data analytics and Internet of Things (IoT) devices to provide cutting-edge insurance products, the Insurtech industry is undergoing a significant transition. For both insurers and policyholders, this paradigm change in risk assessment and coverage customization improves consumer satisfaction and cost effectiveness (Šoša et al., 2022; Hemachandran et al., 2022). Insurtech start-ups can effectively analyze risks and customize insurance plans to individual habits and preferences by utilizing real-time data streams from IoT devices.

A recent study by Yan et al. (2018) emphasizes the potential of Insurtech to streamline the claims processing procedure. Insurers can speed up claims verification and settlement by employing data analytics, ML, and blockchain technology, which will ultimately streamline the customer experience and lower administrative costs.

17.2.5 Open Banking

Initiatives related to open banking are gaining momentum and encouraging cooperative relationships between traditional banks and Fintech firms. The interconnected financial ecosystems that are produced by this cooperative strategy give customers greater control over their financial data (He et al., 2022). Through open banking, customers can easily access a wide range of financial services from different suppliers, encouraging industry competition and innovation.

Research conducted by Unimi et al. (2023) highlights the advantages of open banking for promoting financial inclusion. People with little credit history can now access credit and financial services that were previously out of their grasp by giving users the option to securely disclose their financial data. The Fintech sector's dedication to democratizing financial services and closing access barriers is best demonstrated by open banking.

Unprecedented changes are being made to the financial services industry due to disruptive technologies in Fintech. The widespread use of digital payments, the development of alternative lending platforms, the democratization of wealth management, the revolution in Insurtech, and the rise of open banking initiatives all point to a future in which financial services are more widely available, effective, and suited to specific needs. Consumers and businesses stand to gain from a technologically enabled financial environment that fosters inclusion, efficiency, and creativity as these trends keep evolving.

17.3 Regulatory Environment and Policy Considerations

The emergence of Fintech has brought about significant disruptions in the landscape of traditional financial services, presenting regulators with a complex conundrum: how to effectively promote innovation while concurrently upholding consumer safeguards and ensuring the stability of the financial sector. This intricate balance has prompted the inception of regulatory sandboxes and innovation hubs as pivotal instruments in affording Fintech start-ups the opportunity to try their novel concepts within a controlled framework that adheres to pertinent regulations. The significance of this dynamic is underscored by the observation that, "Regulatory sandboxes provide a safe space for Fintech firms to experiment with new products, services, and business models without immediately being subject to the full regulatory regime" (Amstad, 2019, Ringe & Ruof, 2020).

In this context, policymakers assume a critical role in steering the evolution of Fintech by tackling a spectrum of challenges that intersect with the digital financial realm. Paramount among these challenges are concerns encompassing data privacy, cybersecurity, and the harmonization of regulatory frameworks across international boundaries. Effective handling of these aspects is fundamental to nurturing an environment that is both propitious for Fintech expansion and consistent with the safeguarding of data and systems. To illustrate, it is emphasized that, "Fostering cross-border regulatory harmonization and collaboration is crucial to mitigate potential conflicts and ensure consistent oversight across jurisdictions".

As Fintech perpetuates its transformative trajectory, regulatory entities confront the intricate responsibility of steering the sector's growth in a manner that bolsters innovation, shields consumers, and fortifies financial stability. The utilization of regulatory sandboxes and innovation hubs as experimental arenas serves as a testament to the delicate equilibrium regulators seek to establish. Moreover, the imperative of addressing issues linked to data privacy, cybersecurity, and cross-border regulatory coherence cannot be overstated, as they coalesce to cultivate an environment conducive to the sustained advancement of Fintech.

17.4 Future Trends of Fintech

17.4.1 Integration with Other Industries

The Fintech sector is poised to undergo a profound transformation as it increasingly collaborates with a range of diverse industries, including healthcare, education, and e-commerce. This trend is expected to lead to a convergence of services and the emergence of innovative business models, all aimed at meeting the multifaceted needs of consumers. As Fintech extends its reach beyond traditional financial services, it is anticipated that this integration will pave the way for new avenues of value creation and customer engagement (Siddiqui & Rivera, 2022; Wajid et al., 2022; Gahlot & Ghosh, 2023).

DeFi platforms are rapidly replacing traditional financial intermediaries. DeFi platforms are ready to provide a wide range of decentralized and peer-to-peer financial services, including lending, borrowing, and yield farming, by leveraging the potential of blockchain technology. By circumventing traditional intermediaries, these platforms are set to democratize access to financial services and empower individuals with unprecedented control over their financial activities (Grassi et al., 2022; Azmi & Akhtar, 2022; Trapanese & Lanotte, 2023).

It is anticipated that the integration of AI-driven personalization would completely alter the financial services industry. Financial institutions will increasingly offer specialized goods and services that fit with individual preferences, lifestyles, and life phases as a result of powerful data analytics and ML. According to Azmi et al. (2020), Weber et al. (2023), and Margaret et al. (2023), this trend toward individualized financial experiences is expected to increase consumer happiness, deepen engagement, and promote long-lasting financial connections.

17.4.2 Enhanced Cybersecurity Measures

As the Fintech ecosystem continues to evolve, so do the associated cybersecurity challenges. The dynamic and evolving threat landscape necessitates the implementation of robust cybersecurity measures to safeguard sensitive financial data and transactions. Industry stakeholders are expected to prioritize investments in advanced technologies and practices to ensure the integrity and security of financial operations (Akhtar et al., 2020; Pachare & Bangal, 2022; Jafar et al., 2023).

The Fintech landscape is undergoing a series of transformative shifts driven by integration with diverse industries, the rise of DeFi, personalized financial experiences, and enhanced cybersecurity measures. These trends are poised to reshape the way financial services are delivered, consumed, and secured, paving the way for a more inclusive, efficient, and secure financial ecosystem.

17.5 Implications for Financial Institutions and Traditional Banking

The surge of Fintech is propelling forward, ushering in a transformative era for financial institutions and, consequently, necessitating their adept adjustment to the evolving milieu. In this context, conventional banks find themselves at a juncture wherein their competitive viability hinges upon their capacity to wholeheartedly embrace technological advancements and foster an atmosphere of innovation. One strategic avenue through which this imperative can be fulfilled is by forging strategic alliances and partnerships with burgeoning Fintech start-ups. Such collaborative ventures not only open gateways to pioneering solutions and client-centric services but also culminate in amplified operational efficiency and elevated consumer encounters.

Moreover, the symbiotic association between traditional banks and Fintech start-ups affords multifaceted benefits. Capitalizing on their well-established infrastructural framework and extensive regulatory proficiency, established banks can offer Fintech entities a viable trajectory to expand their operations and broaden their customer outreach. This harmonious integration allows Fintech companies to access the requisite resources for scaling while simultaneously extending the established banks' capabilities to offer innovative solutions and services. Consequently, this collective synergy ushers in a harmonious convergence of strengths and expertise, enabling both entities to remain competitive and resilient in an ever-evolving financial landscape.

The inexorable rise of Fintech underscores an indispensable need for traditional financial institutions to pivot and accommodate this paradigm shift. Collaborative engagement with emerging Fintech start-ups emerges as a strategic pathway to imbue technological innovation and revamp customer interactions, thereby reinvigorating their competitive stance in the dynamic financial domain.

17.6 Conclusion

The future of finance is undeniably intertwined with the evolution of Fintech. The transformative potential of Fintech promises a more inclusive, efficient, and customer-centric financial industry. However, to unlock this potential, stakeholders must navigate regulatory challenges, invest in technological advancements, and foster collaboration between traditional financial institutions and Fintech start-ups. The road ahead is exciting, and as we shape the future of finance, we must remain mindful of the opportunities and challenges that come with it. Through innovation, collaboration, and responsible regulation, Fintech can pave the way for a more resilient and prosperous financial future for all.

References

Agarwal, S., Qian, W., & Tan, R. (2020). Financial inclusion and financial technology. In *Springer eBooks* (pp. 307–346). https://doi.org/10.1007/978-981-15-5526 -8_9

Akhtar, S., Niazi, M. H., & Khan, M. M. (2020). Cascading effect of COVID 19 on Indian economy. *International Journal of Advanced Science and Technology*, 29(9), 4563–4573.

Al-Sabaawi, M. Y. M., Alshaher, A., & Alsalem, M. A. (2021). User trends of electronic payment systems adoption in developing countries: An empirical analysis. *Journal of Science & Technology Policy Management*. https://doi.org/10.1108 /jstpm-11-2020-0162

Amstad, M. (2019). *Regulating Fintech: Objectives, principles, and practices.* Social Science Research Network. https://doi.org/10.2139/ssrn.3541003

Azmi, S., Akhtar, S., & Nadeem, M. (2020). Impact of digitalisation on bank performance: A study of Indian Banks. *Test Engineering and Management*, 83, 23678–23691.

Azmi, S. N., & Akhtar, S. M. J. (2022). Interactions of services export, financial development and growth: Evidence from India. *Quality & Quantity*, 57(5), 4709–4724. https://doi.org/10.1007/s11135-022-01566-8

Byanjankar, A., Mezei, J., & Heikkilä, M. (2021). Data-driven optimization of peer-to-peer lending portfolios based on the expected value framework. *International Journal of Intelligent Systems in Accounting, Finance & Management, 28*(2), 119–129. https://doi.org/10.1002/isaf.1490

Capponi, A., Olafsson, S., & Zariphopoulou, T. (2022). Personalized robo-advising: Enhancing investment through client interaction. *Management Science, 68*(4), 2485–2512. https://doi.org/10.1287/mnsc.2021.4014

Chaturvedi, K., Akhtar, S., Azhar, N., & Shamshad, M. (2021). Impact of corporate social responsibility on financial performance of selected banks in India: Based on camel model. *Studies in Economics and Business Relations, 2*(2).

Gahlot, C. S. S., & Ghosh, S. (2023). Emerging opportunities and challenges in Fintech industry – A comparative study of India with other jurisdictions. In *Advanced series in management* (pp. 21–31). Emerald Publishing Limited. https://doi.org/10.1108/s1877-636120230000031003

Grassi, L., Lanfranchi, D., Faes, A., & Renga, F. (2022). Do we still need financial intermediation? The case of decentralized finance – DeFi. *Qualitative Research in Accounting & Management, 19*(3), 323–347. https://doi.org/10.1108/qram-03-2021-0051

He, X., Liu, D., & Xiao, Y. (2022). Research on building open insurance in the insurance industry based on the concept of open banking. In *Proceedings of the 2022 7th International Conference on Social Sciences and Economic Development (ICSSED)*. https://doi.org/10.2991/aebmr.k.220405.100

Hemachandran, K., Khanra, S., Rodriguez, R. V., & Jaramillo, J. (Eds.). (2022). *Machine learning for business analytics: Real-time data analysis for decision-making*. CRC Press.

Hemachandran, K., Rodriguez, R. V., Toshniwal, R., Junaid, M., & Shaw, L. (2021). Performance analysis of different classification algorithms for bank loan sectors. In *Intelligent sustainable systems: Proceedings of ICISS* (pp. 191–202). Springer Singapore.

Hemachandran, K., Rodriguez, R. V., Subramaniam, U., & Balas, V. E. (2024). Artificial intelligence and knowledge processing: Improved decision-making and prediction.

Hong, X., Li, P., Gong, Y., & Chen, Q. (2023). Robo-advisors and investment intention: A perspective of value-based adoption. *Information & Management, 60*(6), 103832. https://doi.org/10.1016/j.im.2023.103832

Jafar, S. H., Akhtar, S. M. J., El-Chaarani, H., Khan, P. A., & Binsaddig, R. (2023). Forecasting of NIFTY 50 index price by using backward elimination with an LSTM model. *Journal of Risk and Financial Management, 16*(10), 423. https://doi.org/10.3390/jrfm16100423

Ka, H., Georgeb, P. M., Rodriguezc, R. V., Kulkarnid, R. M., & Roye, S. (2021). Performance analysis of KN earest neighbor classification algorithms for bank loan sectors. *Smart Intelligent Computing and Communication Technology, 38*(9).

Margaret, D. S., Elangovan, N., Balaji, V., & Sriram, M. (2023). The influence and impact of AI-powered intelligent assistance for banking services. In *Advances in economics, business and management research* (pp. 374–385). Atlantis Press. https://doi.org/10.2991/978-94-6463-162-3_33

Noguer, M. (2018). Artificial intelligence and the future of finance. *3r Congrés d'Economia i Empresa de Catalunya-Full papers*.

Pachare, S. M., & Bangal, S. (2022). Cyber security in the Fintech industry. In *IGI Global eBooks* (pp. 1–17). https://doi.org/10.4018/978-1-6684-5827-3.ch001

Petrov, D. (2019). *The impact of blockchain and distributed ledger technology on financial services.* University of Economics - Varna. https://stumejournals.com/journals/i4/2019/2/88

Ringe, W., & Ruof, C. (2020). Regulating Fintech in the EU: The case for a guided sandbox. *European Journal of Risk Regulation*, 11(3), 604–629. https://doi.org/10.1017/err.2020.8

Sadiku, A. (2019). Digitalization of banking services in Kosovo: Trends and comparison with the neighborhood countries. ideas.repec.org. https://ideas.repec.org/h/tkp/mklp19/379-392.html

Severino, F., & Thierry, S. (2022). Robo-advisors: A big data challenge. In *Springer eBooks* (pp. 115–131). https://doi.org/10.1007/978-3-031-12240-8_7

Siddiqui, Z., & Rivera, C. A. (2022). Fintech and Fintech ecosystem: A review of literature. *Risk Governance and Control: Financial Markets & Institutions*, 12(1), 63–73. https://doi.org/10.22495/rgcv12i1p5

Šoša, I., & Montes, Ó. R. (2022). Understanding the InsurTech dynamics in the transformation of the insurance sector. *Risk Management and Insurance Review*, 25(1), 35–68. https://doi.org/10.1111/rmir.12203

Trapanese, M., & Lanotte, M. (2023). *Financial intermediation and new technology: Theoretical and regulatory implications of digital financial markets.* Social Science Research Network. https://doi.org/10.2139/ssrn.4464132

Unimi, D. (2023, April 18). *Open banking and financial inclusion - European economy.* European Economy. https://european-economy.eu/2022/open-banking-and-financial-inclusion/

Wajid, A., Sabiha, A., Akhtar, S. M. J., Tabash, M. I., & Daniel, L. N. (2022). Cross-Border acquisitions and shareholders' wealth: The case of the Indian pharmaceutical sector. *Journal of Risk and Financial Management*, 15(10), 437. https://doi.org/10.3390/jrfm15100437

Weber, P., Carl, K. V., & Hinz, O. (2023). Applications of explainable artificial intelligence in finance—A systematic review of finance, information systems, and computer science literature. *Management Review Quarterly.* https://doi.org/10.1007/s11301-023-00320-0

Wilson, C. (2019). Cryptocurrencies: The future of finance? In *Contemporary issues in international political economy* (pp. 359–394). https://doi.org/10.1007/978-981-13-6462-4_16

Yan, T. C., Schulte, P. A., & Chuen, D. L. K. (2018). InsurTech and Fintech: Banking and insurance enablement. In *Elsevier eBooks* (pp. 249–281). https://doi.org/10.1016/b978-0-12-810441-5.00011-7

Chapter 18

Relation between Fintech Trends and Digital Finance: A Bibliometric Analysis

Sana Fatima, Vartika Kapooor, and Aleem Ansari

18.1 Introduction

The financial sector has experienced ongoing advancements in service provision as a result of digitization (Kanungo & Gupta, 2021; Brandl & Hornuf, 2020). This enhancement is characterized by higher levels of interaction and improved data processing in both the client interface as well as back-office operations. In recent times, there has been a notable shift in focus regarding digitization. Initially, the emphasis was on improving the efficiency of traditional tasks. However, the current emphasis has primarily been on generating employment opportunities and developing new business models specifically for financial services firms (Legner et al., 2017; Gomber et al., 2017). "Digital finance" encompasses a wide range of novel financial products, financial institutions, associated financial initiatives, and new modes of customer engagement (Azizi et al., 2021; Anjum et al., 2017). This includes the provision of interactive services by financial technology firms and innovative providers of financial services, as exemplified by Ozili (2018), Gomber et al. (2017), and Barras (1990). Given these facts, scholarly investigations have commenced to explore the aforementioned transformations in the realms of finance and information systems while also delving into the impact of the financial sector on the advancement of digital technologies.

DOI: 10.4324/9781032644165-18

The emergence of financial technology has garnered significant attention from industry professionals within a relatively brief period. The key factor lies in the capacity to transition between supply chain networks across a wide range of industries. The integration of new business models and technological concepts serves as the basis for the development of inventive financing solutions, internal knowledge sharing, and organizational innovation (Abbas et al., 2019a). Additionally, it contributes to the advancement of knowledge management and sustainable organizational innovation (Abbas et al., 2020). This includes the implementation of intelligent and user-friendly financial services that are efficient and cost-effective (Varga, 2017; Gomber et al., 2017; Teece, 2010).

Several scholarly investigations have established a correlation between the divergent and innovative attributes of social media and the avenues for prospective scholarly inquiry. These studies have contributed to a greater understanding of the utilization of online social networks, as evidenced by the works of Liu et al. (2021), Lebni et al. (2017), and Abbas et al. (2019b, 2019c). Furthermore, the findings of the study revealed that the implementation of corporate social responsibility initiatives had a favourable influence on the long-term viability and success of organizations. Hence, it is imperative to utilize media or communication resources in order to attain timely advancements.

Digital finance is posing a significant challenge to existing financial service providers, including banks and insurance companies. Due to the increasing competition posed by Fintech companies, these entities offer distinct opportunities for employers to engage with their newer and more cutting-edge technological customer base (Wang et al., 2021; Joshi, 2020; Arner et al., 2015). In light of this context, there is a current discourse within the realm of traditional financial intermediaries regarding the management of Fintechs. This discussion revolves around the consideration of competitive strategies such as acquisitions, as well as the exploration of alternative approaches such as engaging these firms as service providers that align with their existing business models (Vučinić, 2020; Suprun et al., 2020; Lai, 2020). The advent of technology has provided organizations with novel prospects to sustain their competitive edge and offer innovative and appealing services to their clientele.

Abbas et al. (2019d) demonstrated that firms with a high level of innovation tend to prioritize the establishment of a business network as a means to attain sustainable performance. Moreover, the results of the study revealed that companies that were able to maintain consistent performance levels were able to do so by implementing efficient business networks and adaptable capabilities. It proposed a comprehensive and methodical strategy for attaining sustainable performance by leveraging the dynamic capabilities of businesses.

This study makes a valuable contribution to the existing literature by examining the relationship between digital finance and Fintech. The bibliometric analysis encompasses the comprehensive research findings on digital finance and Fintech available in the ScienceDirect database. The dataset encompassed the time frame spanning from 2006 to 2020, with particular emphasis on the most recent studies conducted, particularly those completed within the last three years (2018, 2019, and 2020).

The subsequent sections of this chapter are organized in the following manner: The section titled "Research Method and Questions" discusses the methodology employed as well as the specific research inquiries that guided the investigation. The section titled "Results and Discussion" presents the findings of our study and provides a comprehensive analysis and interpretation of the data. The concluding section of this paper provides a summary of the main findings and offers suggestions for future research.

18.2 Research Methods and Questions

The bibliometric analysis encompasses various forms of investigation and employs "statistical and mathematical strategies to examine the patterns and advancements in technological and scientific research" (Zhang et al., 2021; Moed, 2006). Reference measurements have been widely employed to ascertain the state of research and track the development trends within a particular field. Citations play a crucial role in enabling researchers to gain a comprehensive understanding of a specific research domain (Vatananan-Thesenvitz et al., 2019; van Oorschot et al., 2018). Furthermore, researchers employ bibliometric techniques to systematically examine publications within the ScienceDirect database, aiming to reveal their historical, current, and prospective contributions. Notably, there has been a proliferation of significant research discoveries in this domain, particularly in recent years. The researchers employed a bibliographic evaluation approach to examine and analyze all publications contained within the database.

The primary objective of conducting a bibliometric analysis had been to systematically gather and assess the existing research pertaining to the specific subject. The aim was to generate unbiased findings that are verifiable and replicable in subsequent studies. In the realm of research findings, a bibliometric analysis is a meticulous methodological evaluation aimed at categorizing extant literature on a particular topic and aiding in the formulation of evidence-based recommendations for practitioners in the respective domain (Prinsen et al., 2018; Kitchenham, 2004). In addition to its primary purpose, a bibliometric analysis must also include the evaluation of the current state of knowledge pertaining to the study (Levy & Ellis, 2006).

The field of financial technology, commonly referred to as Fintech, is receiving increased attention due to the growing impact of digitalization on the financial services industry (Leong & Sung, 2018; Nicoletti et al., 2017). In the realm of financial services, there exists a significant reliance on information, as well as a prevalence of procedures such as online trading platforms (Karagiannaki et al., 2017). The advent of new financing models has created opportunities for extensive and substantial digitization within the financial service industry. This digitization is necessary to enable the ongoing transformation of the value chain, benefiting both service providers and customers. The term "Fintech" is derived from the combination of the words "financial" and "technology," and it is believed that John Reed, the chairman of Citicorp, first used this term in the early 1990s in reference to the establishment of the "Smart Card Forum." In the era of digitalization, the emergence of Fintech applications has revolutionized the prevailing product-centric mindset by incorporating emerging ecosystems. The redundancy of individual channels can occur when financial service designers prioritize hybrid and incompatible interaction modes in consumer operations (Gill et al., 2015; Puschmann, 2017).

The present study conducts a comparative analysis between bibliometric analysis and other research methodologies, namely meta-analysis and systematic review, with a specific emphasis on digital finance and Fintech domains. This study aims to analyze the scope and research trends of digital finance and Fintech.

The study aims to provide academics as well as practitioners with a systematic and categorized perspective of the existing literature related to digital finance and Fintech. To achieve this objective, two research questions are proposed. The question is formulated as follows:

Research Question 1:   "What transformations occurred within the scholarly discourse surrounding digital finance and financial technology (Fintech)?"

The sub-questions presented below have been derived from the primary question.

Research Question 1.1: "What are the most influential research studies, particularly those published in ScienceDirect, that have had a significant impact?"

Research Question 1.2: "What are the significant references that have exerted the greatest influence on the identified studies?"

Research Question 1.3: "Which scholarly journals have garnered the highest readership within the domain of this particular subject matter, and what is the trend in the publication count over the course of time?"

In order to identify relevant literature for the purpose of conducting new studies, a systematic approach was employed. This involved categorizing the primary topics and research questions pertaining to digital finance and Fintech domains, as determined by published materials, into distinct categories. Consequently, the following formulation pertains to the second inquiry in this study:

Research Question 2: "What are the primary subjects and challenges addressed in the academic discourse surrounding digital finance and financial technology (Fintech)?"

This section delineates the methodology employed to conduct the bibliometric literature evaluation, utilizing a pre-established and validated technique. In addition, bibliometric analysis techniques were employed to ascertain the current status of the scholarly literature pertaining to digital finance and Fintech (Ikpaahindi, 1985). The data from the bibliometric study provides an overview of the research conducted on digital finance and Fintech within the ScienceDirect database. The dataset encompassed the time frame spanning from 2006 to 2020. The utilization of digital finance and Fintech was anticipated due to the implementation of closure and quarantine measures amidst the pandemic.

Consequently, a comprehensive examination and analysis were conducted on articles sourced from the ScienceDirect database, specifically focusing on those that contained keywords related to Fintech in their titles, abstracts, and author keywords.

The bibliometric analysis employed various processes and approaches to examine "citation," "co-citation," "bibliographic coupling," and "co-authorship." Specifically, the keywords were analyzed with respect to the study conducted by Zupic and Čater (2015). The research utilized the citation indicator as a means for identifying the primary keywords that were the focus of studies and the notable authors in the area of digital finance and Fintech. In order to ascertain the network of research relationships among them, the phases involved in preparing the bibliometric study were executed, encompassing study design, data collection, analysis, presentation, and guidance (Lobato et al., 2021).

18.3 Results and Discussion

In order to determine the articles that would undergo final review, a three-step process was employed. Initially, a comprehensive compilation of research documents, including research papers, review papers, book chapters, and other relevant sources, was gathered and archived from the ScienceDirect databases. Further, the search was conducted using specific keywords, and the time frame for the search encompassed a wide range of publications up until December 31, 2020, with the aim of including as many relevant sources as feasible.

Published research was obtained by conducting a topic search on digital finance and Fintech in the ScienceDirect database. The search was conducted using the search terms "digital finance," "e-Finance," "Fintech," or "Fintech" in the "title," "abstract," and "keywords" fields from 2006 to 2020. A total of 343 studies were obtained, including 184 research papers, 14 review articles, 111 book chapters, two encyclopaedias, two case reports, and 32 other documents. The distribution of these studies over the 15-year period is presented in Table 18.1. This section provides a description of the database utilized in the bibliometric analysis as well as previous research pertaining to the areas of digital finance and Fintech, specifically employing descriptive statistics.

A list of different contributing publications can facilitate the identification of the most pertinent journal in each respective field. Table 18.1 displays the different publishing ports. Based on the analysis of published literature, research papers have been found to make the most significant contribution, followed by book chapters. According to Table 18.1, the subjects of "digital finance," "Fintech," and "e-finance" represent a contemporary area of knowledge, particularly since major research was conducted within the past three years (2018, 2019, and 2020).

Table 18.1 Statistics of Previous Studies

	Digital Finance (128 Studies)	Fintech (137 Studies)	E-Finance (78 Studies)
Year			
2020	20	34	17
2019	22	28	28
2018	74	52	29
Other Years	12	13	4
Research			
Review Article	4	6	4
Research Article	46	85	53
Encyclopaedia	0	2	0
Book Chapter	59	34	18
Case Report	0	1	1
Discussion	0	1	0
Editorial	2	3	1
News	2	1	0
Short Communication	4	4	1
Other	11	0	0

Additionally, a majority of the aforementioned studies consist of research papers or book chapters. This finding accounts for the substantial volume of output in this particular field of research, as depicted in the subsequent figure.

According to Figure 18.1, a significant portion of the research conducted in the field has been concentrated in recent years, with 155 studies conducted in 2018, followed by 88 studies in 2019, and 71 studies in 2020.

When conducting research on "Fintech regulations," it was observed that the predominant publication types were review and conference papers. Upon analysis of the query results, various types of publications have been identified, including articles, magazines, conference review papers, and book chapters, among others. Between 2006 to 2020, there

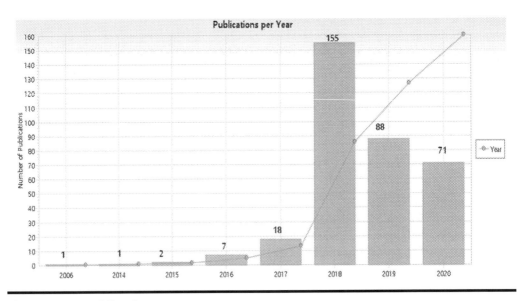

Figure 18.1   Publication per year

has been a noticeable upward trend that has garnered increasing attention and investigation. Figure 18.2 illustrates the observed trend.

Figure 18.2 illustrates that a majority of the studies examined in this analysis employed the keywords such as "Fintech," "blockchain," "financial inclusion," "bitcoin," "banking," "big data," and others. This observation suggests that the prior research primarily concentrated on the subject matter of digital finance and Fintech.

In the past three years, John Hill as well as David Lee Kuo Chuen have emerged as the most influential researchers in the field of digital finance and Fintech. (see Figure 18.3).

The analysis of Figures 18.4A and 18.4B reveals the presence of eight distinct clusters within the network pertaining to the domains of digital finance and Fintech. These clusters can be identified as potential research themes, including "Fintech" along with its associated clusters, "financial inclusion and blockchain," "cryptocurrency and bitcoin," "financial services," "entrepreneurial finance," "P2P lending," "distributed ledger technology," and "trust."

The author conducted further investigation into the domains of Fintech, blockchain, financial inclusion, cryptocurrency, and bitcoin, as indicated by the density as well as the subsequent table in relation to these subjects. These terms should pertain to the investigation and examination conducted by scholars in the domains of digital finance and Fintech.

Table 18.2 presents the relevant data regarding the most cited researchers in this area. Based on the analysis of Figures 18.5A and 18.5B, it can

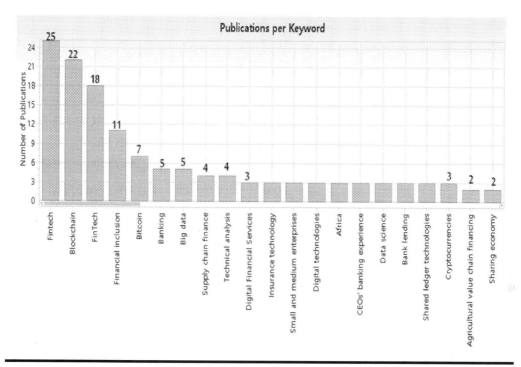

Figure 18.2   Publication per keyword

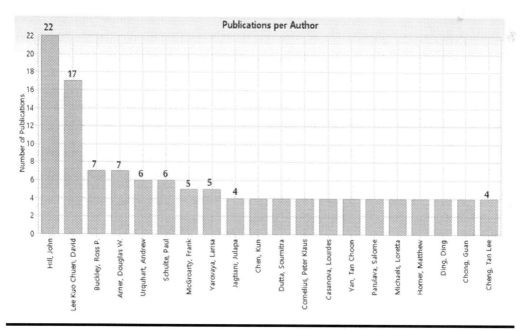

Figure 18.3   Publication per Author

Items: 42 / Clusters: 8 / Links: 194 / Total link strength: 636

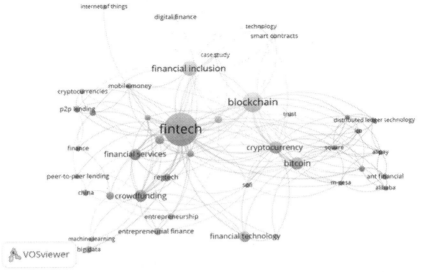

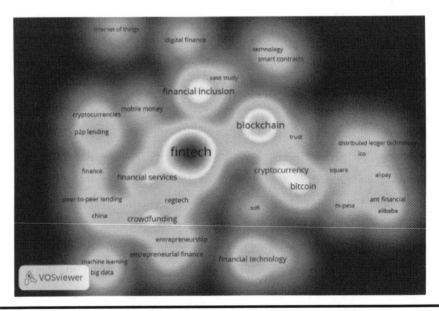

Figure 18.4 Presence of eight distinct clusters within the network pertaining to the domains of digital finance and Fintech

be observed that David Lee Kuo Chuen has been the central figure in the domain of digital finance and Fintech. This indicates the significance of his research in the field, as evidenced by the following studies: Kuo Chuen et al. (2017), Chuen and Deng (2017), Chuen (2015) and Nian and Chuen (2015).

Furthermore, it is worth noting that John Hill's research has not garnered significant attention from other scholars, as evidenced by the absence of

Table 18.2   Occurrence of Keywords in the Network

Keyword	Occurrence	Total Link Strength
Fintech	122	210
Blockchain	52	129
Financial Inclusion	33	59
Bitcoin	25	74
Cryptocurrency	24	92
Financial Services	22	58
Financial Technology	18	26
Innovation	14	51
Regtech	11	27
Regulation	11	20
Mobile Payment	10	21
Entrepreneurial Finance	10	17
Financial Technologies	9	29
P2P Lending	9	15
Big Data	9	11

his name in the network and density analysis. According to the findings presented in Table 18.3, John Hill emerges as a prominent figure in the field of digital finance and Fintech, particularly in relation to his notable research contribution (Hill, 2018). However, his research findings are not widely utilized by other researchers who hold a higher level of prominence within this particular academic domain. Based on this premise, it can be argued that the work conducted by David Lee Kuo Chuen holds greater influence in this particular field compared to the research conducted by John Hill. However, this assertion does not undermine the significance of Hill's research, as it must be acknowledged due to its considerable importance within the field.

18.4 Conclusion

The chapter provides an elucidation of digital finance and Fintech, which are two separate and influential developments within these domains. The

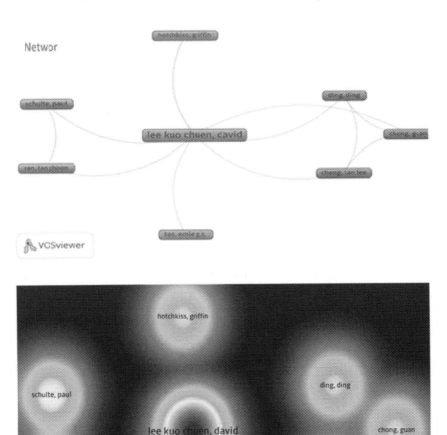

Figure 18.5 Presence of distinct clusters of authors within the network pertaining to the domains of digital finance and Fintech

subsequent section of the chapter employs bibliometric analysis, utilizing the ScienceDirect database, to assess the advancements made in research within the respective field. This indicates that the aforementioned superpowers are also stimulating research in the field, as evidenced by the prominent publications on digital finance and Fintech, leading to the emergence of Fintech in the market (Omarova, 2021). We have identified particular elements that

Table 18.3   Occurrence of Authors in the Network

Author	Occurrence	Total Link Strength
Hill, John	22	0
Lee Kuo Chuen, David	16	19
Arner, Douglas W.	5	8
Buckly, Ross P.	5	8
Urquhart, Andrew	4	1
Ahmed, Shaker	4	8
Casanova, Lourdes	4	8
Cornelius, Peter Klaus	4	8
Dutta, Soumitra	4	8
Grobys, Klaus	4	8
Sapkota, Niranjan	4	8
Schulte, Paul	4	6
Mcgroarty, Frank	4	1

require additional examination, as determined by bibliometric analyses of research pertaining to the implementation of Fintech and digital finance as well as its associated disciplines. The published studies provide comprehensive discussions on the methodologies employed and the main topics explored in the research.

The bibliometric analysis proposes the identification of a fundamental unit of investigation. Thus, it is necessary to consider more than just the number of publications when assessing the influence of research. This entails examining impact centres and analyzing the interconnections between articles within a specific scientific domain (McKiernan et al., 2019; Kim & McMillan, 2008). The utilization of literature in other similar studies is exemplified by the meta-analysis of citations (Timulak, 2009). The utilization of the bibliometric analysis is deemed suitable as a meta-analytic tool to enhance the three aforementioned research objectives.

This study aims to provide valuable insights to academic researchers and financial policymakers who have a keen interest in digital finance. It seeks to enhance their understanding of the present status of Fintech requirements and facilitate the identification of emerging patterns within corporate boardrooms. Furthermore, this research highlights the growing recognition that Fintech will be a pivotal factor in the global pursuit of digital financial advancements.

In addition, there is a consistent development of digital finance and Fintech publications due to the interdisciplinary nature of digital finance and the inclusion of individuals from various disciplines. The literature pertaining to digital finance, whether of high or low quality, is exhibiting improvement, with increasing participation from individuals.

This study has the potential to guide the digital finance and Fintech sectors in formulating effective policies and implementing efficient processes to further advance the evolving digital finance trends. Financial as well as non-financial institutions have the ability to evaluate the financing process as strategic dimensions and in accordance with the vision of policymakers.

References

Abbas, J., Hussain, I., Hussain, S., Akram, S., Shaheen, I., & Niu, B. (2019a). The impact of knowledge sharing and innovation upon sustainable performance in Islamic Banks: A mediation analysis through an SEM approach. *Sustainability*, *11*(15), 4049. https://doi.org/10.3390/su11154049

Abbas, J., Aman, J., Nurunnabi, M., & Bano, S. (2019b). The impact of social media on learning behavior for sustainable education: Evidence of students from selected Universities in Pakistan. *Sustainability*, *11*(6), 1683.

Abbas, J., Mahmood, S., Ali, H., Raza, M. A., Ali, G., Aman, J., Bano, S., & Nurunnabi, M. (2019c). The effects of corporate social responsibility practices and environmental factors through a moderating role of social media marketing on sustainable performance of firms' operating in Multan, Pakistan. *Sustainability*, *11*(12), 3434. https://doi.org/10.3390/su11123434

Abbas, J., Raza, S., Nurunnabi, M., Minai, M. S., & Bano, S. (2019d). The impact of entrepreneurial business networks on firms' performance through a mediating role of dynamic capabilities. *Sustainability*, *11*(11), 3006. https://doi.org/10.3390/su11113006

Abbas, J., Zhang, Q., Hussain, I., Akram, S., Afaq, A., & Shad, M. A. (2020). Sustainable innovation in small medium enterprises: The impact of knowledge management on organizational innovation through a mediation analysis by using SEM approach. *Sustainability*, *12*(6), 2407. https://doi.org/10.3390/su12062407

Anjum, M. N., Xiuchun, B., Abbas, J., & Shuguang, Z. (2017). Analyzing predictors of customer satisfaction and assessment of retail banking problems in Pakistan. *Cogent Business & Management*, *4*(1). https://doi.org/10.1080/23311975.2017.1338842

Arner, D. W., Barberis, J. N., & Buckley, R. P. (2015). The evolution of fintech: A new post-crisis paradigm? *SSRN Electronic Journal, 47*(4). https://doi.org/10.2139/ssrn.2676553

Azizi, M. R., Atlasi, R., Ziapour, A., Abbas, J., & Naemi, R. (2021). Innovative human resource management strategies during the COVID-19 pandemic: A systematic narrative review approach. *Heliyon, 7*(6), e07233. Sciencedirect. https://doi.org/10.1016/j.heliyon.2021.e07233

Barras, R. (1990). Interactive innovation in financial and business services: The vanguard of the service revolution. *Research Policy, 19*(3), 215–237. https://doi.org/10.1016/0048-7333(90)90037-7

Brandl, B., & Hornuf, L. (2020). Where did fintechs come from, and where do they go? The transformation of the financial industry in Germany after digitalization. *Frontiers in Artificial Intelligence, 3*. https://doi.org/10.3389/frai.2020.00008

Chuen, D. L. K. (2015). *Handbook of digital currency : Bitcoin, innovation, financial instruments, and big data.* Elsevier/Ap.

Chuen, D. L. K., & Deng, R. H. (2017). *Handbook of blockchain, digital finance, and inclusion : Cryptocurrency, Fintech, Insurtech, regulation, ChinaTech, mobile security, and distributed ledger.* Elsevier Science.

Gill, A., Bunker, D., & Seltsikas, P. (2015). Moving forward: Emerging themes in financial services technologies' adoption. *Communications of the Association for Information Systems, 36*. https://doi.org/10.17705/1cais.03612

Gomber, P., Koch, J.-A., & Siering, M. (2017). Digital finance and fintech: Current research and future research directions. *Journal of Business Economics, 87*(5), 537–580.

Hill, J. (2018). *Fintech and the remaking of financial institutions.* Academic Press.

Ikpaahindi, L. (1985). An overview of bibliometrics: Its measurements, laws and their applications. *Libri, 35*, 163.

Joshi, V. C. (2020). *Digital finance, bits and bytes: The road ahead.* Springer.

Kanungo, R. P., & Gupta, S. (2021). Financial inclusion through digitalisation of services for well-being. *Technological Forecasting and Social Change, 167*, 120721. https://doi.org/10.1016/j.techfore.2021.120721

Karagiannaki, A., Vergados, G., & Fouskas, K. (2017). The impact of digital transformation in the financial services industry: Insights from an open innovation initiative in fintech in Greece. *MCIS 2017 Proceedings.* http://aisel.aisnet.org/mcis2017/2

Kim, J., & McMillan, S. J. (2008). Evaluation of internet advertising research: A bibliometric analysis of citations from key sources. *Journal of Advertising, 37*(1), 99–112. https://doi.org/10.2753/joa0091-3367370108

Kitchenham, B. (2004). *Procedures for performing systematic reviews.* Keele University.

Kuo Chuen, D. L., Guo, L., & Wang, Y. (2017). Cryptocurrency: A new investment opportunity? *The Journal of Alternative Investments, 20*(3), 16–40. https://doi.org/10.3905/jai.2018.20.3.016

Lai, K. P. Y. (2020). Fintech. In *The Routledge handbook of financial geography*, 440–457. https://doi.org/10.4324/9781351119061-24

Lebni, J., Toghroli, R., Abbas, J., NeJhaddadgar, N., Salahshoor, M., Mansourian, M., Gilan, H., Kianipour, N., Chaboksavar, F., & Azizi, S. (2017). A study of internet addiction and its effects on mental health: A study based on Iranian University StudentsA study of internet addiction and its effects on mental health: A study based on Iranian University Students. *Journal of Education and Health Promotion*, 9(1), 205. https://doi.org/10.4103/jehp.jehp_148_20

Legner, C., Eymann, T., Hess, T., Matt, C., Böhmann, T., Drews, P., Mädche, A., Urbach, N., & Ahlemann, F. (2017). Digitalization: Opportunity and challenge for the business and information systems engineering community. *Business & Information Systems Engineering*, 59(4), 301–308. https://doi.org/10.1007/s12599-017-0484-2

Leong, K., & Sung, A. (2018). Fintech (financial technology): What is it and how to use technologies to create business value in fintech way? *International Journal of Innovation, Management and Technology*, 9(2), 74–78. https://doi.org/10.18178/ijimt.2018.9.2.791

Levy, Y., & Ellis, T. J. (2006). A systems approach to conduct an effective literature review in support of information systems research. *Informing Science: The International Journal of an Emerging Transdiscipline*, 9(1), 181–212. https://doi.org/10.28945/479

Liu, F., Wang, D., Duan, K., & Mubeen, R. (2021). Social media efficacy in crisis management: Effectiveness of Non-pharmaceutical Interventions to manage the COVID-19 challenges [original research]. *Frontiers in Psychiatry*, 12(1099), 626134. https://doi.org/10.3389/fpsyt.2021.626134

Lobato, C. G., Cristino, T. M., Faria Neto, A., & Costa, A. F. B. (2021). Lean system: Analysis of scientific literature and identification of barriers for implementation from a bibliometric study. *Gestão & Produção*, 28(1). https://doi.org/10.1590/1806-9649.2020v28e4769

McKiernan, E. C., Schimanski, L. A., Muñoz Nieves, C., Matthias, L., Niles, M. T., & Alperin, J. P. (2019). Use of the journal impact factor in academic review, promotion, and tenure evaluations. *ELife*, 8, e47338. https://doi.org/10.7554/eLife.47338

Moed, H. F. (2006). *Citation analysis in research evaluation*. Springer.

Nian, L. P., & Chuen, D. L. K. (2015). Introduction to bitcoin. In *Handbook of Digital Currency*, 5–30. https://doi.org/10.1016/b978-0-12-802117-0.00001-1

Nicoletti, B., Nicoletti, W., & Weis (2017). *Future of Fintech*. Palgrave Macmillan.

Omarova, S. T. (2021). Fintech and the limits of financial regulation: A systemic perspective. In *Routledge handbook of financial technology and law*. Routledge, 44–61.

Ozili, P. K. (2018). Impact of digital finance on financial inclusion and stability. *Borsa Istanbul Review*, 18(4), 329–340. Sciencedirect. https://doi.org/10.1016/j.bir.2017.12.003

Prinsen, C. A. C., Mokkink, L. B., Bouter, L. M., Alonso, J., Patrick, D. L., de Vet, H. C. W., & Terwee, C. B. (2018). COSMIN guideline for systematic reviews of patient-reported outcome measures. *Quality of Life Research, 27*(5), 1147–1157. https://doi.org/10.1007/s11136-018-1798-3

Puschmann, T. (2017). Fintech. *Business & Information Systems Engineering, 59*(1), 69–76. https://doi.org/10.1007/s12599-017-0464-6

Suprun, A., Petrishina, T., & Vasylchuk, I. (2020). Competition and cooperation between fintech companies and traditional financial institutions. *E3S Web of Conferences, 166*, 13028. https://doi.org/10.1051/e3sconf/202016613028

Teece, D. J. (2010). Business models, business strategy and innovation. *Long Range Planning, 43*(2–3), 172–194. https://doi.org/10.1016/j.lrp.2009.07.003

Timulak, L. (2009). Meta-analysis of qualitative studies: A tool for reviewing qualitative research findings in psychotherapy. *Psychotherapy Research, 19*(4–5), 591–600. https://doi.org/10.1080/10503300802477989

van Oorschot, J. A. W. H., Hofman, E., & Halman, J. I. M. (2018). A bibliometric review of the innovation adoption literature. *Technological Forecasting and Social Change, 134*, 1–21. https://doi.org/10.1016/j.techfore.2018.04.032

Varga, D. (2017). Fintech, the new era of financial services. *Vezetéstudomány / Budapest Management Review, 48*(11), 22–32. https://doi.org/10.14267/veztud.2017.11.03

Vatananan-Thesenvitz, R., Schaller, A.-A., & Shannon, R. (2019). A bibliometric review of the knowledge base for innovation in sustainable development. *Sustainability, 11*(20), 5783. https://doi.org/10.3390/su11205783

Vučinić, M. (2020). Fintech and financial stability potential influence of fintech on financial stability, risks and benefits. *Journal of Central Banking Theory and Practice, 9*(2), 43–66. https://doi.org/10.2478/jcbtp-2020-0013

Wang, C., Wang, D., Abbas, J., Duan, K., & Mubeen, R. (2021). Global financial crisis, smart lockdown strategies, and the COVID-19 spillover impacts: A global perspective implications from Southeast Asia. *Frontiers in Psychiatry, 12*. Frontiersin. https://doi.org/10.3389/fpsyt.2021.643783

Zhang, J., Jiang, L., Liu, Z., Li, Y., Liu, K., Fang, R., Li, H., Qu, Z., Liu, C., & Li, F. (2021). A bibliometric and visual analysis of indoor occupation environmental health risks: Development, hotspots and trend directions. *Journal of Cleaner Production, 300*, 126824. https://doi.org/10.1016/j.jclepro.2021.126824

Zupic, I., & Čater, T. (2015). Bibliometric methods in management and organization. *Organizational Research Methods, 18*(3), 429–472. https://doi.org/10.1177/1094428114562629

Chapter 19

UPI: Transforming the Way Indians Pay

Hritvik Polumahanti, Monika Verma,
Rachit Garg, and Bala Krishnamoorthy

19.1 Introduction

The Indian government is committed to promoting digital payments as a way to create a more efficient and inclusive economy. This is part of its "Digital India" initiative, which aims to make India a global leader in digital technology. One of the main goals of the Digital India initiative is to create a "faceless, paperless, and cashless" society. This means that the government wants to reduce its reliance on paper and cash transactions and, instead, promote the use of digital payments. There are many different types of digital payments, and they can be implemented in a variety of ways.[1] Digital payments are becoming increasingly popular in India, and there are many different ways to make digital payments. Digital payments are electronic payments that can be made using a variety of methods, such as debit/credit cards, online banking, mobile wallets, and digital payment apps. These methods are convenient and easy to use, and they allow customers to make purchases from anywhere without having to carry cash or cards.

These are viable alternatives to conventional payment systems and have accelerated the speed of transactions and, thus, faster payments. Following the demonetization of currency, people started adopting digital payments, and even small business owners and shopkeepers started taking electronic

DOI: 10.4324/9781032644165-19

payments.[2] One can use a single mobile app to access multiple bank accounts and make payments using the Unified Payments Interface (UPI), a real-time payment system developed by the National Payments Corporation of India (NPCI). One can also use third-party payment aggregators (TPAPs) to combine multiple banking services, such as fund transfers and merchant payments, into a single platform.

UPI also supports peer-to-peer collection requests and peer-to-merchant transactions, which can be scheduled and paid for at the convenience of the parties involved. Many banks in India have their own UPI app for Android, Windows, and iOS devices. Modern cloud computing technologies offer a flexible and easy-to-use platform for teenagers to share resources, store data, and maintain international relationships.[3] The NPCI has modernized and strengthened India's payment and settlement infrastructure. The NPCI governs India's retail payment systems and operates several popular payment platforms, including the UPI.[4] The NPCI has launched a number of new products and services that have made it easier, faster, and more convenient for people to make payments. One of the NPCI's most successful products is RuPay, a debit and credit card network. RuPay is now the preferred card for the Pradhan Mantri Jan Dhan Yojana, a government-sponsored financial inclusion scheme. This means that millions of Indians who previously did not have access to banking services are now able to use RuPay cards to make payments. The NPCI has also launched the Immediate Payment Service (IMPS), which makes India the world leader in real-time retail payments. The IMPS allows users to transfer money between bank accounts instantly, 24/7. This has made it much easier for people to make payments, especially for urgent needs. Other notable NPCI products include the Cheque Truncation System (CTS), the National Financial Switch (NFS), the Bharat Interface for Money (BHIM), and the UPI. These products have all contributed to making the Indian payment system more efficient and inclusive.

19.2 Methodology

The data used in this study is from both primary and secondary sources. Primary data was collected using a structured questionnaire with questions about the topic. A suitable sampling technique was used to select

100 participants who completed the questionnaire. The respondents included people from diverse educational and geographic backgrounds and from various income groups. Small business owners were also surveyed about their experiences with integrating the UPI-enabled payment gateways into their day-to-day business activities. Secondary data was collected from previous research studies on similar topics, as well as from other websites.

19.3 Literature Review

Bappaditya Mukhopadhyay conducted a study of cashless transactions in India. He developed a theoretical model to predict the payment choices of buyers and sellers. His findings showed that the convenience of cashless transactions outweighs the temptation to evade taxes.[5]

Rahul Gochhwal studied the evolution of payment systems using the UPI. He found that the UPI is the most cutting-edge system due to its low transaction fees and speedy settlement due to its lack of intermediaries. The UPI has allowed many banks to communicate with one another and has facilitated interoperability between various bank payment systems.[6]

Vally and Divya (2018) examined the consumer acceptance of electronic payments in India. The use of technology for digital payments has made the banking industry more efficient and helped to achieve the goal of a cashless society. However, a survey shows that only a certain percentage of people are aware of the best practices for using technology securely. Banks should take the initiative to educate the public about these practices.[7]

The UPI and its software, BHIM-UPI, were used to analyze the e-transaction process in Somanjoli Mohapatra's study. The whole payment mechanism and security characteristics are described in this study, and several online payment apps are contrasted. The UPI aims to make financial transactions easy, fast, and convenient.[8]

In his research paper titled "End-user Acceptance of Technology Interface in Transaction-Based Environment," Kartikeya Bolar argued that technology developers and investors need to understand how customers assess technology interfaces based on features and different quality dimensions in order to make strategic decisions about how to improve their interfaces and compete on different quality dimensions.[9]

19.4 Objectives of Study

■ Study the impact of how much digital payment is contributing to the Indian economy.
■ Correlate factors such as data privacy, financial security, and payment defaults for the future scope and development of digital payment platforms.
■ Analyze the possible challenges small business owners and consumers face while using such digital payment systems.

19.5 Data Summary

The survey was distributed using snowball sampling to cover consumers' perspectives about different modes of digital payments regarding factors such as convenience, payment security, and future use in terms of absolute factors enabling the digital payments interface. The sample size for our analysis was 100 respondents.

As evident in Figure 19.1, the sample of respondents was 27.8% female and 72.2% male. This gender imbalance may introduce some bias into the results, but it can also be seen as a reflection of the diversity of the

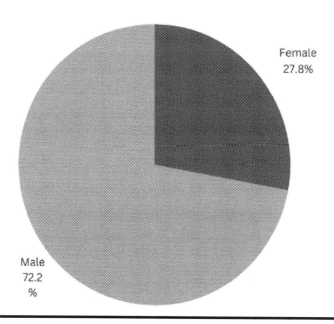

Figure 19.1   Preference of the UPI according to gender

population. The age distribution of the sample was nearly equal across four categories, which is good for ensuring that the results are representative of the wider population.

From Figure 19.3, when considering the occupational aspect, we observe a nearly equal distribution of students and salaried individuals among the sample of UPI users, amounting to 42.2% and 41.1%, respectivelyis shown in figure 19.2.

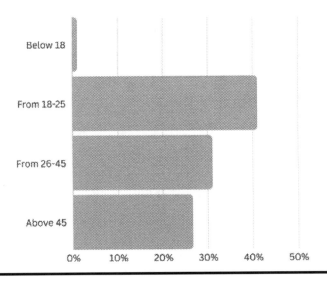

Figure 19.2   Preference of the UPI according to age group

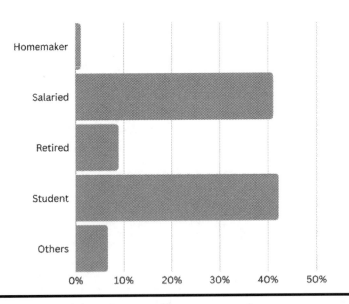

Figure 19.3   Preference of the UPI according to occupation group

Thus, these observations would help us to direct our approach toward determining the usage of digital payments across the population.

Toward determining the reasons for not using digital payment apps, we observe, in Figure 19.4, that there are various reasons, with nearly equal weight, for a few entries and lesser for the remaining.

Regarding the preferred mode of payments for different digital payment gateways, we observe, through Figure 19.5, that the UPI has a majority share, amounting to 86.7% of the respondents. Also, using plastic money in terms

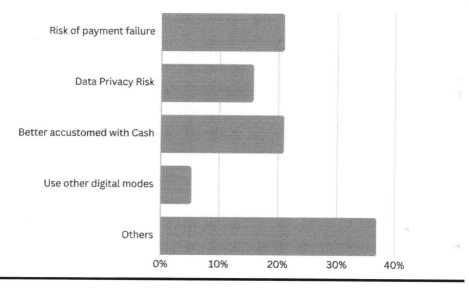

Figure 19.4   Reasons for not using the UPI

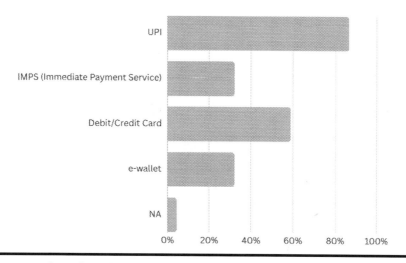

Figure 19.5   Preferred mode of digital payment

of debit cards and credit cards amounted to 58.9% of responses. In this, we considered users to be using more than one mode of payment and to have a better diversity of reactions.

19.6 Findings and Analysis

We analyzed the data we received from our questionnaire considering our primary research, which consisted of questionnaire responses from customers and vendors, which included shopkeepers, retail stores, small food stalls, restaurants, tea stalls, etc. Some results from the responses are presented in the following sections.

19.6.1 Comparative Analysis of Customers' Spending Using Any Digital Payment Mode Based on Their Family Income

Figure 19.6 shows the average transaction amount paid using a digital payment method based on the household's annual income. The most popular

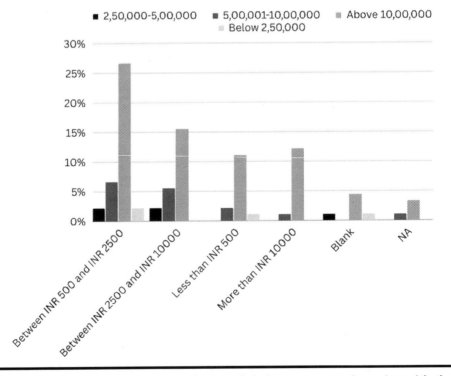

Figure 19.6 How percentage count of using digital payment mode varies with the transaction amount and annual income

digital payment method among those with annual household incomes of more than 10,000,000 Indian rupees is used for purchases between 500 and 2,500 Indian rupees. Spending via digital payment mode is highest for families with annual incomes of more than 10,00,000 Indian rupees, as shown in Figure 19.7, across all transaction amount categories. After that, there is a sizable chasm in digital payment mode adoption between households with an annual income of 5,00,001–10,00,000 Indian rupees and those with an annual income of more than 10,00,000 Indian rupees. It is reasonable to assume that yearly income constraints faced by families prevent some individuals from embracing digital payment methods. While the convenience of online payments has undoubtedly increased since people first started going online during the COVID-19 era, low annual household incomes mean that most people still prefer more traditional payment methods.

19.6.2 Comparative Analysis of People's Preference in Using Digital Payment Mode Based on Their Family Income

Figure 19.8 shows the payment preferences of customers, along with their average household income and the percentage of those who use the UPI.

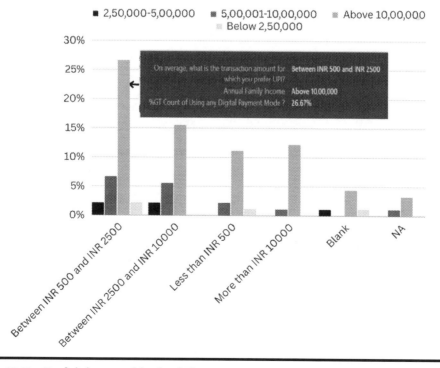

Figure 19.7 Explaining one block of Figure 19.6

Customers with annual household incomes of more than 10,000,000 Indian rupees (black coloured bar in Figure 19.8) have the highest usage of the UPI, IMPS, debit cards, and credit cards. The percentage of customers using the UPI who have a yearly family income between 5,00,001 and 10,00,000 Indian rupees is very close to 35.29%. Families with an annual income of more than 1,000,000 Indian rupees have the same usage proposition for debit cards, credit cards, and electronic wallets. Families with annual incomes of less than 2,500,000 Indian rupees are more likely to use the UPI than those with higher incomes, while the same demographic is less likely to use debit or credit cards.

19.6.3 Comparative Analysis of the Percentage of Customers' Preference in Using Digital Payment Mode Based on Their Geographical Location

To see how different regions use digital payment methods, see Figure 19.9. About 36.67% of all transactions in urban areas are for amounts between 500 and 2,500 Indian rupees. Within the same bracket, the 2,500–10,000 Indian rupee range represents the second-highest transaction amount, roughly 18.89%.

Customers who use digital payment modes and spend between 2,500 and 10,000 Indian rupees are 3.33% of the total in semi-urban areas. Salary

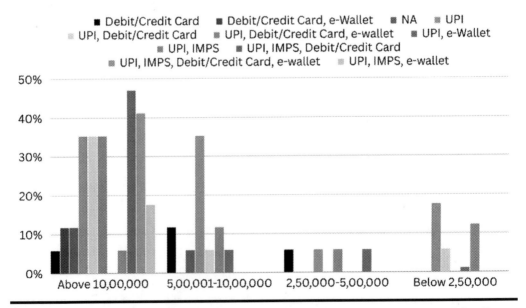

Figure 19.8 Preference of digital payment mode with respect to the annual family income

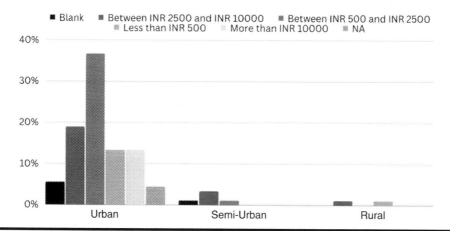

Figure 19.9 **Preference of digital payment mode WRT the occupation and amount transaction**

and student populations in rural areas are even lower, at 1.11%. Based on this data, it can be concluded that the UPI has made great strides as a digital payment mode, but there is still a way to go before it is widely adopted in rural areas. While many know of it, few feel comfortable using it for regular financial transactions.

People with annual household incomes of more than 10,00,000 in urban areas still favour using a combination of payment methods, including the IMPS, UPI, and credit/debit cards. People in rural areas have been observed to prefer cash for the following reasons:

1. **Infrastructure Gap**: A smartphone and reliable internet connection are required to use the UPI, making it difficult for those with fewer financial resources or those living in rural areas to take advantage of the service. Unfortunately, this causes consumers to fall behind the times. The launch of 5G necessitates high-quality smartphones with 5G connectivity, just as with 4G.
2. **Failure to Build Trust**: Consumers lack faith in digital payment methods due to rampant fraud, transaction failure, and instances in which money is withdrawn from an account but cannot be refunded. Your funds could be stolen if you reveal your one-time password (OTP) to an unauthorized third party.
3. **Low Levels of Digital Literacy**: The widespread absence of digital literacy prevents the UPI's widespread adoption. As a result, the general use of English inside the UPI apps contributes to their relatively low uptake. Digital literacy, like other competencies, should start at

the school level. However, many educational systems lack the latest technology and proper infrastructure. Therefore, investments in digital infrastructure, legislation, and governance frameworks in using digital technologies are necessary to address this issue of digital literacy.

4. **The Comfort in Cash**: Cash is always the most convenient form of payment to have on hand. There is no risk of a failed transaction, any possibility of fraud, and no requirement for a computer, smartphone, etc. The transition from cash to online mode might be challenging because having a smartphone with a reliable internet connection can sometimes feel like an extra burden.

19.6.4 Comparative Analysis of Vendor's Data

Figure 19.10 examines the impact of the shift in payment method on the monthly revenue collected from various vendors. Some businesses, such as those selling tea and eggs, recalled when customers would put off making payments until the end of the month, keeping track of their transactions in

	Local Cafe	Kirana Shop Inside Society	Tea and Egg Shop	Street Food Shop
Mode of payment popular before UPI	Cash	Cash	Cash, People used to keep khata book	Cash
Any significant increase in no. of customers using UPI	Yes	No	Yes	Yes
Average amount while paying through UPI	INR 200	INR 600-800	INR 200-300	INR 500-1000
% of monthly receipts through UPI	60%-70%	approx 35%	40-45%	65-70%
Digital payment mode most comfortable with	Google Pay	Paytm, Google Pay, Phone Pe	Paytm, Google Pay	Paytm, Google Pay, Phone Pe

Figure 19.10   Response of interview with different vendors (such as tea and egg shops, local kirana shop, restaurants, local café)

a khata book. However, now that the UPI is an option, suppliers no longer need to worry about being paid late.

UPI is an open protocol, which means that it can be integrated with other technologies to create a more robust and competitive payment network. For example, the UPI can be integrated with blockchain technology to enable faster and more secure cross-border payments. The UPI payments can be made from anywhere in the world, at any time of day or night, using a single mobile app. This is because the UPI is a real-time payment system that is linked to multiple bank accounts.

Before 2016, transferring money between banks could be done using Real Time Gross Settlement (RTGS), Immediate Payment Service (IMPS), or National Electronic Funds Transfer (NEFT). The banking industry desperately needed an update to centralize its processes through a single gateway, automate and standardize its payment infrastructure, and reduce its reliance on many rules, paperwork, and systems.

19.7 Limitations

Some of the limitations included:

1. The persistence of several security issues such as payment defaults, data security, and privacy policies of different platforms.
2. Technological illiteracy among small-scale business owners regarding the checks and balances for the UPI transactions amounted to many disputed transactions.
3. Online payment gateways can be expensive to set up and use, both for merchants and customers. Some firms may charge setup or processing fees, and customers need to have access to the internet and other related services. This can be a significant burden for small businesses and low-income consumers.

19.8 Conclusion

Since the COVID-19 crisis, adopting digital payment methods in India has gained traction. The government of India has been quite effective in promoting digital payment methods. It has made the shift from traditional to digital modes of conducting business seamless and user-friendly. A rise in the number of digital payments was observed in India during the pandemic.[10] For consumers and merchant service providers of essential services to be safe and protected, the NPCI encouraged and advised them to switch to digital payment systems.

In collaboration with the Reserve Bank of India, the government of India launched several awareness efforts via social media intending to encourage the people of India to transition to digital payment methods, which eliminate the need for paperwork and are more convenient.[11] Instead of paying with cash, the government of India has strongly encouraged its people to use digital payment methods, such as the UPI, Unstructured Supplementary Service Data (USSD), and NEFT, which are accessible around the clock. The customer can now make transactions even at odd hours through digital payment, which was impossible earlier. This was made possible by advanced technology and the emergence of smartphones. The digital payment system is bound to delight customers because it is more secure, convenient, and cost-effective than traditional payment methods.

Even though it is subject to cyberattacks and other technological difficulties, the UPI can capitalize on many opportunities in the modern digital environment due to its key strengths. Many consumers are making haste to switch to cashless transactions because they have a limited amount of cash and an imminent cash shortage. The increase in the number of people who use smartphones and the percentage of the population with internet access made it easier for people to use digital payment services. People are gravitating toward using contactless payment methods rather than their other payment options as a result of the COVID-19 pandemic. A mobile payment system is an intriguing option that has emerged as a result of the growing adoption of smartphones and apps that are associated with them.

It has been determined that the expected performance, social impact, price rate, safety, and data privacy are significant elements that influence the adoption of the mobile payment system.[12] Users can take advantage of the ease and swiftness of digital transactions made possible via the UPI. It is gaining popularity, particularly in the retail payment business, as compared to other digital payment solutions, it can be accessed through smartphones at a lower barrier to entry. Regulators could use the UPI to achieve the highest possible level of the country's financial inclusion. If regulators decide to tax the UPI in the future, they should exercise caution and concentrate on improving the banking system so that Fintech companies may offer payment services more efficiently. Focus should be put on enhancing the current banking network if they want to implement a service tax on the UPI.

Payment service providers (PSPs) are required to construct efficient grievance redressal mechanisms to address their customers' concerns. The system's most significant drawback is that the UPI can only be utilized by persons who already have bank accounts. There is an eerie silence in rural areas where people cannot access banks. In the future, research on users' attitudes regarding the UPI and other electronic payment alternatives might be conducted, and the findings of that research could be analyzed with the help of systematic behaviour models.

The launch of e-Rupi is a significant development in the digital payments space. It is a one-time payment platform that allows users to redeem vouchers using a QR code without swiping any cards or even using internet banking. This makes it a very convenient and accessible way to make payments. e-Rupi is also a step toward responsible and transparent digitalization, as it can be used to track and manage payments more effectively.[13]

Notes

1. Ashok G. (2022). Minimum Government and Maximum Governance: Empowering the Impoverished Through Digital India Campaign. Indian Journal of Public Administration, 68(3)
2. Joyojeet P., Priyank C., et al. (2018). Digital payment and its discontents: Street shops and the Indian government's push for cashless transactions. National Science Foundation
3. Abeer I.T., Muhammad S., Bashir H., et al. (2021). A Survey on Modern Cloud Computing Security over Smart City Networks: Threats, Vulnerabilities, Consequences, Countermeasures, and Challenges. Electronics.
4. Surendra N. (2021). National Payments Corporation of India (NPCI) and its Products. Banking School
5. Bappaditya M. (2016). Understanding Cashless Payments in India. Financial Innovation
6. Rahul G. (2017). Unified Payment Interface—An Advancement in Payment Systems. American Journal of Industrial and Business Management - Vol.7 No.10
7. Suma V., Hema D. (2018). A Study on Digital Payments in India. International Journal of Pure and Applied Mathematics - Volume 118 No. 24
8. Somanjoli M. (2017). Unified Payment Interface (UPI): A Cashless Indian. International Journal of Applied Science and Engineering 5(1)
9. Kartikeya B. (2014). End-user Acceptance of Technology Interface in Transaction Based Environment. Journal of Internet Banking and Commerce
10. KPMG Report (2020). Impact of COVID-19 on Digital Payments in India

11. Inder Pal S. S. (2022). Digital Payments Driving the Growth of Digital Economy. National Informatics Centre
12. Ricardo A., Stella M., Darly A. (2016). Intention of Adoption of Mobile Payment: An Analysis in the Light of the Unified Theory of Acceptance and Use of Technology (UTAUT). RAI Revista de Administração e Inovação – Volume 13, Issue 3 (221-230)
13. Government of India (2022). E-RUPI – Digital Payment Solution. National Portal of India

References

Abeer Iftikhar Tahirkheli, M. S.-I. (2021). A Survey on Modern Cloud Computing Security Over Smart City Networks: Threats, Vulnerabilities, Consequences, Countermeasures, and Challenges. *Electronics 10*(15), 1811.

Ashok, G. (2022). Minimum Government and Maximum Governance: Empowering the Impoverished Through Digital India Campaign. *Indian Journal of Public Administration 68*(3), 381–396.

India, G. O. (2022). *e-RUPI - Digital Payment Solution*. From india.gov.in: https://www.india.gov.in/spotlight/e-rupi-digital-payment-solution

Joyojeet Pal, P. C. (2018). *Digital Payment and Its Discontents: Street Shops and the Indian Government's Push for Cashless Transactions*. National Science Foundation.

KPMG. (2020). *Impact of COVID-19 on Digital Payments in India*. KPMG.

Vally, K. S., & Divya, K. H. (2018). A study on digital payments in India with perspective of consumer's adoption. *International Journal of Pure and Applied Mathematics 119*(15), 1259–1267.

Chapter 20

Fintech's Digital Surge: Crafting a Financially Inclusive Future

Mohd Afjal, Chitra Devi Nagarajan,
Payal Sanan, and Ramona Birau

20.1 Introduction

Financial technology (Fintech) has revolutionized the financial sector, creating avenues for increased financial inclusion and economic development. Fintech signifies the fusion of technology and financial services, fostering new product and service designs (Morse, 2015). Its rise has enhanced service efficiency and widened financial institution reach, especially in under-represented markets (Chen, Wu, & Wu, 2020). Financial inclusion, ensuring service accessibility to all societal segments, catalyzes sustainable economic growth and combats poverty (Demirgüç-Kunt et al., 2018). Yet, about 1.7 billion adults remain excluded from formal financial systems, primarily in low- and middle-income nations. This exclusion amplifies income disparities and perpetuates poverty cycles (Banerjee & Duflo, 2011). Fintech, bridging finance and digital technology, encompasses mobile banking, peer-to-peer lending, and blockchain solutions (Zavolokina et al., 2016). It has disrupted conventional financial systems, redefining how users access services. Fintech has the capability to overcome financial inclusion obstacles, such as limited physical banking access, by providing cost-effective, tailored services to marginalized groups, such as low-income or rural individuals (Bhattacharya

DOI: 10.4324/9781032644165-20

et al., 2020). For instance, mobile banking has empowered many in developing countries with essential financial services (Suri, 2017), while peer-to-peer platforms have democratized credit access by linking borrowers directly with lenders (Zhang et al., 2015). Blockchain holds promise for boosting financial inclusion with its transparent, secure transaction processes.

This study homes in on Fintech's specific role in bolstering financial inclusion and economic growth. This study encompasses developments until 2023, capturing recent Fintech advancements. This research not only identifies unexplored research areas but also delivers policy suggestions to stimulate Fintech's advancement, merging academic and practical significance. This study emphasis on interdisciplinary collaboration and global synergy in embracing the fast-paced growth of digital finance offers a fresh perspective.

20.1.1 Objectives of the Study

The objective of this bibliometric analysis is to provide a comprehensive overview of the research on the role of digital financial services in promoting financial access and economic development. Specifically, the study aims to:

1. Map out primary research themes and spotlight emerging topics within Fintech and financial inclusion.
2. Track and evaluate publication trends and citation dynamics over the years.
3. Survey the global spread of publications and patterns of research collaboration.
4. Highlight leading authors, notable institutions, and prominent journals driving the discourse.
5. Identify seminal articles and distil their core findings.
6. Pinpoint existing research voids and suggest directions for upcoming studies.

20.2 Review of Literature

The intersection of Fintech and financial inclusion has witnessed dramatic advancements in recent years. Fintech, born out of technological innovations, has redefined the financial landscape and holds immense potential for bolstering financial access and economic growth (Gomber et al., 2017;

Zavolokina et al., 2016). Particularly in the early twenty-first century, digital advancements such as the internet and mobile technology have expanded financial services to previously inaccessible populations, making innovations such as mobile money pivotal for financial access in developing nations. Recognizing this potential, the World Bank (2014) underscored the role of Fintech in promoting financial access.

Key theoretical frameworks, such as the technology acceptance model (TAM) (Davis, 1989) and the unified theory of acceptance and use of technology (UTAUT) (Venkatesh et al., 2003), have been instrumental in analyzing the adoption of Fintech services. These models spotlight factors such as perceived usefulness and social influence as pivotal for adoption (Shaikh & Karjaluoto, 2015). On the financial inclusion front, frameworks such as the access, usage, and quality (AUQ) (Cull et al., 2009) and the Global Financial Inclusion Index (Global Findex) (Demirgüç-Kunt et al., 2018) have provided valuable metrics and criteria to assess the depth and breadth of financial access.

A growing body of research confirms the transformative effect of digital financial services on financial access. Case studies from Kenya, Mozambique, and Tanzania have showcased mobile money's impact, particularly for marginalized groups (Suri & Jack, 2016; Batista & Vicente, 2018; Mbiti & Weil, 2016). Moreover, the nexus between Fintech and financial literacy has been explored, revealing how digital financial education can enhance financial knowledge and decision-making (Carpena et al., 2011; Xu & Zia, 2012).

This bibliometric analysis aligns with recent studies highlighting various facets of Fintech. Rakshit et al. (2021) emphasize sentiment analytics, while behavioural insights emerge from Sajeev et al. (2021). Afjal's (2022) exploration of Bitcoin and subsequent works (Afjal et al., 2023; Nagarajan & Afjal, 2023; Sajeev & Afjal, 2022) unravel the broader repercussions of Fintech innovations. Lastly, the influence of external factors such as the COVID-19 pandemic on financial markets points to the evolving nature of the Fintech domain (Trivedi et al., 2022).

The economic implications of Fintech are profound. Studies demonstrate that innovations such as mobile money can spur economic growth in rural areas and reduce transaction costs (Aker et al., 2016; Gutiérrez & Singh, 2013). However, the rapid rise of Fintech also underscores the need for adaptable regulatory frameworks, ensuring consumer protection and financial stability.

Akhtar et al.'s (2020) exploration of COVID-19's economic impact lays the groundwork, demonstrating how the pandemic accelerated the need for digital financial solutions. Chaturvedi et al. (2021) further this conversation by linking corporate social responsibility to financial performance, a pivotal aspect in the age of responsible banking and Fintech. Azmi et al. (2020) continue this thread by emphasizing how digitalization enhances banking efficiency, spotlighting technology's crucial role in the sector's evolution. The analysis of the YES Bank crisis by Akhtar et al. (2021) provides a stark contrast, illustrating the challenges faced by traditional banking systems and setting the stage for Fintech's innovative solutions. This perspective is enriched by Akhtar et al.'s (2023) study using the capital adequacy, asset quality, management, earnings, liquidity, and sensitivity (CAMELS0) framework to assess the response of traditional banking to major financial disruptions, such as demonetization. Parallelly, Akhtar et al.'s (2022) investigation using data envelopment window analysis underscores the pressing need for efficiency and innovation in banking, themes that are at the heart of the Fintech revolution.

The narrative extends to Ansari et al.'s (2023) focus on the financial crisis's impact on banks, emphasizing the imperative for robust and resilient financial systems in which Fintech can provide transformative solutions. Complementing this, Jafar et al.'s (2023) exploration into financial forecasting using advanced Fintech tools exemplifies the sector's technological prowess. Azmi and Akhtar (2023) study on the interplay between service exports and financial development, further broadening the understanding of Fintech's economic implications. Conclusively, Wajid et al.'s (2022) research on cross-border acquisitions in the pharmaceutical sector sheds light on the evolving financial strategies in the Fintech era. Together, these studies not only highlight the challenges and opportunities in India's Fintech landscape but also underscore the sector's pivotal role in shaping the future of banking and finance in a rapidly digitalizing world.

20.3 Materials and Methods

This study leveraged the Scopus database by employing a tailored search query, and the gathered data was subsequently imported into a reference management tool. The search string was constructed by integrating terms and keywords typically found in studies exploring the relationship between

Fintech and financial inclusion. The intent was to holistically capture the diverse facets of Fintech, especially its contribution to economic growth and alleviating poverty. To further refine the search results, several filters were applied. The primary constraint was a date range, focusing on publications from 2009 to 2024. Next, the domain filter targeted specific fields: economics, econometrics, and finance; social sciences; business, management, and accounting; computer science; and environmental science. The third layer of filtration centred on document types, including only articles and conference papers. Lastly, a language filter was implemented to retain only English-language documents.

20.3.1 Search String

("financial technology" OR "Fintech" OR "digital financial services" OR "mobile banking" OR "mobile money" OR "digital finance" OR "digital payments") AND ("financial inclusion" OR "financial access" OR "unbanked" OR "underbanked" OR "banking the unbanked" OR "poverty reduction" OR "financial empowerment" OR "financial literacy")

20.4 Results

20.4.1 Analysis Using Biblioshiny

The study began with the use of Biblioshiny, an advanced web application optimized for bibliometric analysis. This tool aids in extracting, organizing, and visualizing intricate academic data, facilitating a closer look at trends within the Fintech and financial inclusion sectors. Table 20.1 displays the dataset on Fintech and financial inclusion, providing key insights into the research in this field.

20.4.1.1 Sources' Production over Time

Table 20.2 reveals a growing trend in research on Fintech and financial inclusion, especially since 2016. This rising interest from 2016 to 2023 highlights the increased importance of digital financial services in enhancing financial access and economic growth. The table specifically emphasizes the dominant role of the top six journals in this area. Between 2010 and 2023, there's a noticeable surge in publications, particularly between

Table 20.1   Main Information about the Dataset

Description	Results
MAIN INFORMATION ABOUT DATA	
Time span	2009–2024
Sources (Journals, Books, etc.)	380
Documents	770
Annual Growth Rate %	0
Average Document Age	2.01
Average Citations per Document	16.09
References	38307
DOCUMENT CONTENTS	
Keywords Plus (ID)	836
Author's Keywords (DE)	1806
AUTHORS	
Authors	1772
Authors of Single-authored Documents	148
AUTHORS COLLABORATION	
Single-authored Documents	158
Co-authors per Document	2.69
International Co-authorship %	27.92
DOCUMENT TYPES	
Article	770

Source: Author's own creation based on the research data

2017 and 2023, when articles rose sharply from just three in 2017 to 98 in 2023. Among the journals, *Sustainability* leads with 41.11% of the total articles, while the *International Journal of Social Economics* contributes the least at 10.74%. The other four journals – *Cogent Economics and Finance, Technological Forecasting and Social Change, Telecommunications Policy,* and *International Journal of Bank Marketing* – contribute between 8.89% and 16.67% as shown in Figure 20.1.

Table 20.2 Number of Articles Published by the Top Journals in Fintech and Financial Inclusion

Year	Sustainability (Switzerland)	Cogent Economics and Finance	Finance Research Letters	Telecommunications Policy	International Journal of Social Economics	Journal of Risk and Financial Management	Technological Forecasting and Social Change
2009	0	0	0	0	0	0	0
2010	0	0	0	0	0	0	0
2011	0	0	0	0	0	0	0
2012	0	0	0	0	0	0	0
2013	0	0	0	1	0	0	0
2014	0	0	0	1	0	0	0
2015	0	0	0	1	0	0	0
2016	0	0	0	2	0	0	0
2017	0	0	0	2	0	0	1
2018	2	0	0	2	0	0	1
2019	3	0	0	2	0	0	1
2020	8	1	1	5	2	1	1
2021	16	4	1	8	5	3	3
2022	28	13	6	10	6	8	4
2023	43	16	13	13	12	12	12
2024	43	16	13	13	12	12	12

Source: Author's own creation based on the research data.

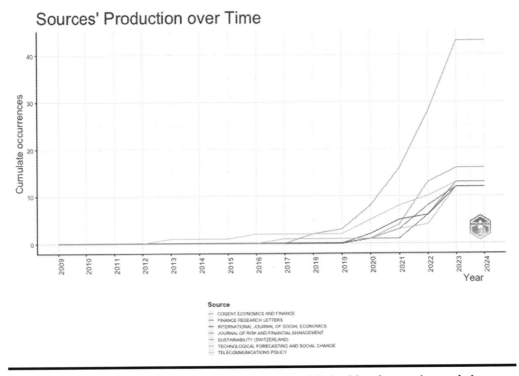

Sources' Production over Time

Source
- COGENT ECONOMICS AND FINANCE
- FINANCE RESEARCH LETTERS
- INTERNATIONAL JOURNAL OF SOCIAL ECONOMICS
- JOURNAL OF RISK AND FINANCIAL MANAGEMENT
- SUSTAINABILITY (SWITZERLAND)
- TECHNOLOGICAL FORECASTING AND SOCIAL CHANGE
- TELECOMMUNICATIONS POLICY

Figure 20.1 Evolution in the number of articles published by the top journals in Fintech and financial inclusion

20.4.1.2 Authors' Production over Time

Figure 20.2 displays the top ten authors' research contributions in the Fintech and financial inclusion sector, emphasizing the role of digital services in promoting economic growth and financial accessibility. The data includes authors' publication years, total citations (TC), and annual citation rates (TCpY). Asongu SA is the leading author, with varied citations between 2020 and 2022 and a peak TC of 45 in 2020. Wang X's significant contribution spans 2018 to 2022, with a high TC of 23 in 2020. Chen Y's most notable year was 2020, with a TC of 160. Okello Candiya Bongomin G had a high TC of 101 in 2018. Other authors, such as Chen S, Ahmad AH, Ozili PK, Iheanachor N, and Zhao Y, also have varied citations. This data highlights the importance and impact of these authors in the evolving Fintech and financial inclusion research landscape.

20.4.1.3 Most Global Cited Documents

Figure 20.3 showcases the top-cited papers in the Fintech and financial inclusion sector, underscoring the influence of digital financial services

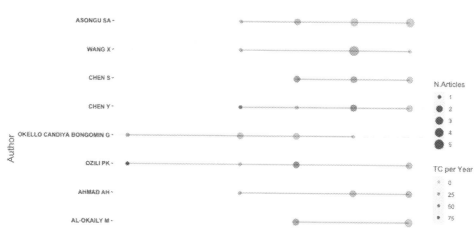

Figure 20.2   Top ten authors' production over time on Fintech and financial inclusion

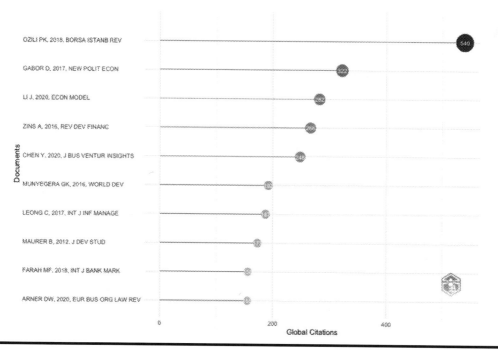

Figure 20.3   Most global cited documents

on economic progress and financial accessibility. Ozili PK's 2018 paper in *Borsa Istanbul Review* leads with 364 total citations and a yearly citation rate of 60.67. This paper's normalized citation value of 11.40 further highlights its significance. Gabor D's 2017 paper in the *New Political Economy* is another key work, boasting 261 total citations and a normalized citation value of 6.93. Other impactful papers include those by Li J, Chen Y, and Munyegera GK. These highly cited works provide insights into dominant themes and findings within the Fintech and financial inclusion domain, guiding future research.

Table 20.3 lists the top-cited papers in the domain of Fintech and financial inclusion, emphasizing their significance within the academic community. The table features ten key papers and their respective metrics, including publication year, total citations, annual citation rate, and normalized citations. . Other notable contributions are from Zins A in 2016 and Li J in 2020, both displaying substantial citation counts and impactful normalized citation scores. The works span from 2012 to 2020, reflecting the sustained research momentum in this sector.

Table 20.3   Most Global Cited Documents

Paper	Year	TC	TC per Year	Normalized TC
OZILI PK, 2018, *BORSA ISTANB REV*	2018	364	60.67	11.40
GABOR D, 2017, *NEW POLIT ECON*	2017	261	37.29	6.93
ZINS A, 2016, *REV DEV FINANC*	2016	207	25.88	5.45
LI J, 2020, *ECON MODEL*	2020	183	45.75	9.64
MUNYEGERA GK, 2016, *WORLD DEV*	2016	164	20.50	4.32
CHEN Y, 2020, *J BUS VENTUR INSIGHTS*	2020	160	40.00	8.43
MAURER B, 2012, *J DEV STUD*	2012	156	13.00	3.44
LEONG C, 2017, *INT J INF MANAGE*	2017	155	22.14	4.12
ALLEN F, 2014, *J AFR ECON*	2014	118	11.80	5.90
FARAH MF, 2018, *INT J BANK MARK*	2018	116	19.33	3.63

Source: Author's own creation based on the research data. *Note: TC-Total Citation*

20.4.1.4 Trend Topics

Figure 20.4 outlines trending topics in the Fintech and financial inclusion arena, revealing shifts in interest over the years using quartiles. Mobile communication's rise, especially from 2015 to 2018, pinpoints mobile devices' pivotal role in accessing digital finance. This transition emphasizes the increasing reliance on mobile tech for financial activities. Microfinance, coming to the fore in 2019, showcases the continued importance of unconventional financing methods. These methods specifically target the financially marginalized, underlining their role in enhancing financial inclusion.

Money services, including remittances and mobile money, have gained traction between 2018 and 2022. This trend illustrates the increasing role of such services in widening financial access. Additionally, the prominence of telecommunication since 2016 underscores telecommunication's crucial part in powering digital finance. Topics such as financial services and banking, prevalent from 2018 onward, spotlight the evolving digital financial offerings and the fusion of traditional banks with Fintech. The consistent mention of

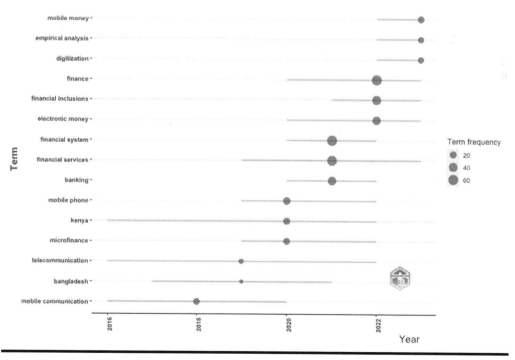

Figure 20.4   Trend topics

mobile phones from 2018 to 2021 accentuates their integral role, particularly in the developing world. The financial system topic's relevance from 2020 to 2022 underlines Fintech and financial inclusion's impact on global finance. Meanwhile, heightened interest in financial inclusion from 2020 to 2022 highlights its cruciality for sustainable economic growth. Finally, the focus on the developing world between 2018 and 2022 reaffirms the potential of Fintech initiatives in addressing financial access issues in these regions. The broader finance topic's peak in 2022 confirms the widespread curiosity about Fintech's role in redefining financial landscapes.

20.4.2 Analysis Using VOSviewer

Subsequently, the study employed VOSviewer, a cutting-edge software application tailored for creating, visualizing, and exploring bibliometric networks.

20.4.2.1 Institutional Collaboration Network Analysis

The institutional collaboration network analysis reveals active collaboration among institutions in Fintech and financial inclusion research (see Figure 20.5). Of 1,381 organizations, 162 met the set thresholds, and 164 were analyzed. Eighteen institutions form a core collaborative group, with the Centre for Economic Policy Research and Imperial College London as leaders. The highest citations are held by Essex Business School, Bristol Business School, and the University of York. Prominent collaborators include the World Bank, African Economic Research Consortium, and Bocconi University, showcasing their significant impact in this field.

20.4.2.2 Co-Occurrence Investigation

The co-occurrence analysis, drawing from 1,700 keywords, showcases the pivotal themes in Fintech and financial inclusion research (see Figure 20.6).

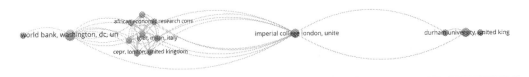

Figure 20.5   Institutional collaboration network analysis

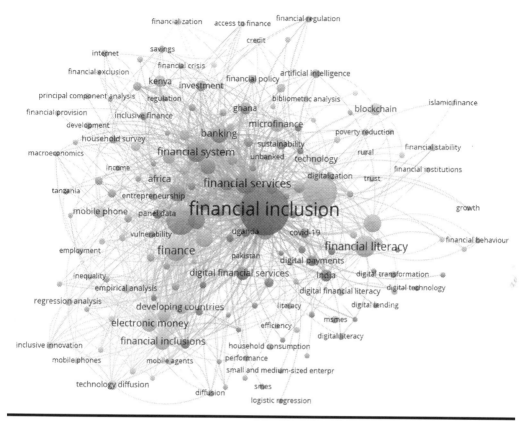

Figure 20.6   Keyword relationship cartography

"Financial inclusion" and "Fintech" dominate with 309 and 165 occurrences, respectively, emphasizing their central role. Keywords such as mobile money, financial literacy, digital finance, and mobile banking underscore the importance of technology. The emergence of "blockchain" and "China" hints at the evolving research dynamics, spotlighting emerging technologies and regional studies.

20.4.2.3 Authors Network Analysis

The authors network analysis, using data from 676 authors, pinpoints influential figures in Fintech and financial inclusion research (see Figure 20.7). Out of these, 70 authors met the set thresholds. The analysis identifies authors with robust bibliographic coupling links, helping researchers navigate the domain's key literature and understand author interconnections. A high total link strength indicates an author's extensive connections, vital for comprehending the intricate research landscape in this domain.

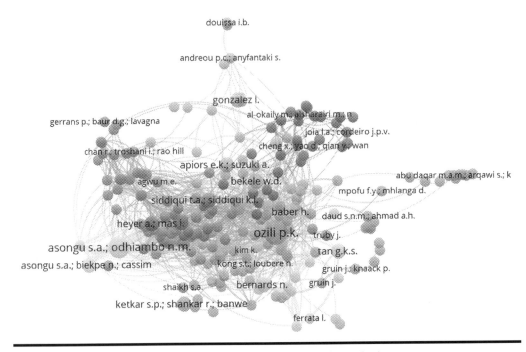

Figure 20.7   Bibliographic coupling – authors network analysis

20.4.2.4 Cited References Analysis

The co-citation-cited references analysis examines the most cited references in Fintech and financial inclusion research, revealing crucial connections (see Figure 20.8). Of 33,127 references, 227 met the citation threshold using the VOSviewer tool. Demirguc-Kunt et al.'s 2018 work on financial inclusion and Fintech is a standout, cited 64 times with a link strength of 306. Similarly, Suri and Jack's 2016 study on mobile money's impact on poverty and gender showcases its pivotal role, with 52 citations and a link strength of 337.

20.5 Discussion

Digital financial services have gained significant academic attention, particularly since 2016, reflecting the growing realization of Fintech's pivotal role in bolstering financial inclusion and its ramifications for sustainable development. This upward trend in research accentuates Fintech's potential to bridge the financial void, especially for marginalized groups. Analyzing the average citations per year indicates that foundational publications (2010–2012) garnered more academic attention due to their pioneering nature, while recent

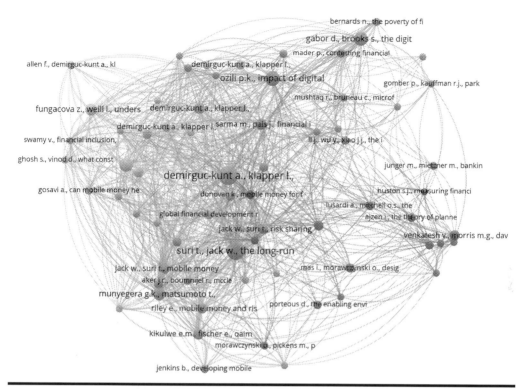

Figure 20.8 Co-citation – cited reference mapping

works (2019–2023) are still establishing their footing in citations. The subject's interdisciplinary approach draws insights from fields such as economics, telecommunications policy, microfinance, and more, underscoring the intricate interplay between technology, society, and the financial ecosystem. The recent surge in research between 2020 and 2022 further emphasizes this synergy, highlighting the evolving digital transformation in the global economy.

Prominent authors in this domain provide a roadmap of impactful research, while globally cited documents offer foundational frameworks guiding the field's trajectory. The global collaboration map showcases the importance of international partnerships in navigating the challenges of this rapidly advancing sector, and thematic maps emphasize the intertwined nature of financial services, technology, and socio-economic growth. Emergent research themes stress the role of connectivity, innovative financing solutions, and the crucial position of telecommunication companies in the digital financial paradigm. In essence, the ever-evolving landscape of Fintech and financial inclusion underscores the transformative potential of digital financial services, emphasizing its implications for a more inclusive and sustainable economic future.

20.6 Implications of the Study

This bibliometric analysis of the Fintech and financial inclusion literature offers invaluable insights for a broad spectrum of stakeholders, including academics, policymakers, and industry practitioners. By systematically mapping out the research landscape, academics can identify research gaps, emergent topics, leading contributors, and potential collaboration opportunities. This in-depth understanding paves the way for innovative research directions and informed academic pursuits. For policymakers, the study provides a comprehensive overview of the existing research, which can inform evidence-based policy decisions. The highlighted significance of digital financial services in promoting financial access and economic growth underscores the need for focused policies and strategies to drive financial inclusion. Industry practitioners, encompassing Fintech start-ups, established financial entities, and non-governmental organizations (NGOs), benefit from a clearer picture of the digital financial services' current state and its potential impact. This knowledge can spur the development of innovative solutions, shape strategic initiatives, and foster partnerships for inclusive growth. Overall, this analysis is a pivotal tool, enriching understanding, guiding policy and industry actions, and setting the direction for future Fintech and financial inclusion research.

20.7 Conclusion

This comprehensive bibliometric analysis sheds light on the rising academic interest in Fintech and financial inclusion, emphasizing the transformative role of digital financial services in enhancing global financial accessibility and advancing economic growth. The interdisciplinary nature of the research mirrors the multifaceted intricacies of the subject and underscores the need for collaborative endeavours across diverse academic disciplines. The surge in research from 2020–2022 testifies to the burgeoning realization of Fintech's potential to bridge the gaps left by conventional financial mechanisms and spearhead the digital economic transformation. Notably, the study spotlights influential contributors and institutions, setting the stage for the academic discourse and potential future collaborations. The global collaboration map accentuates the need for international synergies to navigate the challenges and possibilities of the swiftly evolving Fintech realm. While the research delves deep into existing literature, the inherent limitations call for an extended exploration into areas such as the impact on underserved communities, the efficacy of alternate financing models, and the role of emerging technologies. In summation, this analysis offers a panoramic view of the Fintech and financial inclusion research landscape. As this domain unfolds, it's crucial for scholars and policymakers to stay abreast of changes, ensuring that the perks of financial inclusion are disseminated equitably, fostering a holistic and sustainable economic progression.

References

Afjal, M., & Clanganthuruthil Sajeev, K. (2022). Interconnection between cryptocurrencies and energy markets: An analysis of volatility spillover. *OPEC Energy Review*, 46(3), 287–309.

Afjal, M., Kathiravan, C., Dana, L. P., & Nagarajan, C. D. (2023). The dynamic impact of financial technology and energy consumption on environmental sustainability. *Sustainability*, 15(12), 9327.

Aker, J. C., Boumnijel, R., McClelland, A., & Tierney, N. (2016). Payment mechanisms and antipoverty programs: Evidence from a mobile money cash transfer experiment in Niger. *Economic Development and Cultural Change*, 65(1), 1–37.

Akhtar, S., Alam, M., & Ansari, M. S. (2022). Measuring the performance of the Indian banking industry: Data envelopment window analysis approach. *Benchmarking: An International Journal*, 29(9), 2842–2857.

Akhtar, S., Alam, M., & Khan, M. M. (2021). YES Bank Fiasco: Arrogance or negligence. *Emerging Economies Cases Journal*, 3(2), 95–102.

Akhtar, S., Alam, M., Khan, A. (2023). Measuring technical efficiency of banks vis-à-vis demonetization: An empirical analysis of Indian banking sector using CAMELS framework. *Quality & Quantity*, 57, 1739–1761.

Akhtar, S., Niazi, M. H., & Khan, M. M. (2020). Cascading effect of COVID-19 on the Indian economy. *International Journal of Advanced Science and Technology*, 29(9), 4563–4573.

Ansari, M. S., Akhtar, S., Khan, A., & Shamshad, M. (2023). Consequence of financial crisis on liquidity and profitability of commercial banks in India: An empirical study. *Studies in Economics and Business Relations*, 3(2), 36–50.

Azmi, S., Akhtar, S., & Nadeem, M. (2020). Impact of digitalisation on bank performance: A study of Indian Banks. *Test Engineering and Management*, 83, 23678–23691.

Azmi, S. N., & Akhtar, S. (2023). Interactions of services export, financial development and growth: Evidence from India. *Qual Quant*, 57, 4709–4724.

Banerjee, A., & Duflo, E. (2011). *Poor economics: A radical rethinking of the way to fight global poverty*. PublicAffairs.

Batista, C., & Vicente, P. C. (2018). Introducing mobile money in rural Mozambique: Evidence from a field experiment. *Journal of Development Economics*, 135, 74–91.

Bhattacharya, S., Sarker, S., & Rahman, M. (2020). Digital financial services, financial inclusion and inclusive growth: A review of the literature. *Enterprise Development and Microfinance*, 31(3), 180–198.

Carpena, F., Cole, S., Shapiro, J., & Zia, B. (2011). Unpacking the causal chain of financial literacy. *The World Bank Economic Review*, 26(3), 453–473.

Chaturvedi, K., Akhtar, S., Azhar, N., & Shamshad, M. (2021). Impact of corporate social responsibility on financial performance of selected banks in India: Based on camel model. *Studies in Economics and Business Relations*, 2(2).

Chen, H., Wu, W., & Wu, Y. (2020). A study on the impact of financial technology on individual investors' risk-taking behavior. *Financial Innovation*, 6(1), 37.

Cull, R., Demirgüç-Kunt, A., & Morduch, J. (2009). Microfinance meets the market. *Journal of Economic Perspectives*, 23(1), 167–192.

Davis, F. D. (1989). Perceived usefulness, perceived ease of use, and user acceptance of information technology. *MIS Quarterly*, 13(3), 319–340.

Demirgüç-Kunt, A., Klapper, L., Singer, D., Ansar, S., & Hess, J. (2018). *The global findex database 2017: Measuring financial inclusion and the fintech revolution*. The World Bank.

Gomber, P., Kauffman, R. J., Parker, C., & Weber, B. W. (2017). On the Fintech revolution: Interpreting the forces of innovation, disruption, and transformation in financial services. *Journal of Management Information Systems*, 35(1), 220–265.

Gutiérrez, E., & Singh, S. (2013). Understanding the impact of mobile money on economic growth in Sub-Saharan Africa: A system dynamics approach. *Journal of Modelling in Management*, 8(1), 62–79.

Jafar, S. H., Akhtar, S., El-Chaarani, H., Khan, P. A., & Binsaddig, R. (2023). Forecasting of NIFTY 50 index price by using backward elimination with an LSTM model. *Journal of Risk and Financial Management*, 16(10), 423.

Mbiti, I., & Weil, D. N. (2016). Mobile banking: The impact of M-Pesa in Kenya. In *African successes, volume III: Modernization and development* (pp. 247–293). University of Chicago Press.

Morse, S. (2015). Peer-to-peer lending and the future of the banking industry. *Hastings Business Law Journal*, 11, 277–288.

Nagarajan, C. D., & Afjal, M. (2023). Innovative applications and implementation challenges of blockchain technology in the financial sector. In A. Khang, V. Shah, & S. Rani (Eds.), *Handbook of research on AI-based technologies and applications in the era of the metaverse* (pp. 279–297). IGI Global.

Rakshit, P., Srivastava, P. K., Afjal, M., & Srivastava, S. K. (2021). Sentimental analytics on Indian Big Billion Day of Flip Kart and Amazon. *SN Computer Science*, 2, 1–8.

Sajeev, K. C., & Afjal, M. (2022). Contagion effect of cryptocurrency on the securities market: A study of Bitcoin volatility using diagonal BEKK and DCC GARCH models. *SN Business & Economics*, 2(6), 57.

Sajeev, K. C., Afjal, M., Spulbar, C., Birau, R., & Florescu, I. (2021). Evaluating the linkage between behavioural finance and investment decisions amongst Indian Gen Z investors using structural equation modeling. *Revista de Stiinte Politice*, 72, 41–59.

Shaikh, A. A., & Karjaluoto, H. (2015). Mobile banking adoption: A literature review. *Telematics and Informatics*, 32(1), 129–142.

Suri, T. (2017). Mobile money. *Annual Review of Economics*, 9, 497–520.

Suri, T., & Jack, W. (2016). The long-run poverty and gender impacts of mobile money. *Science*, 354(6317), 1288–1292.

Trivedi et al. (2022). Investigating the impact of COVID-19 pandemic on volatility patterns and its global implication for textile industry: An empirical case study for Shanghai Stock Exchange of China. *Industria Textila*, 73(4).

Venkatesh, V., Morris, M. G., Davis, G. B., & Davis, F. D. (2003). User acceptance of information technology: Toward a unified view. *MIS Quarterly*, 27(3), 425–478.

Wajid, A., Sabiha, A., Akhtar, S., Tabash, M. I., & Daniel, L. N. (2022). Cross-border acquisitions and shareholders' wealth: The case of the Indian pharmaceutical sector. *Journal of Risk and Financial Management*, 15(10), 437.

World Bank. (2014). *Global financial development report 2014: Financial inclusion*. The World Bank.

Xu, L., & Zia, B. (2012). *Financial literacy around the world: An overview of the evidence with practical suggestions for the way forward*. World Bank Policy Research Working Paper (6107).

Zhang, B., Wardrop, R., Rau, R., & Gray, M. (2015). Moving mainstream: The European alternative finance benchmarking report. University of Cambridge and EY.

Zavolokina, L., Dolata, M., & Schwabe, G. (2016). Fintech – What's in a name? In *Proceedings of the 37th International Conference on Information Systems (ICIS 2016)*, Dublin, Ireland.

Chapter 21

A Case Study on Regulatory Compliance and the Repositioning of KFin Technologies of India

Musarrat Shaheen and Farrah Zeba

The purpose of this chapter is to outline a case that narrates the journey and transition of Karvy Stock Broking Ltd. (KSBL) to KFin Technologies within the Indian Fintech industry. The case in this chapter illustrates the challenges, ethical concerns, integrity, and regulatory issues for KSBL, which started as a stockbroking firm but, due regulatory issues and misappropriation of funds, had to transition to a Fintech firm, which provides financial services through technology. The case of KFin highlights the misappropriation of funds and negative outcomes of mismanagement of clients' funds. It raises a concern that regular compliance auditing and internal monitoring of irregularities should be done to protect the integrity and credibility of the financial services in the Fintech industry. Simultaneously, the chapter also outlines the need for transparent communication and ethical responsibility of financial institutions to protect consumers and clients. The chapter concludes by narrating the dire need for a balanced approach to innovation and adherence to government compliance and regulatory standards for the success of the Fintech industry.

DOI: 10.4324/9781032644165-21

21.1 Introduction: Fintech Organizations

Financial technology (Fintech) companies are organizations that deploy technology and digital interfaces to provide financial products and services to people. Innovative technologies are leveraged by these companies to create, enhance, and deliver services across various domains of the financial market, such as banking, transaction and payment processing, investment management, insurance, and more. Some of the common services provided by Fintech companies are digital payments, peer-to-peer lending (P2P), robo-advisors, blockchain and cryptocurrencies, Insurtech, personal finance management, and Regtech.

Digital payment service providers, such as PayPal, Paytm, Google Pay, and PhonePe, facilitate transactions and payments through electronic mediums. The P2P lending companies, such as LendDenClub, India Money Mart, Faircent, and others, provide a platform that connects the borrowers and lenders directly, beyond the functions of traditional financial institutions. Robo-advisors, such as Zerodha Streak, Kristal.ai, and Groww, use algorithms and artificial intelligence (AI) models to provide an automated investment platform that manages customers' investment portfolios. Cryptocurrency exchanges, such as WazirX, CoinSwitch Kuber, and Unocoin, and wallets, such as Coinbase (Coinbase Wallet) and Trust Wallet leverage blockchain technology to provide a secure platform for services pertaining to cryptocurrency exchanges, wallets, and smart contracts. Insurtech, such as Policy Bazaar, Acko General Insurance, and Coverfox, are those tech-driven firms that help in improving and streamlining the products and services of insurance industry in India. Additionally, personal finance management and advisory firms, such as Money Control wealth management and Motilal Oswal wealth management, assist in managing finances and reaching financial goals by tracking expenses and budgeting. Lastly, Regtech companies, such as Cateina Technologies and Comply Advantage, deploy technology to guide business compliance and adherence to government regulations and legal processes.

Fintech companies provide a unique platform to financial markets that are agile, innovative, and focus on customer experiences. There is a debate whether Fintech companies have acted as companions or antagonists, as it disrupted the financial market. Fintech has challenged traditional financial institutions with faster, accessible, reliable, and cost-effective financial services. The Fintech industry has grown exponentially in the past decade and has transformed diverse aspects of the financial market. To answer the question of whether Fintech is a companion or an antagonist, it is necessary to explore some of the services provided by these companies in the Indian financial market.

21.2 Indian Fintech Sector

The Indian Fintech industry is among the top five markets in India by value of capital funding and investments of nearly 270 million US dollars in 2016. The Indian Fintech industry can be broadly categorized across 20 segments and six broad financial services (see Table 21.1).

21.3 Fintech Organizations – Companion or Antagonist?

Fintech organizations are dynamic in nature and a multifaceted phenomenon. It has served the financial market both as a companion and sometimes may look like an antagonist. This duality in nature and service may be due to its transformative nature, which on the one hand, has disrupted the traditional financial services, while on the other hand, has offered innovative and creative solutions to the hurdles associated with financial services. Some of the areas in which Fintech companies acted as a companion are financial inclusion, accessibility, and innovation and creativity in financial services.

When one thinks about financial inclusion, Fintech has emerged as a powerful companion. Financial services such as mobile banking and digital payments have gained momentum due to the increase of Fintech companies. These services are now possible and extended to the underserved populations of rural areas. It has provided access and empowered people to manage their finances and fosters economic participation even to those who were excluded from traditional banking systems. Fintech companies have also streamlined financial processes and made them accessible and more efficient. Fintech services such as digital payment platforms, P2P lending, and robo-advisors have eased the challenges associated with traditional modes of financial services. This ease and accessibility have not only improved the customers' experience but has also made these services available round the clock and across geographical boundaries. Further, Fintech companies also drive innovation and creativity in the financial sector with

Table 21.1   Twenty Segments and Areas of Fintech in India

Areas	Fintech Segments	Brief Description
A. Credit	1. Peer-to-Peer Lending 2. Crowdfunding 3. Marketplace for Loans 4. Online Lenders – on-book lending by Non-Banking Financial Company (NBFC) 5. Credit Scoring Platforms	- All forms of lending marketplaces including peer-to-peer lenders and marketplaces that connect borrowers with both institutions and lenders. - Also includes crowdfunding and equity funding platforms - NBFCs that use alternative scoring and digital channels for acquisition
B. Payments	6. M-wallets and Prepaid Payment Instruments (PPIs) 7. Merchant Payments and point of sale (PoS) Services 8. International Remittance 9. Cryptocurrencies	- Services that enable transfer of funds for various use cases - Person-to-person, person-to-merchant, government-to-person, etc. - Services targeting both payees and merchants by enabling requisite payment infrastructure through mobile or other technologies
C. Investment Management	10. Robo-advisors 11. Discount Brokers 12. Online Financial Advisors	- Wealth advisory services delivered through technology-governed rules and investment strategies
D. Personal Finance Management	13. Tax Filing and Processing 14. Spend Management and Financial Planning 15. Credit Scoring Services	- Tools and services for active management of individual financial profiles (e.g. spend, investments, credit profile, etc.)
E. Bank tech	16. Big Data 17. Blockchain 18. Customer Onboarding Platforms	- Services that utilize many data points, such as financial transactions, and spending patterns to build the risk profile of the customer. This provides an alternate to traditional underwriting methods that are unable to serve people with limited credit data.

Areas	Fintech Segments	Brief Description
		- There is significant value in unstructured data. However, it is difficult to derive value from unstructured data, owing to challenges in analyzing it. A number of new tools are being developed to derive value from large datasets.
F. InsurTech	19. Insurance Aggregator 20. Internet of Things, Wearables and Kinematics	- Small business insurance - Usage-based insurance

Source: Deloitte Analysis*, "Fintech in India- Ready for breakout"

* https://www2.deloitte.com/in/en/pages/financial-services/articles/fintech-india-ready-for-breakout.html

novel services, products, and solutions. Whether it's blockchain-based cryptocurrencies or personalized robo-advisory services, innovations have always been key factors in customer service.

If one looks at Fintech companies from the consumers' perspective, it has been, no doubt, a companion, but when it comes to the financial market, Fintech companies can be also seen as an antagonist. The rapid evolution and fast penetration of quicker services have disrupted traditional financial business models, leading to the extinction of several job roles and functions. Further, automation and AI-based customer service and data analysis have raised concerns about job security and employment sustainability. Added to this, Fintech companies have questioned the norms of the regulatory frameworks, thereby creating several challenges for governments and other regulatory bodies. For instance, cryptocurrencies have posed regulatory dilemmas globally, leading to severe concerns about investor's protection, money laundering, and fraud. Lastly, with respect to financial transactions into digital spaces, cybersecurity threats and risks have escalated. Fintech companies and their tech platforms are repositories of personal and sensitive financial records that may be compromised by cybercriminals.

The ongoing surge in Fintech companies requires more collaborative efforts from the industry players, regulators, consumers, and society to reap the benefits of Fintech companies while mitigating the associated risks. The risk associated with financial services is enormous and may lead to a situation in which a company faces legal allegations and is forced to reposition its identity to survive in the market. The stockbroking firm KSBL, founded in the year 1983 by C. Parthasarathy, was among the established players in the Indian financial sector. It used to provide a range of services such as wealth management, depository services, financial advice, and registrar and transfer agent (RTA) services. Like other financial institutions, KSBL embraced technology in its operation and streamlined its services to create a rich customer experience. As a result, it evolved as one of the fast-growing players in the financial sector of India. But, in KSBL faced a regulatory challenge in 2019, and the Security and Exchange Board of India (SEBI) suspended its licence due to misappropriation of investor funds. Due to the severe regulatory actions and negative brand image, KSBL undertook a significant transformation in its company. The company transitioned into a new entity named Kfin Technologies.

21.4 The Case of Transitioning from KSBL to KFin Technologies

On May 12, 2023, LiveMint reported that the SEBI levied a penalty of 1.9 crore rupees on four former employees of KSBL, which was to be paid within 45 days.[1] On April 28, 2023, the SEBI banned KSBL founder C. Parthasarathy for seven years and levied a penalty of 21 crore rupees for misappropriation of clients' funds. Later, in a series of events, SEBI gave an interim order in November 2023 that prohibited KSBL from acquiring clients until the alleged misappropriation of clients' funds, amounting to more than 2,000 crore rupees, was recovered.[2]

Recently, four different officials at KSBL have been accused of misappropriating their clients' funds. The order, issued by SEBI, mandates the four individuals to pay the fine within 45 days. The alleged corrupt individuals are all top-ranked officials at the firm – Vice President K Hari, Compliance Officer S Gurazada, General Manager S Raju, and Managing Director V Mahesh. This entire controversy yet again unveils a system-level fraud against the customers in which the top-ranked officials raised substantial funds by not only pledging clients' securities but also going to the extent of misusing the power of attorney which was entrusted by clients because of KSBL's goodwill in the financial market. However, with the ethical concern of customer trust or the violation of several legal provisions, these officials diverted the funds to group entities.

SEBI documented all the corruption and manipulation in an 80-page order, which clearly states, "I note that the notices (four persons) were acting as key employees of KSBL when the violations were committed, due to which lakhs of investors have suffered." The officials have allegedly flouted the SEBI's guidelines of not mixing clients' money with investments, utilizing their clients' investments without their knowledge, using the KSBL's money for their sister concerns, and last but not least, even going to the extent of putting clients' investments as collateral for loans from banks and several other financial companies.[3]

21.4.1 The Regulatory Challenge at KSBL

Just after the market ban by SEBI in November 2019, G Naga Sridhar and his team at Hindu Businessline were trying to reach the top management team at KSBL, but they got no response. This made them dig into the background of the company all the way back to its establishment in 1983. They zeroed in on potential ruthless diversification of KSBL, which was beyond its core competencies and might be the core reason for the company's debacle.[4]

Things were not this bad for C Parthasarathy when he and a handful of his friends started the registry business in 1985. In no time, his company took up retail broking with Hyderabad Stock Exchange's financial product distribution in 1990. It was a glorious period for Parthasarathy, as his pet company started growing with debt market broking in 2003, which eventually led to a foray into commodities, insurance, realty, and online brokering in later years.[5]

Over the past decades, analysts observed that the company's overambitious diversification drive pushed the company into high-risk diversified markets, from keeping a record of telecommunications to analyzing data to even making smart IT devices. It was at this time that the company put all its domestic voice business under one umbrella company named Karvy DigiKonnect Ltd. In yet another diversification drive, it acquired HCL Services Ltd. and christened it Karvy Innotech Ltd., and the company quickly jumped into e-commerce support services as Karvy Next Ltd.

Tracing its humble background, in 2019, the Parthasarathy-led company had close to 21 companies in its portfolio, encompassing a business process outsourcing arm, Karvy Global Services Inc. USA and Karvy Inc. USA. Analysts concluded that diversification became the buzzword for growth. But on the side of growth comes the price of the reputation and survival of the company, particularly in times of recession when any kind of diversion of funds means a death knell for the company. This is exactly what happened to KSBL after a National Stock Exchange investigation exposed that a recent inspection revealed that the company illegally moved 1,000 crore rupees to its sister company, Karvy Realty. With the present ban on broking, ongoing investigations, and fresh onslaughts of penal actions, the fate of the entire group now depended on whether renaming KSBL as KFin Technologies could reposition the company in the minds of its clients.[6]

21.5 Background: KFin Technologies

KFin Technologies, now considered as one of India's Fintech companies based at Hyderabad, provides a wide range of financial technology solutions and services. The company is a wholly owned subsidiary of KFin Technologies Holdings Limited and is part of the Karvy Group. KFin Technologies provides services to clients in India as well as globally and has a presence in more than 80 countries. The company provides services and solutions to asset managers and corporate issuers across asset classes and provides several investor solutions, including transaction origination and processing for mutual funds, alternative investment funds (AIFs), pensions, wealth management, and private retirement schemes in Malaysia, the Philippines, and Hong Kong. The company provides software as a service (SaaS) based end-to-end transaction management, data analytics, channel management, compliance solutions, and several other digital services. To date, they have 25 mutual fund asset management companies (AMCs), 23 crore folios, 434 AIFs, and 14.8 tonnes Average Assets Under Management (AAUM). It received the Great Place to Work award in 2020 and 2021. KFin has also been named a mortgage Centre of Excellence (CoE) for the largest registrar and mortgage management company in the world for handling lacs of transactions every year. Refer to Figure 21.1 and 21.2 for the achievements and milestones of KFin Technologies.

The company was initially incorporated under the Companies Act of 2013 as "KCPL Advisory Services Private Limited" and was granted a certificate of incorporation on June 8, 2017. The company's board approved the name change from 'KCPL Advisory Services Private Limited' to 'Karvy Fintech Private Limited' on July 22, 2017, and the company's shareholders

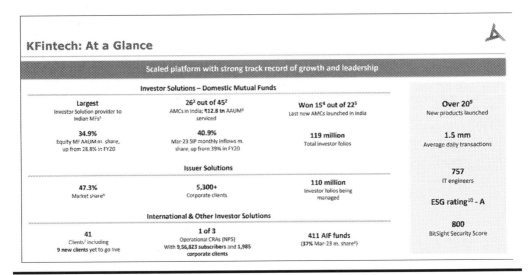

Figure 21.1   Milestones of KFin Technologies Source: Investor's factsheet. Source: https://investor.kfintech.com/wp-content/uploads/2023/05/KFintech-Presentation -Factsheet.pdf

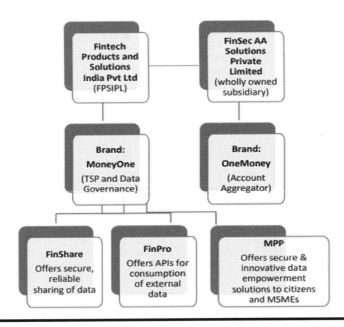

Figure 21.2   FPSIPL Services of KFin Technologies Source: Investor's factsheet. Source: https://investor.kfintech.com/wp-content/uploads/2023/05/KFintech -Presentation-Factsheet.pdf

approved on July 24, 2017, and a fresh certificate of incorporation, under the Companies Act of 2013, was issued on August 10, 2017.

21.6 The Vision and Mission of KFin Technologies

The vision is to create a value- and knowledge-based organization by sustaining a culture of learning, innovation, and teamwork to attain organizational excellence. The mission is to invest efforts in building an inclusive team and culture so that team members feel respected and included, which in turn, empowers and gives them freedom to be creative and effective. Since 2013, the company acquired around a 25.63% stake in Fintech Products and Solutions India Private Limited (FPSIPL).[7] With this acquisition, the company has secured a stable position in the Fintech industry. It enriched its services with FinShare, FinPro, and MPP portals.

21.7 Leader at KFin Technologies

Sreekanth Nadella, CEO of KFin Technologies, is a leading player in the financial service industry. He has more than 25 years of experience working in banking, financial services, and insurance (BFSI). He has held several top leadership positions with organizations such as Franklin Templeton Investments, HSBC, and Standard Chartered Bank. Nadella joined KFin Technologies in 2018 and has since played a key role in accelerating the business's growth and international expansion. KFin Technologies serves more than 90 million investors and more than 200 corporations, making it a top provider of investor and issuer services in India under his direction. Nadella was renowned for his strategic thinking, client-focused style, and proficiency in digital transformation. He received recognition from numerous industry organizations for his efforts in the BFSI sector in India, and in 2021, the *Economic Times*[8] named him one of the top 100 CEOs in India.

21.8 Kfin Technologies and Its Rivals

In December 2022, KFin Technologies launched its initial public offering (IPO). Analysts pitted Computer Age Management Services (CAMS), listed two years ago, as KFin's potential rival. The bone of contention is that the two firms have comparable business models, as both companies furnish services and solutions to asset management companies.[9]

21.9 Repositioning of Karvy as KFin Technologies

Karvy was going through a big-time image crisis in the securities market. Realizing this, the parent company, General Atlantic (GA), a private equity firm headquartered in New York, strategized to reposition its portfolio company — Karvy to Kfin Technologies. GA has been the controlling shareholder for more than a year, with an 83.3% stake in Kfin Technologies.[10]

The newly rechristened brand, KFin Technologies, will be among the largest registrars in India and Southeast Asia. Mavila Vishwanathan Nair was appointed as non-executive chairman with immediate effect. The company will not only provide investment services to 90 million account holders but also close to 2,900 issuers. These issuers amass several banking and non-banking entities such as government organizations, private firms, and mutual funds. Infrastructure-wise, the company boasts 5,000 employees spread across around 200 branches in multiple key locations in India.[11]

21.10 Lesson for the Fintech Industry

The KSBL case suggests strict adherence to regulatory and legal norms and compliance. Compliance to ensure the trust of clients, investors, and regulatory authorities must be the first priority for these companies. Companies, whether traditional or Fintech, providing financial services should ensure that client assets are protected, which is the fundamental responsibility of any financial institution. The case clearly indicates that any misappropriation or mishandling of client funds can lead to severe legal issues, which in turn, may lead to the loss of credibility.

Fintech companies that are engaged in financial services should learn from the regulatory issues KSBL faced and how the wrong diversification decisions using client's funds turned out to be a nightmare for the company. It had to shut down its operation and to reposition itself.

The transition of KSBL to KFin Technologies, thus, offers several key lessons for other firms that are engaged in the financial services sector. A Fintech company can be a companion if it adheres, otherwise it may turn out to be an antagonist. To avoid such situations, Fintech companies should give paramount importance to regulatory compliance.

Another critical lesson is effective risk management. Fintech firms that provide financial services should have rigid and strong risk management frameworks that assist in identifying, mitigating, and assessing operational, regulatory, and other financial risks. Fintech institutions should protect client's assets and function as responsible companies. They should prioritize transparent communication with investors, regulatory bodies, and clients during times of transformations and changes.

The case also outlines the role of strong corporate governance and ethical practices. Corporate governance and ethical practices should be ensured and emphasized and highlight the critical role of transparent, ethical, and high integrity behaviour in operations. Regular auditing and close internal monitoring are important for addressing non-compliance and irregularities issues.

Notes

1. https://www.livemint.com/news/india/karvy-stock-broking-case-sebi-fines-rs-1-9-crore-on-4-former-officials-of-karvy-group-11683910287069.html
2. https://economictimes.indiatimes.com/markets/stocks/news/sebi-bans-ksbl-promoter-from-securities-mkt-for-7-yrs-fines-rs-21-cr/articleshow/99852628.cms
3. https://www.business-standard.com/markets/news/karvy-stock-broking-case-sebi-fines-rs-1-9-crore-on-4-ex-officials-123051200960_1.html
4. https://www.thehindubusinessline.com/markets/rise-and-fall-of-karvy-is-rapid-diversification-source-of-trouble/article30058649.ece
5. https://economictimes.indiatimes.com/the-ipo-scam-crackdown-after/from-a-group-of-friends-to-market-leader/articleshow/1509719.cms
6. https://www.thehindubusinessline.com/markets/rise-and-fall-of-karvy-is-rapid-diversification-source-of-trouble/article30058649.ece
7. FPSIPL is a technology service provider (TSP) having a wholly owned subsidiary, FinSec AA Solutions Private Limited, India's first account aggregator, licensed by the Reserve Bank of India (RBI).
8. A Daily Newspaper in India.
9. https://www.financialexpress.com/market/ipo-news-kfintech-ipo-vs-cams-which-stock-is-better-for-investors-issue-details-price-trend-business-comparison-2921258/

10. http://timesofindia.indiatimes.com/articleshow/72339920.cms?utm_source=
    contentofinterest&utm_medium=text&utm_campaign=cppst
11. https://www.thehindubusinessline.com/markets/general-atlantic-rechristens
    -karvy-fintech-to-kfintech/article30141166.ece

Bibliography

Gomber, P., Kauffman, R. J., Parker, C., & Weber, B. W. (2018). On the Fintech
    Revolution: Interpreting the Forces of Innovation, Disruption, and
    Transformation in Financial Services. *Journal of Management Information
    Systems, 35*(1), 220–265.

IMF (International Monetary Fund). (2017). *Fintech and Financial Services: Initial
    Considerations.* IMF Staff Discuss. Note, June. https://www.imf.org/en/
    Publications/Staff-Discussion-Notes/Issues/2017/06/16/Fintech-and-Financial
    -Services-Initial-Considerations-44985

Kiran, S. C., Dinesh, M., & Naveena, P. (2020). Portfolio Management in Karvy
    Stock Broking a Case Study on Anantapuramu District. *South Asian Journal of
    Marketing & Management Research, 10*(6), 37–52.

Kumar, A. S. (2020). Stock Broking Firms Siphons Off Client Securities. *Global
    Management Review, 14*(1), 1–7.

Mohanraj, D. P., & Kowsalya, P. (2018). *A Study on the Investor's Perception on
    Karvy Stock Broking in Coimbatore District.*

Pejkovska, M. (2018). *Potential Negative Effects of Fintech on the Financial Services
    Sector.* Examples from the European Union, India and the United States of
    America.

Saluja, S. (2022). Identity Theft Fraud-Major Loophole for Fintech Industry in India.
    Journal of Financial Crime, Vol. ahead-of-print No. ahead-of-print. https://doi
    .org/10.1108/JFC-08-2022-0211

Index

Printed in the United States
by Baker & Taylor Publisher Services